TRANSLATING THE QUR'AN IN AN AGE OF NATIONALISM

Over the course of the past two centuries, the central text of Islam has undergone twin revolutions. Around the globe, Muslim communities have embraced the printing and translating of the Qur'an, transforming the scribal text into a modern book that can be read in virtually any language.

What began with the sparse and often contentious publication of vernacular commentaries and translations in the Ottoman Empire and South Asia evolved, by the late twentieth century, into widespread Qur'anic translation and publishing efforts in all quarters of the Muslim world, including Arabic-speaking countries such as Egypt and Saudi Arabia. This is remarkable given that at the dawn of the twentieth century many Muslims considered Qur'an translations to be impossible, impermissible and even impious. Nevertheless, printed and translated versions of the Qur'an have gained widespread acceptance by Muslim communities, and now play a central, and in some quarters, a leading role in how the Qur'an is read and understood in the modern world.

Focusing on the Ottoman Empire and Turkey, and following the debates to Russia, Egypt, Indonesia and India, this book addresses the question of how this revolution in Qur'anic book culture occurred, considering both intellectual history as well the processes by which the Qur'an became a modern book that could be mechanically reproduced and widely owned.

M. BRETT WILSON is Assistant Professor of Religious Studies at Macalester College. He holds a PhD in Religion with a specialisation in Islamic Studies from Duke University. His scholarship has appeared in the *International Journal of Middle East Studies, Comparative Islamic Studies* and the *Encyclopaedia of Women in Islamic Cultures.*

The Institute of Ismaili Studies

Qur'anic Studies Series, 11

Series editor, Omar Alí-de-Unzaga

Previously published titles:

Suha Taji-Farouki, editor,
Modern Muslim Intellectuals and the Qur'an
(2004; Paperback 2006)

Abdullah Saeed, editor,
Approaches to the Qur'an in Contemporary Indonesia
(2005)

Annabel Keeler
Sufi Hermeneutics: The Qur'an Commentary of Rashīd al-Dīn Maybudī
(2006)

Fahmida Suleman, editor,
Word of God, Art of Man: The Qur'an and its Creative Expressions
(2007; Paperback 2010)

Feras Hamza and Sajjad Rizvi, editors, with Farhana Mayer,
An Anthology of Qur'anic Commentaries,
Volume I: On the Nature of the Divine
(2008; Paperback 2010)

Toby Mayer, editor and translator,
Keys to the Arcana: Shahrastānī's Esoteric Commentary on the Qur'an
(2009)

Travis Zadeh,
The Vernacular Qur'an: Translation and the Rise of Persian Exegesis
(2012)

Martin Nguyen,
Sufi Master and Qur'an Scholar: Abū'l-Qāsim al-Qushayrī and the Laṭā'if al-ishārāt
(2012)

Karen Bauer, editor,
Aims, Methods and Contexts of Qur'anic Exegesis (2nd/8th–9th/10th C.)
(2013)

Angelika Neuwirth,
Scripture, Poetry and the Making of a Community: Reading the Qur'an as a Literary Text
(2014)

Translating the Qur'an in an Age of Nationalism

Print Culture and Modern Islam in Turkey

BY

M. Brett Wilson

OXFORD
UNIVERSITY PRESS

in association with

THE INSTITUTE OF ISMAILI STUDIES
LONDON

OXFORD
UNIVERSITY PRESS

Great Clarendon Street, Oxford OX2 6DP
Oxford University Press is a department of the University of Oxford.
It furthers the University's objective of excellence in research, scholarship, and education by publishing worldwide in
Oxford New York
Auckland Cape Town Dar es Salaam Hong Kong Karachi
Kuala Lumpur Madrid Melbourne Mexico City Nairobi
New Delhi Shanghai Taipei Toronto

With offices in

Argentina Austria Brazil Chile Czech Republic France Greece
Guatemala Hungary Italy Japan Poland Portugal Singapore
South Korea Switzerland Thailand Turkey Ukraine Vietnam

Oxford is a registered trade mark of Oxford University Press in the UK and in certain other countries

Published in the United States
by Oxford University Press Inc., New York

First published 2014

British Library Cataloguing in Publication Data
Data available

Library of Congress Cataloging in Publication Data
Data available

Cover illustration:
Kara-Keui (Galata) bridge, Constantinople, Turkey, *circa* 1890–1900.
Courtesy of the Library of Congress.

Cover design: Alnoor Nathani and Russell Harris
Map illustration: Oxford Designers and Illustrators
Index by Meg Davies, Fellow of the Society of Indexers
Typeset by RefineCatch Limited, Bungay, Suffolk
Printed in Great Britain on acid-free paper by
TJ International, Padstow, Cornwall

ISBN 978–0–19–871943–4

The Institute of Ismaili Studies

THE INSTITUTE OF ISMAILI STUDIES was established in 1977 with the objectives of promoting scholarship and learning on Islam, in historical as well as contemporary contexts, and fostering better understanding of Islam's relationship with other societies and faiths.

The Institute's programmes encourage a perspective which is not confined to the theological and religious heritage of Islam, but seeks to explore the relationship of religious ideas to broader dimensions of society and culture. The programmes thus *encourage* an interdisciplinary approach to Islamic history and thought. Particular attention is given to the issues of modernity that arise as Muslims seek to relate their heritage to the contemporary situation.

Within the Islamic tradition, the Institute promotes research on those areas which have, to date, received relatively little attention from scholars. These include the intellectual and literary expressions of Shiʿism in general and Ismailism in particular.

The Institute's objectives are realised through concrete programmes and activities organised by various departments of the Institute, at times in collaboration with other institutions of learning. These programmes and activities are informed by the full range of cultures in which Islam is practised today. From the Middle East, South and Central Asia, and Africa to the industrialised societies in the West, they consider the variety of contexts which shape the ideals, beliefs and practices of the faith.

In facilitating the *Qur'anic Studies Series* and other publications, the Institute's sole purpose is to encourage original research and analysis of relevant issues, which often leads to diverse views and interpretations. While every effort is made to ensure that the publications are of a high academic standard, the opinions expressed in these publications must be understood as belonging to their authors alone.

QUR'ANIC STUDIES SERIES

THE QUR'AN has been an inexhaustible source of intellectual and spiritual reflection in Islamic history, giving rise to ever-proliferating commentaries and interpretations. Many of these have remained a realm for specialists due to their scholarly demands. Others, more widely read, remain untranslated from the primary language of their composition. This series aims to make some of these materials from a broad chronological range – the formative centuries of Islam to the present day – available to a wider readership through translation and publication in English, accompanied where necessary by introductory or explanatory materials. The series will also include contextual-analytical and survey studies of these primary materials.

Throughout this series and others like it which may appear in the future, the aim is to allow the materials to speak for themselves. Not surprisingly, in the Muslim world where its scriptural sources continue to command passionate interest and commitment, the Qur'an has been subject to contending, often antithetical ideas and interpretations. The series takes no sides in these debates. The aim rather is to place on the record the rich diversity and plurality of approaches and opinions which have appealed to the Qur'an throughout history (and even more so today). The breadth of this range, however partisan or controversial individual presentations within it may be, is instructive in itself. While there is always room in such matters for personal preferences, commitment to particular traditions of belief, and scholarly evaluations, much is to be gained by a simple appreciation, not always evident today, of the enormous wealth of intellectual effort that has been devoted to the Qur'an from the earliest times. It is hoped that through this objective, this series will prove of use to scholars and students in Qur'anic Studies as well as other allied and relevant fields.

Contents

List of Illustrations xiii
Note on Transliteration, Conventions and Abbreviations xvii
Acknowledgements xix
Map xxii

Introduction 1
1 'The Mother of Civilisation': The Printing Press and Illegal Copies of the Qur'an 29
2 Ottoman Editions of the Qur'an (1870–1890) 55
3 Vernacular Commentaries and the New Intellectuals 84
4 Politicisation: Neo-Arabism, Missionaries and the Young Turks (1908–1919) 116
5 Translation and the Nation 157
6 Caliph and Qur'an: English Translations, Egypt and the Search for a Centre 184
7 The Elusive Turkish Qur'an 221
8 An Ubiquitous Book 248

Bibliography 261
Index of Qur'anic Citations 279
Index 280

List of Illustrations

(between pages 138 and 139)

Figure 1. Two men reciting the Qur'an by the tombs of sultans Mahmud II and Abdülaziz (late nineteenth century). Courtesy of the Library of Congress.

Figure 2. Namık Kemal (1840–88), journalist, poet and playwright. Courtesy of the University of Texas Libraries, University of Texas at Austin.

Figure 3. Lithographic stone for printing the Qur'an, stored at the Meşihat Archive, Istanbul. Photo by author.

Figure 4. A metal relief printing block for producing small editions of the Qur'an, stored at the Meşihat Archive, Istanbul. Photo by author.

Figure 5. Two students holding copies of the Qur'an in the Eyüp district of Istanbul (between 1880 and 1893). Courtesy of the Library of Congress, Abdul Hamid II Collection.

Figure 6. The final page and colophon of a lithographically printed Qur'an (Matbaa-i Osmaniye, Istanbul, 1301/1884). Calligrapher: Hasan Rıza. Photo by author.

Figure 7. Interior page of a printed Qur'an with illuminations added (Matbaa-i Osmaniye, Istanbul, 1305/1887–8). Calligrapher: Mustafa Nazif. Photo by author.

Figure 8. The Ottoman governor, Ali Ekrem Bey, giving out printed copies of the Qur'an and robes at a ceremony in Beersheba. The banner above reads, *Padişahım çok yaşa* ('Long live the Sultan') (*circa* 1907). Courtesy of the Library of Congress, John D. Whiting Collection.

Figure 9. Musa Carullah Bigiyev (1875–1949), *circa* 1910, translator of the Qur'an into Turkish. Courtesy of –az19, Creative Commons Share Alike 3.0.

Figure 10. Pages from a revised version of Süleyman Tevfik's *Türkçeli Kur'an-ı Kerim* (1927), presenting the Arabic original (inside box) and Turkish translation in parallel columns. Photo by author.

Figure 11. First page of the Egyptian edition of the Qur'an (1924), the most widely used version of modern times. Photo by author.

Figure 12. A translation of the Qur'an resting on the pulpit of Yıldız Hamidiye Mosque, Istanbul (2013). Photo by author.

For my parents,
Elizabeth S. and Michael W. Wilson

Note on Transliteration, Conventions and Abbreviations

Arabic transliterations follow a modified system based on the standard of the *International Journal of Middle East Studies*. Names, terms and toponyms from non-Latin alphabets are transliterated unless common to English. The genealogical sequence Muḥammad ibn Qāsim, etc., is abbreviated with 'b.' for ibn (son) and 'bt.' for bint (daughter); the definite article on the *nisba* and the *laqab* is generally dropped after its first appearance, that is, from 'al-Khargūshī' to 'Khargūshī' or 'al-Jāḥiẓ' to 'Jāḥiẓ', and so forth. Definite articles, however, are by and large maintained for formal titles, that is, al-Ḥakīm. For Ottoman Turkish-language texts and names, the spelling conventions of modern Turkish have been used, but this is not a settled matter given that rapid changes in the Turkish language over the course of the twentieth century and the reintroduction of many Arabic and Persian terms have resulted in diverse methods of spelling. They have been transliterated here in a way that reflects widespread contemporary usage and there is minimal use of diacritical markings (e.g. â, î), since their use varies widely and also makes the text ungainly. Turkish-language works with Arabic titles are translated according to Turkish conventions. In regard to names, square brackets are used for two purposes. There were no surnames in Turkey until 1934, so when brackets are applied to a surname only, they indicate that the surname was not on pre-1934 publications, e.g. Eşref Edip [Fergan]. When square brackets are put around an entire name, they indicate that the article or book was published anonymously but that the name of the author became clear later, e.g. [Mehmet Akif].

Dates

Three different dating systems were in use during the late Ottoman period and the early Turkish Republican period: the Islamic lunar calendar (*hijri*), the Ottoman Fiscal calendar (*Rumi*) and the

Gregorian calendar. For materials with *hijri* or *Rumi* dates, the *hijri* or *Rumi* dates are listed first, followed by the Gregorian year, e.g. 1301/1884. In cases where the Gregorian year is unclear due to the lack of a precise *hijri* or *Rumi* date, both possible years are provided, e.g. 1302/1884–5. Archival documents with full dates are given in a day–month–year format, with the *hijri* or *Rumi* date first, followed by the Gregorian date, e.g. 28 Şubat 1313/12 March 1898. The format of the dating of archival material follows that found in the Ottoman Archives, so that only the initial or, alternatively, the final letter of the name of the month is provided, and this date is separated from the Gregorian date by a dash instead of a forward slash, e.g. 5 C 1323—7 August 1905. In some cases, documents or books have only the Gregorian date; if not noted otherwise, the dates in the text are Gregorian.

Translations of the Qur'an have been taken from Arthur J. Arberry *The Koran Interpreted* (1955), unless otherwise noted.

Abbreviations

BOA	*Ottoman Archives of the Prime Ministry*
EQ	*Encyclopaedia of the Qur'an*, ed. Jane Dammen McAuliffe. Leiden, Brill, 2001–6.
EI	*Encyclopaedia of Islam*, ed. M. Th. Houtsma *et al.* Leiden, Brill, 1913–38.
EI[2]	*Encyclopaedia of Islam*, ed. P. Bearman *et al.*, 2nd edition. Leiden, Brill, 1960–2009.
EI THREE	*Encyclopaedia of Islam*, ed., Kate Fleet *et al.*, 3rd edition. Leiden, Brill, 2007–
TDVİA	*Türkiye Diyanet Vakfı İslam Ansiklopedisi* (*Türk Diyanet Vakfı*).

Acknowledgements

On a recent flight to Istanbul, I ran into a former professor of mine who had been influential in sparking my interest in Turkish and Islamic studies. When I told him that his classes had inspired me to pursue these fields as a profession, he responded with a smile, 'Don't blame me.' From my days as an undergraduate exchange student in Turkey to my recent years as a faculty member, I have had the good fortune of being surrounded by exceptional people whose insight, generosity and humour have ushered me through the labyrinth of scholarly life; and, far from blaming them, as my professor joked, I would like to spill some ink here in gratitude for the variety of ways in which they and others have supported me and made this book possible.

A variety of Sufi teachings warn about the perils of pursuing 'the path' without a guide to lead the way, and the same warning could be applied to a scholarly career. Not one but a host of mentor-guides have steered me along the thin and narrow. Since my first days of graduate school, Bruce Lawrence and Ebrahim Moosa have been generous mentors, providing constant encouragement and invaluable guidance. I was fortunate to have Anne Blackburn, Carl Ernst, Erdağ Göknar, Charles Kurzman, Ken Perkins and Kevin Reinhart as guides as well, all of whom played important roles in shaping my scholarly career. My long-time advisor and friend Anne Blackburn lent me her brilliance yet again and read the entire manuscript, providing insightful feedback, as did Adeeb Khalid. Both are due special thanks. The two anonymous reviewers who recommended this work for publication provided invaluable comments and suggestions. İrvin Cemil Schick kindly shared his knowledge of calligraphy and print history as well as his good company. Over the years, Tony Greenwood has been a kind host at the American Research Institute in Istanbul, which is in many ways my scholarly home away from home. Additionally, he assisted with the translation of some difficult passages.

My colleagues at Macalester College have provided a wonderful community in which to work. The college helped make this book possible with generous institutional support, including Wallace Travel Grants for the summer of 2012 and the spring of 2013 as well as a year-long sabbatical during 2012–13. In particular, I would like to thank Ruth Anne Godollei for sharing her knowledge on the art of lithography and welcoming me into her print shop. I am especially grateful to my colleagues and friends in the Department of Religious Studies – Paula Cooey, Barry Cytron, Erik Davis, Susanna Drake, Jim Laine and Toni Schrantz – whose irreverent humour, good company and thoroughgoing kindness make bearable even the coldest days in *l'Étoile du Nord*.

Writing a book is difficult, while getting it published is seemingly impossible. However, Omar Alí-de-Unzaga, the academic coordinator of the Qur'anic Studies unit at the Institute of Ismaili Studies, his assistant Hena Miah, editor Lisa Morgan and the rest of the staff have smoothed the way at every step and made a long, sometimes arduous, process as pleasant as it could possibly be. I would like to thank them as well as the Qur'anic Studies Series Editorial Board, which closely read and commented on the manuscript.

A number of friends, colleagues and teachers have contributed in various ways to this book: Ceyda Arslan, Cemil Aydın, Shahzad Bashir, Amit Bein, Kemal Beydilli, Johann Büssow, Giancarlo Casale, Sinem Casale, Dücane Cündioğlu, Yorgos Dedes, Selim Deringil, Uğur Derman, Erdal Ekinci, Jamal Elias, Gottfried Hagen, Julianne Hammer, Ayhan Işık, Brian Johnson, Ahmet Karamustafa, Seyfi Kenan, Vangelis Kechriotis, Diyah Larasati, James Meyer, Sait Özervarlı, Wadad Qadi, Recep Şentürk, Şehnaz Tahir-Gürçağlar, Wheeler Thackston, Taylan Toklu and the Toklu family, the Tokatlı family, Yektan Türkyılmaz, Zeynep Türkyılmaz, Joshua White and Travis Zadeh.

Warm wishes go to my graduate school colleagues who shared with me the trials and glories of graduate education. Kenan Tekin deserves special thanks for proofreading the Turkish spelling and transliteration in the manuscript.

The Institute of Turkish Studies provided a sabbatical grant for 2012–13 that was invaluable for completing this book. For assistance during research, I would like to thank the staff of the American Research Institute in Turkey (ARIT), Duke University Library, Macalester College Library, the Islamic Studies Research Center (İSAM), the Ottoman Archives (BOA), the Süleymaniye Library, the Müftülük Arşivi, the Atatürk Library and the Research Centre for Islamic History, Art and Culture (IRCICA).

Thanks to my parents – Michael W. Wilson and Elizabeth S. Wilson – to my sister, Emily W. Geckle, and to my extended family, who have always supported me unconditionally. Finally, I offer my boundless appreciation to my chief muse, Cristina Corduneanu-Huci, who has been a continual source of inspiration and a matchless friend.

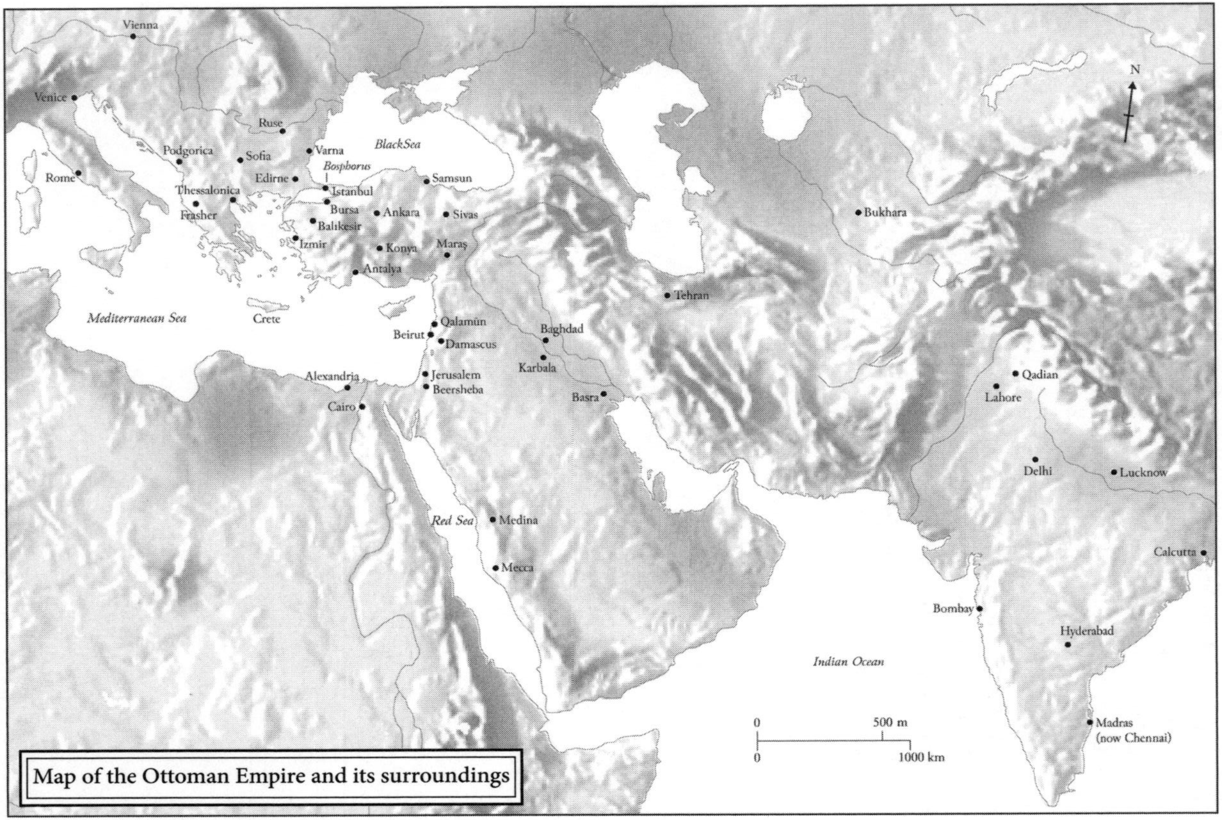

Map of the Ottoman Empire and its surroundings

Introduction

We have sent no Messenger save with the tongue of his people, that he might make all clear to them.

Q. 14:4

If the Prophet had come to this realm, he would have spoken Turkish.

Abdurrahman el-Aksarayi (d. 800/1397)

SEVERAL RECITERS OF THE QUR'AN were summoned to the Dolmabahçe Palace in Istanbul one evening in 1932, and given the nature of the invitation they were rather nervous. The most powerful man in the land, the president of the Turkish Republic, Mustafa Kemal Atatürk (fl. 1923–38), had called them to his salon for a most unusual assignment. He wanted them to recite the Qur'an in Turkish, something that none of these men had ever done or even imagined doing. Like Muslims around the globe, they had memorised and learned to recite the 'Arabic recitation' (*qur'ānan 'arabiyyan*, Q. 43:3–4), a text believed to be divine and composed of inimitable language (See Figure 1, two men reciting the Qur'an). Regardless of any reservations they might have had, they obliged the president and did their best to give a suitable rendition. He listened, directed and even provided feedback. In the following weeks and months, these men went to mosques dressed not in the traditional turbans and robes, but wearing Western suits and without any headgear whatsoever. They recited Turkish renderings of the Qur'an around the country as part of a government campaign to promote worship in the national language.

In another part of town, the brilliant, heavy-smoking Islamic scholar Elmalılı Muhammed Hamdi Yazır (1878–1942) looked on with horror; he did not endorse many policies of the new Turkish state and, like many Muslims, he considered Qur'anic translation impossible. After the fall of the Ottoman Empire, he had faced difficult times, spending a brief period in jail due to his political involvement, and then retreated from public life, passing his days at home. The madrasas where he taught had been closed by the government, leaving him without a job. In the early 1930s, he was offered a contract to compose a Turkish translation of the Qur'an, in addition to the Turkish-language commentary on which he had laboured for years. Considering his views on translation, the down-and-out scholar might have appeared an odd choice for the job. Nevertheless, he accepted the contract and composed a translation (though he did not call it a translation) that became influential and remains widely read in the present day.[1] His behaviour may seem contradictory, but, in fact, it epitomises an approach to translating the Qur'an that pervades modern Muslim societies, whereby writers produce renderings of the text for study (not ritual) while defining them as something other than translations.

Both stories illustrate the changing times during which Islam and the Qur'an were reimagined simultaneously with the creation of a modern nation state. They also reflect major changes that were wrought in the book culture of the Qur'an by the adoption of print technology in various Islamicate societies. Over the course of the past two centuries, Muslims across the globe have embraced printed editions and vernacular renderings of the Qur'an, transforming the scribal text into a modern book which can be read in virtually any language. What began with the sparse and often contentious publication of vernacular commentaries and translations in South Asia and the Ottoman Empire evolved, by the late twentieth century, into widespread Qur'anic translation and publishing efforts in all quarters of the Muslim world, including Arabic-speaking countries such as Egypt and Saudi Arabia.

This is remarkable given that, at the dawn of the twentieth century, the vast majority of Muslim scholars considered Qur'an translations to be impossible, impermissible and even impious. Renderings of the Qur'an have since gained wide acceptance in Muslim communities and play a central, and in some quarters, a leading role in how the Qur'an is read and understood in the modern world. Large-scale publishing ventures sponsored by Muslim-majority states and by Islamic institutions have not only made renderings of the Qur'an widely available but also have given them official sanction. There are now hundreds of translations in major Islamicate languages, and the King Fahd Complex for Printing the Holy Qur'an in Medina, Saudi Arabia, publishes translations in over fifty languages.

This book attempts to answer the question of how this transformation in Qur'anic book culture occurred by considering both the intellectual history surrounding the issue of translation, including the seminal debates, and the processes by which the Qur'an became a modern book that could be mechanically reproduced and widely owned. The rise of modern translations – free-standing, printed renderings that could be read on their own without glosses – requires careful consideration of the evolution of print culture and the ways in which it reshaped approaches to producing and understanding the Qur'an.

Keeping in view these broader shifts, this book explores the emergence of the modern Qur'an in the context of the late Ottoman Empire and the Republic of Turkey from roughly 1840 to 1940. Turkey was not the origin of modern Qur'anic translation and publishing efforts: Muslims in Russia, India and Iran had been printing Arabic editions of the Qur'an well before the Ottomans. In South Asia, the publication of translations had begun in the 1820s, and the efforts of South Asian Muslims were observed and admired by Turkish intellectuals. A case in point is that of the well-known South Asian scholar, Shāh Walī Allāh, who penned an important Persian translation of the Qur'an in the early 1700s (first published in 1866). A well-known but fictitious story circulates that those who disapproved of his efforts attacked him in a mosque in Delhi and dislocated his shoulder in what may have been an assassination attempt. Proponents of vernacularisation and Islamic reform in the late Ottoman Empire and Turkey held him up as a persecuted pioneer of Qur'anic translation and a model for emulation.[2]

Ottoman-Turkish history is crucial for understanding the development of modern printed copies of the Qur'an and vernacular renderings, particularly for the Middle East and North Africa. Encompassing the heartlands of Islam, including the sacred cities of Mecca and Medina, and much of the eastern Mediterranean and the Balkans, the Ottoman Empire had a privileged geographic position and was the most powerful Muslim state in the world for much of its existence. The Ottoman sultans claimed the title of caliph, the leader of the global Muslim community, and in the eyes of many (but certainly not all) Muslims around the globe, the Ottoman sultan was a symbol of Muslim political sovereignty in an age of European colonialism. As part of the late nineteenth-century Islamic Unity (or 'Pan-Islamic') campaign to rally the support of Muslims worldwide for the empire (see Chapter Two), Ottoman Qur'an printing initiatives had far-reaching effects and set new precedents for mass producing the text. After the fall of the empire, the use of Turkish translations in Muslim rituals and nation building within the Turkish Republic shaped modern debates in important ways, pushing the boundaries of how the Qur'an could be conceived as a vernacular scripture and used in the context of the nation state. Reactions to and imitations of events in the Ottoman Empire and Turkey have played a decisive role in the evolution of Qur'an translations and in determining their place in the modern world: Turkish debates on Qur'anic translation in the 1920s (see Chapter Five) sparked debates around the Muslim world (Chapter Six) about the role that renderings of the Qur'an would play in an emerging age of nationalism.

Approaching Qur'anic Translation

One approach to the study of Qur'anic translation has focused on the word choices, styles and inadequacies of existing translations. Finding 'mistakes' and demonstrating that perfect translation is impossible are activities that have become hallmarks of this type of literature.[3] However, in some cases, revealing the imperfections of translations can all too easily slide into serving a theological argument, namely, that the Qur'an is impossible to translate because it is divinely eloquent and therefore inimitable.

An outcome of this tendency is that the interesting choices made by translators are often lost amid compulsive evaluations of accuracy, which is an elusive concept. Additionally, it is rare to find studies that appreciate the beautiful and successful aspects of Qur'anic translations or examine the cases in which translations have been embraced by communities.[4] As the field has been skewed in such a direction, the consequence is that the history of Qur'anic translation has been written as a tragic series of failures rather than as a dynamic and crucial chapter in the history of the Qur'an and Muslim intellectual life. The book in your hands makes no judgement on whether the Qur'an can or should be translated. Instead, it takes a central interest in how and why Muslims viewed translations as vital for coping with the circumstances in which they lived. Indeed, Turkish Muslims debated whether or not certain translations were accurate, but this was a second-order issue that emerged after a critical mass of people had decided that translations were crucial for the modernisation of the Muslim community. To gain insight into this decision, it is imperative to explore the development of the printed Qur'an, the debates about translations, as well as the links between processes related to modernisation and the crystallisation of new nations and nationalisms.

Within the field of Islamic Studies, relatively little attention has been paid to the development of modern versions of the Qur'an. For instance, articles written in the 1930s on the creation of the modern Egyptian recension of the Qur'an, the most widely used Arabic edition of the twentieth and twenty-first centuries, still hold sway as the main sources on the subject.[5] The book history of the Qur'an is a crucial area for understanding modern Islam, given that contemporary piety is increasingly biblio-centric and Qur'an-focused. Drawing upon print history and approaches developed in Translation Studies, this book highlights the fact that the Qur'an as we know it has a modern history. The content and form of translations are products of new technologies as well as political battles and intellectual debates, not simply the word choices and stylistic decisions made by translators.

Looking carefully at the contexts in which modern copies of the Qur'an emerged and flourished, we can gain a sense of why translations were important and why, despite some disenchanted readers, Muslims have continually composed and published renderings of the Qur'an. While focusing on what we might call the cultural history of the Qur'an, this book also explores the actual texts of translations with attention to instances in which specific verses sparked a public controversy or led to reflections on what a translation could or should do. I give special attention to the renderings that mattered to contemporary readers, and on what their concerns can teach us about the social import of Qur'anic translations in the nineteenth and twentieth centuries.

Additionally, this book is intended as an indication of the new directions for research made possible by cross-fertilising Ottoman-Turkish History and Islamic Studies, two fields that have had little intercourse until recently. The scholarship emerging in both fields has much to gain from mutual engagement. At present, the lack of interaction between the two has resulted in a state of affairs in which the basic facts about Islamic reform, the most important intellectuals, and the formative Islamic texts of the Ottoman Empire and Turkey largely remain unknown or poorly understood in the broader fields of Middle Eastern History and Islamic Studies. Meanwhile, scholars of Islam often leave unexplored the wider intellectual, institutional, and technological developments that characterised this period of Ottoman-Turkish history and that of the broader region. Drawing upon Ottoman archival sources, seminal Islamic texts as well as newspapers, memoirs and journals in both Turkish and Arabic, I explore the material and intellectual developments related to the most important Islamic text, and, from this vantage point, attempt to provide a fresh perspective on religious modernisation during the empire-to-republic transition.

The narrative of progress towards nationhood and secularism runs deep in Ottoman-Turkish historiography, and this perspective has included Turkish translations of the Qur'an as a milestone on the path to modernity, enlightenment and civilisation. While this book chronicles the idea of a modern and national Qur'an, it does not intend to replicate the narrative of progress or make value judgements on the emergence of translations. What it does do is show how Ottoman-Turkish narratives of progress aligned themselves with translations and attempted to emplot them on a path of historical evolution that took Europe as a model and considered the Protestant Reformation and its vernacularisation of the Bible exemplars of religious reform. Many Turkish intellectuals and politicians understood religious reform to be the lynchpin of modernisation, and viewed Martin Luther's German translation of the Bible as a defining moment in the rationalisation of religion and the birth of national consciousness. Yet, as we shall see throughout the book, despite attempts to emulate the Reformation, the history of Qur'anic translations developed along a trajectory distinct from that of Biblical translations, playing a different sociopolitical role and adapting to the concerns of existing Islamic institutions and authorities.

'Veiled from the Masses'

Towards the end of the nineteenth century, an Ottoman author named Muallim Naci wrote that commentaries of the Qur'an were 'seen by the elites in the umma' but remained 'veiled from the masses'.[6] For a society in which the memorisation of the Qur'an and the inculcation of Islamic values through Qur'anic precepts and stories formed the cornerstone of Muslim education, what did it mean to claim that the Qur'an was 'veiled from the masses' and, equally importantly, what was at stake in the bombastic claim to unveil it to the people? The aspiration to make the Qur'an accessible reverberates through various kinds of Anatolian-Turkish Islamic literature stretching back as far the 1400s. Writers expressed this intention both for works that were potentially easy to understand and for difficult texts that required substantial erudition and knowledge of multiple languages.[7] Yet when Muallim Naci voiced this refrain in the late nineteenth century it resonated with a different meaning. With the development of print culture and the blooming of national identity in the late Ottoman Empire, intellectuals conceived a new idea of access to the Qur'an, one that favoured individual ownership of the book and valued the direct understanding of the text. This idea combined a pious educational ethos – the imperative to spread the Qur'anic message – with a modern notion of equality that valued broad access, education and enlightenment throughout society. By making the Qur'an accessible, supporters of translation and Qur'anic printing understood their efforts as attempts to challenge the traditional hierarchies of knowledge and provide a more direct way of communicating the central text of Islam. Proponents understood translation as a necessary tool for making the central text of Islam meaningful for non-Arab Muslims in the nineteenth and twentieth centuries. Crucially, as will be discussed in later chapters, they considered increased access to the Qur'an as an integral part of becoming modern and bringing about progress for the Muslim world. In the sphere of religious reform, translating the Qur'an was held to be an indispensable means of imagining and constructing an Islamic modernity that could survive and thrive in the rapidly changing world.

A critical number of intellectuals in the late Ottoman Empire and Turkey came to view direct engagement with, and individual comprehension of, the Qur'an as a necessity for Muslim societies. This view came to hold new power and potential in the nineteenth and early twentieth centuries, bolstered as it was by the spread of literacy via state schools, the emergence of nationalism, efforts at constitutional government, print technology as well as increased knowledge of European history and intellectual currents. In conjunction, these factors made possible the view that disseminating the Qur'an via print and in the language of the people was necessary and even natural.

Ottoman and Turkish reformers – including Haşim Nahid and Hüseyin Kâzım Kadri, both of whom we will come across in later chapters – felt the absence of translations had contributed to the multiple difficulties faced by many Muslim societies from the eighteenth century onwards, including political and economic distress, poverty and illiteracy. Muslim modernists around the globe – such as Musa Carullah Bigiyev – came to view the limited use of Qur'anic translation as a major impediment to the modernisation of Muslim societies. Within this intellectual current, translations of the Qur'an constituted an ideal genre for literate modern citizens who embraced the egalitarian notion that Islamic knowledge should be accessible to every believer. While this approach to Qur'anic translation appeared radical to many Muslims in the Ottoman Empire and Turkey, it gradually moved into the mainstream with rising literacy rates, cheaper books and the spread of public schooling.

It is imperative to explore the connections between the Ottoman-Turkish case and the Qur'anic translation debates in the larger Muslim world during the modern period. The modern history of translating the Qur'an has rarely been approached as an international phenomenon, and the larger story of how modern Qur'an translations emerged remains untold. This calls for a broad historical lens that takes into consideration the overlapping histories of translations in diverse languages. Modern thinking on translation developed on various continents among Muslims who were cosmopolitan and interconnected through travel and print publications. Writers like Muḥammad Rashīd Riḍā and Marmaduke Pickthall followed the same international news, lived either directly or vicariously through World War I (1914–18), and knew each other personally. Given these linkages, it is a story that coheres better in its entirety rather than in its isolated texts and controversial incidents. While exploring this topic will require the work of multiple scholars, the present volume hopes to make a modest contribution in this direction by illuminating the intersections between Qur'anic printing, 'Turkish Qur'an' debates and the conversations about translating the Qur'an into English that occurred in Egypt and on various continents after the abolition of the caliphate.

Despite the challenge to authority implicit in 'revealing' the Qur'an to the masses, over the course of the twentieth century even traditional Islamic authorities – the ulama – gradually came to view renderings of the Qur'an as not only permissible but also necessary and beneficial for modern Muslim societies. Despite initial resistance from many quarters, by and large, the modern ulama have embraced renderings of the Qur'an as an opportunity to heighten Muslims' understanding of the book and to spread its message to non-Muslims. For example, the Turkish Directorate of

Religious Affairs, the Iranian Centre for the Translation of the Holy Qur'an, al-Azhar University in Cairo and the King Fahd Complex for the Printing of the Holy Qur'an are ulama institutions that engage in the production and distribution of translations. While some scholars – such as Elmalılı – abstain from calling any work a 'translation' of the text, vernacular re-writings of the Qur'an under the guise of other genres are considered acceptable by them and are a pervasive type of Qur'anic literature in modern Turkey and beyond. This shift in favour of translations has its roots in the intellectual and technological transformations of the nineteenth and early twentieth centuries.

Any exploration of Qur'anic translation in modern Turkey must take nationalism into consideration, and much has been made of the role of nationalism in the emergence of Turkish translations. A plethora of narratives about the Turkish reforms in the 1920s and 1930s present translations of the Qur'an as a consequence of nationalism and often portray President Mustafa Kemal as the patron and instigator of these texts.[8] However, the role of nationalism has been somewhat misconstrued because these prevalent understandings suffer from anachronism. Whereas most observers point to the 1920s as the beginnings of translation, the perceived need for translations arose from the intellectual milieu of the late Ottoman period, well before the appearance of Turkish nationalism.

The initial impetus for Turkish commentaries and translations emerged from the conviction that the meaning of the Qur'an ought to accessible to those unversed in Arabic. In the Anatolian context, this idea has roots going back to the fourteenth century and attained modern expression, mixed with an Enlightenment ethos, in the Qur'anic commentaries published in the first half of the nineteenth century. This sentiment may have gained support from the proto-nationalist discourses in circulation in the latter half of that century, but vernacular renderings of the Qur'an were rarely construed as nationalist symbols prior to 1918, when Ziya Gökalp (1876–1924) penned a poem that proclaimed the 'Turkish Qur'an' (*Türkçe Kur'an*) to be an essential text for the nation.[9] The need to disseminate and understand its meaning propelled the argument for Turkish-language renderings, and this argument was largely devoid of nationalism until World War I. Even then, this nationalist vision of Qur'an translation was seldom expressed prior to the founding of the Turkish Republic in 1923.

Thus, nationalism was not the initial impetus for Turkish translations of the Qur'an. However, the idea of making the Qur'an accessible – translating it for the 'villager' – meshed seamlessly with the populist message of Turkish nationalism and became a key part of the Kemalist agenda for religious reform.[10] The 1920s and especially the 1930s were periods of intense and experimental nationalism in the Turkish Republic during which identity, language and history were redefined in an attempt to construct a secular nation state upon the ruins of the diverse and polyglot Ottoman Empire. Religious reform played a central role in this effort, and the state attempted to both marginalise and vernacularise Islam in order to create a 'Turkish Islam' that bolstered national solidarity and did not pose a threat to the political stability of the new regime or impede its agenda of cultural reform.

Within this context, modern translations of the Qur'an formed a cornerstone of the new national Islam envisioned by Turkey's leaders. During the rule of Mustafa Kemal Atatürk, the Turkish state experimented with the recitation of translations in mosques and forced imams in certain locations to issue the call to prayer in Turkish. The promotion of translations was central to the attempt to cultivate a national Muslim community that had little connection to the transnational Islamic community. To many Muslims in the region and around the world, it appeared that the Turkish state was attempting to replace the Arabic Qur'an with a translation.

Historical Discourses on Qur'anic Translatability

Circa 1930, the first native English-speaking Muslim to translate the Qur'an, Muhammad Marmaduke Pickthall (1875–1936), summarised an opinion about Qur'anic translation that has been widespread since the eighth century:

> The Koran cannot be translated. That is the belief of old-fashioned Sheykhs and the view of the present writer. The Book is here

> rendered almost literally and every effort has been made to choose befitting language. But the result is not the Glorious Koran, that inimitable symphony, the very sounds of which move men to tears and ecstasy. It is only an attempt to present the meaning of the Koran – and peradventure something of the charm – in English. It can never take the place of the Koran in Arabic, nor is it meant to do so.[11]

Given the fact that Pickthall had translated the Qur'an, it is clear that in the passage above he is defining 'translation' in an unconventional manner. In the language of Islamic scholarship, 'translation' (Ar. *tarjama* or Tr. *tercüme*) has a particular meaning when used in relation to the Qur'an. Most scholars understand translation to mean an exact or equivalent reproduction of the text in another language, and, because of its equivalence, theoretically a translation could replace the original text and supplant its functions in ritual and legal matters. Alternatively, translation in the Islamic lexicon can mean a necessarily imperfect representation of a text that would, by definition, be inappropriate for the Holy Book.

According to the Qur'an and centuries of Muslim scholarship, Qur'anic language is not only divine but also unique; the Qur'an is a linguistic miracle, an instantiation of God's speech wrought in the Arabic language. Numerous passages underline the uniqueness of Qur'anic eloquence, for example, Q. 17:88, which states that even if humankind and the spirit world were to collaborate, they could not produce anything to rival its grandeur. Therefore, to translate, to tamper with the language, runs the risk of undermining the very miracle of the text, and Muslim legal thought, by and large, has deemed the attempt to translate or rival divine language doomed to failure. In this line of thinking, since perfect equivalency cannot be achieved, Qur'anic 'translation' is theoretically and practically impossible.[12] While never universal, this approach to the (im)possibility of translating the Qur'an has been dominant in most historical contexts.

A second factor that colours the discourse on Qur'anic translation is the self-conscious 'Arabicity' of the text. Distinctively, the Qur'an speaks repeatedly about itself as an Arabic revelation.

Unlike the Hebrew Bible or the Greek New Testament, the Qur'an is markedly self-conscious about its own language of communication, mentioning its relationship to Arabic or Arabness on numerous occasions[13] as seen, for instance, in Q. 12:2: *We revealed it as an Arabic recitation so that you might understand* and Q. 20:113: *Even so We have sent it down as an Arabic recitation.*[14] Important scholars such as Abū ʿAbdullāh Muḥammad al-Shāfiʿī (d. 204/820), the eponym of the Shāfiʿī school, argue that these passages and others like them define the text as something that can only exist in Arabic, and contend that its meaning is inextricably bound up with the language. In this view, a common one among legal scholars, the Qur'an is Arabic by definition and no text in another language can be called 'Qur'an'.[15] A Turkish Qur'an, for instance, would be seen as a contradiction in terms.

However, scepticism about Qur'anic translation has never been unanimous. The earliest recorded discussions on translating the Qur'an stemmed from the practical question of how non-Arab converts should perform their obligatory daily prayers (Ar. *ṣalāt*, Tr. *namāz*). Since Muslims are required to pray and those prayers involve the recitation of the Qur'an, how were new converts to perform these prayers if they could not pronounce Arabic correctly and could not understand what they were saying? Would it be preferable to pray in Arabic but mispronounce the words, or would it be better to express the meaning in a language which one could pronounce as well as understand? An important legal thinker of Persian background, Abū Ḥanīfa Nuʿmān b. Thābit (d. 150/767), reasoned that the most important aspect of the Qur'an resided in the meaning it contained, not the language in which it was transmitted. There is potentially support for this view in Qur'anic passages that portray the Qur'an as a message that had been communicated via prophets since time immemorial, for instance, Q. 26:196–7: *Truly it is in the Scriptures of the ancients. Was it not a sign for them, that it is known to the learned of the Children of Israel?* According to one interpretation, the message to the Jewish people was not an Arabic text, therefore, the verse must be referring to a message or meaning that is not determined by any single language.[16] Another verse commonly discussed in this regard is

Q. 14:4: *We have sent no Messenger save with the tongue of his people, that he might make all clear to them.* Abū Ḥanīfa placed emphasis on the importance of meaning for Muslim ritual, granting permission for Persian language prayer, even if the devotees knew Arabic.[17] His approach asserts both the translatability of the Qur'an as well as the legality of ritual prayer in non-Arabic languages.

Though Abū Ḥanīfa's opinion is one of the first recorded meditations on Qur'anic translation in the history of Muslim thought, in retrospect it appears unconventional in its approach to the ritual use of translations. The bulk of subsequent legal thought moved in the opposite direction, defining the Qur'an as intrinsically Arabic and limiting obligatory prayer to Arabic. Even many Ḥanafī scholars came to disagree with the master's opinion, including important members of the late Ottoman ulama and modern Turkish ulama, such as Mustafa Sabri (1869–1954). A controversy rages over whether Abū Ḥanīfa maintained this opinion throughout his lifetime or came to agree with the opinion of his successors. Neither of Abū Ḥanīfa's chief disciples, Muḥammad al-Shaybānī (132–89/750–805) and Abū Yūsuf (113–82/731–98), mentioned that he had second thoughts about this subject. Rather, they modified his opinion, allowing non-Arabs to say their prayers in Persian only if they were incapable of reciting the *Fātiḥa* accurately; this permission to pray in Persian would expire once the person had learned to recite properly in Arabic.[18] Granting conditional, temporary permission for non-Arabic prayer became the dominant position for subsequent generations of the Ḥanafī school, and various writers attempted to harmonise Abū Ḥanīfa's position with that of his disciples.[19] While this may seem only a slight alteration to the opinion of the founder, it in fact posits a radically different hierarchy of language in Muslim ritual. Abū Ḥanīfa had granted equal validity to Persian and, theoretically, to all languages for performing ritual acts, while his disciples' position assumed that Arabic was the exclusively appropriate medium for prayer and that other languages could only serve as a temporary means of attaining proper Arabic ritual.

Other legal schools displayed even less flexibility than the early Ḥanafīs and insisted on rituals being performed exclusively in the

Arabic language. Their position was undergirded by the idea that the Qur'an was uncreated and that Arabic was an essential, not an accidental, aspect of the text. The prevalent view held that Arabic was a sacred language characterised by what Benedict Anderson calls the 'non-arbitrariness of the sign', the notion that a particular language not only conveyed a divine message but also embodied it and was inseparable from its meaning.[20] Broadly speaking, Muslim thought came to regard the Arabic arrangement of the Qur'an as intrinsic, not incidental, to revelation.[21] Mālik b. Anas (d. 179/795), the eponym of the Mālikī school, 'detested' prayer in languages other than Arabic and even loathed it when anyone took an oath using God's name in another tongue.[22] Mālikī scholars often held up Arabic as an example of a unique and superior language, arguing that no language other than Arabic could produce elucidation (*bayān*) or inimitability (*iʿjāz*) and, therefore, prayer in other languages could not be permitted.[23] The Ḥanbalī scholar Shams al-Dīn Muḥammad b. Qudāma al-Maqdisī (d. 682/1283) regarded those of his contemporaries who supported translation as apostates, and believed they were attempting to lead Muslims astray. He lamented that

> some apostatizing non-Arabs in our time began to call for the translation of the Qur'an and other devotions of the prayers, and for the use of such translations in their daily worship. Their true aim is, however, to use this as a means of facilitating apostasy for the rest of their people, and 'the casting of the Qur'an which was sent down from God behind their backs (2:101)'.[24]

The important legal thinker and advocate of the superiority of the Arabic language, Shāfiʿī, argued that reciting the Qur'an in Persian or any other non-Arabic language would invalidate prayer: if a Muslim could not recite in Arabic, he or she should perform the prayers without recitation of the Qur'an and instead recite formulaic praises (for example, *Allāhu akbar, al-ḥamdu li'llāh*). His reasoning is based on the idea that the Qur'an is Arabic and anything non-Arabic is, by definition, not the Qur'an. Therefore, translations are mere human speech and, if recited, they invalidate ritual prayer.[25] Even later Ḥanafīs adopted a more rigid orientation towards the ritual use of translations, and most – including some very prominent thinkers in the Ottoman Empire and Turkey – accepted the idea that Abū Ḥanīfa had changed his opinion and taken a more restrictive view of prayer in the vernacular.

There is substantial agreement between Sunni non-Ḥanafī and Twelver Shiʿi legal scholars on reciting translations during prayer and in viewing Qur'anic inimitability as dependent on the Arabic language. While there are reports of ritual use of Berber translations among Shiʿi groups in North Africa, Twelver Shiʿis largely forbid the reciting of translations during prayer because they view Qur'anic inimitability as inextricably tied to its Arabic form. Travis Zadeh has demonstrated a close correspondence between Twelver and Shāfiʿī positions due to the educational trajectories of some influential Shiʿi scholars who studied with those in Shāfiʿī circles. While most early Shiʿi scholars agreed with the Muʿtazilīs and some early Ḥanafīs that the Qur'an was created in time, the dominant Twelver position went against the Ḥanafīs in regard to praying with translations.[26]

Within the Ottoman context, the most important Shiʿi-affiliated groups were the Bektashi Sufi order and the diverse Alevi communities (often called Kızılbaşlar, 'redheads'), which were and are widespread throughout Anatolia and the Balkans.[27] However, these communities did not enter public debates on translating the Qur'an. Both groups had ritual and legal trajectories distinct from those of the neighbouring Twelver Shiʿis and Sunnis, and they developed a thoroughly vernacular use of the Qur'an within their literature and ritual life. They used Turkish or Kurdish as the primary language of ceremonies and prayers, incorporating phrases and untranslated verses from the Qur'an into rituals and into their rich body of poetry and song. Alevi-Bektashi literature approaches the Qur'an through an esoteric lens, as seen, for example, in this poem that appears to address the reader, '*You* are the meeting place of the two seas (*majmaʿ al-baḥrayn*), both essence and attribute reside in you [. . .] Did you ever realise that you are the one who speaks the Book of God?'[28] The idea that the human being is a locus of divinity and potential producer of Qur'an-like revelation would be viewed as blasphemy (*kufr*) by many Muslim scholars, but for Alevi-Bektashis it is a common trope. These communities interpreted and used the Qur'an very differently from neighbouring Sunnis and Twelver Shi'is. For many such groups, the poetry of their saints and bards held a more prominent place than the Qur'an in shaping their worldview and ritual life. Additionally, the Bektashi order was banned in 1826, making it difficult to publicly express Bektashi views for most of the late nineteenth and early twentieth centuries.[29] Because of this combination of factors, they did not play a visible role in the debates on Qur'anic translation in the late Ottoman Empire and early Turkish Republic.

All things considered, it is important to keep in mind that the views of the jurists have never been homogenous or hegemonic. There have always been jurists of various legal schools who supported translations as well as a range of different approaches to vernacular renderings and conceptions of the Qur'an by Sufis, litterateurs and non-jurists. For instance, the Islamicate literary world has often called the *Mathnawī* of Jalāl al-Dīn Rūmī 'The Persian Qur'an', though it is not a translation of the Qur'an but rather a massive work of rhymed verse that takes a great deal of inspiration from the Qur'an. It is a 'Qur'an' in the sense that it is thought by some to be the most eloquent piece of literature in the Persian language, much as the Qur'an is for the Arabic language, and perhaps also divinely inspired.[30]

Muslim scholars were not unique in considering scriptural language sacred language. Given the ties between politics, religious authorities and holy writ, changing the medium of religious texts by altering either their mode of production or their language has proven to be a sensitive matter in diverse societies and traditions. From the translation of the Jewish scriptures into Greek to the vernacular renderings of the Bible in early modern Europe, the history of scriptural translation has been fraught with controversy and, at times, even violence. For instance, because the Catholic Church considered Latin a sacred language and the idiom of its religio-political authority, it severely punished those who translated the official Latin version of the Bible (itself a translation) into European vernaculars. To translate was to challenge church authority and reject the dominance of Latin scripture. During the sixteenth century, Biblical translators like the English scholar William Tyndale (1494–1536) were excommunicated, imprisoned and even executed because they were considered opponents of Catholic authority.[31]

While Islamic legal opinion often rejects Qur'anic translation, there is not a similar history of violent suppression of such works and, in fact, Islamic societies have often used other forms of rewriting the text or of 'bringing it to understanding'.[32] The term *tafsīr* plays an important role in Arabic and in Islamic discourse for genres that explain and communicate the meaning of the Qur'an. The most basic, pre-technical meaning of *tafsīr* is to make plain what is concealed or to open up what is closed. As a genre, the word *tafsīr* is usually translated in English as commentary, interpretation or exegesis. Jews and Christians writing in Arabic use *tafsīr* to refer to translations of, as well as commentaries on, the Bible.[33] In Islamic literature, it suggests a range of explanations and expansions on the Qur'anic text. Some texts with the name *tafsīr* include multiple types of explanation which involves applying etymology, commenting on the text, expanding at length on individual words, citing relevant narrative material and, in other places, translating or paraphrasing.

Similar to the relationship between *translation* and *interpretation* in English, the boundary between *tarjama* and *tafsīr* is sometimes clear and other times blurred in traditions of Islamicate letters. The Arabic dictionary *Lisān al-ʿArab* by Ibn Manẓūr (d. 711/1312) defines 'translator' (*tarjumān*) as 'an interpreter of language' (*al-mufassir li'l-lisān*), that is, one who performs *tafsīr* on language.[34] In similar fashion, the late Ottoman dictionary *Lûgat-i Ebüzziya* defines translation as 'explaining (*tefsir*) and clarifying one language with another'.[35] The fact that Islamicate linguistic traditions often use these terms to define one another underlines the idea that the activities of translation (*tarjama*) and interpretation (*tafsīr*) are closely linked and difficult to distinguish, thereby reflecting the contemporary truism that *every translation is an interpretation*.

The Shāfiʿī jurist Muḥammad b. Bahādur al-Zarkashī (d. 794/1392) reports a conversation in which a teacher tells his students that translating (*tarjama*) the Qur'an is forbidden. A student then asks him if that means that no one is permitted to interpret (*tafsīr*) the Qur'an. This astute question points to the heart of the matter: the distinction between *tafsīr* and *tarjama* is often hazy. The teacher responds by attempting to distinguish between the two: translation can potentially replace the original text, whereas interpretation merely informs the hearer of what the interpreter understands.[36] The distinction between replacement and explanatory supplement is crucial. For renderings of the Qur'an, Muslim scholars almost unanimously rejected the former and embraced the latter. Unlike the case of the canonised Christian Bibles, which were replaced by translations in Syriac, Latin and Coptic, and later German, Dutch and English, the Qur'an in its original language has been defended vigorously as a central component of Islamic ritual and scholarship.

Despite the formal prohibitions of translations in legal compendia, oral and written translations have played an important role in the propagation and teaching of Islam. The social realities of Muslim ritual often departed dramatically from the letter of Islamic legal manuals. The ritual use of translations in Bukhara and along the Volga is well attested, and it is likely that similar uses occurred in other regions as well. Zadeh argues that Abū Ḥanīfa's pro-translation fatwa probably granted *post factum* legitimacy to an already existing phenomenon of the performance of ritual in the Persian language.[37] Moreover, some jurists like the Shāfiʿī scholar al-Isfarāʾīnī (d. 471/1078–9) broke ranks with their legal schools and argued that translation (*tarjama*) was crucial for propagating and teaching Islam among non-Arabs.[38] He wrote that the necessity of translation was clear, given that 'the Arabs and those who know Arabic are fewer in number than those who do not know [Arabic]', a refrain that would often be heard in the debates on the subject in the Ottoman era as well.[39] Evidence suggests that non-Arab Muslims in Transoxiana and Khurasan had 'fully integrated' the Persian language as a means of interpreting and transmitting the Qur'an by the eleventh century.[40]

Turkish-speaking Muslims in Anatolia and the Balkans made similar arguments in favour of Qur'anic translation. For the predominately Ḥanafī Muslims in these regions, the (for some) controversial opinion of Abū Ḥanīfa was the paradigmatic reference for validating Turkish language as a medium of ritual, scripture and religious knowledge. For instance, the rhyming Ottoman legal manual *Vikaye-i Manzume* invokes his views:

> He saw the Persian Qur'an as valid no less
> Whoever reads it in prayer may he do it with zest
> In whatever language, in whatever tongue it may be,
> words are mere tools, meaning is the key[41]

The verses diminish the importance of Qur'anic Arabic, claiming that any idiom, even Turkish – a language often viewed as coarse, even barbaric, by Arabs and Persians – could convey divine meaning. As in the Persianate world, the ghost of Abū Ḥanīfa would loom large in the Ottoman-Turkish debates of the coming centuries.

Turkish Translations of the Qur'an

The earliest known translations in Old Anatolian Turkish, the most direct predecessor of Ottoman and modern Turkish, date back to the fourteenth and fifteenth centuries, the oldest dated copy bearing the year 827/1424.[42] Building on a Central Asian tradition of multilingual interlinear Qur'anic translations, these interlinear texts are either bilingual (Arabic–Turkish) or trilingual (Arabic–Persian–Turkish), and they began to appear in the fourteenth century following the break-up of the Anatolian Seljuk state into territories governed by Turkish-speaking rulers.[43] Some works provide word-for-word Turkish equivalents underneath Arabic terms, forming a running glossary for the Arabic.[44] However, many translations from this period translate and paraphrase complete verses or chapters.[45]

Manuscripts of interlinear Qur'an translations were supplementary texts that did not threaten to replace the Arabic Qur'an. The translation is subordinated graphically on the page, written or scribbled in smaller script underneath the Arabic original in a different colour. This format stands in sharp contrast to modern bilingual translations where the translations are found in columns parallel to the Arabic, suggesting equivalence in meaning and prestige. The earliest Turkic and Turkish translations do not rhyme, nor are they written in metre as were some early Persian translations. This suggests that they did not function as texts to be recited ritually. Moreover, reports of Turkish-language prayer and the use of translations in ritual are notably lacking in historical accounts from the early Ottoman and pre-Ottoman periods. While the evidence for constructing a social history of how such texts were used is fragmentary, it seems that literate elites and the ulama used interlinear translations to aid their reading of the Arabic text and in educational settings.

Additionally, interlinear texts occasioned no controversies in the early Ottoman context and seem to have been composed and used by the ulama. The uncontroversial nature of these books underscores the importance of historical context in determining what was at stake when controversies over the translation of the Qur'an did erupt in later centuries. It was only with the coming of print that translations of the Qur'an began to appear threatening in the Ottoman Empire, causing Muslim scholars to reopen the classical debates on translation and acceptable genres of interpretation. In the modern period, the question of access to books and control of interpretation hinged largely on print technology and its ability to amplify the dissemination of texts, transform written culture and give voice to competing ideas.

Modern Factors, New Conversations

To make sense of Qur'anic translation debates in the modern period, we must not only understand the classical positions but also consider the new factors that reshaped conversations among intellectuals and enabled vernacular renderings to blossom. When late Ottoman and Turkish thinkers discussed translation they did so in a print-based public sphere, within the context of a centralised modern state that had steadily diminished the power of the ulama, and at a time when Muslims had intimate knowledge of European history, intellectual currents and Christian missionary activities. These contexts were radically different from that of Abū Ḥanīfa or any other scholar of the premodern period, and the evolving opinions on Qur'anic translation sought to meet the needs of the modern period, not to rehash theoretical debates from centuries before. Qur'anic translations re-emerged as controversial books in the modern period because they were consequential for the modernisation of Ottoman and Turkish societies during a period of political and intellectual crisis. Far from being a subject of scholastic debate, translation involved actual dramatic shifts in political authority and the economy of knowledge production.

One issue to take into consideration is the unequal balance of power between the Ottoman Empire and Europe during the nineteenth century. European states exerted immense political and cultural influence on the late Ottoman Empire, and, as a result, European historical trajectories provided the empire with models for imitation, adaptation or rejection. Many Ottoman intellectuals envisioned Islamic reform along the lines of European developments and presented the Reformation, nationalism and liberalism as viable sources of inspiration. Additionally, the ascent of Euro-American power enabled widespread Christian missionary activities across the eastern Mediterranean which included translating and refuting the Qur'an.[46] These attacks on the Qur'an created a sense of urgency among Muslims to defend their sacred book. The power disparity between the Ottomans and the European empires coloured the way in which Turkish Muslims weighed the pros and cons of Qur'anic translation and charted new courses for reform and renewal.

Translation itself meant something distinct in this period. The concept had new connotations and layers of meaning shaped by modern history. In addition to the traditional understanding of the Arabic terms *tarjama* and *tafsīr*, Turkish and European notions of translation influenced the debates about rendering the Qur'an into the vernacular. The translation of European, especially French, literary works led to vibrant discussions on the role and meaning of translation in Ottoman society,[47] and the transfer of scientific and technical knowledge via translation played a prominent role in the process of Ottoman-Turkish modernisation. Şehnaz Tahir-Gürçağlar writes that, 'Translation came to be regarded as an instrument of enlightenment and modernization in the late Ottoman Empire and early Republican period both by the ruling elite and the intellectuals of the country.'[48] In other words, translation was no mere linguistic endeavour; it was seen as a tool of progress.

Within late Ottoman society, the decline of the ulama's institutional power and the development of a print-based public sphere granted new opportunities for non-ulama intellectuals to influence public opinion on Islamic issues. Muhammad Qasim Zaman has shown that the ulama in South Asia were successful in competing with the new intellectuals via print media. In the late Ottoman Empire, this was true to a certain extent, but devout non-ulama intellectuals were far more successful. The ulama progressively lost authority and public influence as the state curtailed their political power and social standing during the last decades of the empire and in the early years of the Turkish Republic.[49] For non-ulama intellectuals, the assertion of *tarjama* was metonymic for a new vision of Islamic authority that demanded more democratic access to Qur'anic knowledge and asserted the right of the non-ulama to weigh in on Islamic matters. The modern genre of Qur'anic translation emerged simultaneously with these new intellectuals and challenged the authority of the ulama to act as the official interpreters of the Qur'an. Supporters of Qur'anic translation in the late Ottoman Empire and Turkey argued for a revival of the opinion of Abū Ḥanīfa and for an imitation of Martin Luther's German Bible in the form of a Turkish Qur'an in order to challenge the ulama's monopoly of Qur'anic interpretation and reveal the meaning of the sacred book to larger swathes of Ottoman society.

Given the threat to ulama authority, many late Ottoman and early republican ulama strongly opposed translation in order to protect the community from what they believed were the insufficiencies and excesses of the new intellectuals and, moreover, to safeguard their position as the custodians of Islamic knowledge. In the eyes of many ulama, the Qur'an needed to be protected and preserved during these difficult times, not opened up to potentially radical reinterpretation by self-styled intellectuals influenced by European literature and learning. For them, *tarjama* of the Qur'an amounted to a breakdown in Islamic authority that could very well lead to chaos.

Despite these fears, even during the heyday of Turkish nationalism in the 1920s and 1930s, Turkish translators encountered an immense 'intervening body of commentary' that limited the range of licit translations they could make.[50] Devout intellectuals and the ulama expected translations of the Qur'an to be informed by, and to agree with, the commentaries, so to varying degrees translators practised *tarjama* through *tafsīr*, consulting works of Qur'anic commentary to guarantee the correctness of their translations. Print media enabled translators to disseminate new renderings of the Qur'an far and wide, but it also made their task more difficult. Because of this new media, modern translators faced a great deal of scrutiny and criticism since their audience – which included those who had spent their entire life reciting, studying and revering the text – could attack their renderings publicly in newspapers, journals and pamphlets. This context made radical reinterpretations of the text unfeasible and gave traditional commentaries significant influence in shaping modern translations.

The influence of Europe, an expanding print culture and the crisis of ulama authority added new dynamics to the traditional scholarly debates on Qur'anic translation. Throughout this book, these factors will be considered while tracing the emergence of Qur'anic translation from the earliest printed Turkish commentaries on the Qur'an in the mid-nineteenth century to those produced shortly before World War II. This period, from roughly 1840–1940, marks the crucial transition in which translations of the Qur'an broke through scholarly and legal taboos and became mainstream Islamic literature, both in Turkey and in the larger Muslim world.

Structure of the Book

Since print media is crucial to the popularisation of Qur'an translations, examining print history and attitudes towards print technology figure prominently in this exploration. The history of the printing of the Qur'an in the late Ottoman Empire will be dealt with in Chapter One and Chapter Two; both use materials from the Ottoman archives to provide an account of how the Ottomans came to print the Qur'an and how printed copies helped to bring about the broader shift towards Qur'anic accessibility. Next follows an examination, in Chapter Three, of the rise of Turkish as an Islamic language via the Turkish-language Qur'anic commentaries that became prevalent in the latter half of the nineteenth century. Additionally, it probes the ethos of vernacular access – the notion that Muslims should have access to renderings in their own language – that crystallised at the turn of the century.

Chapter Four examines the translation debates from 1908 to 1918 through the perspectives of the prominent Egyptian writer Muḥammad Rashīd Riḍā (1865–1935), Christian missionaries and the Russian Tatar reformist Musa Carullah Bigiyev (1875–1949). Moreover, it considers the relationship between translation, narratives of progress and emerging discourses of Turkish nationalism. Chapter Five explores the controversial translations published during the early years of the Republic of Turkey that dismayed the public and instigated the state to sponsor an official translation project in response. Following on from this, Chapter Six will demonstrate how Arab, South Asian and English Muslims wrestled with the question of translation in the period following the Turkish Qur'an controversy; it will also examine the emergence of seminal English-language translations in the light of Turkish debates. On the heels of the developments in Turkey, Egyptian scholars reignited the debate about the necessity of translations to properly represent and spread Islam to the rest of the world. Chapter Seven examines the state-sponsored translation project in Turkey, the experiments with Turkish-language ritual and the difficulties that were encountered in attempting to create an official translation. Chapter Eight provides a summation of the discussions of previous chapters.

NOTES

1 Elmalılı Muhammed Hamdi Yazır, *Hak Dini Kur'an Dili: Yeni Mealli Türkçe Tefsir* (Istanbul, Matbaa-i Ebüzziya, 1935–9).

2 Ömer Rıza [Doğrul], *Kur'an Nedir?* (Istanbul, Amedi Matbaası, 1927), pp. 88–9.
3 For example, Hussein Abdul-Raof, *Qur'an Translation: Discourse, Texture and Exegesis* (Richmond, Curzon, 2001); idem, 'The Qur'an: Limits of Translatability', in Said Faiq, ed., *Cultural Encounters in Translation from Arabic* (Clevedon, Multilingual Matters, 2004), pp. 91–106; A.R. Kidawi, 'Translating the Untranslatable: A Survey of English Translations of the Quran', *Muslim World Book Review* 7, no. 4 (1987), pp. 66–71.
4 Notable exceptions to this trend include Travis Zadeh, *The Vernacular Qur'an: Translation and the Rise of Persian Exegesis* (Oxford, Oxford University Press in association with The Institute of Ismaili Studies, 2012) and Sufia Uddin, *Constructing Bangladesh* (Chapel Hill, University of North Carolina Press, 2006).
5 Gotthelf Bergsträsser, 'Koranlesung in Kairo', *Der Islam* 20 (1932), pp. 1–42; idem, 'Koranlesung in Kairo', *Der Islam* 21 (1933), pp. 110–34.
6 Muallim Ömer Naci, *Hülasatü'l-İhlas*, ed. Ahmed Sabri (Istanbul, Matbaa-i Ebüzziya, 1304/1886–7), p. 4.
7 Gottfried Hagen, 'Translations and Translators in a Multilingual Society: A Case Study of Persian–Ottoman Translations, Late Fifteenth to Early Seventeenth Century', *Eurasian Studies* 2, no. 1 (2003), p. 131.
8 Niyazi Berkes, *The Development of Secularism in Turkey* (New York, Routledge, 1998), p. 487; Mahmut Esat Bozkurt, *Atatürk İhtilâli* (Istanbul, Burhaneddin Matbaası, 1940), p. 313; Charles H. Sherrill, *A Year's Embassy to Mustafa Kemal* (New York, Charles Scribner's Sons, 1934), pp. 193–6.
9 Ziya Gökalp, *Ziya Gökalp Külliyatı*, vol. I: *Şiirler ve Halk Masalları*, ed. Fevziye Abdullah Tansel (Ankara, Türk Tarih Kurumu Basımevi, 1952), p. 113.
10 Ibid.
11 Marmaduke Pickthall, *The Meaning of the Glorious Koran* (New York, Dorset, 1985), p. vii.
12 Richard C. Martin, 'Inimitability', *EQ*, vol. II, pp. 526–36.
13 On the topic of Qur'anic self-consciousness, see Daniel A. Madigan, *The Qur'ân's Self Image: Writing and Authority in Islam's Scripture* (Princeton, NJ, Princeton University Press, 2001); Stefan Wild, *Self-Referentiality in the Qur'ān* (Wiesbaden, Harrassowitz, 2006); idem, ed., *The Qur'an as Text* (Leiden, Brill, 1996).
14 Q. 12:2 and Q. 20:113 have been modified by the author.
15 A. Kevin Reinhart, 'Jurisprudence', in Andrew Rippin, ed., *The Blackwell Companion to the Qur'ān* (Malden, MA, Blackwell, 2006), p. 439.
16 Zadeh, *Vernacular Qur'an*, p. 114.
17 Zadeh, *Vernacular Qur'an*, pp. 60–61; Mahmoud Ayoub, 'Translating the Meanings of the Qur'an: Traditional Opinions and Modern Debates', *Afkar/Inquiry* 3, no. 5 (1986), p. 35.
18 Reinhart, 'Jurisprudence', p. 437.
19 Zadeh, *Vernacular Qur'an*, p. 118.
20 Benedict Anderson, *Imagined Communities: Reflections on the Origin and Spread of Nationalism* (New York, Verso, 1991), p. 14.
21 Ibid., p. 41.
22 Zadeh, *Vernacular Qur'an*, p. 73.

23 Ayoub, 'Translating', p. 35.
24 Ibid, p. 36.
25 Zadeh, *Vernacular Qu'ran*, pp. 75–7.
26 Ibid., pp. 126–9.
27 See John Kingsley Birge, *The Bektashi Order of Dervishes* (London, Luzac, 1937); Markus Dressler, *Writing Religion: The Making of Turkish Alevi Islam* (Oxford, Oxford University Press, 2013).
28 A favourite concept for mystical contemplation, 'the confluence of the two seas' is mentioned in Q. 18:60; see Bedri Noyan, *Bektaşilik Alevilik Nedir?* (Ankara, Doğuş Matbaacılık, 1985), p. 249.
29 Birge, *The Bektashi Order*, p. 16.
30 It was the poet Nūr al-Dīn ʿAbd al-Raḥmān Jāmī (817/1414–898/1492) who originally called Rūmī's work the Persian Qur'an (*Qur'ān dar zabān-e pahlawī*); Nile Green, *Bombay Islam: The Religious Economy of the West Indian Ocean, 1840–1915* (Cambridge, Cambridge University Press, 2011), p. 100.
31 'Tyndale, William', *Oxford Encyclopedia of the Reformation* (Oxford, Oxford University Press, 1996)
32 Richard E. Palmer, *Hermeneutics* (Evanston, IL, Northwestern University Press, 1969), p. 13.
33 Andrew Rippin, 'Tafsīr', *EI*[2], vol. X, pp. 85–8.
34 Muḥammad b. Mukarram Ibn Manẓūr, *Lisān al-ʿarab* (Beirut, Dār Iḥyāʾ Turāth al-ʿArabī, 1997), II, p. 26.
35 Ebüzziya Tevfik, *Lûgat-i Ebüzziya* (Istanbul, Matbaa-i Ebüzziya, 1306/1888–9), p. 319.
36 Muḥammad b. Bahādur al-Zarkashī, *Baḥr al-muḥīṭ fī uṣūl al-fiqh* (Beirut, Dār al-Kutub al-ʿIlmiyya, 2000), p. 361.
37 Travis Zadeh, 'Translation, Geography, and the Divine Word: Mediating Frontiers in Pre-Modern Islam' (PhD Dissertation, Harvard University, 2006), pp. 477–8. On Bukharan translations, see Ashirbek Muminov, 'Disputes in Bukhara on the Persian Translation of the Qur'ān', *Mélanges de l'Université Saint-Joseph* 59 (2006), pp. 301–8.
38 Zadeh, 'Translation', pp. 518–21.
39 Ibid., p. 520.
40 Ibid., p. 522.
41 Balıkesirli Devletoğlu Yusuf, *Vikaye-i Manzume*, MS İzmir 762 (Süleymaniye Library, Istanbul), p. 3.
42 Türk-İslam Eserler Müzesi no. 40 (827/1424), Istanbul, Turkey.
43 Mehmet bin Hamza and Ahmet Topaloğlu, *XV. Yüzyıl Başlarında Yapılmış Satır-Arası Kur'an Tercümesi* (Istanbul, Devlet Kitapları, 1976), p. xvii. On Central Asian Turkic translations, see János Eckmann, *Middle Turkic Glosses of the Rylands Interlinear Koran Translation* (Budapest, Akadémiai Kiadó, 1976); Gülden Sağol, ed., *An Interlinear Translation of the Qur'an into Khwarzm Turkish* (Cambridge, MA, Harvard University – Department of Near Eastern Languages and Civilizations, 1993); Zeki Velidi Togan, 'The Earliest Translation of the Qur'an into Turkish', *İslam Tetkikleri Enstitüsü Dergisi* 4 (1964), pp. 1–19.
44 Hamza and Topaloğlu, *XV. Yüzyıl Başlarında Yapılmış Satır-Arası Kur'an Tercümesi*, p. 3.

45 Ibid., p. xviii. See, for example, Esra Karabacak, *An Inter-Linear Translation of the Qur'an into Old Anatolian Turkish* (Cambridge, MA, Harvard University - Department of Near Eastern Languages and Civilizations, 1994).
46 See Chapter Four in this book.
47 Cemal Demircioğlu, 'From Discourse to Practice: Rethinking "Translation" (*Terceme*) and Related Practices of Text Production in the Late Ottoman Literary Tradition' (PhD Thesis, Boğaziçi University, 2005), pp. 3–14.
48 Şehnaz Tahir-Gürçağlar, 'The Translation Bureau Revisited', in María Calzada Pérez, ed., *Apropos of Ideology: Translation Studies on Ideology - Ideologies in Translation Studies* (Manchester, St Jerome Publishing, 2003), p. 114.
49 Muhammad Qasim Zaman, 'Commentaries, Print and Patronage: "Ḥadīth" and the Madrasas in Modern South Asia', *Bulletin of the School of Oriental and African Studies* 62, no. 1 (1999), pp. 60–81.
50 George Steiner, *After Babel: Aspects of Language and Translation*, 2nd edn (Oxford, Oxford University Press, 1992), p. 262.

1

'The Mother of Civilisation': The Printing Press and Illegal Copies of the Qur'an

> The craft of printing and publishing is worthy of being characterised as the mother of civilisation. It is a magnificent technology, without equal, deserving to be called the most useful and highest of human inventions.
>
> Ahmet Cevdet Pasha (1822–95), *Tarih-i Cevdet*

In mid-nineteenth century Istanbul, a copy of the Qur'an (*muṣḥaf*) would have been made by hand over the course of a month, many months or even years, depending upon the speed and circumstance of the scribe. Since an average copy numbered around six hundred pages, producing an accurate, readable book was no small task. Copies varied widely in terms of artistry, the quality of materials and the skill of the scribe, which could range from that of a master calligrapher (*hattat*) to a less talented copyist (*nessah, müstensih*). As a consequence of the manual mode of production, even the most humble copy of the Qur'an was an expensive object that few people could afford to own.

While the method of reproducing manuscript copies of the Qur'an changed relatively little over the centuries, the demand for books had changed quite dramatically by the mid-nineteenth century. The expansion of Ottoman bureaucracy and state schools in the 1800s created an unprecedented need for affordable books as more Ottoman subjects learned to read and used books for education, cultural edification and religious instruction. The first attempts to build a modern educational system organised by the state began during the Tanzimat era (1839–76). The first state middle schools (*rüşdiyye*) were opened in Istanbul in 1847 and gradually spread to the provinces. During the 1840s and 1860s, traditional Qur'an schools that taught memorisation of the text were also increased in number and, in some cases, reformed to teach basic literacy in order to prepare students for middle school.[1] In 1869, new regulations created a standardised curriculum for state schools and made attendance mandatory for certain age groups of boys and girls. Additionally, they created a system of high schools (*idadi* and *sultani*) for larger towns and cities.[2] As we shall see below, controversies over the printing of the Qur'an began precisely in this context of educational expansion and increasing demand for books.

The printing press made it possible to meet this need in various fields, but it could not be used for the Qur'an as the reproduction of the Holy Book was controlled by scribes with close ties to the ulama who opposed its printing for a combination of economic, religious and cultural reasons. They were concerned about the economic ramifications of print technology for their livelihoods and worried about the ritual purity of an unknown method of reproduction. Also, the use of heavy machinery imported from Europe to produce the Muslim Holy Book appeared to be sacrilegious and disrespectful. Opposition from the book copyists and certain segments of the ulama influenced state policy on this issue and prevented the mechanisation of Qur'anic reproduction for some time.

When Ottoman Muslims in Istanbul began to use the printing press in 1727, establishing the first Muslim-run press in the world, they were not granted permission to print copies of the Qur'an and did not do so until the late nineteenth century, decades after their co-religionists in Russia, Iran, Egypt and India. Additionally, the state forbade the publishing of the Qur'an in other regions within its realm and banned the importing of printed copies from abroad, thereby making any printed Qur'an in the empire an illicit object. However, demand for affordable copies was strong, and, as a result, imported and illegally printed copies of the Qur'an flooded the Ottoman book market. The state responded by enforcing an embargo on printed copies of the Qur'an for most of the nineteenth century, but the ubiquitous illegal Qur'an copies and the increasing demand for them presented the traditional bookmakers with a robust challenge.

Affordability and Access

For Ottoman Muslims, learning to recite and, in some cases, read the Qur'an formed the foundation of education for both rich and poor. Oral recitation could be taught via rote methods to a broad swathe of society in mosques and madrasas. Yet, the vast majority of Ottoman Muslims did not own a copy of the Qur'an because of its high price. The fact that most Ottoman subjects were illiterate did not mean that families or individuals did not want to possess a copy; for many, the value of the book as a sacred object that adorned and protected the home was more important than reading or reciting it. The prohibitive cost, not illiteracy, explains why most Ottoman Muslims before the twentieth century did not own a copy of the Holy Book.

Estate records from Ottoman Sofia (modern-day Bulgaria) reveal that the price of a copy had reached 1,000–2,000 Ottoman *akçe* by the second half of the eighteenth century when the average price of a cow was between 600 and 1,000 *akçe*,[3] and a skilled worker in Istanbul earned 113.4 *akçe* per day.[4] By the early nineteenth century, the average price in Sofia ranged from 3,600 to 6,000 *akçe* (30–50 *kuruş*), when the daily wage for a skilled worker in Istanbul averaged 401.2 *akçe* (1810–19).[5] Thus, such a labourer would have needed wages from nine days of work to purchase one of the less expensive copies, and an unskilled labourer would have had to work twice that to pay for a copy. What this means is that it was rare or, at the very least, difficult for the less well-to-do to buy a copy of the Qur'an.[6]

Muslims had access to written copies of the Qur'an located in mosques and libraries, but the ability to own a *muṣḥaf* for the home or for private study was constrained. While this did not pose a serious problem for much of Ottoman history, the newly established school systems of the nineteenth century expanded the need for copies of the Qur'an; more broadly, the spread of printing made books of all varieties cheaper and book ownership more common, thereby increasing the expectation that printed copies of the Qur'an should be affordable and accessible. These factors colluded to make possession of a physical copy of the Qur'an more desirable than ever. The high price of manuscript copies, however, made this desire difficult to fulfil.

Printed Copies of the Qur'an in Europe

The first encounter of Ottoman Muslims with printed copies of the Qur'an occurred in the sixteenth century when Venetian merchants brought a printed edition to sell in the Ottoman domains. The printing of the Qur'an in Arabic and in translation began as European ventures in the 1500s, when Ottoman armies and occupations extended into Central Europe and Europeans saw the Ottomans as an impending threat. Ottoman victories over European armies spurred an interest among Christian leaders in 'the Turks' and their religion. The German reformer Martin Luther and others initially understood Islam to be a heresy – not a distinct religion – and viewed the Ottoman threat as a punishment from God for the wicked ways of Christians. The quest to understand and undermine the Ottomans in sixteenth-century Europe led Luther and others to support publishing a Latin translation of the Qur'an. Some Europeans opposed printing such a translation because they felt that the Qur'an was a dangerous book. These opponents accepted the necessity for European scholars to read and understand the Qur'an, but they insisted that only pious scholars do so, suggesting concern about the possibility of conversions to Islam.[7]

Nevertheless, important Protestant reformers supported the publication of a Latin translation of the Qur'an and supported its publication. The scholar Theodor Bibliander believed that God had given Christians the printing press in order to attack the Antichrist, and argued that publishing a translation of the Qur'an would assist in the struggle to convert Muslims.[8] Martin Luther was the key advocate of the project and he laid out an extensive rationale, arguing that Christian Europe faced two devils, the inner devil, the Pope, and the outer devil, the Turks. For Luther, translating scripture was a means of defeating both the inner and outer devils; he believed the vernacular Bible would break the Catholic Church's control over the scriptures and the translation of the Qur'an would expose the theological error of the Turks. Luther knew that many Muslims did not favour translating the text and explained Muslim opposition to translation in a novel way, claiming that Muslims opposed translation in order to hide what he considered its falsity and ridiculous legends. In stark contrast to the doctrine of Qur'anic inimitability, Luther recast Muslim opposition to translation as a way of covering up an embarrassing text. For Luther, the printed, translated Qur'an would be a powerful weapon in the arsenal of Protestant pastors, exposing the text and revealing the depravity of the Muslim religion.[9]

Luther's desire became reality in 1543, when Bibliander and Johannes Oporinus printed a twelfth-century Latin translation of the Qur'an titled *Lex Mahumet pseudoprophete* (The Law of Muhammad the False Prophet) by an English monk named Robert of Ketton (fl. 1141–57).[10] The volume enjoyed resounding commercial success, leading Bibliander to publish a second edition in 1550. Early Protestants printed Latin renderings of the Qur'an in order to discredit the text, and, to ensure this effect, they printed it together with explicit refutations. Luther himself translated Ricoldo da Monte Croce's Latin refutation of the Qur'an into German in 1542.[11] Protestant printers envisioned the Latin translation as a weapon for use in a bodily and spiritual battle against the Ottoman Turks.

The rise in printing in the fifteenth and sixteenth centuries that had bolstered the Protestant cause by rapidly spreading its literature and pamphlets also made possible a new, expanded commerce for books in which thousands of copies could be produced and substantial fortunes could be made. Benedict Anderson has called this new business of the book 'print-capitalism'.[12] During the same period, European publishers began to print Arabic editions of the Qur'an. Given that Luther's German translations of the Bible had sold an astounding number of copies, it stood to reason that there might be an equally vast market for the Muslim Holy Book. With this in mind, the Venetian publisher Paganino de' Paganini published the first ever full-length printed Qur'an in 1537/1538. Unlike the Latin translation, these Arabic-only editions were not intended for a European audience but rather for Muslims. Very few

Europeans could read Arabic in this period, and the first Arabic grammar for readers of Latin was not published until 1540.[13]

Paganini planned to export this Venetian-printed edition to the Ottoman Empire and possibly other Mediterranean ports as well. Viewing the eastern Mediterranean as a vast potential market, Paganini sought to include the Qur'an in the commercial sphere of early modern print capitalism. It was a bold idea for a Christian publisher to attempt to sell printed copies of the Qur'an to Muslims. Jurists traditionally forbade Muslim warriors from carrying copies of the Qur'an into non-Muslim territories due to fears that the books would fall into non-Muslim possession, which would defile the text.[14] Discussions of non-Muslim impurity in relation to the Qur'an centre around Q. 56:77–80: *it is surely a noble Koran in a hidden Book none but the purified shall touch, a sending down from the Lord of all Being.* The idea of Christians producing the text and selling it to Muslims would have been scandalous to the Ottoman ulama, just as it would have been unlikely for sixteenth-century Christians to welcome the opportunity to purchase copies of the Bible from Ottoman Muslims. It is unclear whether Paganini fully grasped this; moreover, it appears that he did not fully understand Ottoman laws prohibiting the importation of printed books in the Arabic script.

When Paganini's printed copies of the Qur'an arrived in Istanbul, Ottoman authorities intercepted, confiscated and reportedly destroyed them. Scholars have pointed out that not only would these Qur'an copies have been found objectionable on account of their Christian provenance, but it is unlikely that they would have satisfied the aesthetic tastes of Ottoman Muslims because the Arabic text included numerous errors and was stilted and clumsy in appearance. However, it is important to keep in mind that regardless of their appearance, elegant or ugly, non-Qur'anic printed books in the Arabic script were not permitted to circulate in the Ottoman domains until 1588, and printed editions of the Qur'an did not become legal, as we shall see below, until several centuries later. Quite simply, Paganini's books were illegal, regardless of whether they had defects in content or style. Ottoman authorities would have recognised the illegality of Paganini's imported books at first glance. Paganini was detained and then later released due to the intervention of the Venetian ambassador. Jean Bodin's *Colloque entre sept scavans* suggests that Ottoman authorities intended to execute Paganini and that the intervention of a Venetian ambassador managed to spare his life.[15] Ultimately, Paganini's venture to sell printed copies of the Qur'an to Muslims ended in financial ruin, and only one copy of the text is known to have survived. This sole surviving Venetian edition was found in the library of the Franciscan Friars of San Michel in Isola, Venice.[16]

In sixteenth-century Europe, two distinct motives led to the printing of the Qur'an: polemic and profit. Printed Latin translations were designed to serve as polemic propaganda against the Ottoman Empire and Islam. By endeavouring to expose and refute the Qur'an, they helped construct ideological opposition against the threat of Ottoman invasion and conversion to Islam. In sharp contrast, Venetian publishers printed Arabic versions for financial gain without any polemic agenda whatsoever. They did not have any qualms about printing books that would potentially be used for Muslim ritual and education, that is, activities that would perpetuate and potentially strengthen Islam. These two motives, polemics and profit, marked the first encounters of the Qur'an with the printing press. Both of these ventures – firsts in the history of Qur'anic printing – revealed the conflicting relationship between European Christians and Ottoman Muslims, who were enemies in some instances and trading partners in others.

Sephardic Jews, refugees from the Spanish expulsion of Iberian Jews and Muslims, had established the first printing press in Istanbul in the early 1490s. The Ottoman state granted permission for non-Muslim religious communities to use the press in the late fifteenth century, but did not allow Ottoman Muslims to do so. The question of why Ottoman Muslims did not embrace print technology at the same time has fuelled an ongoing conversation among historians. Though this subject is outside the parameters of this study, a brief word here is in order as Ottoman Muslim attitudes and policies towards print technology in general shed light on the reluctance of the Ottomans to print the Qur'an.

The Ottoman state followed a path of cautious acceptance and control of print for the non-Muslim communities, allowing them to use printing presses for their own communal and religious works. While Christian and Jewish communities had the right to use the press, the Ottoman state forbade the printing of any texts in the Arabic script, regardless of their content, and no Muslims were allowed to operate presses. In the sixteenth century, the Holy Roman Empire's ambassador Ogier Ghiselin de Busbecq remarked that the Ottoman Turks have 'never been able to bring themselves to print books . . . [and] . . . [held] that their scriptures, that is, their sacred books would no longer be scriptures if they were printed'.[17]

Though printing remained illegal for Muslims, Sultan Murat III (r. 1574–95) gave permission, in 1588, for the European merchants Branton and Orazio Bandini to import and sell Turkish, Persian and Arabic books on non-religious subjects. A printed version of the edict in Ottoman Turkish was appended to one of the books sold by the Bandinis, Nāṣir al-Dīn al-Ṭūsī's Arabic recension of a text by the Greek mathematician Euclid.[18] This edict was the first example of printing in the Turkish language and suggests that, though the Ottoman state was unwilling to allow Muslims to engage in printing, it did permit printed texts in the Arabic alphabet to be bought and sold in Ottoman territories.[19] The Ottoman distaste for printed books has been widely discussed, but there were also those who clearly supported the adoption of print technology. The seventeenth-century intellectual Kâtip Çelebi (aka Ḥājī Khalīfa, d. 1067/1657) complained that the lack of printing made it difficult for knowledge to be spread in the Ottoman Empire, especially with respect to the accurate and consistent reproduction of maps. In the absence of the press, he describes Ottoman book culture as beholden to scribes who could not make error-free copies.[20] In a similar vein, another observer in the early 1600s – the historian İbrahim Peçevi – wrote that 'printing a thousand volumes causes less drudgery than writing one manuscript'.[21] It is clear that the benefits of print were known and appreciated by some Ottoman Muslim statesmen and intellectuals.

The Printing of Non-Islamic Books in the Ottoman Empire

In the early eighteenth century, the state gave permission for the first Muslim-run press in the Muslim world, Darü'l-Tiba, to print books in the Arabic script. A convert to Islam from Transylvania named İbrahim Müteferrika (d. 1745) led the venture to establish a press in Istanbul. Müteferrika championed the cause of printing, obtained permission from Sultan Ahmet III (r. 1703–30) and oversaw the operations of the press from its establishment in 1727 until his death in 1745. In 1726, he wrote a treatise titled 'The Usefulness of Printing' in which he pleads for the adoption of printing by Ottoman Muslims. In it, he extols the virtues of the printed text, arguing that it has more clarity, is useful for education, passes on knowledge, enables error-free replication, lasts longer, makes books less expensive, improves organisation, permits greater dissemination and fights ignorance. Müteferrika also makes reference to the destruction and loss of many books in war and fires, suggesting that the resultant scarcity of books poses the danger of certain works being permanently lost in the Ottoman domains if printing is not embraced. He also notes that Europeans profit financially from the book trade and urges Ottoman Muslims to do so as well.[22]

The ulama played an integral part in the operation and oversight of this press. Their support was essential for legitimising Muslim use of this technology, and it is clear that they wanted some level of control over the production of books and the dissemination of knowledge. Therefore, a precondition of opening the press was that the ulama have a significant role in proofreading and oversight. The upper echelons of the ulama penned a formal opinion (*fatwa*) granting permission for printing and wrote statements supporting the venture. Furthermore, ulama members worked as proofreaders for the press and, after Müteferrika's death, they took over the day-to-day operations in addition to serving on committees overseeing the publications.[23] These endorsements and ulama participation in book culture were necessary to prevent the ulama ranks from opposing the venture. However, the ulama were not a homogenous group and there were divisions among them about how the press would reshape the bookmaking industry.

Several studies have depicted the book copyists and others in the book production trades linked to the ulama as the main source of opposition to the press. A powerful group of guilds with thousands of members, they reportedly staged a demonstration in Istanbul in the 1720s against the press and attempted to incite the people to rebel against it.[24] However, some scholars have recently cast doubt upon scribal opposition to printing. Ali Birinci argues that reports of calligraphers opposing the printing press are nothing but legends. He holds that the late adoption of the press occurred because Ottoman society did not feel a need for the technology.[25] Conventional narratives, however, explain that the copyists feared that the press would eliminate their jobs and leave them destitute and, moreover, that they viewed the manual production of books in the Arabic script as the Islamic method of transmitting texts and saw the printing press as an expression of European influence on Ottoman society. Additionally, these narratives note that, given that non-Muslims operated most presses, the Muslim bookmakers feared that Greeks, Armenians and Jews would seize the lion's share of the book trade if printing were legalised for works in the Arabic script.[26]

Ottoman scribes spent the bulk of their time copying the Qur'an and other religious texts. It was the core of their trade and their primary source of income. During the eighteenth century, Islamic works – particularly the Qur'an – were the most sought after books in Ottoman society. While book ownership was rare in general, estate registries demonstrate that the Qur'an was the most commonly owned book and that Islamic works constituted more than three-quarters of all books owned by members of the ruling (*askeri*) class.[27] On the other hand, only a small circle of educated elites wanted to purchase works of history, geography and other non-Islamic genres which were geared towards the literati. Therefore, in order to avoid a confrontation with the scribes, Müteferrika stipulated, in 'The Usefulness of Printing', that only 'books other than those of Islamic jurisprudence (*fiqh*), Qur'anic commentary, Prophetic traditions (*ḥadīth*) and theology (*kalām*)' would be printed. The imperial edict which supported the foundation of the press states that it has the licence to publish scientific works on subjects such as astronomy, philosophy and language, but not Islamic genres. With these guarantees that the press would not print Islamic works, and that the ulama viewed the technology as useful and permissible, the opposition subsided rapidly and a press was established without further obstacles.[28]

The Ottoman calligraphic tradition and its close relationship to the reproduction of the Qur'anic text contributed to the initial opposition to the printing of the sacred text, and the process by which the first Muslim printing press was established reinforced the idea that the calligraphic tradition constituted the Ottoman-Islamic way of making books. By the eighteenth century, the Ottomans had developed a rich calligraphic tradition, particularly in the domain of Qur'anic scripts. The reverence for the skill of the Ottomans in this arena is illustrated by a Turkish saying, which quips that 'the Qur'an was revealed in Mecca, recited in Cairo and written in Istanbul'.[29]

Calligraphers went through intensive training with a master. After years of study, the master granted the disciples a licence that permitted them to sign their own works and included them in a lineage of calligraphic masters which traced its origins back to the family of the Prophet Muhammad. The transmission of knowledge and skills from Muhammad, his Companions and the great scholars and saints of the past was and is fundamental for validating and authenticating practices and traditions as Islamic. The *isnād*, a genealogical chain of masters and disciples that outlines the lineage of transmission, forms the key textual device for illustrating these lineages. Ultimately, most calligraphic genealogies can be traced back to ʿAlī b. Abī Ṭālib (d. 40/661) who was the cousin of the Prophet, the first imam of the Shiʿa and the fourth caliph of Islam. Given these links, works signed by an Ottoman calligrapher bore a stamp of authenticity that traces back generations to the early Muslim community, and ostensibly guaranteed the quality and reliability of the work.

Moreover, the calligraphic tradition traces its roots to the Qur'an itself, which frequently mentions and even invokes the tools of scribal culture; the Qur'an refers to ink (*midād*, Q. 18:109), parchment (*qirṭās*, pl. *qirāṭīs*, Q. 6:7, 91) and the pen (*qalam*, pl. *aqlām*, Q. 31:27; Q. 68:1; Q. 96:4), for instance.[30] Such an example is seen in *Sūrat al-Qalam* (Q. 68, Chapter of the Pen), which begins with the oath *Nūn. By the Pen, and what they inscribe*. Some commentators have interpreted the mysterious Arabic letter *Nūn* (ن) at the beginning of the verse as a graphic depiction of an inkpot, while others view the 'Pen' as the Divine Intellect or the Agent of Creation.[31] The

Qur'anic concepts of the Preserved Tablet (*lawḥ al-maḥfūẓ*) and the Mother of the Book (*umm al-kitāb*) mentioned in the Qur'an are integral to Muslim understandings of cosmology, including the origins of revelation, God's will and the records of human deeds that determine one's entrance to either heaven or hell.[32] The tools of the scribal craft – pens, ink, books and scrolls – play a prominent role in the Qur'anic text and symbolise important elements of Muslim cosmology. All of these elements contributed to what Walter Benjamin calls the 'aura' of a work of art embedded in tradition and ritual, in this case, the aura of the Qur'anic manuscript.[33]

Printing, unlike calligraphy and writing, could not trace its origins back to the early Muslim community, but rather to fifteenth-century Germany and to the non-Muslim printers who developed the technology. Therefore, printed books lacked a lineage that provided Islamic authenticity and guaranteed the quality of work. Such a guarantee did not necessarily mean that books produced by said copyists would be error-free. In fact, it appears that Muslim scribes committed just as many errors as other men of the pen, but, nevertheless, the Ottoman calligraphic tradition was linked to a past of well-known and respected Muslim figures, which gave the practitioner an aura of reliability or, at the very least, included him in an explicitly Islamic tradition. Print technology bore a completely different lineage that was foreign and of dubious ritual purity, given that Ottoman scribes knew little about the technical aspects of the printing process. Moreover, in order to open and maintain a press, Ottoman printers relied heavily on imported technology and expertise from Europe. Within the empire, the Christian and Jewish communities pioneered the craft of printing and had far more experience and expertise than Ottoman Muslims, whereas the scribal reproduction of the Qur'an was a time-honoured and hallowed tradition for Muslims. Print technology and the vast majority of its practitioners stood outside the Islamic book traditions.

In one sense, copying the Qur'an was an act of piety. Calligraphic albums are replete with sayings that emphasise the meritorious and divine character of the scribal craft. A well-known tradition attributed to the Prophet says, 'Whoever writes *in the name of God* (*bismillāh*) in a beautiful script will enter Heaven without judgement.'[34] A calligrapher had to be in a state of ritual purity to copy the sacred text, and the practice was thought to possess great religious merit. However, copying the Qur'an was also a trade and one must be careful not to romanticise the occupation of the scribe or the calligraphic tradition in general. Scholarship on calligraphy tends to focus on elite calligraphers who produced ornate masterpieces commissioned by pashas and sultans, while paying less attention to the typical scribes and copyists (*müstensih*) who produced the average and mediocre copies of the Qur'an, which were far more common. While Islamicate intellectual traditions demonstrate reverence for the scribal craft, they also express distrust and derision towards it. For instance, the poet Fuzuli's (d. 1556) witty rant against scribal error, 'the omission of one dot makes the [Turkish word for] "eye" "blind"' (*gâh bir nokta kusuriyle gözü kör eyler*), also reinforces this view.[35] These examples reveal a complex range of sentiments towards scribes in Islamicate societies, ranging from adoration to condescension.

Beyond genealogies and cultural attitudes, it is important to bear in mind that Ottoman scribes constituted an important and powerful group in Istanbul. The number of copyists and bookmakers in Istanbul during the eighteenth century has been estimated to have been as high as 90,000.[36] Crucially, they were closely related to the ulama – another very influential group in Ottoman society and politics; writing about the processions of guilds for the Ottoman sultan, Kâtip Çelebi describes the booksellers as 'a guild which wears the clothing of the ulama and which is in the service of the ulama'.[37] The ulama and their students in the madrasa were the primary consumers of manuscript books in the Ottoman Empire, and it is no surprise that they had a close relationship with the makers and sellers of Islamic texts. In fact, the ulama controlled the booksellers' guild and managed to control the manuscript trade even after the advent of printing.[38] In tandem, the ulama and the book tradesmen comprised a powerful bloc which used its clout to shield Islamic texts from the printing press and maintain control of the Qur'an trade under the traditional bookmaker guilds.

As Muslims in neighbouring regions began to print the Qur'an in the first half of the nineteenth century, the ulama–scribal bloc rejected the trend and preserved the handwritten text, which was at the heart of their intellectual culture and their economic interests. The poet Mehmet Akif [Ersoy] (1873–1936) satirised the pious attachment to scribal texts and the distrust of the printed word in a famous poem. In it, a preacher tells his audience that the world rests on a bull, on top of a fish, under which is a sea and then rocks. The audience is sceptical, and they ask him if this is correct; he responds, 'What I am saying comes from handwritten, not printed, books. Know that whoever doubts it is a heinous heretic.'[39] For some segments of the population, scribal works alone had religious authority, and the spread of printing accented the importance of manuscript works in Islamic intellectual and ritual life. Brinkley Messick has noted a similar disdain for printed books in post-Ottoman Yemen, where the leader, Imam Yaḥyā, banned the use of printed works in certain schools.[40]

The Beginning of Islamic Printing in the Ottoman Empire

The Ottoman state embarked on significant reforms focusing on the modernisation of the Ottoman army in the late eighteenth and early nineteenth centuries. In a related development, the first printed Islamic text in Ottoman history appeared in 1803 when Sultan Mustafa III's daughter Hadice Sultan (1766–1821) financed the printing of one thousand copies of a book called *The Last Will and Testament* (*Vasiyetname*), a treatise on the basic articles of faith by the well-known Ottoman scholar Mehmet Birgivi (d. 981/1573). Birgivi was an eminent Ḥanafī jurist who clashed with the famous Shaykh al-Islam Ebu Suud (d. 1574) on a number of matters.[41] Hadice Sultan sponsored Birgivi's publication for the edification of the soldiers of the new European-style army, the New Order corps (Nizam-ı Cedid), which Sultan Selim III (r. 1789–1807) had founded in 1793. Following numerous Ottoman military defeats by European forces, the Ottoman state created this army – trained by European drill masters – with hopes of modernising the military forces.

Designed for the troops, the printed text was in simple Ottoman Turkish and included vowel markings. Hadice Sultan sponsored this venture so that the soldiers and the people would gain the basic knowledge of religion and learn how to perform the daily prayers.[42] Its format made it conducive to being read aloud, and the text may thus have been used for instructional purposes. In addition to printing this work, Hadice Sultan intended for a mosque to be built near the barracks in which the soldiers could hear sermons and receive advice from imams.[43]

Despite this attempt to instil piety via printed texts, the abstention from publishing the Qur'an itself continued well into the nineteenth century. In Istanbul, the Qur'an remained the exceptional text par excellence, exempt from the rigours of the moveable-type printing press. In fact, it is unclear whether there was any interest in printing the Qur'an in Istanbul prior to the mid-nineteenth century. The scribal Qur'an appeared to serve its purpose as there is no evidence of demand for printed copies, and, moreover, Ottoman statesmen did not wish to upset the delicate political balance by antagonising the scribes and the ulama.

However, the situation in Cairo was rather different. There, the governor of Ottoman Egypt, Mehmet Ali (1769–1849), had created a de facto autonomous country, and pushed forward a modernisation programme that was more aggressive and progressive than that of Istanbul. Though autonomous in reality, Mehmet Ali's Egypt formally remained a part of the Ottoman Empire, and intellectual life between Cairo and Istanbul remained closely connected. Under his leadership, a new printing press was established (in Bulaq) along with a range of publications including the first Ottoman language newspaper, works of history, science and religion. In the 1830s, the press in Bulaq printed partial editions of the Qur'an which contained the first chapters for children to memorise, and, given their small size, were cheaper and more portable than full-length copies and therefore easier to use for educational purposes. These appear to have been the first editions of the Qur'an printed in the Ottoman territories.

The emergence of public education provided the impetus for printing copies of the Qur'an in Mehmet Ali's Egypt. To create a modern army and bureaucracy, Mehmet Ali needed officers and officials who could read documents and maps. The expansion of education created a need for more books, and not just any sort, but standardised books. In order to provide a modern education in which students received a uniform education, printed books were preferable to manuscripts both in terms of content and cost. In 1832, the government newspaper *al-Waqāʾiʿ al-Miṣriyya* announced plans to print selected portions of the Qur'an (*ajzāʾ*) for student use in the government schools, and the first editions appeared in April 1833.[44] Unfortunately, no copies from this early printing have survived.

As in Istanbul, the Egyptian ulama had reservations about printing the Qur'an. Their wariness of this project reflects the concerns of a scribal class forced to cede their authority over sacred texts to state powers, for Mehmet Ali's modernisation campaign encroached on their domain as guardians of the textual tradition. Many of the ulama also viewed the practices of the press as *bidʿa*, that is, as a deviation from tradition or an inauspicious addition to the way of the Prophet. They raised concerns about the proper preservation of the Qur'anic content and the maintenance of ritual purity during the printing process. Specifically, they questioned whether printing involved the use of dog skins, a ritually impure material which would defile the text. As a precautionary measure, Mehmet Ali requested that the mufti of Egypt, Shaykh al-Tamīmī, place his seal on the printed copy to demonstrate the approval of the upper levels of the ulama establishment. However, it seems that these assurances did little to assuage the concerns of many in the ulama ranks, and some of their worries proved to be well founded. In the 1850s, these copies were re-examined and found to contain mistakes, leading to their recall by the Ministry of Education.[45]

The first experience with official Qur'anic printing in Ottoman Egypt provides a good example of the tension between a modernising state, ambitious to mechanise book production, and a reluctant ulama corps, fearful of how the transition to print would transform Islamic books and religious authority. In the Egyptian case, the state had the power to push the project through, perhaps hastily so, despite the opposition of many Islamic scholars. The ultimate product – a flawed, later recalled edition – did not please the ulama and reflected the lack of full collaboration between the state and the ulama. This initiative in Cairo did not inspire a similar effort in Istanbul, where the political balance favoured dealing with the ulama and their books in a more deferential manner.

Illicit Books

North and east of the Ottoman territories, Qur'an printing had developed more rapidly. Bolstered by the support of Empress Catherine II, Muslims from various cities in the Russian Empire printed the Qur'an beginning in the late eighteenth century. In St Petersburg alone, three editions had been published before the end of the eighteenth century.[46] Presses in Iran printed copies by the 1820s at the latest,[47] and in India, copies of the Qur'an were printed in Bombay, Lucknow and Calcutta in the 1850s. Evidence from the Ottoman archives shows that these printed *muṣḥaf*s from Iran, Russia and India had entered the Ottoman Empire by the 1850s and were circulating in both the capital and the provinces. In India, for instance, print capitalism developed several decades earlier than in the Ottoman domains and even non-Muslim presses like the Hindu-owned Nawal Kishore Press in Lucknow printed copies of the Qur'an for sale abroad.[48] Additionally, entrepreneurial printers in Istanbul began to publish and sell editions without the permission of the Ottoman state. These illegal copies of the Qur'an precipitated a great deal of controversy among the Ottoman ulama and state officials who viewed them as economic, religious and political threats. This deluge of imported and illegally printed copies of the Qur'an would ultimately force Ottoman statesmen and the ulama to rethink the long-standing ban on printing the Qur'an.

Most printed copies came from Iran or from Iranian printers in Istanbul, and the Ottoman Empire's response to the circulation of Iranian editions was coloured by the contentious rivalry that existed between it and the Iranian Qajar Empire.[49] The Ottomans and the Qajars had a long history of dispute over territories and subjects in eastern Anatolia. They were on the verge of war in the 1830s, but this was circumvented by the second Treaty of Erzurum in 1847, which divided the disputed eastern Anatolian territory between the two empires and established a boundary commission to define the entire border.[50] Even so, this treaty did not defuse the tensions between the two states over the eastern Anatolian region. When Nāṣir al-Dīn (d. 1896) acceded to the throne in Iran in 1848, he contended for recognition as the world leader of the Shi'i Muslims.[51] The shah was keen to assert his claim to be the sultan of the Shi'a, and to extend his protection to the Shi'a living in Ottoman Iraq and eastern Anatolia who had been subject to various persecutions. In the past, Ottoman authorities had turned a blind eye to Kurdish Sunni tribes' periodic raids into Shi'i towns and villages in Western Azerbaijan and Kurdistan, and, according to Abbas Amanat, the Ottomans also ignored, perhaps even encouraged, the persecution of the Shi'a in Iraq; for example, this was said to be the case for the violent attacks against the Shi'a in Karbala in 1843.[52] These tensions formed the backdrop to Ottoman reaction to the importation of Iranian-printed copies of the Qur'an.

The wealth of documents on printed copies of the Qur'an in the Ottoman archives reveals that the Ottoman state and ulama were deeply concerned about the circulation of non-Ottoman versions of the Holy Book. Selim Deringil has observed that the state viewed them as symbols of foreign sovereigns, akin to flags, medals and other symbols of imperial power;[53] for the ulama, they constituted Islamic books created outside of their networks and control, by unknown persons, via an unapproved method of reproduction. The first mention of these illicit books occurs in documents related to the troubles with Iran, where the Ottoman government invokes the long-standing ban on importing copies of the Qur'an that had been in place since the time of the Venetian Qur'an in the sixteenth century. In 1852, for example, the office of the grand vizier notified authorities in the eastern provinces that Iranians were prohibited from importing and selling printed copies of the Qur'an in the Ottoman Empire.[54] A second reference to illicit copies of the Qur'an is found in a memorandum of 1853 which describes the 'nefarious activities' of the consuls in the eastern Anatolian town of Erzurum, and orders their dismissal and replacement. This memorandum states that copies of the Qur'an printed in Iran should not be allowed to enter Ottoman territories and that Iranians travelling to Kurdistan, Iraq and Erzurum 'should be observed closely'.[55] However, aside from the suspicion of political intrigue on the part of Iranians, the memorandum does not provide any substantive reason why the copies of the Qur'an printed in Iran should not be allowed to circulate in Ottoman territories. There is no mention of the content of these books or any suggestion of textual corruption. The books were illegal, firstly, due to the continuing ban on imported printed copies of the Qur'an, and, secondly, because they were politically suspect as imperial symbols of the Qajar state, which was both Shi'i and a rival to the Ottoman Empire.[56]

Iran, however, was not the only source of printed editions. Versions from the Russian Empire, British India, Europe and even semi-autonomous Ottoman Egypt flowed across the Ottoman borders as well. The state and ulama regarded these versions as equally unacceptable, and gave orders for them to be seized at the borders and wherever they turned up in the territories of the empire. In response to the influx of books, the Ottoman state and ulama declared an embargo on printed copies of the Qur'an, making the calligraphic Qur'an the only licit form of the Holy Book.

The implementation of the ban on foreign copies of the Qur'an took its toll on cross-border travellers in various ways. In 1863, a Crimean refugee named Emir Salih was detained when customs officials found thirty-six printed copies of the Qur'an and one hundred and twenty copies of the last thirtieth of the Qur'an (*amme cüzü*) in his possession. He told the customs officials that 'he had some property in the Crimea which he attempted to sell, but was unable to do so. In exchange for the property, he was given thirty-six copies of the Qur'an and one hundred and twenty copies of the last thirtieth of the Qur'an.'[57] The Crimean traveller was thus carrying his wealth in the form of printed Qur'anic texts which he probably intended to sell inside the Ottoman territories. Seeing that Emir Salih was 'from the impoverished class and . . . also elderly', customs officials were hesitant to leave the refugee destitute. They appealed to their superiors in search of 'compassionate measures' that would both enforce the law and protect the meagre assets of Emir Salih.[58] In the end, the authorities decided that the books had to be seized, stored and preserved according to the law, but they deemed that Emir Salih should be compensated for the losses, and gave him a lump sum for his books and expenses.[59] In addition to showing some of the complicated human stories associated with the Qur'an printing embargo, this instance reveals yet another way in which this policy was difficult and, at times, expensive for the Ottoman state to enforce. In cases like Emir Salih's, Ottoman officials actually succeeded in preventing the circulation of foreign printed copies of the Qur'an. However, on the whole, this policy failed to stem the tide, and the flow of printed works from Iran and elsewhere did not cease. In March 1861, a strongly worded memorandum reiterated and intensified the order to stop and seize copies of the Qur'an of Iranian provenance. The customs officials were given orders to enact an 'absolute prohibition' of Iranian copies of the Qur'an. This document introduced a new aspect to the conversation by emphasising that the texts were 'not free of errors and mistakes' but suffered from 'printing defects'.[60] However, this memo does not detail the nature of the insufficiencies, and, therefore, it is difficult to gauge how one should understand the accusation of error and distortion. On one hand, it is probable that there existed some minor errors such as those that occur in many handwritten *muṣḥaf*s and in almost all early printings of the Qur'an. On the other hand, for political purposes, Ottoman officials may have exaggerated the gravity of the mistakes in order to justify banning books which Ottoman subjects wanted to purchase. It is important to remember that printed foreign Qur'an copies would have been illegal even if they were perfectly accurate.

In October 1861 Ottoman officials again sent reminders to the various branches of government, and particularly the customs officials in the provinces, to be more vigilant and scrupulous about enforcing the law that forbade the selling and buying of foreign copies of the Qur'an.[61] This fresh flurry of concern was precipitated when officials observed that printed copies could be found in schools and in the hands of children in the eastern province of Sivas.[62] The issue of textual corruption cropped up again, yet in a different guise. A message to the grand vizier's office said that the copies of the Qur'an could not be allowed to circulate because during the printing process the text had not been treated with the proper respect.[63] It remains unclear whether this document indicates that the printers were not careful enough, and therefore committed errors, or that the standards of ritual purity for handling the Qur'an were ignored.

However, officials in Istanbul were not pleased with the implementation of the embargo and threatened to launch an investigation into the activities of customs officials, who had responded to the order sluggishly and committed errors in its enforcement.[64] It is likely they were suspected of illicit activities, perhaps of benefiting from bribes or other perks from the book traders. Nevertheless, Ottoman customs officers and police confiscated printed copies of the Qur'an over a broad geographic area. In addition to the eastern Anatolian region bordering Iran, reports mention seizures in Baghdad and Basra (Iraq), Beirut (Lebanon), Istanbul and Samsun (Turkey), Varna and Ruse (Bulgaria), and Crete and Thessaloniki (Greece) among many others. Thousands of seized books were sent to Istanbul to be stored in the library of the Ministry of Education and also given to the Shaykh al-Islam's office – the head of the Islamic establishment in the Ottoman state – for evaluation. Because of their illegal status, the books could not be sold or given away, and, instead, they collected dust in a depot for the better part of two decades.

Black-market Copies of the Qur'an

Despite all efforts, copies of the Qur'an from Iran, India, Russia and elsewhere increasingly found a receptive market in Istanbul and Anatolia. They were a less expensive alternative to manuscript copies, and demand for cheaper versions was robust. This phenomenon did not escape the notice of entrepreneurs in Istanbul, who began to secretly print and sell copies of the Qur'an in the city. Qur'an printing became a black-market business venture in the Ottoman capital and presents a fascinating case of Islamicate print capitalism.

In 1856, an Ottoman Muslim named Hafız Ahmet attempted to secretly print the Qur'an in the Kocamustafapaşa neighbourhood in Istanbul. The police detained and interrogated him and his associates, whereupon they confessed their crimes.[65] After an investigation into their activities and connections, they were released on bail.[66] Hafız Ahmet was found to be the chief protagonist of the printing scheme and to have a contract with an Iranian by the name of Taki Efendi.[67] The title 'Hafız' may indicate that Ahmet had memorised the entire Qur'an, and perhaps worked as a professional reciter of the text. This example is telling because most illegal printing operations involved members of the ulama and madrasa students, suggesting that their expertise was needed and also that a certain segment of the ulama supported the printing of the text despite the opposition of the leadership. Their involvement presents a more complicated picture of the ulama's attitudes towards, and participation in, Qur'anic printing prior to legalisation. A divide existed between the Shaykh al-Islam's office, which vigorously opposed printing, and the madrasa students, who very likely wanted to own their own copies of the book and make them available for purchase.

Working together with Ottoman partners, Iranian booksellers connected to the Qajar consulate in Istanbul dominated the black-market trade. Benefitting from diplomatic protection, Iranians in Istanbul faced less risk and were able to maintain their position in this trade through an organisation known as the Sahaflar Şirketi (Bookseller's Company).[68] In addition to *muṣḥaf*s, the company printed a range of non-forbidden books including important works on hadith and Qur'anic commentaries. The black-market printers and smugglers had frequent run-ins with the Ottoman authorities, but in most cases they were released with little penalty other than the confiscation of their books, and, in some instances, they even succeeded in recovering the seized goods. The appearance of illegally printed copies of the Qur'an in sundry locations around Istanbul disturbed the ulama repeatedly. When discarded pages from these printings appeared in grocery stores around the capital, where grocers allegedly used them to wrap up fruit and vegetables, the ulama complained to the authorities, demanding that stricter measures be taken to prevent clandestine printing activities.[69]

Ultimately, the Ottoman embargo on printed copies of the Qur'an was a resounding failure. State archives reveal that printed editions continued to circulate, as confirmed by the continuous repetition of orders from Istanbul to enforce the ban and the frequency of reported confiscations. The continued smuggling and illegal printing point to an imbalance between the supply of and demand for affordable copies of the Qur'an. Despite the efforts of the state, the illegal trade thrived, and Ottoman subjects purchased printed editions regardless of their origin. It is also notable that Ottoman Muslims, including some members of the ulama who purchased or produced such books, did not feel beholden to protect or support traditional bookmakers. Handwritten copies were expensive and, in some cases, of inferior quality to printed versions. Most of them were written not by calligraphers but by copyists, who produced the bulk of the books for use by the less affluent.[70] It seems that for many madrasa students and others lacking financial resources, the printed copies provided a welcome alternative to traditionally copied books.

NOTES

1 Selçuk Aksin Somel, *The Modernization of Public Education in the Ottoman Empire, 1839–1908: Islamization, Autocracy, and Discipline* (Leiden, Brill, 2001), pp. 59, 74–5.

2 Ekmeleddin İhsanoğlu, 'Education', *Encyclopedia of the Ottoman Empire*, ed. Gábor Ágoston and Bruce Masters (New York, Infobase Publishing, 2001), pp. 202–3. On late Ottoman education, also see Benjamin C. Fortna, *Imperial Classroom: Islam, the State, and Education in the Late Ottoman Empire* (Oxford, Oxford University Press, 2002).

3 Orlin Sabev, 'Private Book Collections in Ottoman Sofia, 1671–1833 (Preliminary Notes)', *Etudes Balkaniques* 39, no. 1 (2003), p. 41.

4 Wage information for the years 1780–89 comes from Süleyman Özmucur and Şevket Pamuk, 'Real Wages and Standards of Living in the Ottoman Empire, 1489–1914', *Journal of Economic History* 62, no. 2 (2002), Table 1, p. 301.

5 Ibid.

6 Ibid.

7 Hartmut Bobzin, '"A Treasure of Heresies": Christian Polemics against the Qur'an', in Stefan Wild, ed., *The Qur'an as Text* (Leiden, Brill, 1996), pp. 162–3.

8 Harry Clark, 'The Publication of the Koran in Latin: A Reformation Dilemma', *Sixteenth Century Journal* 15, no. 1 (1984), p. 6.

9 Ibid., pp. 10–11.

10 Thomas E. Burman, '*Tafsīr* and Translation: Traditional Arabic Qur'ān Exegesis and the Latin Qur'āns of Robert of Ketton and Mark of Toledo', *Speculum* 73, no. 3 (1998), p. 705, n. 9. See idem, *Reading the Qur'an in Latin Christendom, 1140–1560* (Philadelphia, University of Pennsylvania Press, 2007).

11 Bobzin, 'Treasure', p. 167.

12 Anderson, *Imagined Communities*, p. 36.

13 Angela Nuovo, 'A Lost Arabic Koran Rediscovered', *Library* 12, no. 4 (1990), p. 282.
14 Michael Cook, *The Koran: A Very Short Introduction* (Oxford, Oxford University Press, 2000), p. 56.
15 Jean Bodin, *Colloque entre sept scavans qui sont de differens sentimens: Des secrets cachez, des choses relevées* (Geneva, Droz, 1984), p. 352.
16 Nuovo, 'Lost Arabic Koran', p. 273.
17 Ogier Ghiselin de Busbecq, *The Turkish Letters of Ogier Ghiselin de Busbecq, Imperial Ambassador at Constantinople, 1554–1562*, tr. Edmund Seymour Forster (Oxford, Clarendon Press, 1968), p. 135.
18 Euclid, *Euclidis elementorum geometricorum libri tredecim; Ex traditione doctissimi Nasiridini Tusini* (Rome, Typographia Medicea, 1594).
19 Günay Alpay Kut, 'Maṭbaʿa: In Turkey', *EI*², Brill Online 2014.
20 Mustafa b. Abdullah Kâtip Çelebi, *Cihânnümâ* (Kostantiniyye, Istanbul, Darü'l-Tıbaati'l-Amire, 1144/1732), pp. 55–6.
21 İbrahim Peçevi, *Tarih-i Peçevi* (Istanbul, 1281/1864–5), I, p. 363, cited in Reinhart Schulze, 'The Birth of Tradition and Modernity in 18th and 19th Century Islamic Culture: The Case of Printing', *Culture and History* 16 (1997), p. 43.
22 See İbrahim Müteferrika's tract, 'The Usefulness of Printing', in George N. Atiyeh, ed., *The Book in the Islamic World: The Written Word and Communication in the Middle East* (Albany, State University of New York Press, 1995), pp. 289–92.
23 Kemal Beydilli, 'Matbaa', *TDVİA*, vol. XXVIII, p. 108.
24 Berkes, *Development of Secularism*, p. 40; Imre Karácson, 'İbrahim Müteferrika', *Tarih-i Osmani Mecmuası* 1, no. 3 (August 1910), pp. 183–4; Selim Nüzhet Gerçek, *Türk Matbaacılığı*, vol. I: *Müteferrika Matbaası* (Istanbul, Devlet Basımevi, 1939), p. 58.
25 Ali Birinci, 'Osman Bey ve Matbaası: Ser-Kurenâ Osman Bey'in Hikayesine ve Matbaa-i Osmaniye'nin Tarihçesine Medhal', *Müteferrika* 39, no. 1 (Summer 2011), pp. 4–5.
26 İsmet Binark, *Eski Kitapçılık Santalarımız* (Ankara, Kazan Türkleri Kültür ve Yardımlaşma Derneği Yayınları, 1975), pp. 76–7.
27 Şükrü Hanioğlu, *A Brief History of the Late Ottoman Empire* (Princeton, NJ, Princeton University Press, 2008), pp. 38–40.
28 Ahmet Cevdet Pasha, *Tarih-i Cevdet* (Istanbul, Matbaa-i Osmaniye, 1309/1891–2), I, p. 74. The press went unscathed in the Patrona Halil uprising of 1730–31 that denounced the Frankish tendencies of the court, toppled Sultan Ahmet III, and resulted in the execution of grand vizier Ibrahim Paşa; Robert Olson, 'The Ottoman Empire in the Middle of the Eighteenth Century and the Fragmentation of Tradition: Relations of the Nationalities (Millets), Guilds (Esnaf) and the Sultan, 1740–1768', *Die Welt des Islams* 17, no. 1/4 (1976–7), pp. 329–44.
29 Binark, *Eski Kitapçılık*, p. 78.
30 See İrvin Cemil Schick, 'Text', in Jamal J. Elias, ed., *Key Themes for the Study of Islam* (Oxford, Oneworld, 2010), pp. 321–5.
31 See, for example, Ṭabarī's interpretation of Q. 68:1; Abū Jaʿfar Muḥammad b. Jarīr b. Yazīd al-Ṭabarī, *Jāmiʿ al-bayān ʿan taʾwīl āy al-Qurʾān* (Beirut, Dār al-Fikr, 1984), XIV, pp. 14–15.

32 Daniel A. Madigan, 'Preserved Tablet', *EQ*, vol. IV, pp. 261–2.
33 On the aura of the Arabic manuscript, see Nadia al-Bagdadi, 'From Heaven to Dust: Metamorphosis of the Book in Pre-Modern Arab Culture', *Medieval History Journal* 8, no. 1 (2005), pp. 83–107.
34 David J. Roxburgh, *Prefacing the Image: The Writing of Art History in Sixteenth-Century Iran* (Leiden, Brill, 2001), p. 112, n. 113. For further examples, see İrvin Cemil Schick, 'The Iconicity of Islamic Calligraphy in Turkey', *RES: Anthropology and Aesthetics* 53/54 (2008), pp. 211–24.
35 In Ottoman Turkish, the word for eye is written كوز (*göz*). If the dot on the last character is left out, كور, it spells the word *kör* (blind). Mehmed bin Süleyman Fuzuli, *Divan*, cited in Muhammet Nur Doğan, *Fuzûli'nin Poetikası* (Cağaloğlu, Istanbul, Kitabevi, 1997), p. 37.
36 Binark, *Eski Kitapçılık*, p. 76; Beydilli, 'Matbaa', p. 108.
37 Binark, *Eski Kitapçılık*, p. 94.
38 Schulze, 'The Birth of Tradition and Modernity', p. 42.
39 Mehmet Akif Ersoy, *Safahat: Asım*, Part VI (Istanbul, İnkılap Kitabevi, 1958), p. 407.
40 Brinkley Messick, *The Calligraphic State: Textual Domination and History in a Muslim Society* (Berkeley, University of California Press, 1993), p. 116.
41 Birgivi rejected attempts by Ottoman jurists to adapt or bend the rules of classical Ḥanafī fiqh for contemporary exigencies. The choice of a text by Birgivi for the first printed Islamic work may have been symbolic, since it appears to reflect a broader effort by the Ottoman Palace in the early nineteenth century to promote a Sunni–Ḥanafī collective ethos. On Birgivi, see Colin Imber, *Ebu's-Su'ud: The Islamic Legal Tradition* (Stanford, CA, Stanford University Press, 1997), p. 144. Christoph K. Neumann, 'Book and Newspaper Printing in Turkish, 18th–20th Century', in Eva Hanebutt-Benz, Dagmar Glass and Geoffrey Roper, eds., *Middle Eastern Languages and the Print Revolution* (Westhofen, WVA-Verlag Skulima, 2002), p. 233.
42 Ali Birinci, '"Birgivi Risalesi": İlk Dinî Kitab Niçin ve Nasıl Basıldı?' in *Tarih Yolunda: Yakın Mazî Siyasî ve Fikrî Ahvâli* (Istanbul, Dergâh Yayınları, 2001), p. 194.
43 Ibid., p. 195.
44 Michael W. Albin, 'Printing of the Qur'an', *EQ*, vol. IV, pp. 264–76. The Qur'an is traditionally divided by reciters into thirty portions (*juz'*), one for each day of the month. These divisions govern the recitation of the Qur'an, and many early Qur'anic printings followed this structure.
45 Ibid., pp. 269–70.
46 Ibid.
47 Nile Green, 'Journeymen, Middlemen: Travel, Transculture, and Technology in the Origins of Muslim Printing', *International Journal of Middle East Studies* 41, no. 2 (2009), p. 215.
48 Green, *Bombay Islam*, p. 95.
49 Selim Deringil touches upon the issue of foreign printed copies of the Qur'an; see Selim Deringil, *The Well-Protected Domains: Ideology and the Legitimation of Power in the Ottoman Empire, 1876–1909* (London, I.B. Tauris, 1998), pp. 53–4.
50 Firoozeh Kashani-Sabet, *Frontier Fictions* (Princeton, NJ, Princeton University Press, 1999), pp. 24–6.

51 Abbas Amanat, *Pivot of the Universe: Nasir al-Din Shah Qajar and the Iranian Monarchy, 1831-1896* (Berkeley, University of California Press, 1997), pp. 232–7.
52 Ibid., p. 233. Also, see Selim Deringil, 'The Struggle against Shiism in Hamidian Iraq: A Study in Ottoman Counter-Propaganda', *Die Welt des Islams* 30, no. 1 (1990), pp. 45–62.
53 On the Ottoman use of imperial symbols see Deringil, *Well Protected Domains*, chapters 1–2.
54 BOA A.MKT.UM 113/99 (6/S/1269—19 November 1852).
55 BOA A.AMD 42/61 (2/C/1269—13 March 1853).
56 It is worth mentioning that during the same years (1853–4), Protestant missionaries distributed some 20,000 copies of Armeno-Turkish and Kurdish Bibles in the Ottoman Empire. Zeynep Turkyilmaz, 'Anxieties of Conversion: Missionaries, State and Heterodox Communities in the Late Ottoman Empire' (Unpublished PhD Thesis, University of California, Los Angeles, 2009), pp. 228–9.
57 BOA İ.MVL 484/21939 (Arzuhal: 26/Ş/1279—16 February 1863) (Catalogue: 19/Za/1279).
58 Ibid.
59 Ibid.
60 BOA A.MKT.UM 463/115 (13/N/1277—25 March 1861).
61 BOA A.MKT.UM 509/80 (11/R/1278—16 October 1861) [Catalogue has been mislabelled as 18/R]; also e.g. BOA A.MKT.UM 509/90 (19/R/1278—24 October 1861); BOA A.MKT.UM 513/50 (19/R/1278—24 October 1861).
62 BOA A.MKT.UM 515/47 (19/R/1278—24 October 1861) (Catalogue: 8/Ca/1278).
63 BOA A.MKT.UM 513/84 (22/Ra/1278—27 September 1861) (Catalogue: 2/Ca/1278).
64 BOA A.MKT.UM 515/47 (25/R/1278—30 October 1861) (Catalogue: 8/Ca/1278).
65 BOA A.MKT.NZD 180/35 (22/B/1272—29 March 1856).
66 BOA A.MKT.NZD 184/61 (2/N/1272—7 May 1856).
67 BOA A.MKT.NZD 185/11 (8/N/1272—13 May 1856).
68 Ahmet İhsan Tokgöz, *Matbuat Hatıralarım*, ed. Alpay Kabacalı (Istanbul, İletişim Yayıncılık, 1993), p. 105.
69 Ahmet Cevdet Paşa, *Tezâkir*, ed. Cavid Baysun, 2nd edn (Ankara, Türk Tarih Kurumu Basımevi, 1986), IV, p. 128.
70 M. Uğur Derman, 'Hattat', *TDVİA*, vol. XVI, p. 497.

2

Ottoman Editions of the Qur'an (1870–1890)

But a still more wonderful conjuror fashioned for himself a mighty thing that was neither man nor beast, but which had brains of lead, intermixed with a black matter like pitch, and fingers that it employed with such incredible speed and dexterity that it would have had no trouble in writing out twenty thousand copies of the Koran in an hour; and this with so exquisite a precision, that in all the copies there should not be found one to vary from another by the breadth of the finest hair. This thing was of prodigious strength, so that it erected or overthrew the mightiest empires at a breath; but its powers were exercised equally for evil and for good.

Edgar Allen Poe, *The Thousand-and-Second Tale of Scheherazade* (1850)

In 1871, the Ottoman state officially conceded that its embargo on foreign copies of the Qur'an had failed. The unsuccessful embargo against printed editions caused some intellectuals and statesmen to consider the idea of printing the text in Istanbul under government supervision. By not printing the text, the Ottoman state was forfeiting a profitable sector of the book trade to foreigners and smugglers and, moreover, was placed in a position where it could not control the quality or the content. Supporters of printing reasoned that if the state provided affordable, high-quality copies, then the demand would be met and illegal versions would lose their appeal. Yet, in order to pursue this, the government would need to gain the approval of the ulama for the project. The Sublime Porte (the government of the Ottoman Empire) had petitioned the ulama authorities to grant permission for printing the Qur'an on several occasions in the mid-nineteenth century but had received negative replies.[1] In response, supporters waged a campaign to convince Ottoman society that printing copies of the Qur'an was a necessary technological advance that would be a benefit, and not a detriment, to the vitality of Islam in the Ottoman Empire.

The London Edition

Unable to print the Qur'an within the Ottoman Empire, the Ottoman statesman and Egyptian prince Mustafa Fazıl Pasha (1829–75) explored the possibility of importing copies printed in London. Mustafa Fazıl, the grandson of Mehmet Ali and the brother of the Egyptian khedive Ismail Pasha, was a leader and key patron of the Young Ottomans (*Genç Osmanlılar*), a group of intellectuals that called for the establishment of Islamic constitutionalism, imagined as a form of representative government based on the Islamic principle of consultation.[2] During a stint in Paris in 1866, Mustafa Fazıl wrote an open letter to Sultan Abdülaziz (r. 1861–76) criticising his reign and lamenting the current state of the Ottoman Empire. Additionally, he orchestrated the opposition abroad, financing the publication of opposition newspapers – such as *Hürriyet* (*Freedom*) – by Ottoman political exiles in Europe and bankrolling their living expenses. One of the Young Ottomans supported by Mustafa Fazıl was the famous journalist, poet and playwright Namık Kemal (1840–88), who is known for injecting the concepts of the fatherland (*vatan*) and freedom (*hürriyet*) into late Ottoman political discourse (See Figure 2). Additionally, he played a central role in discussions about civilisation (*medeniyet*) and what it should mean for Ottoman society.[3]

In the late 1860s, Kemal presented Mustafa Fazıl with the idea of printing a lithographic edition of the Qur'an in London and importing it into the Ottoman Empire. It was to be based on the manuscript of the renowned Ottoman calligrapher Hafız Osman (1642–98), who had produced one of the most famous and frequently reproduced *muṣḥaf*s of the Ottoman period. This project was intended to solve the problem of illegally imported copies and provide Ottoman subjects with an affordable, reliable copy. Additionally, as critics pointed out, the agents of this project also expected to make a substantial profit from this arrangement.

The prince accepted Kemal's proposition, and, upon request, provided from his capacious personal library a rare copy of the Qur'an written by Hafız Osman.[4] An entrepreneur named Aristidis Fanton, who had given Kemal lessons in law in England, was intimately involved in the plan to print the Qur'an in London. Fanton worked out the financial and legal details of producing and then importing the books into the Ottoman Empire. He acted as Kemal's partner and agent, taking care of all the details in Istanbul since, as a political exile, Kemal could not travel there. In fact, it was Fanton who journeyed to Istanbul, presented the proposal of the project to the prince and obtained the Hafız Osman *muṣḥaf* from him. While there, Fanton skilfully used his connection with Kemal to gain audiences with high Ottoman officials and to seek out business opportunities of all kinds. In addition to ensuring that he acquired the Qur'an printing venture, Fanton was involved in making a bid to build a railroad from Baghdad to Istanbul, in trying to obtain an exclusive contract to print maps for the Ottoman Ministry of Education, and in attempting to set up a publishing house to make photolithographic prints of Turkish and Arabic manuscripts.[5] Besides seeking out these larger projects, he also imported and sold wine, gold watches, rifles and musical instruments.[6] It is clear that, for Fanton, obtaining an exclusive contract to import and sell copies of the Qur'an in the Ottoman Empire was, first and foremost, an outstanding business opportunity.

As Fanton politicked and negotiated in Istanbul, Kemal's job was to oversee the printing process in London, assist Fanton in his other business affairs and watch over Fanton's family. The letters he wrote to Kemal reveal that Fanton was the more determined partner in bringing the project to completion, and suggest that he may have been the driving force behind the whole endeavour. Fanton wrote a steady stream of letters to Kemal detailing his dealings in their various projects and providing news about Kemal's family. In contrast, Kemal was far less engaged in the project and failed to send regular news. To Fanton's dismay, Kemal was remiss in supervising the printing project, and, on more than one occasion, he left his duties in London to spend time in Paris, where he was known to indulge in the pleasures of the city.[7] At a critical juncture in the project, for instance, Kemal travelled to Paris and, in Fanton's view, jeopardised the entire plan.[8] As a highly educated Ottoman gentleman familiar with the Arabic script and Islamic texts, Kemal was responsible for overseeing the production process of the Qur'an and making sure that the English print master produced a suitable edition. Fanton implored Kemal to return to London to fulfil his duties, pointing out that the entire venture hinged upon its quality.[9] Moreover, he tried to convince Kemal to stop drinking alcohol, as it was harming their partnership and damaging Kemal's reputation in Istanbul.[10] This last bit was particularly important because Kemal's primary contribution to the project was his name and the doors that it could open, since it had been thanks to Kemal's introduction that Fanton had been able to gain access to the highest echelons of Ottoman society.

Despite the sometimes challenging partnership with Kemal, Fanton maintained remarkable optimism about the prospects for their printed edition of the Qur'an. He told Kemal that the government would purchase a large quantity and that Mustafa Fazıl wanted to print between 50,000 and 100,000 copies.[11] When he obtained the contract to print and the permission to import the books, he assured Kemal: 'our fortune is guaranteed'.[12] The contract amounted to an exclusive lease for Fanton to import printed copies of the Qur'an, which the Ottoman Ministry of Education would then send to schools around the empire (See Figure 5, students holding copies of the Qur'an).

Although the level of Kemal's input was at times questionable, he did make efforts that proved beneficial in bringing the project to fruition. In addition to opening the doors to elite Ottoman society for Fanton, Kemal took charge of the campaign to sway public opinion in favour of the printing project, using his nimble pen to counter the opposition that emerged from various sectors. For those who were opposed to the printing of the Qur'an, the prospect of printing copies in England and importing them to Istanbul was just as undesirable as the vending of black-market versions from Iran or Russia, if not more so. A political activist and journalist named Ali Suavi (1839–78) opposed the London printing project. Like Kemal, Suavi had fled to Europe in order to criticise the regime from abroad, where he engaged in energetic publishing activities. Unlike Kemal, Suavi did not come from an elite background and was more revolutionary than intellectual in temperament. Trained in the madrasa system, he also had a more religiously conservative outlook than other Young Ottomans and often wore the turban rather than the fez. By the time of the Qur'an printing project, Suavi had broken ranks with the Young Ottomans and taken up residence in France, first in Paris and later in Lyon. In his Lyon-based Turkish-language newspaper *Ulum*, Suavi denounced Kemal's printing project and claimed that the ink used to print it had been mixed with pig's grease (*hınzır yağı*) and was therefore ritually unclean.[13] The use of pig's grease in the lithographic process for this project seems very unlikely. Lithographers generally mixed inks with vegetable-based oils like linseed, or, if animal fat were used, it was typically from mutton, not swine.[14] It is probable that Suavi simply wanted to discredit Kemal's project, and defend the interests of the copyists and calligraphers.

In 1871, the London edition was published and imported to Istanbul. After the book began to be sold, Kemal wrote a newspaper article which defends the printing of the Holy Book against the arguments of an anonymous opponent of Qur'anic printing. The exchanges between Kemal and this author reveal the nature of the debate on the necessity of printed editions in Ottoman lands. The anonymous piece argues that the publishers were greedy profiteers who had set their sights on the livelihood of calligraphers. It claims that printing the Qur'an would leave the calligraphers destitute, and represented a heinous case of predatory capitalism.[15] Moreover, the commodification of the Qur'an deeply perturbed the author, who believed the marketing strategies and advertisements which Fanton and Kemal employed to promote the sale of the book were unethical and completely inappropriate. In the author's view, they were also attempting to deceive the public into welcoming a printed version of the Qur'an from England through advertisements about the ritual purity of the Book.[16]

The issue of ritual purity figured prominently in the arguments against the printing of the Qur'an. Whereas Suavi had suggested that the ink was impure and mixed with pig's grease, the anonymous writer accused Kemal's edition of using olive oil, suggesting that it was unbefitting due to its odour.[17] Additionally, this piece emphasises the impure locations through which these copies would have to pass in order to make the journey from London to Istanbul. First and foremost, the author criticises the fact that the books were being 'printed in Frankistan to be sold in Turkistan', that is, being printed by non-Muslims in a non-Muslim land for consumption by Ottoman subjects.[18] The author then questions whether it is fitting to 'drag the Well-Preserved Book, which is the sublime scroll of the Hidden Tablet, through ferry storehouses and customs offices' for financial gain.[19] For the author, the clear connection between the impurity of the physical location and the impurity of the financial motivation made the enterprise doubly foul.

The author also questions if it is even desirable for there to be so many copies of the Qur'an available due to the possibility that they may end up in sundry impure locations. This concern was guided by the situation in Europe where, the author notes, so many copies of the Bible had been produced that even hotels, where prostitution and gambling occur, '[were] full of Bibles'.[20] In this view, a plenitude of copies implies an undesirable ubiquity that increases the risk of impurity. The author, therefore, deemed the process impure in terms of the production (ink), the location of printing (London), the motivation for publishing (financial) and the ritually unclean physical spaces where copies of the Qur'an would reside or pass through (warehouses, ships, hotels).

The calligraphic Qur'an became a focal point of resistance to the sweeping and often disruptive changes confronted by Ottoman Muslims in the nineteenth century, including the diminution of ulama power, the centralisation of the state, and the influx of European culture and technology. For those who opposed various aspects of the modernisation process, of which Qur'anic printing was a part, the Qur'anic manuscript became synonymous with the preservation of Islam and traditional Ottoman culture.

In response, Kemal defended the printing of the Holy Book, and printing in general, as an advance in technology – much like the tramway and photography – which would improve the lives of Ottoman Muslims.[21] He noted that manuscript copies of the Qur'an for schoolchildren were expensive items and expressed his bemusement that men of religion would impede a technology that would make them more affordable.[22] Furthermore, Kemal pointed out that printed copies were already a reality in Istanbul: 'For fifteen years, copies of the Qur'an from every corner of Europe and especially from Iran have come to Istanbul and remained.'[23] He argued that refusing to print was to ignore the present reality and to reject inevitable technological advances. As for the charge of attempting to cultivate demand via deceptive advertising, Kemal replied that the publishers had no need to do so because there was already a great demand from various classes, 'from the most learned of the ulama to the porters' in the bazaar, for inexpensive copies of the Qur'an.[24] According to him, even the calligraphers were purchasing this version in order to imitate the script of Hafız Osman, to which most of them had never had direct access.[25]

In regard to the accusation that Qur'an printing was nothing more than a profit-making venture, Kemal points out that the trade of copying the Qur'an was similarly a business venture for the traditional calligraphers. He asks sarcastically, 'Do the calligraphers write out the Qur'an for free as a good deed?'[26] The answer to this question was an emphatic 'no', as the copyists charged a price which allowed, in Kemal's words, 'wretched' farmers to purchase only a single page at a time, and forced fathers to skip meals in order to obtain the text for their children.[27] Given that theirs was a business like any other, Kemal argues that calligraphers should not be allowed to impede technological and social progress based on the claim that their trade was somehow sacrosanct and different from all other occupations threatened by modernisation. After all, he adds, no one protested on behalf of the row-boat paddlers when the steam ferries were introduced.[28] For Kemal, Qur'an printing was a critical part of modernisation, and the argument that traditional modes of book production should be protected held no more weight than the claim that the Ottoman state should reject steamships, railroads and electricity.

As for the accusations about impure conditions of production and transportation, Kemal assured the critics that all such claims were baseless and that this project had taken every precaution to ensure the text's physical sanctity. The lithographers had used an odourless, vegetable-based liquid for the ink, and the volumes were transported in sealed, waterproof chests that were stored in ulama-approved locations.[29] Kemal challenges his critics to prove that manuscript copies were treated in a more respectful fashion, mentioning that these versions were usually transported to Istanbul on horses and mules, and in the hands of smugglers from 'diverse' religious sects. In any case, Kemal posits, these criticisms were all baseless anyway, because there is no prohibition against having a copy of the Qur'an in a place that contains profane or impure things, such as a person's home or a warehouse; he asks, 'should we not have a [copy of the] Qur'an in our homes and should we climb up to the Exalted Throne in order to be worthy of having a copy of the sacred Book?'[30]

The question of who held Islamic authority played an important role in this debate. The critics of the project presented themselves as defending the interests of Ottoman Muslims by protecting them against the predations of profiteers and the sacrilege of the defiling of the Qur'anic *muṣḥaf*. They expressed doubts about all facets of the project from production to transportation to motive, and dubbed these methods contrary to Islamic bookmaking traditions. Additionally, they went so far as to allege that the project violated sacred law and constituted an instance of disbelief.[31] Kemal found this line of reasoning, and its claim to Islamic authority, to be completely groundless. Firstly, he held that this project would make an accurate, beautifully written copy of the Qur'an available to the public at an affordable price. More Ottoman Muslims could own a copy of the text whose quality would exceed, by far, that of the average scribal *muṣḥaf*. Rather than purchasing an expensive copy that was 'illegible' and 'unsound', the less well-to-do could obtain a beautiful edition in the writ of none other than Hafız Osman, one of the greatest Ottoman calligraphers.[32] Therefore, in Kemal's thinking, it meshes perfectly with the Islamic ethical imperative of acting in the public interest. To oppose this aim, he contended, was contrary to the egalitarian ethos of Islam, and constituted nothing more than preservation of self-interest on the part of the scribal class.

In regard to Islamic legitimacy, Kemal pointed out that the Ottoman caliph's ministers, including the Shaykh al-Islam, had approved the project and deemed it to be in accordance with the sharia, and in the best interests of the Muslim world. With the backing of the Ottoman state, Kemal questioned how these critics could dare to question the Islamic legitimacy of the project. In challenging the legality of the caliph's will, he reasoned, 'you accuse of incorrect belief all the officials of the caliphate of the Islamic World which is the defender of the Muhammadan religion'.[33]

Giving a foreigner – in this case Aristidis Fanton – a concession to import a particular product had a long history and, in the case of books, it followed the same pattern as the importation of non-Islamic printed works in the Arabic script in the late sixteenth century. The historian and statesman Ahmet Cevdet Pasha reports that the Sublime Porte had wanted to print the Qur'an for many years, but had been unable to secure permission from the ulama to move forward with the venture.[34] Of the London edition, Cevdet writes that 'the Sublime Porte gave them permission [to import] and they sold them, but these prints did not come out properly'.[35] Cevdet does not explain the nature of their insufficiencies, but the text includes a statement by a committee of scholars who found mistakes in Hafız Osman's rendering, alluding to a table listing the errors and their corrections:

> The copies of the Qur'an al-Karīm that the famous calligrapher Hafız Osman produced in the year 1094/1682–3 have been multiplied and reproduced by photograph [i.e. photolithography] and have been read aloud by us from start to finish. It is certified that they contain no error in any word other than those mistakes of diacritic marks and short vowels that are shown in the table that we arranged.[36]

It is unclear whether these are the insufficiencies to which Cevdet refers. We may surmise, however, that the problematic nature of these books really stemmed from their European, non-Muslim provenance.[37]

Additionally, it is essential to consider that the issue of price may have been a factor. Fanton and Kemal had a monopoly on printed copies of the Qur'an: they faced little competition – other than the black market – and therefore had no reason to sell the books cheaply. As mentioned earlier, it is clear that this monopolistic venture was embarked upon to make a profit, even a fortune, at least as far as Fanton was concerned. Circumstantial evidence also indicates that this edition may have been expensive. Black-market printing and smuggling continued to flourish, suggesting that illegal copies remained significantly cheaper. The various perceived problems of this edition – its foreignness, the financial ambition of its producers and its expense – strengthened the perception that the state needed to take direct control of the printing process.

The First Istanbul Edition of the Qur'an

On 2 May 1873, the Ottoman state took the historic decision to print the Qur'an itself, and it did so in grandiose fashion. The office of the grand vizier stated its ambitious intention to print 500,000 copies, a large print run by the standards of the nineteenth century and perhaps the largest ever in the history of Ottoman printing.[38] This was an immense undertaking that would create an unprecedented number of copies of the Qur'an within the empire, enough to provide copies for use in schools and mosques, and for any other purposes as well. The document ordering this project states that 'handwritten copies of the Qur'an had become scarce', causing hardship for Ottoman Muslims and that, 'out of necessity', those who wanted a Qur'an had turned to the 'faulty editions' sold by illegal presses and smugglers who had 'subverted the embargo by various tricks'.[39]

The person chosen to lead the project was Ahmet Cevdet, a celebrated scholar and statesman who had both the ulama credentials and the political acumen to successfully bring the project to completion. In the middle of 1873, he was transferred to the Ministry of Education, which became the institutional headquarters from which Ottoman Qur'an printing and distribution were directed. Cevdet had to successfully navigate the interests of the ulama and address their concerns about the ritual purity and accuracy of the printing process.[40] In particular, they had misgivings about the application of heavy pressure upon the text, and feared the possibility of impure materials being found in the machinery, brushes (animal hair, skins) and the ink (pig's fat, olive oil).[41] Echoing this concern, archival documents that recommend the printing of the Qur'an make repeated reference to the care that would be taken to respect and preserve the text during the process. The grand vizierate stipulated that representatives of state ministries should oversee the project in order to ensure the most pristine and amenable conditions. It further specified that in the course of printing, 'not one sheet of paper is to be wasted or destroyed'.[42] Documents from subsequent decades insist that those in the print shop cannot work 'without doing ritual ablutions' beforehand, and some stipulate that Christians and other non-Muslims cannot work on Qur'anic printing projects or even enter the premises.[43]

Cevdet recounted that, at one point in history, Islamic scholars had debated whether or not the process of binding books showed disrespect towards the Qur'an. He claimed that some scholars found the process objectionable because of the manner in which the binder had to strike the pages with a metal tool and smash the sheets in a wooden press. These acts, Cevdet explained, were viewed as inconsistent with the displays of reverence and purity required when interacting with the written Qur'an. Yet, binding had become permissible because it protected the pages of the text by preventing them from being scattered about and damaged, thereby serving a greater good. Cevdet theorised that such a case embodied the Islamic legal principle by which 'matters are judged by their intentions' (*al-umūr bi-maqāsidihā*), and that, in comparison with binding, the printing process was not as rough on the text and that the good of multiplying copies outweighed the bad in the mechanical violence of the process.[44]

Once the Ottoman government had decided to go ahead and print the Qur'an, they had to choose a method of printing. For decades, Ottoman presses and the presses in Egypt and Russia had been producing Qur'anic commentaries and other Islamic works with movable-type printing, a process in which small metal or wooden blocks containing individual letters had to be arranged manually one by one (See Figure 4, metal printing block). The process was labour intensive, expensive and, in its initial phases, encountered difficulties producing elegant Arabic script. However, technological advances offered an alternative method.

The development of photolithography in the 1860s provided an inexpensive new method of reproducing texts and images. Since government officials were concerned with producing a 'high-quality, accurate' *muṣḥaf*, and, crucially, doing so cost-effectively, they chose to use photolithographic printing. Archival evidence shows that the state took the decision to print without choosing a method beforehand.[45] In lithographic printing, grease is drawn onto blocks of special limestone. The ink adheres to the image where the grease was applied, which can then be printed onto paper using a press. The most basic form of lithography produces a print that is a mirror image (i.e. in reverse) of that on the stone. This required an artist or scribe to work directly on the stone in reverse, making the reproduction of texts difficult and impractical. However, with photolithography, printers developed a process whereby a photographic image could be applied to the stone, enabling the reproduction of any text or image (See Figure 3, lithographic stone). In Europe, this technology was used primarily for printing images, whereas Islamicate printers employed it mostly for reproducing texts.[46] For Qur'anic printing, this meant that highly esteemed calligraphic editions of the Qur'an could be reproduced accurately and inexpensively.

This new technique made it possible for there to be a smooth transition from manuscript to print, avoiding abrupt change and maintaining aesthetic sensibilities. In theory, it also resolved the concern about error because it involved no typesetting as did letter-block printing. Printers could simply choose a venerable manuscript copied by a respected calligrapher and transform it into a printed book, as had been the case with the London edition of Hafız Osman's *muṣḥaf*. In many editions, the colour was lost, but the shape of the letters and the arrangement of the page remained the same. In these respects, photolithography also enabled the Ottoman government to link the manuscript tradition with the new technology.[47] Having settled upon photolithography, the government decided to reproduce the acclaimed *muṣḥaf* of Şekerzade Mehmed Efendi (d. 1752), a renowned Ottoman calligrapher of the twelfth/eighteenth century.

The first official (i.e. legal) Ottoman *muṣḥaf* in Istanbul was published towards the end of Ramadan, in the year 1874. In order to assuage concerns about the printing of the text, an announcement composed by Cevdet was appended to this version. It makes reverential reference to the calligraphic text, and, by its inclusion, emphasised the continuity between the calligraphic and print traditions: 'For four hundred years, most of the copies of the Qur'an have been handwritten with the *naskh* (Tr. *nesih*) style script, and many talented masters in this art have come and gone.'[48] The announcement pays homage to the master calligraphers of the Ottoman Empire, Şeyh Hamdullah (1429–1520), Hafız Osman (1642–98), Seyyid Abdullah Efendi (d. 1731) and Şekerzade Mehmed Efendi whose text the government chose to reproduce for the first photolithographic edition (See Figure 6, a lithographic Qur'an page).

The announcement also recounts that Sultan Ahmet III, the same sultan who gave permission for the opening of the Müteferrika printing press in 1729, sent Şekerzade to Medina to make a copy of a renowned *muṣḥaf* in the mosque adjoining the tomb of the Prophet Muhammad. Şekerzade had remained in Medina for several years and copied this Qur'an 'letter by letter', bringing the final product to Istanbul where it gained acclaim as a Qur'an of unparalleled beauty.[49] The inclusion of this historical detail cleverly served to connect the 1874 Istanbul edition of the Qur'an with Medina, the city of the Prophet. It is only at the end that the announcement mentions printing and photolithography.

In order to further bolster the acceptability of the project, the announcement indicates that the highest ranking members of both the ulama and the calligraphers participated in the production of the book. However, after invoking the authority and gravitas associated with first-/seventh-century Medina and four hundred years of Ottoman calligraphic tradition, the announcement presents a somewhat surprising bit of information. It states that, upon examination, the nineteenth-century scholars had found 'errors' (*görülen yanlışlar*) in the venerable *muṣḥaf* of Şekerzade and corrected them. Whereas the preceding portion of the announcement builds confidence in the text, these final lines cast a shadow of doubt upon it:

> On this occasion, the text was read to the head reciter Timur Hafız in Istanbul and the errors seen therein were corrected by the shaykh of the calligraphers and the head of the ulama İzzet Mustafa Efendi and printed via the art that has appeared in our age, photolithography, in the Military Lithographic Printing Press with the expertise of Kolağası Hafız Ali Efendi.[50]

It is interesting that scholars felt the need to question Şekerzade's text, given its status as one of the great Ottoman *muṣḥaf*s. However, the ulama insisted on an inspection committee as a condition for approving the project, thereby giving themselves a supervisory role in the process. Studying the 1288/1871 edition imported from London, Malissa Taylor found that a proofreading committee of no less than ten Islamic scholars had signed their names to ensure the quality of the book, but, like the edition of 1874, it mentions the presence of errors in the text.[51] One argument against printing had been the fear of introducing errors, but Ottoman Qur'anic printings reveal that the printing process sometimes exposed the 'mistakes' of the calligraphic tradition or at least the discrepancies between what was perceived as correct at different points in history.[52] Printing, and the various procedures of checking and correction surrounding it, resulted in a very similar circumstance in early modern Europe, where greater scrutiny led to the cross-checking of manuscript texts and the subsequent revision of the printed versions.[53] This dynamic contributed to the development of critical editions and the discipline of text criticism. In the quest for a standard edition, the Ottoman printings of the Qur'an in the late nineteenth century led to the scrutiny of even the most prestigious *muṣḥaf*s. This process of establishing an accurate, standard edition continued into the early twentieth century when the Egyptian state organised the printing of a new edition that became the most widely used version in the twentieth century.

A Qur'an for all

The Ottoman state emphasised the fact that handwritten copies had become prohibitively expensive and that printing the text would make them affordable to more members of the public. With printing, 'even the poorest man', the Ministry of Education stressed, 'will be able to buy the quantity he needs, either for himself or for his children'.[54] To this end, the sultan decided to sell the copies at an affordable price, 'without making one cent (*akçe*) of profit' as he claimed.[55] In 1875, copies were sold at a price of twenty *kuruş* plus the cost of binding – ten *kuruş* extra for the standard binding or fifteen *kuruş* extra for the deluxe binding. To put this in perspective, the average skilled worker in Istanbul made approximately sixteen and a half *kuruş* per day, so two days' wages would suffice to purchase a copy, a significant improvement over the nine days' wages needed to buy a manuscript version in the early nineteenth century.[56]

As production and efficiency increased, prices dropped even further. Beginning in 1882, bound copies of the Şekerzade edition sold for twelve *kuruş* and those of the calligrapher Kadırgalı for ten *kuruş*, and by 1891, those prices fell to eleven *kuruş* and nine *kuruş* respectively. Unbound versions (*ecza*) from the approved state press could be purchased for even less: in 1882 they cost eight *kuruş* and six and a half *kuruş* respectively, and in 1891 they sold for seven and a half *kuruş* and six *kuruş* respectively. Mass production via print technology succeeded in making copies more economical, and the falling prices aligned with the Ottoman state's discourse that emphasised that Qur'an printing was a not-for-profit venture designed to make the book affordable, a rationale that was included in the colophons of many Ottoman editions.[57]

In early modern Europe, printing was a lucrative business and profits enabled printing operations to expand and diversify rapidly.[58] The central religious text and most coveted book – the Bible – was the first printed work, and presses enabled Protestant tracts and vernacular translations of the Bible to spread rapidly across Europe. Since, at the outset, printing was in the hands of private entrepreneurs and Protestant reformers, religious separatism, profit-seeking and non-conformism surrounded print culture there. In stark contrast, the Ottoman state controlled the printing business, impeding the emergence of print capitalism and, for the most part, succeeding in that aim. Unlike the Bible, the Qur'an was printed long after other types of works, and its printing was restricted to the press approved by the state; further, for roughly the first one hundred and fifty years, Ottoman printing was not profitable. The printing of Islamic works, including the Qur'an, did not have any association with a separatist religious group or a political movement. There were of course Ottoman subjects who printed the Qur'an surreptitiously and imported copies from abroad, showing an entrepreneurial spirit akin to that of their predecessors in early modern Europe and in South Asia, but they did so in order to make a profit and provide inexpensive books, not to challenge the religious establishment. Even in this case, the Ottoman state did everything in its power to stymie entrepreneurial printing by controlling the book trade closely, preventing unsanctioned Islamic publications and allowing only limited printing under the strict supervision of the ulama.

This pattern continued for the Qur'an even after the Ottoman state opted to make Qur'anic publishing a state-managed venture, leasing the printing rights to publishers linked to the palace. The government entrusted the initial Qur'an printing operations to the Matbaa-i Amire, the revamped successor of the oldest Muslim press in the empire founded by Ibrahim Müteferrika. However, with the ascension of Sultan Abdülhamid II (r. 1876–1908), the Matbaa-i Osmaniye – a press run by Osman Zeki Bey (d. 1890), a close friend of Abdülhamid II – gradually took over the coveted Qur'an printing contracts. In 1880, it received a concession to print the *muṣḥaf*s of several famous calligraphers for a duration of twenty-five years. These books were approved and stamped by the Ministry of Education, which allowed them to pass through customs and be exported abroad.[59] From this point onwards, Osman Bey's contract was renewed numerous times and, despite challenges from other publishers, his press maintained a legal monopoly on Qur'anic printing until Abdülhamid II's downfall in 1908–9.

Facing European encroachment and nationalist separatist movements in the Ottoman Empire, the famously paranoid sultan gained greater control over the printing process by putting a close ally at the helm of what would become, with his patronage, the premier press in Istanbul. Osman Bey came from a family of elite calligraphers who had close ties to the palace and had produced high quality copies of the Qur'an for previous sultans.[60] Raised in the milieu of the palace, Osman Bey continued the family tradition and was trained as a calligrapher. He remained in the inner circle of Abdülhamid II for the duration of his reign and benefited from the state's patronage of his press. The monopoly proved to be extremely profitable and Osman Bey amassed a sizeable fortune from the printing business, some of which he used to purchase a large plot of land on the northern outskirts of Istanbul where he built a European-style mansion. This area of Istanbul north of Taksim – Osmanbey – currently bears his name.[61]

Other printers resented the fact that a single printing house, and one closely linked to the sultan, had the exclusive right to print the Qur'an. There was no reason why multiple publishers could not be granted permission to print. In fact, competition in this field would have lowered the price of the books even further, thereby helping the Ottoman government of Abdülhamid II to achieve its stated aim of 'multiplying them until they can be obtained by both rich and poor'.[62] However, it is likely that the Shaykh al-Islam's office worried that allowing widespread printing would lead to quality control issues of the sort that had appeared in printed versions from Iran, Russia, India and Europe. In short, it would be more difficult to monitor the printing process as well as the accuracy of texts if multiple publishers entered the market. Evidence suggests that the Ottoman state preferred to maintain firm control over one publisher and to block others from participating in what was very likely the most lucrative sector of the publishing business.

Excluded from this sector, Ottoman and Iranian printers in Istanbul continued to print copies illegally.[63] Moreover, reports about illegal printing operations and discarded pages of the Qur'an appearing in grocery stores (allegedly used to wrap fruit and vegetables) surfaced long after the Ottoman state began to allow legal but limited printing.[64] The Iranians in Istanbul were still publishing black-market copies a decade after the first Istanbul editions, and, when harassed by Ottoman officials, they went so far as to lodge complaints, albeit unsuccessfully, with the government for inhibiting their printing activities.[65] The extent of illegal Qur'an printing and importing activities in this period was impressively diverse and widespread, reflecting the continuing profitability and demand for such books and highlighting the difficulty of maintaining exclusive control over the text.

Despite these unsanctioned printings of the Qur'an, it is clear that the press of Osman Bey carried out the vast majority of Qur'an publishing and received the substantial orders for copies from the Ministry of Education for use in the education system and in Abdülhamid's various propaganda activities. In 1882, for instance, the government placed an order with Osman Bey's press for 500,000 copies.[66] If this target figure was actually achieved, then the Ottoman state alone sponsored the printing of over one million copies in Istanbul between 1874 and 1883. In comparison, the centre of Muslim publishing in the Russian Empire – Kazan – published 82,300 *muṣḥaf*s between 1852 and 1859. During the same period in Kazan, 169,900 partial versions (*Haftyak*) were published as well.[67] By 1896, Osman Bey's press had printed 2.5 million copies of the Qur'an.[68] While figures from other presses are elusive, Ottoman Qur'an printing in this period was almost certainly the most prodigious publishing of the Muslim Holy Book that the world had ever seen.

Disseminating the Word: Education and Islamic Unity

Even before the advent of printing, the Ottoman state often took on the responsibility of providing copies of the Qur'an for mosques, not only in the capital but across the empire. The provision of copies of the Qur'an constituted a form of munificence on the part of the sultan, an honour akin to that of providing the shroud to cover the Kaaba in Mecca, or building monumental architecture, or funding public works. The Ottoman state and its subjects, to some extent, understood the provision of copies of the Qur'an for mosques to be a responsibility of the state or of wealthy patrons who usually had close ties to the state. The Ottoman archives contain many requests from provincial mosques and remote schools for copies of the Qur'an or for the repair of existing copies, and the state usually obliged such requests.[69]

With the advent and development of Qur'an printing, the state amplified its distribution of *muṣḥaf*s exponentially. Whereas the state had previously given a few dozen manuscript copies to mosques in a given year, in the last quarter of the nineteenth century, it began to provide tens of thousands of printed copies to schools across the empire, and, moreover, to send them far beyond its boundaries to Muslims around the world. Two main factors influenced this trend: the rapidly growing Ottoman school system and the Islamic Unity (or 'Pan-Islamic') campaign of Abdülhamid II.

Education

One of Namık Kemal's main arguments for printing the Qur'an was that students had to pay unreasonably high prices for handwritten copies. He reasoned correctly that students would be important consumers and beneficiaries of the printed text. The modernising state and its expanding bureaucracy required a larger educational system to provide literate officials for government service. This led to the opening of new schools across the empire that created considerable demand for printed books, including the Qur'an. Under Abdülhamid II, state schools began to inculcate in their students the values of morality and loyalty to the sultan to a greater extent than was the case during the Tanzimat era (1839–76). The reason for this emphasis was that many in the society perceived a crisis of morality which they believed threatened the social fibre of the empire; education, particularly religious education, was one tool which the state attempted to use to remedy this looming threat.[70]

Schools knew about the printing ventures at an early point in the process and petitioned the government to supply them with copies. In 1871, for instance, the very first year that the lithographic editions of the Qur'an had been imported from London, Ottoman officials on the island of Crete requested five hundred copies for impoverished elementary school students.[71] Their counterparts in Montenegro issued a very similar petition with an emphasis on religious necessity. They wrote that, for lack of books, the people of the towns of Podgorica and Işbozi 'had not been able to learn their religious duties and obligations and had fallen into a state of ignorance'.[72] Noting the poverty of the local residents, they asked the state to provide copies of the Qur'an and religious treatises that would teach the basic precepts and practices of Islam.

Having enforced the embargo for so many years, the Ministry of Education had accumulated a large stockpile of printed copies of the Qur'an. Seeing these books rot away for years on the shelves, Ottoman officials devised a way to put them to good use in educational and morality boosting campaigns. The books were sent to the Shaykh al-Islam's office for inspection. Copies deemed to be sound were given away to children, the poor and even soldiers, although the vast majority would go to students in the expanding school system.[73] While some 'problematic' editions could be corrected and sent, others were 'beyond repair'.[74]

Islamic unity

In response to the rapid expansion of European colonialism and political influence in the nineteenth century, not only in the Muslim world but around the globe, Abdülhamid II embarked on a campaign to unite Muslims behind the Ottoman Empire, the only remaining formidable Muslim polity. To unite disparate people in far-flung corners of the world, even on a level of common sympathy, would seem to be a considerable and difficult undertaking. Yet many colonised peoples, for instance, the Acehnese under Dutch rule in the Indonesian archipelago and the South Asian Muslims under British colonial rule in India, responded to the Ottoman sultan's symbolic leadership with enthusiasm. Central to this campaign was Abdülhamid's conferring upon himself the title of the 'Protector of the Two Holy Cities' (Mecca and Medina) and his claim to be the 'caliph of all Muslims'.[75] Ottoman sultans had staked a claim to the title of caliph for centuries, but Abdülhamid II emphasised and publicised these titles to an unprecedented degree around the Muslim world, using print technology and benefiting from improvements in travel and communication between different continents.

As one component of the Islamic Unity campaign, the Ottoman state used printed copies of the Qur'an to proclaim the Ottoman caliph as the symbolic leader of the Muslim world. During Abdülhamid's reign, many printings invoked the name of the sultan as patron and leader, saying in Arabic that the book was printed at the command of 'the possessor of sound opinion and felicitous effort, the Sultan Ghazi Abdülhamid, son of the Sultan Ghazi Abdülmecid, may his enemies be vanquished, may his heart be glad and may his realm continue to flourish'.[76] Another edition printed in 1884–5 has a full page at the end with a large, ornate heading 'Abdülhamid Khan', under which it states that 'Our Master, His Excellence' issued special orders to provide the book as a gift to assist Muslims who want to recite the Qur'an 'at all times'.[77] Invoking the sultan's name and calling for the protection of his domains, the editions printed in Istanbul became emblems of the Ottoman claim to global Muslim leadership and were often given as gifts to win and sustain the loyalty of Muslims in various regions within and beyond the empire. The state directed the Qur'an-giving campaign primarily towards Ottoman subjects in regions where loyalty to Istanbul was in question, but it also gave copies to Muslims in different parts of the world.

The Ottoman archives contain a wealth of documents on Qur'anic distribution policies that provide glimpses into the evolution of state-led Qur'anic publication. An interesting example of global distribution is seen in the Ottoman overtures to Muslims in South East Asia, an area densely populated with Muslims living under European colonial rule. An archival document from the Ministry of Foreign Affairs provides a glimpse of Ottoman intentions in the area; it states that 'since there are eighteen to twenty million Muslims on the island of Java in the Dutch colonies', certain notables there were to be given printed copies of the Qur'an 'in the name of the sultan with the intention of making a favourable impression'.[78] Beyond sympathy, it is unclear what the sultan hoped to gain by fostering good relations with colonised Muslims in a region as distant as South East Asia.

Rather than any formal alliance, it seems that the desire to be recognised as caliph and to further solidarity among Muslims fuelled such efforts, and the circumstances of Dutch colonial rule made some Javanese and Acheans enthusiastic proponents of the Ottoman sultan/caliph. In 1899, a Javanese Muslim named Aḥmad b. Salīm wrote a fascinating letter in Arabic, preserved in the Ottoman archives, to the Sublime Porte that must have been very gratifying to the Ottomans. He complained of Dutch colonial oppression and described the Ottoman Empire as a ray of hope for the Muslims of the region. He wrote: 'How much I hope that an envoy of our brothers the Turks will come to these lands to inspire our hearts'.[79] He was especially impressed by the experience of two Muslims from South East Asia who had travelled to Singapore and Japan dressed in Ottoman clothes. On account of their apparel, he recounts, they were greeted with the utmost hospitality and respect because of the esteem that the Japanese held for the Ottoman state. For Aḥmad b. Salīm, this story provided an example of what an affiliation with the Ottoman caliphate could do to improve the plight of his embattled co-religionists if a similar influence were felt in Java.

In connection with this appeal for Ottoman support, Aḥmad b. Salīm requested that the Ottomans send printed copies of the Qur'an for his small town. Having heard that the Ottoman consul in Batavia (the Dutch name for modern-day Jakarta) had given away several hundred copies, he informed the Ottomans that none of these books had reached the town where he lived. In his words, there was 'a great need among the poor students' for these books; he offered his prayers for the sultan, 'our Master, Commander of the Faithful (*Amīr al-Mu'minīn*)'.[80] He insisted that even twenty copies would suffice to do significant good. The Ottomans responded by sending a shipment of four hundred copies, which were photolithographic editions of Hafız Osman's and Şekerzade's famous *muṣḥafs*. Poor students received 375 copies, while twenty-five specially illuminated copies were sent to the local notables (See Figure 7, example of illuminated Qur'an page). Additionally, the Sublime Porte decided to award Aḥmad b. Salīm with a medal for his good works and favourable inclination towards the Ottoman sultan, whom he recognised as caliph.[81] Java was not alone. The Ottomans also sent copies of the Qur'an to communities in Sumatra and rewarded local leaders who aided Muslim communities. In the same region, the Muslim leadership of Singapore petitioned Ottoman emissaries for copies of the Qur'an printed in the abode of the caliph.[82]

While the volume of Ottoman Qur'an distribution in South East Asia was impressive, it paled in comparison with similar efforts in the Arabic-speaking territories closer to home, where the sultan gave away many more books. Within the territories of the empire, the government sought to secure the loyalty of its diverse subject populations, especially Kurdish and Arab tribes that had little direct contact with the state and were largely autonomous. In the campaign to promote loyalty to the sultan/caliph, the Ottoman state strengthened connections with tribal leaders and showered them with largess, providing copies of the Qur'an printed in Istanbul and other gifts. Some of these distributions were voluminous. In 1889, for instance, the government sent 8,200 copies of the Qur'an to the sparsely populated Najd region of the Arabian peninsula and two thousand Arabic grammar books; a small fortune in watches, headgear (*kūfīyas*) and robes accompanied the crates of books.[83] This sizeable shipment for the Najd reveals the impressive scale of the Ottomans' Qur'anic publication and distribution activities.[84] To commemorate the handing over of these gifts from the sultan, provincial governors organised ceremonies in which Ottoman officials presented the townspeople and local leaders with copies of the Qur'an underneath a banner proclaiming 'Long live the Sultan!' (*Padişahım çok yaşa*!). There is also documentation that the son of Namık Kemal, Ali Ekrem Bey, the chief administrative official (*mutasarrıf*) of Jerusalem, gave copies of the Qur'an to the Bedouins of Beersheba in 1907 and also to the city dwellers in Jerusalem (See Figure 8).[85]

These editions of the Qur'an were not only expedient gifts intended to purchase the favour of local notables and, thereby, to keep them loyal to Ottoman interests. In addition, they possessed a symbolic dimension: they represented and projected a sense of Ottoman modernity. Along with the invocation of the name of Sultan Abdülhamid II, early printings reflect the modernising ethos of the Ottoman state. The colophons locate the books within a context of progress and enlightenment when, for example, they state that the sultan printed the text 'in the age of spreading knowledge and science'.[86]

This connection between loyalty to the Ottoman state, modernisation and the presence of printed copies of the Qur'an appears in an interesting document from the province of Ottoman Yemen, which was reconquered by the Ottomans between 1871 and 1872. The Ottomans had introduced the first printing press and the use of printed text books to Yemen in the late 1870s, giving printing a distinctly Ottoman association in the province.[87] In 1890, an official named Muhammad Hilal Efendi drew attention, in a memorandum to the Sublime Porte, to the 'strange publications' and air of dissention that circulated in Yemen. He argued that there was a need for a display of beneficence from the sultan in order to win the favour of the local population and quell the commotion surrounding the Zaydī Shi'i treatises making their way around the province. Muhammad Hilal noted that in the local mosques 'the copies of the Qur'an are all handwritten. There is not a single printed copy.'[88] For him, this was significant because, 'However many [printed] copies there are in the local mosques, that is how much Qur'an recitation there will be.'[89] In Muhammad Hilal's mind, there was a clear relationship between printed copies of the Qur'an (symbols of modernity and imperial investment) and the loyalty of Yemeni subjects to central power, manifested as Sunni observance. Printed *muṣḥaf*s embodied Ottoman modernity and cosmopolitan Sunnism, while manuscripts represented traditionalism and Zaydī localism. This example reflects the broader Ottoman campaign to 'correct' the religious beliefs of non-Sunni Ottoman subjects, including Yezidis, Nusayris and the Alevis, and to instil Ḥanafī doctrine via schools.[90]

Muhammad Hilal recommended that the sultan send printed copies of the Qur'an as a gift to the province, suggesting that benefits would ensue for the empire. This, he argued, would make a 'favourable impression', and, secondly, 'further acquaint the people with the Exalted State' and increase their obedience and submission.[91] This official pinned high hopes on the efficacy of printed copies from the sultan to improve the state of religious observance, dissuade Yemenis from what he saw as heretical (i.e. Zaydī) inclinations and enhance governance in his respective province. Whether these purposes were likely to succeed is less interesting than the fact that an Ottoman official connected such concerns with books. For this Ottoman official, the printed *muṣḥaf* was a symbol of the Ottoman sultan's authority and the path to Sunni loyalty in a distant province.

The political symbolism affiliated with the printed Qur'an in the nineteenth century has parallels with the transformation of calligraphic Qur'anic manuscripts in the ʿAbbāsid Empire. Yasser Tabbaa's research demonstrates the relationship between what he calls the Sunni Revival and the shift from angular to cursive script in Qur'anic manuscripts beginning around the fourth/tenth century. He argues that the ʿAbbāsid's development of a more legible Arabic script based upon a new recension of the Qur'an appeared as a direct response to the Ismaili Fatimid state, which continued to use the angular Kufic script. According to Tabaa, the cursive script clearly distinguished ʿAbbāsid versions and visually expressed the state's control over the sacred text.[92]

In Ottoman Yemen and elsewhere, the printed Qur'an served a similar function. Controlled and distributed by the Ottoman state and clearly different from manuscript copies, the printed Qur'an was an unmistakable emblem of the Ottoman sultan and his control over the sacred text. The Ottoman state gave thousands upon thousands of free copies to poor students, economically strapped mosques and, additionally, distributed large quantities as gifts to Muslims in the Balkans, the Arabian peninsula, Afghanistan, the Cape of Good Hope and as far east as Java and Sumatra.

During the same period that the printed Qur'an was being promoted as an imperial symbol in the Islamic Unity campaign, Sultan Abdülhamid's censorship and surveillance of books intensified and, in 1889, a committee was established to scrutinise all books before publication in order to ensure that they did not contain material that was politically or culturally subversive. Under the regime of heightened sensitivity with respect to books, Ottoman officials continued to enforce the embargo on foreign *muṣḥaf*s, confiscating copies originating from a diverse array of locations outside the empire, including Vienna, India and Russia. The attention to illegal printing within the empire remained equally stringent as Iranians and others continued to reap profits, since they were the only competitors and providers of the most affordable copies. Frustrated by incursions on its business, the Matbaa-i Osmaniye defended its exclusive right to print the Qur'an and pressured the government to protect its privileged position in the printing business.[93] The lack of competition created by the state monopoly caused prices to remain higher than necessary and sustained the demand for illegally printed copies.

Printing the Qur'an was also an important step in the emergence of modern Qur'an translations. The battle over who would control the production of physical copies of the Qur'an served as a prelude to the debate about transmitting the content of the Qur'an via translation. The way in which the state used printed copies laid the groundwork for a mass-produced religious text that was both an educational tool and a symbol of state authority. The projection of the printed Qur'an as an emblem of the sultan-caliph's authority set a precedent for the view that a Turkish translation could serve as an emblem of the Turkish nation. The government's distrust of foreign copies of the Qur'an and unauthorised prints demonstrates that the Ottoman sultan, supported by ulama, claimed an exclusive right to control the sacred text within the borders of the empire. Just as the printed Qur'an became a symbol of Ottoman modernisation, later reformers would argue that late Ottoman society needed translations of the Qur'an to progress on the path towards full modernity.

NOTES

1 Cevdet, *Tezâkir*, IV, p. 128.

2 Şerif Mardin, *The Genesis of Young Ottoman Thought: A Study in the Modernization of Turkish Political Ideas* (Princeton, NJ, Princeton University Press, 1962; repr. Syracuse, NJ, Syracuse University Press, 2000).

3 A. Kevin Reinhart, 'Civilization and its Discussants', in Dennis Washburn and A. Kevin Reinhart, eds., *Converting Cultures: Religion, Ideology, and Transformations of Modernity* (Leiden, Brill, 2007), pp. 267–89.

4 Mithat Cemal Kuntay, *Namık Kemal: Devrinin İnsanları ve Olayları arasında* (Istanbul, Maarif Basımevi, 1944), I, pp. 539–40.

5 BOA HR.TO 456/32 (7 August 1872); Mithat Cemal Kuntay, *Namık Kemal: Devrinin İnsanları ve Olayları arasında* (Istanbul, Milli Eğitim Basımevi, 1949), II, p. 35.

6 Kuntay, *Namık Kemal*, II, pp. 35–7.

7 Letter from A. Fanton to Namık Kemal (5 April 1870) in Kuntay, *Namık Kemal*, II, pp. 2–3.
8 Letter from Fanton to Kemal (n.d.) in Kuntay, *Namık Kemal*, II, p. 47.
9 Kuntay, *Namık Kemal*, II, p. 47.
10 Ibid., II, p. 49
11 Ibid., II, pp. 23–8.
12 Letter from Fanton to Kemal (20 July 1870) in ibid., II, p. 32.
13 Ali Suavi, 'İstanbul'da Mektup', *Ulum*, 15 Şaban 1287/9 November 1870, pp. 82–3.
14 I would like to thank Ruth Anne Godollei for sharing her knowledge on this subject.
15 Namık Kemal, 'Kemal'ın Müdafaası', *Mecmua-i Ebüzziya* 3, no. 25 (1300/1882), pp. 769–70. The journal printed the article ten years after its composition.
16 Ibid., p. 771.
17 Ibid., p. 773.
18 Ibid., p. 771.
19 Ibid., p. 772.
20 Ibid., p. 775.
21 On ulama criticism of modernisation in the Ottoman Empire, see Rudolf Peters, 'Religious Attitudes toward Modernization in the Ottoman Empire: A Nineteenth Century Pious Text on Steamships, Factories and the Telegraph', *Die Welt des Islams* 26, no. 1 (1986), pp. 76–105.
22 Namık Kemal, 'Kemal'ın Müdafaası', p. 770.
23 Ibid.
24 Ibid., p. 771.
25 Ibid., p. 775.
26 Ibid., p. 771.
27 Ibid., pp. 779–80.
28 Ibid., p. 770.
29 Ibid., pp. 772–3.
30 Ibid., p. 773.
31 Ibid., p. 778.
32 Ibid., p. 780.
33 Ibid., pp. 778–9.
34 Cevdet, *Tezâkir*, IV, p. 128.
35 Ibid. Also, see Ahmet Hamdi Tanpınar, *XIX. Asır Türk Edebiyatı Tarihi* (Istanbul, Yapı Kredi Yayınları, 2006), p. 319.
36 *Mushaf-ı Şerif*, MS Hacı Mahmud Efendi 6, Süleymaniye Library, Istanbul, final page, cited in Malissa Taylor, 'The Anxiety of Sanctity: Censorship and Sacred Texts', in Seyfi Kenan, ed., *Osmanlı ve Avrupa: Seyahat, Karşılaşma ve Etkileşim (18. Yüzyıl Sonuna Kadar)/ Ottomans and Europe: Travel, Encounter and Interaction (Until the End of the 18th Century)* (Istanbul, İSAM Yayınları, 2010), pp. 536–7. Translation is by Malissa Taylor.
37 Adding confusion to the situation, Victor Chauvin lists Constantinople and London as the places of printing. He appears to be mistaken regarding the former. Victor Chauvin, *Bibliographie des ouvrages arabes ou relatifs aux Arabes, publiés dans l'Europe Chrétienne de 1810 à 1885* (Liège, H. Vaillant-Carmanne, 1907), X, pp. 30–31.

38 BOA A.MKT.MHM 453/60 (4/Ra/1290—2 May 1873).
39 Ibid.
40 Cevdet, *Tarih-i Cevdet*, I, p. 76.
41 Albin, 'Printing of the Qur'an'; Kuntay, *Namık Kemal*, II, p. 773.
42 BOA A.MKT.MHM 453/60.
43 Birinci, 'Osman Bey', pp. 33 and 37.
44 Cevdet, *Tarih-i Cevdet*, I, p. 76.
45 See BOA A.MKT.MHM 453/60.
46 For further information on Islamicate use of lithography, see Nile Green, 'Stones from Bavaria: Iranian Lithography in Its Global Contexts', *Iranian Studies* 43, no. 3 (2010), pp. 305–31.
47 Albin, 'Printing of the Qur'an'; Ian Proudfoot, 'Mass Producing Houri's Moles', in Peter G. Riddell and Tony Street, eds., *Islam: Essays on Scripture, Thought, and Society* (Leiden, Brill, 1997), pp. 161–86.
48 Cevdet, *Tezâkir*, IV, p. 128.
49 Ibid.
50 Ibid., IV, pp. 128–9.
51 Taylor, 'The Anxiety of Sanctity', p. 536.
52 Ibid., p. 537.
53 Elizabeth L. Eisenstein, *The Printing Revolution in Early Modern Europe*, 2nd edn (Cambridge, Cambridge University Press, 2005), pp. 48–9.
54 BOA MF.MKT 23/77 (22/Za/1291—31 December 1874).
55 Ibid.
56 Wage figures are for the period 1870–79 and come from Özmucur and Pamuk, 'Real Wages', Table 1, p. 301.
57 See, for example, the colophon in *Mushaf-ı Şerif* (Istanbul, Matbaa-i Osmaniye, 1301/1884).
58 Anderson, *Imagined Communities*, pp. 43–4.
59 Birinci, *Osman Bey*, pp. 26–7.
60 Nedret Kuran Burçoğlu, 'Matbaacı Osman Bey: Saray'dan İlk Defa Kur'an-ı Kerim Basma İznini Alan Hattat', *Tarih ve Toplum* 209 (2001), pp. 33–4.
61 Ibid., p. 40.
62 *Mushaf-ı Şerif*, p. 614.
63 Tokgöz, *Matbuat Hatıralarım*, p. 105.
64 BOA MF.MKT 27/208 (28/Ra/1292—4 May 1875).
65 BOA MF.MKT 60/12 (03/Ra/1296—24 February 1879).
66 BOA İ.DH 68339 (22/Ca/1299—11 April 1882).
67 Mahmut Gündüz, 'Matbaa Tarihçesi ve İlk Kur'an-ı Kerim Basımları', *Vakıf Dergisi* 12 (1978), p. 348.
68 Birinci, 'Osman Bey', p. 39.
69 BOA İ.DH 308/19645 (5/R/1271—26 December 1854); A.MKT.NZD 124/95 (7/R/1271—28 December 1854); BOA İ.MVL 525 23572 (16/Ş/1281—14 January 1865).
70 Fortna, *Imperial Classroom*, pp. 202–3.
71 BOA İ.MTZ.GR 13/427 (20/R/1288—9 July 1871).
72 BOA İ.ŞD 34/1661 (26/S/1294—12 March 1877).
73 BOA MF.MKT 299/55 (16/B/1313—1 January 1896).
74 BOA MF.MKT 118/22 (29/L/1307—17 June 1890).

75 See Deringil, *The Well-Protected Domains*, pp. 46–67.
76 *Mushaf-ı Şerif*, p. 614.
77 *Amme Cüzü* [Juz' 30] (Istanbul, Matbaa-i Osmaniye, 1302/1884–5), p. 41.
78 BOA İ.HR 290.18200 (29/C/1300—7 May 1883); BOA İ.HR 290/18200-2 (10/B/1300—17 May 1883).
79 BOA. MF.MKT 462.35 (19/R/1317– 26 August 1899).
80 Ibid.
81 Ibid.
82 Tokgöz, *Matbuat Hatıralarım*, pp. 116–17.
83 BOA İ.DH v. 87416 dol. 121 (27/Ca/1306—29 January 1889).
84 Ottoman envoy Muhammad Başala recommended similar gifts for the rulers of the Sudan; see Selim Deringil, 'Legitimacy Structures in the Ottoman State: The Reign of Abdulhamid II (1876–1909)', *International Journal of Middle East Studies* 23, no. 3 (1991), p. 353.
85 BOA BEO 3018/226298 (8/S/1325—23 March 1907); ʿĀrif al-ʿĀrif, *Tārīkh Biʾr al-Sabʿ wa qabāʾilihā* (Jerusalem, Maṭbaʿat Bayt al-Maqdis, 1934), pp. 246–7; David Kushner, *To Be Governor of Jerusalem* (Istanbul, Isis, 2005), pp. 97–8.
86 *Mushaf-ı Şerif*, p. 614.
87 Messick, *The Calligraphic State*, pp. 115–17.
88 BOA İ.DH v. 94394 dol. 122 (13/Ra/1308—27 October 1890).
89 Ibid.
90 Deringil, *Well-Protected Domains*, pp. 69–84.
91 Ibid.
92 Yasser Tabbaa, *The Transformation of Islamic Art during the Sunni Revival* (Seattle, University of Washington Press, 2001), pp. 43–4.
93 BOA BEO 2637/197759 (5/C/1323—7 August 1905).

3

Vernacular Commentaries and the New Intellectuals

There is a long tradition in Islamicate literature of looking down upon and belittling the Turkish language because it was deemed coarse and unrefined in comparison with Arabic and Persian. While this line of thinking was especially popular among Arabic- and Persian-speaking authors, many Turkish-speaking authors have also voiced such sentiments. The lack of regard for Turkish is also evident in the paucity of Turkish dictionaries and grammar books prior to the nineteenth century. Nevertheless, at various points in history, Turkish-speaking Muslims have in fact expressed discomfort with the dominance of the Arabic and Persian languages and the lowly state of the Turkish language, and some protested against the hegemony of Arabic in Muslim ritual and intellectual discourse as well. Following the disintegration of Seljuk rule in Anatolia during the seventh/thirteenth century, a number of Turkish-speaking rulers (*beyler*) held sway over small principalities in Anatolia. As a result, this era witnessed attempts to dignify Turkish Islamic literature when rulers who wanted to understand Islamic works commissioned their translation into Turkish, and when the ulama worked to teach Islam and carry out legal matters for Turkish-speaking populations.

In the late 800s/1300s, a little-known author named Abdurrahman el-Aksarayi lamented the prevalent disrespect for the Turkish language among his ulama colleagues and argued that Islamic literature needed to be composed in the language of the people. Perceiving the inability of most Muslims in Anatolia to derive guidance from Persian and Arabic legal texts, Aksarayi composed a book that would teach local Muslims the basic elements of Islamic worship. However, due to his use of Turkish, other scholars were unwilling to read it, causing him to complain, 'It is unfair that they do not pay any attention to this book ... In times of need, it is common practice to express the religious rulings in another language so that the people understand, and the benefit is the same.'[1] He supports his reasoning with a quotation from the Qur'an, *We have sent no Messenger save with the tongue of his people, that he might make all clear to them* (Q. 14:4), and asserts that the Prophet Muhammad would have spoken Turkish had he come to Anatolia. Invoking the importance of language as a means rather than an end, he argues that the goal of the ulama should be to convey knowledge that is useful and intelligible for 'the people' (*halk*).[2]

We must, however, be cautious when reading statements about writing in an accessible way for 'the people'. In many cases, this trope conveying the desire that the work should be broadly accessible is merely a convention that authors use, even for texts that are quite complex and require knowledge of multiple languages. Most Ottoman Islamic literature requires its readers to have some level of competency in Arabic and, in many cases, Persian as well.[3] We must also keep in mind the fact that the population was largely illiterate and came into contact with these works in distilled form through oral teaching and preaching. During the Ottoman period, various kinds of Turkish-language Islamic literature circulated in Anatolia and the Balkans, including interlinear translations of the Qur'an and Qur'anic commentaries (*tefsir*), but these works were used for study by scholars and the cultural elite, not by unlettered Muslims.

Full of miraculous adventures and fantastic episodes, popular stories of the prophets (*kısas-ı enbiya*) played a far greater role in the teaching of the Qur'an and the shaping of popular understandings of Islam than Qur'anic translations or commentaries. Gottfried Hagen has argued that these stories 'constitute nothing less than a translation of the scripture of Islam into the symbolic language of myth', which a large swathe of the population could understand, and that it effectively replaced the use of the Qur'an for didactic purposes among Turkish-speaking Muslims.[4] Tijana

Krstić's research on conversion to Islam in the Ottoman Balkans demonstrates the centrality of Turkish-language catechisms (*ilm-i hal*) for conveying Muslim beliefs and practices to converts, while the Qur'an remained an 'ever-remote authority for most new Muslims', a book that was more revered and recited than read.[5] The importance of these catechismal books carried over into the nineteenth century, when Mehmet Birgivi's catechismal work was the first Islamic text to be printed in 1803. Whereas commentaries and interlinear translations were largely scholastic, these easy-to-understand genres played a decisive role in communicating the Qur'an to non-elite Muslims in the premodern period. They conveyed the Qur'an and the essentials of Islamic practice and belief in a format and language that served the needs of Muslims living in Ottoman territories.

The shift towards more people directly engaging with the Qur'an occurred with the rise of printing and the spread of state schools in the nineteenth century, when a revolution in Ottoman literature took place on several fronts. The broad circulation of printed books, the beginning of Ottoman journalism, the emergence of the Ottoman novel, and the increased translation of European and Islamicate works into Turkish created a new intellectual context in which the production and consumption of knowledge became more egalitarian. Translation played such a key role in cultural life during this period (1850–1914) that Saliha Paker dubbed it the Ottoman 'age of translation'.[6] The need for Ottomans to learn European military methods and science and technology in order to defend the empire supplied the initial impetus to translate Western works into Turkish. A series of military losses convinced many Ottoman statesmen and literati that reform, even drastic reform, was necessary. They came to see the acquisition of European science and martial prowess as integral to the survival of the empire, and became interested in European history as a model for reform.[7] Biographies of great leaders in Europe figured among the earliest printed translations in the nineteenth century, including works like *The History of Catherine the Great* (*Katerina Tarihi*, Cairo, 1829) and *The History of Napoleon Bonaparte* (*Bonapart Tarihi*, Alexandria, 1833).

However, the translation movement in the early part of the century went beyond works on history, geography and the military. Translations of Islamic texts held an important place in the literary trajectory of the period as well. Historical and literary scholarship has largely neglected this phenomenon and focused on the shift towards Western genres.[8] This oversight is unfortunate because the publication of religious works in Turkish marks an important period of transformation in Ottoman Islamic literature; it marks a time during which greater access to traditional Islamic knowledge was provided and the genre of Qur'anic commentary was reshaped. Printed Islamic works of this period use clear, direct – even simplified – Turkish prose that was accessible to the less sophisticated readers. It reflects the spread of public education which had created a new class of students and literate low-level bureaucrats who had become consumers of literature of this type. As the number of readers increased, the difficulty of religious texts decreased, and a genre of easy-to-read, Turkish Islamic literature emerged that was clear, condensed and available for purchase at bookshops towards the latter quarter of the century.[9] The florescence of translation and vernacular Islamic literature in print transformed the way in which late Ottoman readers engaged with the Qur'an. Oral teaching in mosques, madrasas and Sufi lodges, stories of the prophets, and Arabic and Persian commentaries had facilitated the understanding of the Qur'an among the wider public prior to the nineteenth century. However, with the publication of simplified Turkish-language commentaries during the middle of the century, printed books became an increasingly viable means by which literate Muslims could learn about the Qur'an.

Ayıntâbî Mehmet's Turkish Commentary – *Tibyan*

It was in Cairo, not Istanbul, that Turkish commentaries of the Qur'an first entered the realm of print. In the nineteenth century, an influential population of Turkish speakers lived in Cairo and ruled Egypt. This 'Ottoman-Egyptian elite' used Turkish as the language of polite society, literature and government.[10] Cairo's 'age of translation' of works into Turkish preceded the similar trend in Istanbul by at least two decades.[11] The reformist Ottoman governor of Egypt, Mehmet Ali, hailed from the Ottoman Balkans and, in fact, knew very little Arabic. In 1257/1841–2, the press he established at Bulaq published *Tefsir-i Tibyan* (*The Elucidation*) by Ayıntâbî Mehmet Efendi (d. 1111/1698–9), a Turkish-language commentary that draws heavily on ʿAbd Allāh b. ʿUmar al-Bayḍāwī's *Anwār al-tanzīl*.[12] Some scholars consider this work to be the first printed Turkish translation of the Qur'an.[13] That judgement, however, depends wholly upon how one defines *translation*, and agreeing on a definition is no simple matter. In the case of renderings and commentaries of the Qur'an, we encounter a variety of texts that involve some degree of – for lack of a better phrase – *direct* translation (i.e. translations without extra-Qur'anic material), but often such texts are embedded in or accompanied by extensive digressions, extensions and glosses. In the Turkish context, deeming a text a 'translation' rather than a commentary has largely depended upon how succinct it is. This is an inexact science and, on a theoretical level, it may be more helpful to think of these works as longer or shorter representations of the Qur'an. On a technical level, the issue of format – how the text is actually arranged – plays an important role. How prominent and how accessible is the translated portion? Is it divided up into fragments that are scattered amongst the original text and commentary, or can it be read as a freestanding text? The classic interlinear manuscript/handwritten translation placed translated text below the original, usually in smaller script with a different colour and often in inelegant handwriting. Paraphrastic commentaries usually placed it after each verse or phrase of the Qur'an; it was divided and impossible to read as a flowing, independent text. The evolution of commentary into translation bears witness to an increasing independence and readability of the translated text. The freestanding vernacular translation of the Qur'an, in the absence of the original Arabic text, is a modern phenomenon in the Turcophone world.

While Ayıntâbî's *Tibyan* contains a great deal of direct translation and paraphrase, it also includes considerable extra-Qur'anic material: occasions of revelation explaining the context in which particular verses were revealed, hadiths (i.e. oral reports about the sayings and actions of the Prophet), as well as narrative traditions known as 'Hebrew folklore' (*Isrā'īliyyāt*) that were often used to elaborate upon and interpret Qur'anic verses. The glosses are structured in the style of a traditional commentary, and there is no attempt to mimic Qur'anic style or create a flowing text. On points of disagreement among classical commentators, Ayıntâbî provides the various positions and opinions of respected authorities. Given this material, the book bears closer resemblance to a traditional commentary than a modern translation of the sort that attempts to produce an equivalent representation of a text. One can certainly find many passages rendered in Turkish within the text, making it a landmark in the history of printed Turkish exegesis, but it is a far cry from a freestanding literary translation.

For a seventeenth-century work, Ayıntâbî's *Tibyan* is remarkably easy to read, an asset that helped make it the most popular and frequently reprinted Qur'anic commentary in the late Ottoman Empire. Its simple style points to a distinct trajectory in the history of Ottoman translation: whereas translators rendered literary and historical works into the elaborate Ottoman Turkish of the literati, for Qur'anic commentaries and other Islamic literature they employed a simple, direct style. This trend reflects the phenomenon observed by André Lefevere, whereby authors tend to translate important religious or cultural texts in a more literal and conservative fashion than other forms of literature.[14] Additionally, it suggests that Islamic works were designed to be accessible to a broader swathe of readers and to be used in oral teaching, unlike translated European literary works. This was certainly the case for Ayıntâbî's *Tibyan*, which began to be used in Ottoman madrasas soon after its publication.[15] Additionally, it became an important source for the emerging cadres of writers, statesmen and intellectuals who were educated in largely secular subjects, had less and less interaction with the ulama, and lacked the ability to read the Arabic language. Though the structure and content of Ayıntâbî's *Tibyan* differ little from conventional commentaries, its publication marks the important transmutation of Turkish-language commentary into print medium. It was the first Turkish commentary work to be printed, and it continued to be used well into the twentieth century.

Since the early nineteenth century, the centralisation of state power, the creation of a civil court system and the establishment of state-run schools progressively marginalised the ulama and the madrasas.[16] Many ulama worked in the new schools, particularly as religious teachers, but they worked within the framework of a state-organised curriculum, not the traditional Ottoman madrasa system. The new schools expanded literacy and created a new class of secularly educated Ottomans who were familiar with European learning and less beholden to the ulama.[17]

Within this context, printed texts enabled the mass distribution of Islamic knowledge directly to the people, thus bypassing the traditional intermediaries – the Islamic scholars and jurists. The madrasa system had extolled the virtues of person-to-person knowledge transmission in order to ensure that the student had not only read but properly understood a particular text; in addition, the presence of a living, breathing teacher guaranteed an interpretation that fit within the parameters of the discursive tradition. The increasing supply of inexpensive, easy-to-read religious books opened new avenues for the transmission of Islamic knowledge and abetted the decline of the Ottoman ulama.

İsmail Ferruh Efendi's *Mevakib,* and the New Translators

On the western shore of the Bosphorus, a waterfront mansion regularly welcomed the finest minds in Istanbul to share their intellectual pursuits in gatherings among like-minded friends. The group was thought of as the vanguard of intellectual life in the capital during the early nineteenth century, as its conversations and lessons included philosophy, science, religion, medicine, mathematics and literature from Islamic and European traditions. Men well versed in Islamicate belles-lettres and Western thought cultivated this salon where the intellectually curious could both learn and teach. Its co-founder and host was İsmail Ferruh Efendi (d. 1840).

With the rise of printing and increased intellectual contact with Europe, a new genus of Ottoman Muslim authors emerged. Writers from outside of the ulama, typically well-educated gentlemen, began to write and translate books dealing with Islamic subjects, topics which the ulama had previously dominated. This emerging intelligentsia would come to play a leading role in the campaign to translate the Qur'an, and the broadminded statesman Ferruh epitomised this new cadre of intellectuals. In the 1820s, he composed a book called *Mevakib*, posthumously published in 1864, which became an important source of information on the Qur'an for readers of Turkish.[18] *Mevakib* is an adapted translation of the popular Persian Qur'anic commentary *Mawākib-i ʿaliyya* by Ḥusayn Wāʿiẓ al-Kāshifī (d. 910/1505).[19]

Reflecting the spirit of the times, Ferruh intended to create an accessible commentary that would be meaningful to people in his own day. The introduction lays out the rationale for creating a text that spoke to a broader swathe of readers than the conventional literature written by men of his pedigree and stature. It also reveals the set of difficulties that his foray into the translation of a Qur'anic commentary might encounter. The author pre-emptively confronts potential concerns about his questionable status as an authority on religious matters, the use of the Turkish language, the mode of translation employed, the format of the work as well as the style of Turkish used. Ferruh makes it clear that virtually every aspect of this project was potentially subject to criticism for violating the conventions and protocols of Islamic scholarship.

From a Crimean family, Ferruh was the son of a wealthy merchant and became a successful trader in his own right. He entered the employ of the state as overseer of the imperial storehouses and belonged to the reform programme known, during Sultan Selim III's reign, as The New Order (*Nizam-ı Cedid*).[20] The modernisation of the Ottoman army constituted the primary thrust of this reform effort, but it also included the development of Ottoman foreign embassies and measures to bring Western sciences to the empire. Among various bureaucratic posts, Ferruh served as the Ottoman ambassador to England between 1797 and 1800, becoming one of the few statesmen to have spent an extended period in a European country. He participated actively in English social life and reportedly joined the Masonic lodge, an affiliation that has caused controversy among some devout Turkish writers who find it difficult to believe that Ferruh was a Freemason.[21]

Nevertheless, his affiliation with the Freemasons appeared to be well known in social circles in London. Mirza Abu Taleb Khan (1752–1806) of Lucknow made Ferruh's acquaintance in London and wrote the following on his initiation into the Masonic brotherhood:

> I was frequently urged by several of the Freemasons to become one of their brethren; but as I was not perfectly convinced that their principles were comfortable to my mode of thinking, I begged leave to decline the honour. They however prevailed upon Effendi Ismael, the Turkish ambassador, and Effendi Yusuf, his secretary, to embrace their tenets; and both these Mohammedans were initiated into all the mysteries of Freemasonry.[22]

Upon his return to Istanbul, Ferruh established The Beşiktaş Scientific Society, a group dedicated to the discussion of Western scientific and philosophical topics as well as literature. This assembly of learned gentlemen gathered in his mansion by the Bosphorus in the Istanbul neighbourhood of Ortaköy.[23] Some historians have called this society the first Freemasonic lodge in the Ottoman Empire. However, this designation is questionable. It is more probable that the group's interest in European science and philosophy as well as Ferruh's alleged involvement with Freemasonry in London led some to brand it a Masonic lodge. Regardless, it is certain that this salon brought together some of the best minds in Istanbul. The polymath Şanizade Ataullah Efendi (d. 1826) and the philosopher Kethüdazade Arif Efendi (d. 1849) figured among the frequent participants.[24]

The reign of Sultan Mahmud II (r. 1808–39), during which Ferruh lived, did not bode well for groups perceived as secret societies. Combining state centralisation with a policy emphasising Sunni identity, conformity and stringency of religious practice, Mahmud attacked the power of provincial notables and eliminated the military unit known as the Janissaries (in 1826) in order to consolidate and centralise power. Mahmud also persecuted the Bektashi Sufi Order – an order with Shi'i leanings and ties to the Janissary corps – confiscating its properties and exiling or executing many of its leaders. Ferruh's Scientific Society was not a Bektashi lodge, but given its profile and association – real or imagined – with Freemasonry, it remained vulnerable to charges of Bektashism, as 'Bektashi' had become a catch-all term for those practising social and religious non-conformism; it therefore applied to non-Sunnis and to liberal intellectuals alike. At this sensitive juncture, a personal dispute erupted between a key member of the Scientific Society, Şanizade, and the sultan's head physician, Behçet Molla. Behçet accused the Scientific Society of being a Bektashi group, and, being close to the sultan, his claim resulted in the persecution of the group and its members by the authorities. The state exiled Ferruh to the Anatolian city of Bursa, but later commuted his sentence to Kadıköy, a neighbourhood on the Asian shore of the Bosphorus near Istanbul, allegedly because he was at work on a Qur'anic commentary. The historian Ahmet Cevdet saw the accusations against Ferruh as baseless and suggested that his participation in a pious project served as evidence that he was not a religious deviant.[25]

Ferruh was known as a 'learned man of literary talents', and he led discussions on literature within the Scientific Society.[26] In addition to his work on the Qur'an, he composed a treatise on logic and possessed a high level of expertise in the Persian language.[27] It was Persian, not Arabic, which served as the vehicle for Ferruh's engagement with and knowledge of the Qur'an.

Conscious that he lacked the credentials of the ulama, in the introduction Ferruh cites his immersion in Qur'anic commentaries to bolster his credibility: 'Since the days of my youth, I passed my time studying most of the Arabic, Persian and Turkish Qur'anic commentaries.'[28] He also mentions that, during the translation, he consulted four well-known Qur'anic commentaries 'for comparison and agreement'.[29] Ferruh complains that most commentaries have a 'word-by-word' arrangement, whereby the meanings of individual words are given below the Qur'anic text in glossary-like fashion. In many such works, the meanings are not linked in grammatically consistent sentences, and Ferruh argues 'it has been a difficult matter for the common people to bring together, make sense of and connect the meaning of these texts'.[30] The old-style interlinear translations often assumed that the reader understood

Arabic, whereas Ferruh wanted to present a flowing text that could be easily understood by readers 'who are neither familiar with nor conversant in the Arabic language'.[31]

Writing in Turkish alone would not guarantee any greater level of accessibility. Due to the ornate style and voluminous vocabulary of literary Ottoman Turkish, it could be just as foreign to Turkish speakers as Arabic. Ferruh knew this very well, and explained why he used the simpler style of Turkish prose that he did: 'I have opted to compose this in succinct, common Turkish, avoiding the subtleties of the literati in order to facilitate the understanding of the common people and make it easy to consult, which is the fundamental goal.'[32] Since most of the common people could not read, we might assume that the author thought his work could be used in oral pedagogy, but it also seems likely that by 'common people', Ferruh meant those who were not a part of elite literary circles but were literate, for example, madrasa students, segments of the ulama and professionals who had gone through secularly oriented schools. A short time after its publication in 1864, Ottoman madrasas began to use Ferruh's *Mevakib* in their curricula and the book became rather popular.[33] Along with *Tıbyan*, it became one of the few printed resources for studying the Qur'an in Turkish during the nineteenth century.

Like Ayıntâbî's *Tibyan* before it, Ferruh's *Mevakib* is a commentary-translation providing direct translations of verses but also including occasions of revelation and other elements of exegetical literature alongside the Arabic text of the Qur'an. Its style is expansive; for instance, Ferruh's *Mevakib* expands Q. 2:2, *That is the Book, wherein is no doubt, a guidance to the godfearing*, into 'In this book – that is, in the Qur'an – there is certainly no doubt or suspicion that it is the perfect Book that God Almighty promised by revelation in the preceding Holy Books. It shows the path for the godfearing – i.e. those who keep away from mortal sins and prostitutes.'[34] In other ways as well, this work remains far from the modern conception of a translation, for it is not a text that can stand alone from the original. It follows a verse-by-verse format, providing the Arabic verse followed by Turkish parsing which makes it impossible to read the Turkish renderings as a continuous text. Ferruh's

Mevakib and Ayıntâbî's *Tibyan* were frequently discussed and cited by intellectuals in the periods of the late Ottoman Empire and the early Turkish Republic. These two works constituted key references for the Turkish literati well into the first quarter of the twentieth century.

In addition to Ayıntâbî's *Tibyan* and Ferruh's *Mevakib*, two other full-length Turkish commentary-translations were published in the late nineteenth century. The first – *Zübed-i asari'l-Mevahib ve'l-Envar* – was a distillation of Kāshifī's and Bayḍāwī's commentaries by Ahmet b. Abdullah,[35] and the second – *el-Tefsirü'l-Cemali* – was a Turkish translation of the Arabic commentary *Jalālayn* with a running Turkish translation of Shāh Walī Allāh's Persian translation *Fatḥ al-Raḥmān*.[36] While less frequently published and cited than the works above, they too helped delineate a new trajectory for Turkish renderings of the sacred text and point to the emerging variety of interpretive literature.

Rise of the Commoners: Qur'anic Commentary for the Public

In addition to Ayıntâbî's *Tibyan* and Ferruh's *Mevakib*, a number of Turkish-language commentaries and translations on particular chapters of the Qur'an appeared throughout the nineteenth century. In the main, these texts were adapted translations of Arabic and Persian works, thus following the pattern set by the *Mevakib* and *Tıbyan*; yet, they often included original Turkish translations of the Qur'anic text. After 1850, succinct Turkish commentary-translations appeared in print with increasing frequency. Echoing Ferruh's populist ethos, these works speak to a broader readership and reiterate the importance of comprehension versus mere recitation by extolling the virtues of understanding.

Pre-nineteenth century works often identified a particular ruler, madrasa students or Sufi novices as the intended audience. However, in the nineteenth century, authors began to designate the public at large as the imagined readership. Johann Strauss points out that many translations of literary and scientific works remained in manuscript form and were 'destined for a select readership of statesmen and government officials who had commissioned them'.[37] He has dubbed this kind of text a 'translation of restricted access' and argues that printing these works for general consumption was revolutionary.[38] Like the historical and literary works he discusses, a parallel class of restricted-access translations of Islamic works circulated among the ulama and Sufi circles. In the seventeenth century, for instance, Ankaralı İsmail (d. 1042/1631) wrote a Turkish commentary on *Sūrat al-Fātiḥa* (Q. 1) with the intention of writing an accessible work for a limited audience. In it, he says, 'This exquisite book and noble compilation has been written and composed in Turkish so that it will be useful to all the students and easy for the novices to understand', thereby indicating that initiates in his Sufi order were the intended readers.[39] However, Ankaralı, a scholar and commentator on Jalāl al-Dīn Rūmī's *Mathnawī*, could not refrain from 'adorning and embellishing' the work with quotes from the Sufi figures and the ulama. He cites long passages of Persian poetry every two or three pages, often using them to make an argument or prove a point. The ease of reading in Turkish that he intended for his students no doubt suffered due to his copious embellishments, but, to his credit, the Turkish passages are remarkably lucid. İbrahim Gözübüyükzade Kayserivi (d. 1834) wrote for a similar, limited audience in the early nineteenth century when he composed *Tercüme-i Süre-i Duha* – his translation of *Sūrat al-Ḍuḥā* (Q. 93), *Sūrat al-Qadr* (Q. 97) and *Sūrat al-ʿAṣr* (Q. 103). He says it was in response to 'repeated requests from a group of pure pupils among the students' that he translated these Qur'anic chapters 'in a Turkish of unrivalled clarity'.[40]

Apart from translations of restricted access, there had been intermittent efforts to address the commoners in religious literature. Such works did not necessarily assume that the masses could read; rather, they took it for granted that they would be read to in mosques and reading circles. It was more common for imams or shaykhs to orally translate books for their audiences than for works to be composed in the vernacular and directly address the commoner.

The shift from restricted access translations to what we might call public Islamic texts written for the average Ottoman reader occurred only with the evolution of a print-based public sphere in the last third of the nineteenth century. The first seventy years of the century had indeed witnessed exciting new developments – the beginning of religious printing, the first Ottoman Turkish newspapers and the translation of European literature. Nevertheless, compared to international standards, the number of different books, the quality of printed works, the publishing capacity, the accessibility and diversity of reading materials remained rather low. In the first century of printing (1727–1830), Ottoman presses had only published 180 different titles, a miniscule figure considering that the first fifty years of publishing in Europe produced between ten and fifteen thousand. By 1876, the figure totalled just over 3,000 distinct books in Turkish, still a comparatively small number.[41]

Sultan Abdülhamid II, who came to power in 1876, sought to redress the situation during his thirty-two-year reign. During that time, he promoted the technical refinement of the Ottoman press in order to improve the level of intellectual life and create a positive image abroad by publishing books that, as one publisher put it, would 'reflect well upon the Ottomans'.[42] Another publisher in the city of İzmir remarked that Ottoman progress 'in the finest of all crafts, the craft of printing', due to the sultan's support, made a positive impact on education, even in Islamic studies. The state recognised that printing ventures remained in an unsatisfactory state and actively promoted its evolution as a means of Ottoman self-representation and as an educational tool. These efforts resulted in technically higher quality products, larger distributions and more diverse publications.[43]

Despite its support for the printing industry, the Hamidian regime was autocratic, and tightly controlled the press, censoring the publication of any material reflecting liberal thought or containing discussions on Islamic reform. In retaliation, opposition forces established presses abroad in Europe and Egypt where they could publish on the need for constitutionalism and Muslim reform. The regime's concern about the potential for public Islamic discourse to mobilise opposition forces led to restrictions that also constrained and weakened the ulama. Abdülhamid II feared the ulama and the potential for Islam to be used as a rallying-point against his rule. Despite the discourse of Islamic unity propounded by the Hamidian regime, in many ways the sultan's rule continued and deepened the conditions that had been instigated by the state reform in the previous Tanzimat era, which had reorganised and created new state institutions, and, by and large, weakened the political and social power of the ulama.

The policy to marginalise the ulama was evident in the Hamidian policy towards religious publications. While projecting himself as caliph to the rest of the world, Abdülhamid's administration took special care to remove many Islamic works from circulation. At one point, the sultan ordered his censors to burn such works, along with other 'subversive' books, in the furnace of a Turkish bathhouse in Istanbul.[44] Meanwhile, works on Western science, materialism and evolution by Ludwig Büchner, Charles Darwin, Herbert Spencer and John Stuart Mill 'were sold freely in the Istanbul bookshops'.[45] Public discussion about Islam, except when it affirmed the sultan's role as caliph, was effectively suppressed during Abdülhamid's reign, and few books on Islam were allowed to be published after the establishment of a publication oversight committee in 1889. This policy severely limited the opportunities for Muslim reformers to publish, and constrained the development of Qur'anic interpretation in the late Ottoman period. Whereas intellectuals like Muḥammad 'Abduh (1849–1905) and Muḥammad Rashīd Riḍā in Egypt, and Sayyid Ahmad Khan and Muhammad Iqbal (1877–1938) in British India could push the boundaries of Muslim thought at the turn of the century in print, Ottoman intellectuals faced a strict and stifling regime of censorship.

Despite these limits, the progress of the press served as the midwife to the birth of a more pervasive and broader-reaching public sphere, and it was within this sphere that Islamic texts came to address the commoners in the vernacular with rising frequency. Kemal Karpat points out that a similar trend occurred in the scholarly debates held in the sultan's presence during the month of Ramadan (*huzur dersleri*). Whereas these contests were traditionally held in Arabic, Sultan Abdülhamid II ordered the scholars to converse in Turkish so that a larger portion of the audience could understand.[46] Muallim Naci composed a concise Turkish commentary on *Sūrat al-Ikhlāṣ* (Q. 112) in which he notes with regret that information on this important Qur'anic chapter has remained inaccessible to most believers. As mentioned earlier, he complains that the books of the ulama on *Sūrat al-Ikhlāṣ* have been seen by the 'elites in the umma' but have remained 'veiled from the masses'.[47] The divide between the elite (*has*) and the masses (*amme*), or the literate and the illiterate, or the select few and the commoner, was a standard topic of Islamic discourse, just as it was in ancient Greek and other intellectual traditions. As the medieval scholar Abū Ḥāmid al-Ghazālī (d. 505/1111) made clear in his treatise *Iljām al-ʿawām ʿan ʿilm al-kalām* (*Warding off the Masses from Theology*), many members of the ulama did not think that all Muslims should have access to all kinds of knowledge.[48] The Enlightenment-based ideals of universal access to knowledge and rationality that pervaded the nineteenth century directly challenged this understanding of restricted knowledge. One of the key questions for Islamic thought in this period was how the elite/masses divide would be understood in relation to Islamic knowledge and scholarship in the modern age, and this uncertainty was at the heart of vernacularisation debates in relation to the Qur'an. Even in the 1880s, Muallim Naci still found it necessary to justify his work. He argued that the simplified style of commentary embodied in his work should be considered equal to other genres of interpretation and that reading it should be a duty for Muslims because it would expand their understanding of the Qur'an.[49] The new ethos of breadth of propagation over depth in content became increasingly common, but still required apologia.

Popular Qur'anic commentary reached new levels of simplicity in short Turkish commentaries on particular chapters of the Qur'an that appeared after 1850. In addition to clear language, they exhibit a heightened sense of the importance of comprehension as opposed to ritual recitation. Reciting the Arabic text of the Qur'an is a key feature of Muslim ritual, required for daily prayers, and is practised widely as an expression of piety and as a means of education. For centuries, non-Arab Muslims had memorised and recited the Arabic verses regardless of whether they understood them, but, in the nineteenth century, many of the Ottoman intelligentsia began to emphasise comprehension. The mufti of Edirne, Mehmet Fevzi

Kureyşizade (d. 1900), came to argue, like many others in his generation, that merely reciting Qur'anic verses – without understanding them – did not suffice for the predicament of contemporary Muslims. He wrote that even when someone recites the Qur'an without understanding the meaning, God still accepts their effort, 'however, it cannot be denied that the . . . effect of reciting it with understanding' would produce a more significant experience.[50]

To this end, Kureyşizade composed a short book 'clarifying in the Turkish language' the meaning of *Sūrat al-Wāqiʿa* (Q. 56). This printed work, aimed at a general audience, exemplifies a profound level of popularisation. Before even stating the purpose of the work in the introduction, the author is quick to mention the popular tradition that whoever recites *Sūrat al-Wāqiʿa* 'regularly at the appointed time will never be poor . . .'[51] At the bottom of the same page, the pertinent prophetic reports are cited, reaffirming this talismanic property of the sura. In addition to the appeal to a general audience, the structure and style of the book demonstrate the deep vernacularisation of commentary works from the period, which address those in a lower stratum of literacy and education than previous commentaries. The Turkish prose is remarkably simple and easy to read, and, structurally, the author explains and re-explains the meaning of the verses in progressively easier-to-understand formats. Through constant summary, simplification and review, Kureyşizade ensures that he leaves no one in the dark.

Though Kureyşizade wrote for the newly literate classes, he takes care to defend himself against the potential critiques of the elite. Explaining why the work is so simple, he writes, 'I saw it appropriate to make clear only the gist and meanings such that they would settle nicely in the minds of the commoners and [the masses who] are not versed in the letter and spirit [of the text].'[52] Evidently, the author feared that more adept readers might confuse the simplicity of the text with that of his own intelligence, so he wanted to make it clear that he had descended into simplistic explanations and common language for the benefit of inferior minds. Composing Islamic literature in the popular register held the potential to hurt his reputation as a competent scholar, as challenging the traditional categories of knowledge for the elites and masses had its own risks.

Nevertheless, the vernacularisation and simplification of commentary works proceeded steadily. When Ferruh's *Mevakib* was reprinted in 1902 (along with Ayıntâbî's *Tibyan*), the publisher testified to the expansion of the audience and public sphere, explaining that the decision to reprint the work was due to the demand of the public (*amme*), not of the literati. He explained that the book was being reprinted because Ferruh's work was eloquent, reliable and had 'gained the appreciation and good will of the public'.[53] Sentiments such as these illustrate the fact that, over the course of the nineteenth century, the 'public' and the 'commoners' began to matter as readers of Qur'anic interpretation; they were no longer mere listeners. The spread of new state schools and the corresponding rise in literacy caused a gradual erosion of the traditional elite/commoner dichotomy. Though overall literacy rates remained low well into the twentieth century, the newly educated classes created a demand for religious literature that shaped the content and form of publications.

Over the course of the nineteenth century, conventional categories of authorship were becoming outmoded as well. The composition and compilation of Qur'anic exegesis historically was the purview of the ulama corps. Beginning with İsmail Ferruh Efendi, a number of non-ulama authors, typically state functionaries, entered the realm of Qur'anic interpretation, most often as translators or compilers of classical *tafsīr* works. Giridi Selim Sırrı (1844–95) is a prime example of this phenomenon. He spent his career working in different bureaucratic and administrative posts for the Ottoman state. Known as a meticulous and demanding leader, he held important governorships and was a decorated public servant. He was one of Abdülhamid II's most trusted officials. However, in addition to his political career, Sırrı Pasha wrote prolifically on Islamic matters, language and literature, and composed a number of partial Qur'anic commentaries.[54] The authorship of works on Qur'anic commentary came to reflect the bifurcation of the Ottoman education system into madrasas and state schools as well as the larger divide between *a la Turca* (traditional Ottoman) and *a la Franca* (modernist Ottoman, European-inclined) cultural orientations. Some authors had madrasa backgrounds while others studied in state institutions or with private tutors. Some worked in the ulama corps while others spent their careers as government officials.

The idea that Muslims needed to understand the meaning of the Qur'an also had its sceptics. Writing from Paris in 1869, the journalist/activist Ali Suavi conceded that it was beneficial to know the meaning of the Qur'an but questioned the necessity of its direct study. He rejected the argument that most Muslims were ignorant of the text and contended that everyone, even jurists, knew the Qur'an *indirectly* through various intermediaries. He argued that the meaning of the Qur'an had been divided up and disseminated through doctrinal pamphlets, works on ethics, biographies of the Prophet and sermons in clear language that everyone could understand; therefore, all Muslims, with or without education, knew the meaning of the Qur'an indirectly through these various avenues. Suavi admitted that studying the Qur'an itself holds benefits for those who have the time to do so, but maintained that direct study would always remain secondary because the Qur'an pervades Islamicate culture in so many ways that one is confronted with it simply by being a part of Muslim society.[55] Suavi's notion of the pervasiveness of the Qur'an in general culture resembles Susan Bassnett and André Lefevre's concept of the cultural 'image of the text', which often has more impact on society than the actual contents of the text itself.[56]

The new importance of Turkish as a language of media and mass communication occasioned meditation on the place of Arabic in Ottoman society. Suavi explored the question of whether Arabic is the language of the Arabs or the *lingua Islamica*, common to all Muslims. Responding to Ottoman writers who defined Arabic as a foreign language, Suavi puts forth a cosmopolitan view of Islamicate civilisation and rejects the idea that Arabic is somehow non-native to Ottoman society. He argues that Arabic is the language of Islam and Muslim societies, not the property of a single ethnic group; he contends that most people who use the Arabic language are either non-Arabs or Arabised Muslims (*mustaʿrab*), and that it has been Persians and Turks, not Arabs, who had actually organised Arabic grammar historically.[57] In less contentious fashion, Suavi writes that his Ottoman ancestors 'did not see Arabic as a foreign language',[58] since, along with Turkish and Persian, it was an organic part of Ottoman scholarly and literary culture for the preceding generations. Only with the vernacular turn in Ottoman textual practices and the emerging nationalist view of languages as the property of particular peoples did Arabic begin to appear foreign.[59]

For Suavi, viewing Arabic as the language of ritual and scripture served a purely pragmatic purpose: it supported Muslim unity. 'This is not a religious matter,' he writes, 'but rather an attempt to avoid differences of opinion and unite all the Muslim peoples under one language.'[60] For Suavi, the Arabic language per se is not important because of its intrinsic linguistic or miraculous qualities. Instead, Arabic matters for the spiritual and political unity of Muslims because it is the tie that binds them together. Severing that tie holds the potential to divide the multilingual, multiethnic Muslim umma and weaken it further vis-à-vis Europe. His claim that the medium of Arabic is not religiously significant marks a sharp departure from the prevalent notion that Qur'anic Arabic is an inimitable and sacred language, possessing intrinsic value. This view represents a pragmatic turn in the view of Islamic language during a period of political, military and economic weakness in the Ottoman Empire and Islamdom as a whole. Suavi's political understanding of Arabic's importance foreshadowed Rashīd Riḍā's similar position on the matter by several decades.[61]

Across the Muslim world, the question of which language could serve as the medium of Islamic knowledge and ritual constituted a crucial intellectual question of the late nineteenth and early twentieth centuries. As literacy, print media and Enlightenment ideals (as well as Christian missionaries) spread, the role of Arabic as a sacred language, one in which most Ottoman subjects and Muslims around the globe lacked functional literacy, came under increased scrutiny. The result was a polarisation of attitudes, with some camps supporting vernacular ritual and translations, and others striving to preserve and expand the role of Arabic.

On 13 February 1880, the ulama leaders in the south-eastern Indian city of Madras (contemporary Chennai) publicly pronounced a fatwa that condemned a South Asian Muslim as an 'infidel, an atheist and a wanderer from the truth' who should not be buried in a Muslim cemetery or greeted in public, and whose marriages were dissolved. He earned this censure by composing and publishing a 'Hindustani' translation of the Qur'an, claiming that it was equal to the original in eloquence and arguing that it was incumbent upon local Muslims to recite such a translation during the obligatory daily prayers, his reasoning being that prayers are valid only when they are understood.[62] The alleged claims of the translator as well as the harsh response of the ulama exemplify the heightened concern about translations that spanned various continents.

Various Islamicate languages experienced a period of Arabisation, incorporating more Arabic vocabulary and coining neologisms, and many Arab intellectuals worked for a revival of Arabic itself. In the Ottoman Empire, political and educational support for Arabic was dwindling as the ulama corps weakened and state schools took prominence over the course of the nineteenth century.

The (Re)Opening and Limits of the Qur'an Translation Debate

As Ottoman schools and institutions prioritised adopting modern sciences as well as European literature and culture, Western languages – especially French – came to play important roles as the media of knowledge, civilisation and polite society, gradually displacing Arabic and Persian. The importance of the French language in late Ottoman intellectual life should not be underestimated, even in the domain of Islamic thought. Someone living in nineteenth-century Istanbul could easily purchase a French translation of the Qur'an, complete and freestanding, without the Arabic text or the glosses of commentators. He or she could not find a similar book in Turkish, aside from the commentaries discussed in this chapter, which in many ways did not appear modern as they retained the feel and style of traditional commentaries. It is all but certain that the most widely read translation in the late Ottoman period was the French-language *Le Koran* by Albert de Biberstein-Kazimirski, originally published in 1841.[63] It was in this context that Ottoman Muslim intellectuals began to discuss the need for a Turkish translation that resembled those in European languages.

Under the reign of Abdülhamid II, strict control of the press – particularly with respect to religious publications – made it impossible to publish a work titled 'translation of the Qur'an' (*Kur'an tercümesi*) because of the ulama's opposition to the concept of Qur'anic translation and due to the fear that they could harm efforts to foster Islamic unity. The state permitted the publication of Turkish-language Islamic texts, including Qur'anic commentary, but not outright translations. As the Shaykh al-Islam deemed translations 'impermissible', the state also forbade the importation and circulation of Qur'an translations in all languages, paralleling the policy against foreign-printed Arabic *muṣḥaf*s.[64] At a time when the Ottoman state promoted Islamic unity, the sultan did not want to alienate his Muslim subjects, especially his Arab subjects, with controversial works like translations of the Qur'an. Many perceived Turkish translations as a threat to the authority of the Arabic Qur'an, and equated the abandonment of the Arabic language with the abandonment of Islam and the rise of ethno-linguistic divisions in the umma. Additionally, as we shall see in the next chapter, many Ottoman Muslim scholars/ulama drew negative associations between scriptural translation and both Christian missionaries and European colonial projects. Along with the impossibility of publishing a translation, the public conversations on the subject during this period were limited due to the fact that serious public discussion about Islamic subjects was severely curtailed.[65] Thus, what we have with these published works are only glimpses of the various opinions that were at large during this period. The Ottoman intelligentsia began to argue for the necessity of translating the Qur'an in the late nineteenth century. However, we know about them mostly via counterarguments and censorship because publicly supporting translation during the Hamidian period stood at odds with the sultan's campaign for Islamic unity and had overtones of liberal, dissident thought.

The prolific novelist, publisher and popular writer, Ahmet Midhat (1844–1913), raised the subject of translations in a book published in 1894–5 that provides an extensive defence of Islam against European critics. The book takes the format of a conversation between Midhat and his friends, and one of the author's interlocutors notes that among the Muslims of the world, Arabic speakers constitute a minority and suggests that this demographic imbalance will likely lead to a growing desire to translate the Qur'an.[66] In response, Midhat agrees that the translation of the Qur'an is an important issue in contemporary Islam and suggests reasons why no decision or conclusion on the matter of translation has been reached:

> Firstly, since Qur'anic eloquence is inimitable, it is impossible to translate it exactly. Secondly, since many words in the language that will be translated have no equivalents or counterparts, it would be necessary to change these words, and this is expected to open the door to distorting the Noble Book from translation to translation. Thirdly, some legal rulings are made by analysing and evaluating the words of divine books, and changing these words in a translation will close the door to these methods.[67]

This is a reasonable summary of prevalent thinking on the matter, with which he appears to concur. However, Midhat recognises that the printed vernacular commentaries have already come close to making Qur'anic translation a reality, writing that 'the commentaries like Ferruh's *Mevakib* and Ayıntâbî's *Tibyan* are so succinct that they can be seen more as translations than commentaries'.[68] Additionally, Midhat acknowledges the existence and legitimacy of interlinear translations: 'The Persians even created a way of making copies of the Qur'an with one line of Arabic and one line of Persian. However, no one from Islam has granted permission to do a free-standing Qur'anic translation without the Arabic text accompanying it or to regard such a translation as the Book of God.'[69] Referring to Persian interlinear translations, Midhat appears to be unaware that the same type of works had existed in the Turkish language for centuries. It is likely that such texts circulated among particular ulama circles and the court, yet it appears that Midhat and the broader Ottoman readership were unaware that they existed. Only the printed works like Ayıntâbî's *Tibyan* and Ferruh's *Mevakib* were broadly known and consulted in the late nineteenth century. It is notable that Midhat views the translations as permissible as long as they include the original Arabic text and are not regarded as *being* the Qur'an itself.

Nevertheless, Midhat had ambivalent feelings about translations, which he viewed as a genre of commentary. He argued that even the commentary tradition was not as reliable as the prophetic Hadith because no one understood the Qur'an as well as the Prophet himself. Accordingly, he displayed more enthusiasm for the project of his contemporary, Hacı Zihni Efendi (1846–1912), to translate hadiths into Turkish.[70] Commenting on the atheist writer Beşir Fuad (1852–77), who committed suicide at the age of twenty-five, Midhat attributed his tragedy to not knowing Arabic or Persian, being ignorant of Islamic knowledge and reading French translations of the Qur'an. 'One can imagine the grave consequences of such deficiencies in a Muslim and Ottoman', writes Midhat.[71]

Ahmet Cevdet, the well-known historian and statesman and Midhat's contemporary, held that fully translating the Qur'an was a formal impossibility, but demonstrated a reserved support for its necessity. In the introduction to his unfinished Arabic-Turkish lexicon on Qur'anic vocabulary, he writes that 'in order to appreciate the refinement of the Qur'an, one must be quite skilled in Arabic. Each person enjoys the Qur'an according to his or her ability and skill in Arabic.' Yet he adds that 'it is not possible to truly translate the Qur'an into other languages'.[72] In these brief sentences, Cevdet illustrates the conundrum that the Qur'an as a linguistic miracle presents – an individual can only appreciate the Qur'an according to his or her proficiency in Arabic, yet translation cannot effectively transmit the miracle contained therein. According to this logic, a seemingly unbridgeable linguistic chasm stands between the Qur'an and the Muslim unlettered in Arabic.

After acknowledging the imperfection of translation, however, Cevdet makes a case for writing a Turkish lexicon of Qur'anic vocabulary. First, he notes that 'some notable figures in the past have translated [the Qur'an] into Turkish so that those who do not know Arabic can understand the apparent meanings'.[73] By recognising that translations only convey apparent or literal meanings, Cevdet avoids claiming that a translation could stand in the place of the Arabic Qur'an while, at the same time, affirming their value. Cevdet felt that existing translations like Ayıntâbî's *Tibyan* had begun to encounter trouble transmitting even the literal or apparent meaning because of their archaic language. This problem prompted him to 'set about translating the Qur'an in the Turkish dialect that is current in Istanbul',[74] that is, to write a lexicon of Qur'anic terms.

Despite the caution demonstrated by late Ottoman supporters of translation, there was in fact an attempt to translate the Qur'an in the late nineteenth century by an important scholar and linguist. Born in the city of Frasher in the Balkan provinces of the Ottoman Empire (modern-day Albania), Şemseddin Sami (1850–1904) was an ardent proponent of elevating the Turkish language to new levels of importance and refinement. His most famous works include the first Turkish novel (*Taaşşuk-ı Tal'at ve Fıtnat*, 1872/3), a Turkish language encyclopaedia (*Kamusü'l-alam*, 1889) and a Turkish dictionary (*Kamus-i Türki*, 1899).[75] In the introduction to the dictionary, Sami stresses the need for bringing Turkish up to par with other literary languages by creating a comprehensive dictionary and grammar. He laments the fact that despite having a literary tradition of one thousand years, Turkish speakers have neglected to produce proper dictionaries and grammar books for their own language, and have failed to preserve their language, evinced by the substantial accumulation of Persian and Arabic vocabulary at the expense of Turkish words. Moreover, on the basis of grammar and syntax, he argues that the tongues spoken in the Turkic East, Central Asia, and West Anatolia and the Balkans, are not different languages but rather different dialects of the same language – Turkish. Crucial to his perception of the language, Sami contends that the language commonly known as Ottoman (*Osmanlıca*) should be called Turkish (*Türkçe* or *Türki*).[76]

Sami's lexicographic and encyclopaedic works shaped the emergence and conception of the Turkish language, and later gained renown as canonical texts of the Turkish nation. Yet few know of his Qur'anic commentary and translation project called *Tefsir-i Cedid* ('The New Commentary'). Sami finished the work around 1898 and submitted it to the Ministry of Education for approval to be published, a required procedure. The ministry's documents indicate that it provided the meanings of the verses along with helpful explanations in 'a language that everyone would be able to understand'.[77] The ministry sent Sami's manuscript to the Shaykh al-Islam, Mehmet Cemaleddin (1848–1917), for examination, a required procedure in the publication of Islamic works, and this stage proved to be the death knell for its prospects. After a month of analysis, the Shaykh al-Islam wrote that Sami had translated the verses in a way that 'contradicted the explanations and interpretations' of the great Qur'anic commentators and could 'never' be published.[78] Unfortunately, these brief descriptions are all that remain of the book. It fell victim to the censorship of the Hamidian period and never reached the presses, much less the bookshops. After being denied permission for publication, the manuscript version was destroyed or lost.

Numerous sources indicate that Sami faced public censure and, possibly, some type of punishment for translating the Qur'an into Turkish. The musician, poet and public intellectual Samih Rifat (1874–1932) lambasted Sami, who was not an Islamic scholar, for attempting, as an unqualified person, to undertake a translation project of such magnitude for Ottoman Muslims: 'Did you forget that three days ago your book was rejected . . . by the Religious Examination Committee and you were warned not to enter this kind of research after quickly learning a few words of Arabic?'[79] As to the fate of Sami's translation, the prominent Turkist thinker Yusuf Akçura (1876–1935) wrote: 'Sami Bey even undertook a translation of the Qur'an, but because the Ottoman government definitively prohibited this venture, the portion which he translated had to be destroyed.'[80] A later defender of Sami, Vala Nurettin (1901–67), claimed in 1943 that Sami had been 'condemned to the death penalty' because he undertook a Qur'an translation, but that the government later pardoned him.[81] A conversation, real or imaginary, reported by the journalist Yunus Nadi (1880–1945) portrays another version of the affair that depicts Sami as a victim, persecuted for the nationalist cause. The students of a religious scholar, Hafız Refi Efendi, asked him one day:

- Teacher, are you upset?
  He began:
- Don't ask, children. Since yesterday, I've been choked up with anger.

- Why, Teacher?
- How can I not be angry? Didn't an imbecile named Şemseddin Sami translate the Qur'an? Not only that, this buffoon translated the Qur'an and gave it to the Ministry of Education. The ignoramuses over there rather liked this translation, said 'congratulations', and showered the idiot with compliments. They recommended it for publication. Nevertheless, the book came to me because someone with common sense said that the Shaykh al-Islam's Office should take a look at this translation.
- You read it and found it to be bad, Teacher?
- What do you mean 'Did I read it?' Would I ever read something like that?
- Then what did you do, Teacher?
- What am I going to do? I decided to destroy the translation and give that ignorant buffoon eighty paddle strikes on the buttocks.[82]

Whether Sami was sentenced to death or to a disciplinary paddling or (most likely) to neither, it is certain that he caught the attention of the regime because he was from an influential Albanian family and was a prominent writer. Fearing his potential as a leader of Albanian separatism, Sultan Abdülhamid II placed Sami under house arrest. He was forbidden to receive guests from 1899 onwards, and he spent his remaining years on scholarly projects until his death in 1904.[83]

Given the constrictions of the late Ottoman public sphere, it should come as no surprise that the most radical affirmation of Turkish as a religious language came from a dissident who was located not in the empire but abroad. Mehmet Ubeydullah Efendi (1858–1937) was a madrasa-trained, turban-clad author, translator, spy, adventurer and partisan of the Young Turk movement that had developed in opposition to the regime of Abdülhamid II. In a work on Islamic reform published in Cairo, Ubeydullah contended that in order to truly understand Islam, Turks would have to translate both the Qur'an and Hadith into Turkish. He writes, 'No one can prevent those among us who want to learn about religion by reading

Arabic. However, we categorically cannot accept that religion be restricted *only* to Arabic.' Because many Turks could not understand Arabic, he continues, a number of them had attempted 'to read and understand the Qur'an from French and English'.[84]

Ubeydullah indicates that Turkish translations would not necessarily replace reading the Arabic Qur'an but rather the translations in European languages that educated Ottomans were already reading. It seemed ridiculous to Ubeydullah and others that Ottoman subjects could not read translations in Turkish and remained beholden to translations by non-Muslim Europeans. Beyond supporting translation, Ubeydullah took the matter one step further and proposed the idea of a 'Turkish Qur'an'. That is, he not only argued for a Turkish translation of the text, but also for the production of a Turkish version that might not only explain, but potentially replace the original text for prayer and study, and for use in sermons. The potential for substitution is precisely the contingency that the ulama had laboured so diligently over the centuries to prevent. Mehmet Ubeydullah championed the cause of the Turkish Qur'an with zeal and preached the virtues of translation to all who would listen. During his exile in Egypt, Ubeydullah met with the Egyptian scholar Rashīd Riḍā and horrified him with the idea of a 'Turkish Qur'an'. Riḍā went on to write vehemently against Turkish translations in the coming years, as we shall see in the following chapter.

Over the course of the nineteenth century, a far-reaching vernacularisation of Islamic literature and Qur'anic commentary occurred through printed Turkish commentaries. The notion that Turkish was a language of importance that could serve as a medium of religion became more and more appealing to the late Ottoman literati and to Muslims in the Russian Empire who spoke related languages and sought to unite Turkic Muslims across Eurasia. Though outright translations (*tercüme*) were prohibited, a number of Turkish-language commentaries with renderings of Qur'anic verses had appeared in print by the turn of the twentieth century. Ubeydullah's assertion of a Turkish Qur'an was both revolutionary and deviant. It required not only a textual, but political revolution for that assertion to transcend the hushed conversations of political dissidents and liberal thinkers.[85]

NOTES

1 el-Aksarayi, *İmadü'l-İslâm fi tercemeti Ümdeti'l-İslam*, MS Nurosmaniye Kütüphanesi 34 NK 1770, cited in Osman Nuri Ergin, *Türkiye Maarif Tarihi* (Istanbul, Osman Bey Matbaası, 1943), V, pp. 1604–5. Translation is my own.

2 Ibid., V, p. 1605.

3 Hagen, 'Translations and Translators', p. 131.

4 Gottfried Hagen, 'From Haggadic Exegesis to Myth: Popular Stories of the Prophets in Islam', in Roberta Sterman Sabbath, ed., *Sacred Tropes: Tanakh, New Testament, and Qur'an as Literature and Culture* (Leiden, Brill, 2009), pp. 305 and 314.

5 Tijana Krstić, *Contested Conversions to Islam: Narratives of Religious Change in the Early Modern Ottoman Empire* (Stanford, CA, Stanford University Press, 2011), p. 29.

6 Saliha Paker, 'The Age of Translation and Adaptation, 1850–1914: Turkey', in Robin Ostle, ed., *Modern Literature in the Near and Middle East, 1850–1970* (London, Routledge, 1991), pp. 17–32.

7 Johann Strauss, 'Turkish Translations from Mehmed Ali's Egypt: A Pioneering Effort and Its Results', in Saliha Paker, ed., *Translations: (Re)Shaping of Literature and Culture* (Istanbul, Boğaziçi University Press, 2002), p. 112.

8 Tanpınar, *XIX. Asır Türk Edebiyatı Tarihi*, p. 118.

9 Johann Strauss, 'Who Read What in the Ottoman Empire (19th–20th Centuries)?' *Middle Eastern Literatures* 6, no. 1 (2003), p. 47.

10 Ehud R. Toledano, *State and Society in Mid-Nineteenth-Century Egypt* (Cambridge, Cambridge University Press, 1990), pp. 157–8. For detailed information on Turkish-language publishing in Egypt, see Ekmeleddin İhsanoğlu, *The Turks in Egypt and Their Cultural Legacy* (Cairo, American University in Cairo Press, 2012).

11 Strauss, 'Turkish Translations', p. 111.

12 The first printing was Ayıntâbî Mehmet, *Tercüme-i Tefsir-i Tibyan* (Cairo, Bulaq, 1257/1841–2). Susan Gunasti, 'Approaches to Islam in the Thought of Elmalılı Muhammed Hamdi Yazır (1878–1942)' (Unpublished PhD Thesis, Princeton University, 2011), p. 51.

13 The editors of *The World Bibliography of Translations of the Meanings of the Holy Qur'an* consider Ayıntâbî's *Tibyan* to be the first printed translation; İsmet Binark and Halit Eren, *World Bibliography of Translations of the Meanings of the Holy Qur'an: Printed Translations, 1515–1980*, ed. Ekmeleddin İhsanoğlu (Istanbul, IRCICA, 1986), pp. xxx, 790.

14 See the introduction in Susan Bassnett and André Lefevere, *Constructing Cultures: Essays on Literary Translation* (Clevedon, Multilingual Matters, 1998), p. 7.

15 Gunasti, 'Approaches', p. 52.

16 İsmail Kara, 'Turban and Fez: *Ulema* as Opposition', in Elisabeth Özdalga, ed., *Late Ottoman Society: The Intellectual Legacy* (London, Routledge Curzon, 2005), p. 164.

17 On literacy and reading practices, see Benjamin Fortna, 'Learning to Read in the Late Ottoman Empire and Early Turkish Republic', *Comparative Studies of South Asia, Africa and the Middle East* 21, nos. 1–2 (2002), pp. 33–41; idem,

Learning to Read in the Late Ottoman Empire and the Early Turkish Republic (New York, Palgrave-MacMillan, 2011).

18 İsmail Ferruh, *Tefsir-i Mevakib* (Istanbul, Matbaa-i Amire, 1281/1864). Several publications list 1282/1865 as the first publication, but the Süleymaniye Library (Nazif Paşa Collection no. 1522), Istanbul, holds a copy from 1281/1864.

19 Kristin Zahra Sands, 'On the Popularity of Husayn Vaʿiz-i Kashifi's *Mavāhib-i ʿaliyya*: A Persian Commentary on the Qur'an', *Iranian Studies* 36, no. 4 (2003), pp. 469–83.

20 Mehmet Alaadin Yalçınkaya, 'İsmail Ferruh Efendi'nin Londra Büyükelçiliği ve Siyasi Faaliyetleri (1797–1800)', in Kemal Çiçek, ed., *Pax Ottomana: Studies in Memoriam, Prof. Dr. Nejat Göyünç* (Ankara, Sota-Yeni Türkiye, 2001), p. 383.

21 Dücane Cündioğlu has cast doubt upon Ferruh's relationship with Masonic lodges; see Dücane Cündioğlu, '"Mason" Olduğu Söylenen Kur'an Mütercimi (1)', *Yeni Şafak*, 3 October 2000, http://yenisafak.com.tr/arsiv/2000/ekim/03/dcundioglu.html; idem, '"Mason" Olduğu Söylenen Kur'an Mütercimi (2)', *Yeni Şafak*, 6 October 2000, http://yenisafak.com.tr/arsiv/2000/ekim/06/dcundioglu.html.

22 Abu Taleb Khan, *Travels of Mirza Abu Taleb Khan in Asia, Africa, and Europe During the Years 1799 to 1803*, tr. Charles Stewart (New Delhi, Sona Publications, 1972), p. 98.

23 Cevdet, *Tarih-i Cevdet*, XII, p. 184.

24 Kâzım Yetiş, 'Beşiktaş Cemʿiyyet-i İlmiyyesi', *TDVİA*, vol. V, pp. 552–3.

25 Cevdet, *Tarih-i Cevdet*, XII, p. 183.

26 Thomas Naff, 'Reform and the Conduct of Ottoman Diplomacy in the Reign of Selim III, 1789–1807', *Journal of the American Oriental Society* 83, no. 3 (1963), p. 304.

27 Richard Chambers, 'The Education of a Nineteenth-Century Ottoman Alim, Ahmed Cevdet Paşa', *International Journal of Middle East Studies* 4, no. 4 (1973), p. 457.

28 İsmail Ferruh, *Tefsir-i Mevakib* (Istanbul, Matbaa-i Amire, 1281/1864), I, p. 2.

29 Ibid., I, p. 4.

30 Ibid., I, p. 2.

31 Ibid.

32 Ibid., I, p. 3.

33 Gunasti, 'Approaches', p. 52.

34 Ferruh, *Tefsir-i Mevakib*, I, p. 8.

35 Ahmet Salih b. Abdullah, *Zübed-i asari'l-Mevahib ve'l-Envar* (Istanbul, Rıza Efendi Matbaası, 1292/1875).

36 Muḥammad Jamāl al-Dīn al-Dihlawī, *el-Tefsirü'l-Cemali ala'l-tenzil il-Celali*, tr. Muḥammad Khayr al-Dīn Hindī al-Haydarābādī (Cairo, Bulak Matbaası, 1294/1877). Gunasti argues that this work is likely a translation of the commentary *Fatḥ al-ʿAzīz* composed by Shāh Walī Allāh's son ʿAbd al-ʿAzīz al-Dihlawī; Gunasti, 'Approaches', pp. 53–4.

37 Strauss, 'Turkish Translations', p. 114.

38 Ibid., pp. 114–15.

39 Ankaralı İsmail, *Fatiha Tefsiri: Fütuhat-ı Ayniye* (Istanbul, Matbaa-i Ahmed Kamil, 1328/1910–11), p. 5.

40 İbrahim Gözübüyükzade Kayserivi, *Tercüme-i Süre-i Duha*, ed. Mahmud Raci (Istanbul, Ali Şevki Efendi Matbaası, 1287/1870–71), p. 2.
41 İrvin Cemil Schick, 'Print Capitalism and Women's Sexual Agency in the Late Ottoman Empire', *Comparative Studies of South Asia, Africa and the Middle East* 31, no. 1 (2011), p. 197.
42 Naci, *Hülasatü'l-İhlas*, pp. 3–4.
43 Precise figures and helpful graphs can be found in Schick, 'Print Capitalism', pp. 197–8.
44 Raşit Çavaş and Fatmagül Demirel, 'Yeni Bulunan Belgelerin Işığında II. Abdülhamid'in Yaktırdığı Kitapların bir Listesi', *Müteferrika* 28, no. 2 (2005), pp. 3–24.
45 Deringil, *Well Protected Domains*, p. 54.
46 Kemal Karpat, *The Politicization of Islam: Reconstructing Identity, State, Faith, and Community in the Late Ottoman State* (New York, Oxford University Press, 2001), pp. 337–8.
47 Naci, *Hülasatü'l-İhlas*, p. 3.
48 Abū Ḥāmid al-Ghazālī, *Iljām al-ʿawāmm ʿan ʿilm al-kalām* (Cairo, al-Maktaba al-Azhariyya li'l-Turāth, 1998).
49 Naci, *Hülasatü'l-İhlas*, p. 4. Naci also wrote on the mysterious separated letters that come at the beginning of numerous Qur'anic suras: Muallim Ömer Naci, *Muamma-ı ilahi yahud bazı süver-i Kur'aniyenin evailindeki huruf-ı tehecci* (Istanbul, 1302/1884–5).
50 Mehmet Fevzi Kureyşizade, *el-Havasü'n-nafia fi tefsir suret el-Vakia* (Istanbul, 1313/1895–6), p. 3.
51 Ibid., p. 3.
52 Ibid., p. 7.
53 Ayıntâbî Mehmet and İsmail Ferruh, *Tefsir-i Tibyan ve Tefsir-i Mevakib* [published together in one volume] (Dersaadet, Istanbul, Şirket-i Sahafiye-i Osmaniye, 1902), p. 2.
54 Cemal Kurnaz, 'Sırrı Paşa', *TDVİA*, vol. XXXVII, pp. 127–9; Giridi Sırrı Paşa, *Sırr-ı Tenzil* (Diyarbakır, Diyarbakır Matbaası, 1311/1893–4); idem, *Ahsenü'l-kasas: Tefsir-i Sure-i Yusuf aleyhisselam* (Istanbul, Şirket-i Mürettibiyye Matbaası, 1893); idem, *Sırr-ı İnsan: Tefsir-i Sure-i İnsan* (Istanbul, Eski Zabtiye Caddesinde 61 numaralı Matbaa, 1312/1894–5); idem, *Sırr-ı Furkan: Tefsir-i Sure-i Furkan* (Istanbul, Matbaa-i Osmaniye, 1312/1894–5); idem, *Sırr-ı Meryem: Tefsir-i Sure-i Meryem* (Diyarbakır, Vilayet Matbaası, 1312/1894–5).
55 Ali Suavi, 'Lisan u Hatt-ı Türki', *Ulum* (1286/1869), cited in Dücane Cündioğlu, *Türkçe İbadet* (Istanbul, Kitabevi, 1999), p. 159.
56 Susan Bassnett and André Lefevere, *Translation, History, and Culture* (London, Pinter Publishers, 1990), pp. 9–10.
57 Suavi, 'Lisan', cited in Cündioğlu, *Türkçe İbadet*, pp. 157–8.
58 Ibid., p. 158.
59 Anderson, *Imagined Communities*, p. 36.
60 Suavi, 'Lisan', cited in Cündioğlu, *Türkçe İbadet*, p. 160.
61 See Muḥammad Rashīd Riḍā, 'Tarjamat al-Qur'ān', *al-Manār* 11, no. 4 (1908), pp. 268–74; for a detailed discussion of his views, see Chapter Four in this book.
62 Edward Sell, *The Faith of Islam* (London, Trübner, 1880), pp. 233–6.

63 Albert de Biberstein-Kazimirski, *Le Koran* (Paris, Charpentier, 1841). It was reprinted in sundry editions and can still be found in many libraries in Istanbul.
64 BOA MF.MKT 178/123 (8/S/1311—21 August 1893); BOA MF.MKT 179/115 (14/Z/1310—28 June 1893) (Catalogue: 20/S/1311).
65 Hanioğlu, *Brief History*, p. 140.
66 Ahmet Midhat, *Beşair: Sıdk-ı Muhammediye* (Istanbul, Kırk Anbar Matbaası, 1312/1894–5), p. 97.
67 Ibid., p. 98.
68 Ibid., p. 99.
69 Ibid., pp. 99–100.
70 Ibid., pp. 102–3. Midhat is probably referring to Mehmet Zihni; Jalāl al-Dīn al-Suyūṭī, *el-Hakaik: Mimma fil-cami is-sagir vel-mesarik min hadis-i hayr il-halaik* (Istanbul, Bab-i Ali Caddesinde 25 Numaralı Matbaa, 1310–11/1892).
71 Berkes, *Development of Secularism*, p. 293.
72 Ahmet Cevdet Pasha, [Introduction], *Lûgat-i Kur'aniye*, in Süleyman Tevfik, *Tercümeli Kur'an-ı Kerim* (Istanbul, Maarif Kütüphanesi, 1927), p. 4.
73 Ibid. It is noteworthy that Cevdet uses the term translation (*tercüme*) to describe Turkish rewritings of the Qur'an instead of commentary (*tefsir*) or synopsis (*meal*). These latter terms were far more acceptable for referring to Turkish renderings during the Hamidian period.
74 Ibid.
75 Şemseddin Sami, *Taaşşuk-ı Tal'at ve Fıtnat* (Istanbul, Elcevaip Matbaası, 1289/1872–3); idem, *Kamusü'l-Alam: Tarih ve Coğrafya Lûgati ve Tabir-i Esahhiyle Kâffe-i Esma-i Hassa-i Camidir* (Istanbul, Mihran Matbaası, 1306–16/1889–98); idem, *Kamus-i Türki* (Istanbul, İkdam Matbaası, 1317/1899).
76 Şemseddin Sami, *Kamus-i Türki* (Istanbul, Çağrı Yayınları, 1987), p. 2.
77 BOA A. MF.MKT 28/389 (28 Ş 1313—12 March 1898).
78 BOA MF.MKT 429/1 (21/B/1316—5 December 1898).
79 Agah Sırrı Levend, *Şemsettin Sami* (Ankara, Üniversitesi Basımevi, 1969), p. 99.
80 Yusuf Akçura, *Türk Yılı, 1928*, p. 354, cited in Levend, *Şemsettin Sami*, p. 99.
81 Va-Nu [Vala Nurettin], 'Şemseddin Sami Sinsi bir Türk Düşmanı mıydı? Hâşa', *Akşam*, 15 October 1943, p. 3.
82 Yunus Nadi, 'Türkçe Kuran, Türkçe İbadet', *Cumhuriyet*, 25 January 1932, p. 4.
83 Çiğdem Balim, 'Sāmī', *EI*^{2}, vol. VIII, pp. 1043–4.
84 Azmzâde Refik Bey, *Kıvam-ı İslam*, tr. Mehmet Ubeydullah (Cairo, 1324/1906), pp. 157–8.
85 On the decline of madrasas and the ulama, see Amit Bein, *Ottoman Ulema, Turkish Republic: Agents of Change and Guardians of Tradition* (Stanford, CA, Stanford University Press, 2011).

4

Politicisation: Neo-Arabism, Missionaries and the Young Turks (1908–1919)

And hold you fast to God's bond, together, and do not scatter
(Q. 3:103)

WITH THE RISE OF Middle Eastern nationalisms and the prospect of colonisation by European powers, the question of Muslim unity and political survival loomed large in the minds of Muslim intellectuals in the early twentieth century and injected a strong dose of politicisation into the debate on Qur'an translation. As visions of the Muslim community transformed and national consciousness became heightened, traditional arguments about Qur'anic inimitability and the privileged status of the Arabic language appeared, to reform-minded intellectuals and politicians, more and more at odds with the zeitgeist. The inimitability of Qur'anic language continued to be discussed and debated by both the ulama and devout intellectuals, but such discussions now occurred in the shadow of concerns about the political survival of the Ottoman Empire in the face of both European encroachment and internal bureaucratic changes which emphasised the primary role of the Turkish language in state affairs. The political consequences of translation acquired a newfound prominence across the empire as currents of proto-nationalist and anti-nationalist thought recalibrated discussions, shifting the topic of concern away from Qur'anic inimitability to Muslim revival and unity. Crucially, the emergence of Arab nationalism presented an important new source of opposition to translating the Qur'an.

The New Arabism and Muḥammad Rashīd Riḍā

As the language of the Qur'an, Muslim ritual and much of Islamic scholarship, Arabic held a privileged position and served an important function in medieval Muslim societies straight through to early-modern Muslim societies. In addition to its religious significance, many scholars saw Arabic as a uniquely eloquent and superior language. The age of nationalism, however, brought about new views of Arabic as intellectuals probed the nature of Arabness in literary societies, cultural associations and missionary colleges. Early twentieth-century Arabism was a variety of Romantic linguistic nationalism that viewed language as the soul of the nation. Proto-Arab nationalists defined the Arabs as a people bound together as a nation by the Arabic language, and by a shared history and culture. They took pride in the historical accomplishments of the Arabs, including the establishment of a powerful empire, the scientific and mathematical discoveries of Arab intellectuals as well as the development of an impressive oeuvre of poetry, historiography and sacred texts. Though many Arabists were Christians or secularists, they often looked to the Qur'an as the pinnacle of the Arabic language and made the Qur'an a symbol of Arab national identity.[1]

The Egyptian modernist movement led by Muḥammad ʿAbduh and Rashīd Riḍā adopted many aspects of nationalist discourse, combining its Romantic vision of Arab history and language with a programme of Islamic reform based on fresh interpretation of the Qur'an and Hadith, the revival of *ijtihād* (independent legal reasoning) and the modernisation of state and society. ʿAbduh and Rashīd Riḍā argued for a revival of Islam led by the Arabs and called for the revitalisation of the Arabic language. Born in the village of Qalamūn in Ottoman Syria, Rashīd Riḍā became one of the best-known and most influential Muslim intellectuals of the early twentieth century. He was a disciple of the Egyptian reformist thinker ʿAbduh, with whom he established the journal *al-Manār* (*The Lighthouse*) in Cairo. *Al-Manār* became the vanguard organ of Muslim modernist thought and enjoyed circulation throughout the Muslim world. Readers of Arabic from around the globe read the journal, contributed articles and sought Rashīd Riḍā's opinion via written correspondence. Following ʿAbduh's death, Riḍā took over the operations of the journal and wrote a prodigious number of articles, fatwas and opinion pieces on the full spectrum of issues concerning the modern Muslim world and reformist thought. A proponent of *ijtihād* and the unification of the legal schools, he was also an ardent advocate for propagating the Arabic language and a stalwart opponent of translating the Qur'an.

Around the turn of the twentieth century, conversations among Turkic Muslims about translating the Qur'an had begun to perturb Rashīd Riḍā. The dissident from Izmir, Mehmet Ubeydullah, had been exiled to the Hijaz due to his opposition to Sultan Abdülhamid II. Ubeydullah, however, escaped to Cairo, an abode of press liberty for Muslim reformists, where he met Rashīd Riḍā and discussed the idea of creating a 'Turkish Qur'an'.[2] A 'Turkish Qur'an' was inimical to traditional definitions of the 'Arabic Qur'an' as well as the neo-Arabist agenda of Rashīd Riḍā (and of the journal *al-Manār*), who hoped to revive – not diminish – the use and prestige of the Arabic language. Rashīd Riḍā was less than pleased to hear of vernacular conceptions of the Qur'an, but the issue continued to confront him in various guises. In 1908, for example, a Muslim shaykh in the Russian Empire, Aḥsan Shāh Aḥmad al-Samarī, wrote to Rashīd Riḍā asking about the permissibility of translating the Qur'an. Samarī had become curious about this question by reading books from Istanbul as well as from the conversation among intellectuals in his own milieu.[3] He wrote:

> As for our Russian-Turkish men of letters, they insist on translating it and they say: there is no meaning in saying that it is not permissible to translate the Qur'an except that it must remain incomprehensible. Therefore, they conclude that translating it is obligatory. It is now being translated in the city of Kazan and the translation is being published in segments. And so Zayn al-ʿAbidīn Ḥājī al-Bakuwī, one of the volunteer fighters in the Caucasus, is intent on translating it into the Turkish language (*al-lisān al-turkī*). We request, dear sir, that you give consideration to this matter.[4]

Rashīd Riḍā responded to this inquiry with a lengthy fatwa published in *al-Manār* on 30 May 1908.[5] He used this fatwa to reply to the rising chorus of voices that promoted translations, particularly Turkish translations, of the Qur'an. For Rashīd Riḍā, translations threatened to displace the inimitable revealed text and open a Pandora's box of ethnic and linguistic divisions among the Muslim umma. This was in conflict with his vision of Muslim reform, in which the Arabs would play the leading role in politically and intellectually reviving the umma.

Against the tide of European military and economic power, Rashīd Riḍā advocated a vision of Arab renaissance, which was imagined as a revival of the Arab leadership of the early Muslim empires with an emphasis on the Arabic language. According to him, Muslim unity

> was only obtained in past centuries thanks to the Arabs, and will not return in this century except through them, united and in agreement with all other races. The basis of the union is Islam itself, and Islam is none other than the Book of God Almighty, and the Sunna of His prophet . . . Both are in Arabic. No one can understand them properly unless he understands their noble language.[6]

Under the Arabs and united in the Arabic language, argued Rashīd Riḍā, Islam had risen to greatness and established a flourishing civilisation. He emphasised, perhaps more than any other writer, that linguistic unity was an essential component in the success of Islam as a religio-political phenomenon. He also contended that Muslim societies began to decline when non-Arabs 'pounced on their thrones, and the non-Arab ulama issued opinions that permitted worship, recitation of the Qur'an and recitation during *ṣalāt* in non-Arabic languages'.[7] According to Riḍā, Muslims had neglected the importance of using a common language; this distanced non-Arabs from the message of the Qur'an and allowed divisions to persist among Muslim peoples. From this perspective, he viewed the need to translate the Qur'an as a mark of Muslim negligence to sufficiently explain its meanings to people in their own languages.[8] For Rashīd Riḍā and most reformist intellectuals, greater understanding of and engagement with the Qur'an formed a key component in reviving Islam and strengthening Muslim societies.

Whereas some reformists saw translation as an ideal means to these ends, Rashīd Riḍā viewed it as a path to misunderstanding and disunity. For him, the division of Muslims into nation states revealed a lack of faith, which caused some Muslims to be content with translations rather than the original, Arabic, Qur'an. 'This wavering', he writes, 'is one of the effects of Europe's political and civil struggle against Muslims. It allured us to be disunited and divided into different races, each of which thinks that its life lies within it, but which is none other than the death of all.'[9] Riḍā does no less than frame Qur'an translation as a part of a broader European effort against the peoples of Islam, defining translations as tools of colonisation and the translators as imitators of Europe who were attempting to 'liberate' Muslims from the revealed Arabic text.[10]

Rather than abet the purported European agenda to divide and conquer through translation, Rashīd Riḍā urged Muslims to make translation unnecessary by reviving and spreading the Arabic language. Central to this effort was educational reform and language instruction, including the 'use of modern educational methods' and making the study of Arabic compulsory in all Muslim schools.[11] Rashīd Riḍā consistently urged Muslims to learn and propagate the Arabic language in order to foster communal unity and understand the Qur'an. He went so far as to argue that learning Arabic was obligatory for every Muslim, a view that provoked several rebuttals from other Islamic scholars.[12] Rashīd Riḍā encountered much opposition to his idea that propagating Arabic was a religious imperative, but he dismissed his opponents as imitators who simply followed their legal schools and did not independently evaluate the proof for his unconventional argument.[13] Never one to mince his words, he argued that without agreement on the language of the community's most central text – the Qur'an itself – the chances for collaboration on education, governance and resistance to imperialism would be impossible.

In addition to his political rationale, Rashīd Riḍā opposed Qur'an translation on linguistic and theological grounds. Rashīd Riḍā defined translation as 'the understanding of a translator, who may or may not be correct',[14] and asked sarcastically how the interpretation of one fallible person could be made into the 'creed for an entire nation'.[15] Since translations are not the verbatim text that had been revealed to Muhammad, Rashīd Riḍā saw them as unreliable for independent legal reasoning (*ijtihād*). This concept was a cornerstone of the Muslim modernist programme, the intellectual tool through which the modernists hoped to reform Islamic law, and reinvigorate intellectual and cultural life. Since Rashīd Riḍā firmly believed that translations made *ijtihād* impossible, and thereby threatened his vision of reform, he sought to present arguments that would suppress the acceptance of translations before it became too prevalent.

To this end, Rashīd Riḍā offered the novel perspective that using translations of the Qur'an constituted an act of imitation (*taqlīd*). He argued that 'the Quran prohibited imitation in religion and denounced the imitators. Deriving religion from the translation of the Qur'an is imitating its translator; therefore it is a deviation from the guidance of the Qur'an and does not follow it.'[16] Because of this prohibition of *taqlīd*, those who depend on a translation cannot fulfil the ability of the believers described in Q. 12:108 to 'call to God with sure knowledge': *Say: This is my way. I call to God with sure knowledge, I and whoever follows after me.* Rashīd Riḍā interprets this verse to mean that God obliges Muslims to use their minds and be independent, critical thinkers. As translations lead to imitation, they are useless for original thinking and cannot be considered Islamic.[17]

The editor of *al-Manār* also felt that translating the Qur'an's polyvalent and infinite meanings could limit the range of possibilities to a single meaning and deprive readers of the potential for new understandings. As Rashīd Riḍā says, the Qur'an is constantly renewing itself, 'inundating the reader [with new perspectives] according to his preparation and wisdom'.[18] He reasons that new wisdom and secrets might appear to contemporary readers which had not become manifest in previous generations. However, if translated, the text will only yield what the translator has understood, denying subsequent generations the opportunity to profit from new discoveries yielded by the inimitable Arabic text.[19] Translation also posed the danger of distortion. Echoing a traditional Muslim view of the Christian Bible as a text that had undergone distortion, Rashīd Riḍā opined that translations in different languages would have discrepancies between them 'akin to those between the different translations of the Old and New Testaments among the Christians'.[20] Given the contradictions in these texts, Riḍā questioned how Muslims could wish to subject the Qur'an to corruption and dissimilarities, since, unlike the Qur'an itself, translations are not protected from alteration.[21]

Finally, Rashīd Riḍā reiterates the widely held opinion that some aspects of the Qur'an are simply untranslatable due to the subtlety and richness of its language. As an example, he refers to Q. 15:22, a verse that describes the wind and the rain as forces controlled by God that provide sustenance for humankind.[22] He points out that the translator might render this verse in the metaphorical sense that some commentators have suggested, namely, that the mention of the wind and the sky with the occurrence of rain represents the male impregnating the female and the birth of a child afterwards. If one translates this metaphorically, he holds, the reader would not understand the literal sense of the verse whereby the wind 'carries pollen from male trees to female ones'.[23] Citing the prominent Sunni scholar Abū Ḥāmid al-Ghazālī, Rashīd Riḍā notes that some other aspects of the Qur'an are equally untranslatable, for instance the Beautiful Names of God (*al-asmā' al-ḥusnā*). In *Warding off the Masses from Theology*, Ghazālī writes that translating the Beautiful Names is forbidden because they number among the ambiguous verses (*mutashābihāt*) mentioned in Q. 3:7. Following his lead, Rashīd Riḍā holds that translating the Names – as many Turkish translations did – amounts to blasphemy (*kufr*).[24] Again referring to Ghazālī, he contends that Persian, Turkish and other languages lack equivalents to some Arabic words, and that the translator who uses his own understanding to fill in the gaps may induce the reader to hold beliefs not intended by the Qur'an. Even Arabic words with Persian equivalents can be misleading because they may be used metaphorically in one language but not in another. Likewise, some words may be homonyms in one language and not in the other. All these pitfalls, in Rashīd Riḍā's eyes, make perfect translation impossible.[25]

Since Rashīd Riḍā advocated comprehension of the Qur'an but rejected Qur'anic translations, what then were modern Muslims to do in order to deepen their personal engagement with the Book? In contrast to some of his reformist views, Rashīd Riḍā's prescription for non-Arab Muslims was surprisingly conservative as he recommended adhering to the pedagogical status quo. Uneducated, ordinary Muslims should 'memorise *Sūrat al-Fātiḥa* and some short suras so that they may recite them in prayer; interpretations of these should be translated for them. In addition, some verses should be read to them in religious lessons and interpreted for them in their own language, as is the practice of many non-Arab Muslims, even in China.'[26] Riḍā simply urged the ulama to fulfil their traditional duty to explain the text to the people, a duty which he argued they had neglected. Religious scholars, on the other hand, he believed, ought to learn Arabic, understand the Qur'an independently and refer to the exegetical tradition.[27] Hence, for Rashīd Riḍā, the traditional division between the religious experts and laypersons should not be eliminated, but rather the duties of the experts should be properly practised. The ulama remain front and centre as the custodians of the text for the common Muslim in his writings.

Vis-à-vis the Qur'an, Rashīd Riḍā opted decisively for Muslim unity via the Arabic Qur'an; direct, personal comprehension of the Qur'an was a secondary concern. The programme suggested for non-Arabs – traditional pedagogy or learning Arabic – did not hold the prospect of ushering in broad comprehension of the sort that nationalists and educational reformers envisioned and laboured towards. Rather than mass comprehension, Riḍā's answer to the dilemmas facing Muslims was to preserve the Qur'an in its original language and propagate Arabic to eliminate linguistic and ethnic differences among Muslims, following the model of the early Muslim community.

Many late Ottoman and Turkish intellectuals held similar views, advocating the propagation of the Arabic language and opposing

Qur'anic translation on theological and political grounds. The Istanbul-based journal *Sebilürreşad* (*The Path of the Rightly Guided*) – an important venue for writings of devout intellectuals and the elaboration of Muslim modernist thought during the latter part of the empire and the early republic – argued that Ottoman schools needed to pay more attention to Arabic as opposed to French, which was widely taught.[28] A writer for the journal, Ahmed Naim, argued that it was obligatory to love the Arabs above all others 'for their Islamic zeal, for their racial affinity to Muhammad, for their language being the language of the Qur'an, and for the sake of our gratitude to them for having brought Islam'.[29] The Islamic scholar and two-time Shaykh al-Islam of the Ottoman Empire (1919 and 1920), Mustafa Sabri (1869–1954), was the most outspoken Turkish opponent of Qur'anic translation. Sabri opposed not only Turkish translations but also Turkish-language commentaries. A staunch advocate of the traditional pedagogical role of the ulama, he placed little value on common Muslims' understanding of Islam and doubted their ability to understand commentaries properly on their own. Instead of embracing the push for comprehension, Sabri reminded Muslims that reciting the Qur'an without understanding it was a praiseworthy act linked to the preservation of the Qur'an.[30] If a Muslim wanted to understand the meaning of the verses, Sabri recommended that he consult someone qualified to explain them.[31] Like Rashīd Riḍā, Sabri held that it was a duty for Muslims to propagate Arabic amongst themselves as a shared language. If all the linguistic communities were to use their own language, he wrote, it would 'deliver a blow to the harmony and unity of Islam'.[32] Sabri went so far as to lament the fact that Turks had not been fully Arabised, and thought it was unfortunate that, like the Persians, they had retained their language instead of adopting Arabic.[33] An opponent of religious reform, Sabri suspected that proponents of Qur'anic translation wanted to replace the revealed text. For this late Ottoman scholar and leader of the conservative opposition, the promotion of translations was a misguided enterprise led by unqualified persons, a project that threatened to injure both the textual sanctity and communal solidarity of Islam.[34]

Riḍā's vision of circling the wagons around Arabic, spreading Arabic literacy and disavowing translations in national languages was highly impractical and swam against the powerful currents of national awakening and educational reform among Muslim intellectuals in Istanbul, Kazan, Tehran, Java, the Indian subcontinent and Central Asia, not to mention Arabic centres like Cairo. In many respects, those who promoted the revitalisation of Arabic were presenting a final case for the revival of premodern Arabic cosmopolitanism.

Protestant Missionaries and Qur'anic Translation

A specific instance of how translation could be seen as injuring Muslim unity appeared in the form of Christian missionary activities and translations. Protestant missionaries followed Qur'an translation activities with great interest and diligently announced their publication in missionary journals. Many missionaries themselves translated the Qur'an into Asian and African languages with the intention of demonstrating its inferiority to the Bible.[35] According to one prominent thread of missionary thinking, translations resulted in textual transparency and enabled rational comprehension of the Qur'an. The prevalent missionary rationale was that this scripture was a confused mass of distorted Biblical stories which most Muslims could not comprehend because they did not know Arabic. Translations allowed missionaries to demonstrate the content of the Qur'an and compare and contrast it with the Bible. Once Muslims learned what the Qur'an actually said and compared it with the Christian Bible, so the thinking went, they would realise the superiority and truth of the Bible.

In 1924, for instance, the Australian Qur'anic scholar Arthur Jeffery (1892–1959) argued that comparing the Bible and the Qur'an presented one of the best avenues for preaching Christianity among Muslims.

> We should welcome the claim that they have a sacred book, encourage them to study it (for, particularly outside of Arabic speaking countries, Moslems are frequently sadly deficient in

> knowledge of their own book), and invite them freely to make their own choice after examination of the two books. Christianity has nothing to fear from the most searching examination of its Scriptures. Islam has everything to fear, particularly as education becomes more and more widespread.[36]

Repeating Martin Luther's arguments centuries before, Protestant missionaries submitted that making the Qur'an's meaning transparent would demonstrate its deficiencies and win converts.[37]

To this end, missionary publications often cheered on the publication of translations. The journal *The Moslem World* had as its subtitle *A Quarterly Review of Current Events, Literature, and Thought among Muhammedans and the Progress of Christian Missions in Moslem Lands*. It took a keen interest in translations by both missionaries and Muslims. Its founder, Rev. Samuel Zwemer (1867–1952), explained the paucity of Muslim translations by reinterpreting the idea of Qur'anic inimitability: 'Islam has never had its Pentecostal gift of tongues . . . The Bible, in contrast to the Koran, has this unique quality, that it can be rendered into all the languages of mankind without losing its majesty, beauty, and spiritual power. The secret lies in the subject matter of the scriptures.'[38] Whereas he deems the Bible's content to be of the highest quality, the beauty of the Qur'an is 'altogether in its style, and, therefore, necessarily artificial'.[39] The Qur'an, for Zwemer, was untranslatable because the rhyme, rhythm and music of the text could not be conveyed via translation, and, stripped of these stylistic qualities, the content was extremely disappointing. Therefore, to translate was to disarm.

Zwemer published a bibliography of translations in 1915 that demonstrates a common missionary approach to Qur'anic translation in the early twentieth century. He wrote that the first translation of the Qur'an was composed 'due to the missionary spirit of Petrus Venerabilis, Abbot of Cluny'.[40] After describing the history of translations in various languages, he highlights a Bengali-language translation 'with Christian comment and explanation' published in 1908 by an Australian missionary that 'can be made a schoolmaster to lead Moslems to Christ'.[41] Zwemer encourages those in other mission fields to compose similar texts. In conclusion, he writes:

> When we remember that this work of translation has, with a few exceptions, been the work of Western scholars, Orientalists and missionaries, the contrast between the Arabic Koran and the Bible, the Book for all nations, is strikingly evident. And from the missionary standpoint we have nothing to fear from modern Koran translations; rather may we not hope that the contrast between the Bible and the Koran will be evident to all readers when they compare them in their vernacular?[42]

As for the Ottoman Empire, Zwemer pointed out the difficulties encountered in publishing a Turkish translation and expressed concern that translations would not circulate freely in Muslim lands as long as 'orthodox Islam' remained prevalent.

After the Young Turks Revolution of 1908 (also known as the Constitutional Revolution) that dethroned Abdülhamid II, Julius Richter (1862–1940), a German Protestant missionary, drew a connection between the translation of the Qur'an and religious freedom, including the right to 'change one's religion according to the convictions of conscience'.[43] He hoped that the Young Turks' rise to power would facilitate the right of Muslims to convert to Christianity. An article in a Young Turk-affiliated newspaper, which demanded the translation of the Qur'an into Turkish, gave Richter hope for the future of religious freedom, but an official proclamation denouncing the article dampened his expectations. Nevertheless, the restoration of the Ottoman constitution and the growing demand for translation still marked a changing scene for Protestant missions. Richter thought that Turkey was about to enter a 'new chapter . . . an unheard of "day of opportunity"' for missionary work in the 'Turkish East'.[44]

Missionary support for translations of the Qur'an injected a new cause for concern into the traditional Muslim linguistic and theological arguments about the genre. The effect of this concern was mixed. On one hand, some Muslims came to view the emergence of translations as a European conspiracy to destroy the

Qur'an, and they became even more firmly opposed to such ventures.[45] On the other hand, missionary rhetoric against the Qur'an, together with polemic translations by missionaries, inspired some Muslims to compose translations in order to rectify the image and elucidate the content of the Qur'an, which they believed Christians had maligned and misrepresented. An English translation of the Qur'an published in 1915 by a South Asian community called the Anjuman-i Taraqqi-i Islam in Qadian (Punjab) reflects this sentiment:

> No other religion has been so cruelly misrepresented as that of the Holy Qur'an. Besides answering the objections of the hostile critics we intend to present to the readers of all creeds and nationalities a true picture of Islam . . . It is with these objects in view that we have undertaken this translation of the Holy Qur'an . . . to convey the true sense of the Holy Book and to remove the misunderstandings under which many people are labouring, thanks to the misrepresentations of Christian writers on Islam.[46]

In the late Ottoman Empire, many Muslims shared these sentiments about the maligned image of Islam and the need to counteract it.

European-language translations, with which many educated Ottomans were familiar, often provided the impetus to translate the Qur'an into Turkish. After reading a French textbook for schoolchildren that contained translated Qur'anic verses, the late Ottoman writer İsmail Hakkı Bereketzade (1850–1918) quipped that it appeared as if the authors had compiled all possible mistakes in one place. In order to show the true sense of the text, he began writing a regular column in which he translated passages into Turkish with an explanation.[47] Refutations of missionary and Western portrayals of Islam became a popular genre.

Heightened missionary efforts to injure the credibility of the Qur'an, often via translation, had thus precipitated a new kind of suspicion of the genre of translations and of reformist translators, many of whom advocated emulation of the Protestant Reformation. Yet, despite these new connotations, reformist visions of the Qur'an gained currency in the public sphere with the political revolution that occurred in 1908. The emerging political scene in Istanbul, undergirded by rising literacy rates and inspired by the ideals of the French Revolution, '*liberté, egalité, fraternité*', favoured the push for direct comprehension of the text.

Revolutionary Comprehension: The 1908 Revolution

In July of 1908, a secret organisation of young bureaucrats and military officers, called the Committee of Union and Progress (CUP, *İttihat ve Terakki Cemiyeti*), also known as the 'Young Turks' (Fr. *Les Jeunes Turcs*, Tr. *Jön Türkler*) forced Abdülhamid II on 24 July 1908 to restore the Ottoman Constitution of 1876. Abdülhamid II was first reduced to a ceremonial role and then, following an unsuccessful counterrevolution, he was deposed in 1909. To prevent separatism in the Balkans and Arab provinces and strengthen the empire, the new government worked to centralise power by establishing a firmer grip on the Arab provinces. The centralisation policy encroached upon the traditional domains of local Arab leaders, stoking opposition and fuelling nationalist sentiment. The CUP took measures to ensure Turkish leadership of the empire and implemented measures that gave the Turkish language a more prominent role in administrative offices, courts and schools, ostensibly to streamline official communication and cultivate an imperial elite with a shared language. The CUP made Turkish-language classes compulsory in elementary schools throughout the empire, and made Turkish the language of instruction in secondary and higher education. Whereas previously courts had used regional languages such as Arabic, in 1909 the government began to require the use of Turkish in all courts of the empire, 'a measure that led to discontent, inconvenienced judicial officials and litigants, and threatened the administration of justice'.[48]

Opposition to CUP centralisation focused on the issue of language, and the CUP was accused of Turkification policies, ethnic chauvinism and irreligiousness. Though centralisation was at the heart of the issue, critics exploited the symbolic power of language policies, framing the expanded use of Turkish as proof that the CUP was abandoning Arabic, the language of the Qur'an and the

Prophet. Arab critics equated Turkification with the elimination of religion from public life and framed a departure from Arabic as a departure from Islam. A surge of complaints about the irreligious behaviour of CUP officials lent credence to these claims.[49] Amid accusations that the new regime in Istanbul was abandoning Arabic and apostatising from Islam, the sensitivity towards translating the Qur'an became accentuated and gained new political resonance.

The case of Rashīd Riḍā is instructive as an instance of discontentment with the Young Turks. He initially supported the 1908 revolution and went to Istanbul in 1909 with a request for the Ottoman government to establish a school to train Muslim missionaries in modern fields of study as well as Islamic studies. In 1910, the government offered to support the school under the conditions that it be governed by the Ottoman Shaykh al-Islam and that Turkish would be its language of instruction. However, Riḍā viewed the Shaykh al-Islam's involvement as a politicisation of the school and claimed that the CUP wanted to use it as a tool of Turkification. After this episode, Rashīd Riḍā became a staunch opponent of the CUP, whom he thereafter lambasted as atheists and Freemasons.[50] Moreover, his views on Muslim unity changed and he began to manoeuvre for the establishment of an Arab Muslim empire. He led efforts to establish an Arab caliphate and founded a secret society whose *raison d'être* was to foster unity between the Arabian peninsula and the Arab provinces of the Ottoman Empire.[51] Having lost faith in the Ottomans, Rashīd Riḍā and others accepted funds from the British to incite revolt in the Ottoman provinces.[52]

The Constitutional Revolution and the rise of the CUP eliminated the restrictive press laws enacted by the deposed sultan. Press freedom unleashed a deluge of new publications on previously taboo subjects. 'Freedom', 'progress', 'civilisation' and 'reform' figured among the buzzwords of the day. Dozens of new newspapers and journals appeared shortly after the proclamation of the constitution on 24 July 1908, and an effervescence of enthusiasm for public expression overwhelmed Istanbul. Free of Abdülhamid's censors, the Ottoman media was able to diversify and mature, thus enabling an environment in which nationalism and Muslim modernism could thrive.[53]

The leaders of the CUP and many writers of post-revolutionary literature were influenced by Turkist thought. Turkism (*Türkçülük*) was the proto-nationalist discourse that emphasised the importance of the Turkish language, culture and identity. Drawing inspiration from the European field of Turkology, which developed in Russia and Central Europe in the nineteenth century, Turkists sought to uncover and revive elements of the Turkish language and culture that had been submerged within Islamicate civilisation.[54] For Turkists like Ziya Gökalp, the awakening of Turkish identity was integral to the modernisation and renewal of the Ottoman state and society. A related Pan-Turkist (*Türklük*) movement envisioned a cultural-political union of Turkic peoples from the Ottoman and Russian empires, stretching from the Balkans to Central Asia. Both Turkism and Pan-Turkism gained currency after the 1908 revolution, as did Arab, Armenian and other nationalist discourses. Though the CUP supported Turkist organisations and publications, it continued to promote Islamic unity and Ottoman solidarity, goals that nationalism of any variety would threaten.[55] Therefore, Unionist efforts should not be seen as Turkish nationalism in the sense of establishing a separate state for the Turkish nation. The primary mission of the CUP was to save the Ottoman Empire.

In addition to nationalist currents, the freer public sphere made it possible for Islamic intellectual activity to thrive in the capital. Prior to the revolution of 1908, Abdülhamid II had sent intellectuals into exile because he feared their ability to unleash criticism against the regime. The exiles included a number of 'devout intellectuals' – non-ulama writers and activists – who valued the Islamic tradition and approached the problems of the day with reference to Islam as a key source of public values.[56] Moreover, the sultan's press censor had precluded any meaningful religious debate in the public sphere. In fact, the pious opposition to Abdülhamid had worked with the Young Turks abroad, and the Constitutional Revolution in 1908 opened the doors to devout intellectuals and to the public debate on Islamic matters in general.[57] Both the devout intellectuals and the ulama established journals and newspapers dedicated to Islamic subjects that provided novel forums for the debate and exploration of contemporary Muslim concerns.

The periodicals allowed new voices to publicly express a wide range of ideas about religion in the abstract and about the reform of Islam in particular. Beset by the threat of European colonisation and troubled by separatist movements within the empire, the conversations of Ottoman intellectuals focused on the question of how to revitalise state and society in order to survive the difficult political and economic circumstances of the empire and the larger Muslim world. The question of why Islamic civilisation had declined and how Muslims would again rise filled the pages of newspapers, journals and treatises such as *Sebilürreşad* and *al-Manār*. The role of religion and the need to reform Islam figured prominently in these discussions.[58] Muslim reformist thought that had been suppressed by Abdülhamid II found full public expression and elaboration in the post-revolutionary public sphere. Ottoman thinkers appropriated reformist thought in diverse combinations. Though different in their principles and approach, competing intellectual outlooks were in agreement that the existing Islamic institutions needed to be reformed.[59]

A reformed-minded trend known as Muslim modernism evolved as the intelligentsia in various Islamicate lands wrestled with the military, economic, cultural and intellectual forces of modern Europe that increasingly shaped the fortunes of Muslim domains. Torn between the threat and opportunity presented by Europe, Muslim modernists worked to develop an understanding of Islam that was in harmony with modern European civilisation, one based on the sacred sources of Islam that could make use of modern institutions, knowledge and technology for the benefit of Muslim societies. Charles Kurzman argues that modernists pursued four main goals: cultural revival, political reform, science and education promotion, and women's rights.[60] He argues that freedom of speech or 'the right to say novel things in an Islamic discourse' was the central issue for Muslim modernist intellectuals around the globe.[61]

Modernists argued for the renewal of *ijtihād* and its use in addressing a wider range of issues, the unification of Islamic legal schools, and the right to read and interpret the Qur'an and the Hadith without intermediaries. Additionally, they sought to harmonise the sacred sources with human reason, and to connect Islamic concepts with facets of modern civilisation, for example, by equating the concept of *shūra* (consultation) with democracy.[62] Modernists such as Mehmet Akif and Musa Carullah Bigiyev tended to emphasise the centrality of the Qur'an, criticise the scholasticism of the ulama and take a critical approach to Hadith. Some supported capitalism, most championed constitutionalism, and virtually all stressed the importance of expanding and improving educational institutions as the eradication of ignorance, superstition and backwardness was a pervasive theme.[63] To convey their ideas, they used traditional literary forms with altered content, novel forms of religious writing including novels, plays and translations as well as newspapers and journals.[64]

Muslim modernists argued that negligence and misinterpretation of the Qur'an had played a significant role in the decline of Muslim civilisation. This negligence stemmed in part from the ulama, whom reformists criticised for indulging in arcane intellectual pursuits, protecting their own interests and failing to teach Muslims the meaning of the Qur'an. The modernists held that excessive reliance upon classical Qur'anic commentaries, the inflated position of the ulama as intermediaries, and the closing of the 'Gate of Independent Reasoning' had distracted and distanced Muslims from the fundamental imperatives and spirit of the Qur'an. According to this school of thought, the Qur'an advocated the pursuit of science, rational investigation and progress, and did not contradict the necessities of a modern society. Central to the history of Qur'anic translation, modernists advocated a fresh reading of the Qur'an as an essential step in spurring Islamicate revival. Many modernists viewed opposition to Qur'anic translation as an outdated dogma of the ulama, designed to preserve their control of interpretation and keep the masses in the dark.

As press freedom opened up the public sphere to reformist Muslim thought, it also precipitated unprecedented criticism of the religious establishment. Never before had the ulama faced such harsh, public attacks.[65] For instance, the physician and public intellectual Abdullah Cevdet (1869–1932) published a steady stream of criticism directed not only at the ulama but also at Islam itself.[66] In 1914, the journal *İslam Mecmuası* published an article that accused the ulama of poisoning 'the minds of the students with superstitions and absurdities'.[67] This critical barrage was matched by state policy. CUP policies eroded the power of the ulama, marginalising their political and institutional power. In 1909, the government forbade sharia courts from hearing private cases after a civil court had issued a verdict.[68] The CUP took all necessary measures to marginalise the ulama's political organisation and deny them any significant role in the legislative process.[69] In 1916, the powers of the ulama diminished significantly as the government removed the Shaykh al-Islam from the Ottoman cabinet, transferred his oversight of the religious courts to the Ministry of Justice and placed the madrasas – formerly administered by the Shaykh al-Islam – under the administration of the Ministry of Education.[70]

With the decline of the ulama's power and the expansion of press freedom, Islamic authority became an increasingly contested matter, and this contestation had clear implications for access to religious knowledge and texts. Abdullah Cevdet described the changing of the guard via new forums. He commented: 'The mosque pulpits are no longer the only intellectual centres, no longer the only educators: [now, they include] books, magazines, in short, the press; this European institution dramatically decreased the influence of the ulama.'[71] The diminution of the ulama establishment coincided with a new ethos where universal accessibility to Islamic knowledge and sacred sources was valued and trumpeted publicly. In post-1908 Istanbul, support became pervasive for Qur'anic transparency – the idea that the text could be clearly understood via translation – and for personal engagement with the Qur'an. An article titled 'Our Neglect of the Qur'an and its Causes' published in the journal *İslam Dünyası* (*The World of Islam*) contains a representative argument for this kind of comprehension. The author accuses madrasas of having for centuries neglected teaching the Qur'an and *tafsīr*, and argues that imitation of juristic and intellectual predecessors had deprived Muslims of direct engagement with the text itself. The consequences were dire, the author says, since 'two of the greatest reasons for the misfortunes of the people of Islam are their neglect (*gaflet*) of the Qur'an and the Hadith. Therefore every Muslim should approach the Qur'an and

Hadith, which are the bases of the Islamic religion.' The author concludes, 'There is nothing as shameful as not trying to read and understand the Noble Qur'an.'[72] The sentiments exemplified by this article were widespread among the intelligentsia, and contributed to the emergence of translations and commentaries in the late Ottoman public sphere.

Translations debuted not in book format, but in the columns of the newly established Islamic journals, usually in sections dedicated to *tafsīr*. Just a few weeks after press freedom was established, in August 1908, the journal *Sırat-ı Müstakim* began to feature columns by Bereketzade that translated and then commented on verses of the Qur'an. Yet these translations do not bear the name 'translation' (*tercüme*) in light of the fact that the term remained a sensitive subject, even for many Muslim modernists, and due to the fact that it remained illegal to publish them.[73] The editor of *Sırat-ı Müstakim*, Mehmet Akif Ersoy, also composed his own renderings as well. Interpreting Q. 3:103, Akif reflects the dominant concerns of the day, pleading for Muslim unity: 'Oh Believers! Hold fast all together to the bond of God, the sublime religion of Islam, obey the commands of God and the Prophet, keep away from what they forbid, and never be divided so that your hearts and souls might be bound tightly together always.'[74] In the commentary section, titled 'Unity Brings Life and Excellence; Division Demolishes and Kills', he warns that Muslim infighting – very likely referring to the tension between Arabs and Turks – threatens to destroy the entire umma. United under the mantle of the Prophet, Akif continues, Muslims conquered the world and enlightened peoples who were living in darkness; everyone worked for the progress of Islam with no selfish interests. In a thinly veiled commentary on the current state of affairs, he describes the lapse of unity: 'While among Muslims there was no nationality other than religion, [in recent days] every group began to make a claim to nationality. They sowed hypocrisy among Muslims and then began to fight among themselves.'[75] Akif's is a vernacular rendering of the Qur'an with decidedly anti-nationalist aims.

In subsequent years, other journals like *İslam Mecmuası* and *Hayrü'l-Kelam* followed suit, regularly publishing partial Qur'anic translations followed by explanations. Pointing to the broad interest in translation in the public sphere, prominent Turkist writer Ahmet Ağaoğlu (1869–1939) was impressed that translation efforts had 'begun in quarters utterly at variance with each other in their tendencies' and that 'protests against the translation have been remarkably feeble'.[76] Opinion among intellectuals, so it seemed, had moved decisively in favour of Qur'anic accessibility. However, what Ağaoğlu failed to mention was that between 1908 and 1912 virtually no one called the translated texts 'translations', and there was a notable absence of discussion about translating the Qur'an. Akçura expressed surprise that the translations printed in periodicals had not sparked significant conversation or even attracted much attention. In contrast, he wrote, Muslims in Russia had debated the merits of translations for years before actually printing them.[77] Devout Ottoman modernist authors like Bereketzade and Akif did not believe in the formal possibility of translating the Qur'an, and it seems that the prevalent opinion among devout intellectuals and the ulama remained opposed to the notion of a translation. As long as the passages were called commentaries (*tefsir*), summaries (*meal*) or explanations (*beyan*) no opposition arose. Avoiding the term *tercüme*, authors went about the task of translation with gusto, establishing a modus vivendi in which they composed and published translated passages of the Qur'an that neither disturbed their consciences nor upset the doctrine of Qur'anic untranslatability.

Incorruptible Meaning: Musa Carullah Bigiyev

This modus vivendi of translation by any other name was fragile since the practice was veiled by a thin shield of legitimacy. Like most novel or controversial activities, it called out for theorisation, which came in 1912 when a Muslim from Russia published a popular manifesto in support of Qur'anic translation.

A native of Kazan and an ethnic Tatar, Musa Carullah Bigiyev (See Figure 9) established himself as one of the best-known and most controversial reformist intellectuals in Russia and the Ottoman Empire. A man of cosmopolitan learning, Bigiyev began his education at a Russian elementary school and then pursued further studies at madrasas in Kazan, Bukhara, Istanbul and Cairo.[78] Bigiyev's articles and book excerpts frequently appeared in Istanbul-based journals, and Ottoman writers engaged with and challenged his ideas. Bigiyev harshly criticised classical Muslim scholarship for its conservatism, its scholasticism – that distanced Muslims from the sacred sources – and for what he saw as its failure to maintain Islamic intellectual vitality. He distinguished himself as an ardent supporter of Islamic reform, promoting the adoption of modern schools and engagement with Western science. In one of his most controversial opinions, for which he was vociferously attacked by the ulama, he argued that God's mercy extended not only to Muslims but also universally to all humans of whatever faith. This view brought him into a heated conflict with traditionally minded scholars in Russia and Istanbul. Due to this and other iconoclastic views, traditionalist journals in Russia branded him a heretic (*murtad*) and the Ottoman Empire banned his works for a period, as the Shaykh al-Islam retained considerable control over the publication and circulation of religious books.[79]

The controversies that made Bigiyev enemies, however, also won him many supporters. In the same year of the Constitutional Revolution in Istanbul, 1908, the Tatar author began to compose a Turkish translation of the Qur'an. Bigiyev generally wrote in the Pan-Turkic idiom advocated by journalist Ismail Gaspirali (Gasprinsky) (1851–1914), who hoped to foster communication and collaboration among Turkic peoples from the Balkans to Central Asia. Designed to be intelligible to Turkic Muslims in the Russian and Ottoman Empires, this language was a clear and simplified form of Ottoman Turkish.[80] When Bigiyev completed the translation in 1911/1912, the Muslim Religious Committee in the Russian city of Ufa denied permission for its publication. The traditionalist ulama journals *Beyanü'l-Hak* (Istanbul) and *Din ve Maişet* (Kazan) applauded the committee's decision.[81] Bigiyev then established his own press in St Petersburg, where he planned to print his translation as well as a newspaper. Several publications in Istanbul enthusiastically announced the coming of his translation.[82] Despite expectations, Bigiyev did not succeed in publishing the work, and the manuscript version has reportedly not survived.[83]

Though the translation never appeared in print, Bigiyev published his thoughts on Qur'an translation in his popular book *Halk Nazarında bir Niçe Mesele* (*Several Issues for Public Consideration*) published in 1912 in Kazan. Along with Bigiyev's advocacy for Qur'an translation, this controversial book addresses the causes of Muslim decline, the definition of faith, the future of Islam and the contemporary state of Turkic language and literature. Popular among madrasa students, the book sold swimmingly, and Bigiyev received letters from Istanbul urging his publisher to ship more copies from Kazan.[84] However, the Shaykh al-Islam's office in Istanbul banned the book along with his three other works based on the accusation that they circulated 'heretical ideas'.[85] The Shaykh al-Islam later retracted the ban.[86]

In *Halk Nazarında bir Niçe Mesele*, Bigiyev constructs an unconventional scholarly argument in support of translating the Qur'an. In consideration of the view that Arabic is the only valid language for Qur'anic recitation and obligatory prayer, he concludes that the exclusive use of Arabic was a logical and useful measure designed by the early religious scholars to preserve the Qur'an.[87] The early Muslim community had two duties: first, to preserve the verbatim text of the Qur'an, and, second, to explain and propagate its meaning. Bigiyev argues that the community achieved the first duty, the preservation of the text, via detailed attention to memorisation and ritual recitation in Arabic, and by developing reliable methods of producing written copies. However, he continues, the Prophet did not provide specific instructions for explaining the Qur'an and for transmitting it to non-Arabs;[88] thus, in a sense, Muslims were left to figure this out on their own.

Extending the argument, Bigiyev contends that not only was the verbatim text established and preserved, but so too its meaning: 'As every word, every vowel of the Qur'an is preserved, so too are the meanings of the words and sentences preserved.'[89] The Muslim linguistic disciplines, he continues, were developed in order to preserve the meanings of the words and sentences of the Qur'an, protecting them from alteration. In this manner, 'the blameless Muslim umma zealously established both the consonantal text and meaning of the Qur'an without alteration (*bi-la taghyīr*)'.[90]

Figure 1. Two men reciting the Qur'an by the tombs of sultans Mahmud II and Abdülaziz (late nineteenth century). Courtesy of the Library of Congress. See page 1.

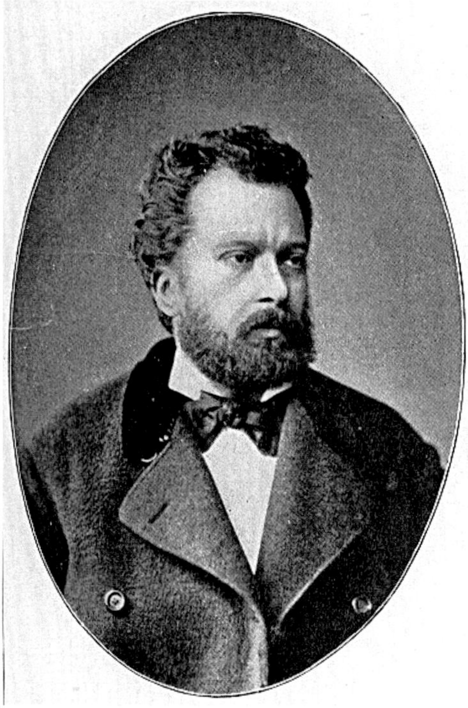

Figure 2. Namık Kemal (1840–88), journalist, poet and playwright. Courtesy of the University of Texas Libraries, University of Texas at Austin. See page 56.

Figure 3. Lithographic stone for printing the Qur'an, stored at the Meşihat Archive, Istanbul. Photo by author. See page 66.

Figure 4. A metal relief printing block for producing small editions of the Qur'an, stored at the Meşihat Archive, Istanbul. Photo by author. See page 66.

Figure 5. Two students holding copies of the Qur'an in the Eyüp district of Istanbul (between 1880 and 1893). Courtesy of the Library of Congress, Abdul Hamid II Collection. See page 58.

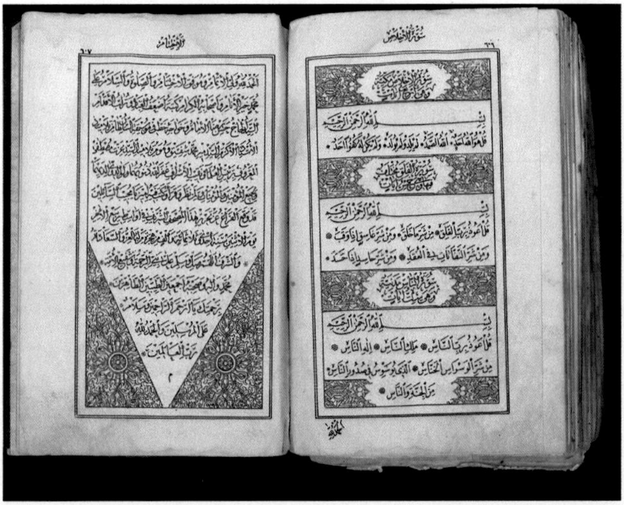

Figure 6. The final page and colophon of a lithographically printed Qur'an (Matbaa-i Osmaniye, Istanbul, 1301/1884). Calligrapher: Hasan Rıza. Photo by author. See page 67.

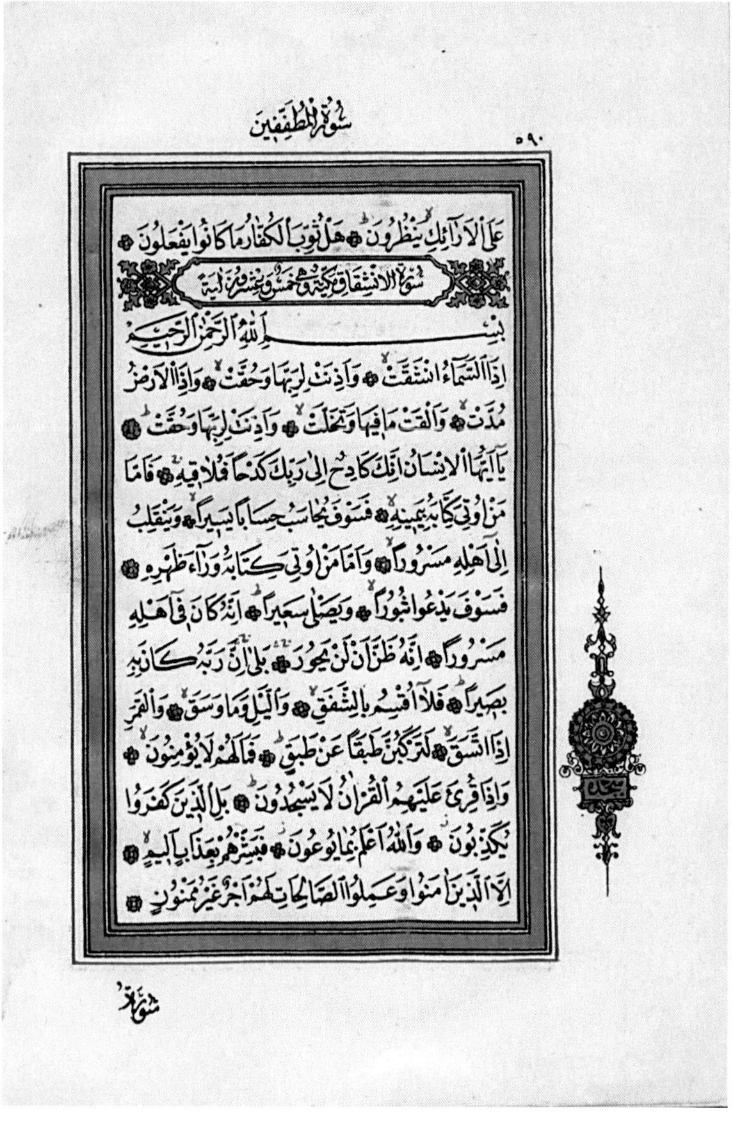

Figure 7. Interior page of a printed Qur'an with illuminations added (Matbaa-i Osmaniye, Istanbul, 1305/1887–8). Calligrapher: Mustafa Nazif. Photo by author. See page 76.

Figure 8. The Ottoman governor, Ali Ekrem Bey, giving out printed copies of the Qur'an and robes at a ceremony in Beersheba. The banner above reads, *Padişahim çok yaşa* ('Long live the Sultan') (*circa* 1907). Courtesy of the Library of Congress, John D. Whiting Collection. See page 77.

Figure 9. Musa Carullah Bigiyev (1875–1949), *circa* 1910, a translator of the Qur'an into Turkish. Courtesy of –az19, Creative Commons Share Alike 3.0. See page 136.

Figure 10. Pages from a revised version of Süleyman Tevfik's *Türkçeli Kur'an-ı Kerim* (1927), presenting the Arabic original (inside box) and Turkish translation in parallel columns. Photo by author. See page 162.

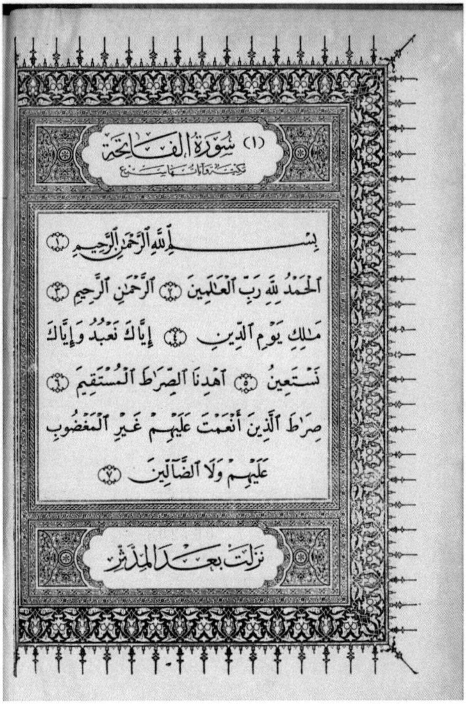

Figure 11. First page of the Egyptian edition of the Qur'an (1924), the most widely used version of modern times. Photo by author. See page 189.

Figure 12. A translation of the Qur'an resting on the pulpit of Yıldız Hamidiye Mosque, Istanbul (2013). Photo by author. See page 253.

According to Bigiyev, Qur'anic meaning was preserved not in works of Qur'anic commentary – which could be fanciful glosses that departed from the text – but in the dictionaries, grammars and other linguistic genres that developed around the Qur'an. He suggests that, theoretically, one could retrieve original meanings through the language and linguistic apparatus: formalised language was the guarantor of Qur'anic meaning.

The presumption of fixed meaning, frozen in the language itself, formed the foundation of Bigiyev's rationale for translating the Qur'an: 'If the meaning is established like the Arabic arrangement of the text (*naẓm*), by necessity translating the Qur'an is possible. After the meaning has been preserved, saying that translation is not possible is equivalent to saying that the meanings of the Noble Qur'an can never be understood.'[91] By locating the meaning of the Qur'an in the language of the text itself – not in Qur'anic commentaries – Bigiyev constructs a rationale for independent interpretation via translation that bypasses the scholastic commentary traditions which he distrusted and blamed for the stagnation of creative interpretation.

The question of how to use Qur'anic commentaries when translating is a key methodological issue for all translators. Does one seek to explain unknown words with the aid of the commentaries? Should one rely primarily on what the letter of the text suggests or should one refer to the interpretative tradition for guidance? In order to make a fresh interpretation and derive new inspiration for the present, as many modernist thinkers sought to do, some level of independence from commentary works was necessary. However, given the difficulty and ambiguity of the Qur'an, most translators made use – sometimes extensive – of the commentary corpus. With a text that has an immense commentary tradition spanning a millennium, the modern translator has to decide not only how close to bring the reader to the text or the text to the reader but also how close to bring the text and the reader to the exegetical corpus. Bigiyev heavily criticised Muslim commentators for distorting the meaning of the Qur'an and pursuing partisan aims. Yet, despite his distaste for and distrust of *tafsīr* works, he consulted them extensively during his own translation project.[92] In describing his methodology, though, he makes it clear that language and linguistic indicators played a much greater role in the project than the opinions of commentators.

Bigiyev projects language as a transparent and unbiased conveyer of information that could guarantee the reliability of a translation. This faith in language and the letter of the text was a reaction to what he saw as liberties taken by commentators, as he felt that commentators all too often went outside the actual text and interpolated their own understandings, distorting the meaning. Consider his approach to Q. 7:117, a passage in reference to the confrontation between Moses and Pharaoh's sorcerers who had turned their ropes and staffs into snakes: *And We revealed to Moses: 'Cast thy staff!' And lo, it forthwith swallowed up their lying invention*. Many commentators interpret the verse to mean that the staff of Moses came alive and ate the cords and staffs of the Pharaoh's sorcerers, but Bigiyev found this interpretation to be nonsensical, 'There is not a single letter in this verse . . . to justify the translation that it ate their ropes and staffs.'[93] For Bigiyev, the commentators had ignored other verses in the Qur'an that clarify this verse. In this instance, Bigiyev invokes intra-textual interpretation, the use of different verses in the Qur'an to interpret other verses, a method which he openly endorses in the treatise.[94] Though Q. 7:117 does not specify what the staff of Moses 'swallowed up', Q. 20:66 says that *their ropes and their staffs were sliding*, indicating that they had become snakes as depicted in the Biblical narrative in Exodus.[95] Bigiyev argues that Moses' staff could not have eaten the ropes and staffs of the sorcerers because they had taken on the form of snakes through the sorcerers' magic; thus, it is 'a distortion (*tahrif*) of the inimitable *naẓm* to say that they ate the ropes and staffs themselves'.[96] The stiff literalism of some interpreters was, for Bigiyev, an example of the intellectual aridity and stagnation that plagued Islamic thought.

Additionally, Bigiyev criticises the commentators for declaring certain verses null through abrogation (*naskh*) and for editing the meaning of other verses in order to ensure the text conforms to certain theological agendas. As an example, Bigiyev refers to Q. 17:16: *And when We desire to destroy a city, We command its men who live at ease, and they commit ungodliness therein, then the Word is realized against it, and We destroy it utterly.* This verse is replete with ambiguity due to its succinct style: the second phrase, *We command its men who live at ease* (*aradnā mutrafīhā*), does not clarify what is commanded. The third phrase, *and they commit ungodliness* (*fa-fasaqū*), fails to specify what type of ungodliness is being committed. These ambiguities concerned the commentators; Abū Jaʿfar Muḥammad b. Jarīr b. Yazīd al-Ṭabarī (224/839–310/923), for instance, describes a prevalent interpretation in his time as that which fills in the blanks to mean *We command those who live at ease to obey God, and they commit ungodliness by their rebellion against God.*[97] Bigiyev disapproves of this method of translation because it inserts the understanding of the interpreter into a translation and potentially distorts the meaning of the original.[98]

Bigiyev dubbed both *tafsīr* and *ta'wīl* mere 'human thought' (*insanın fikri*).[99] In order to derive meaning directly from the text, Bigiyev considered translation the most reliable method and understood it to be a transfer of meanings from one language to another without interpretation. In contrast to the axiom that every translation is an interpretation, Bigiyev defines them as distinct activities:

> In the translation, I only considered the customary meanings and the indications of the Arabic language. I did not rely on a human's perspective for even a single letter. I refrained from writing my small, pathetic ideas next to the awe-inspiring, sacred meanings of the Qur'an. I too will curse any buffoons (*herifler*) who attempt to do such a thing.[100]

Bigiyev suggests that divine meaning can be accessed seamlessly through human language and then transmitted into another language without interference from the translator. In this way, the 'human perspective' does not contaminate the divine message. The dictates of formal, established language safeguard the meaning from the whims of the translator. Language, and Qur'anic language in particular, appears transparent. For Bigiyev, the translator's role is to convey this transparency without interference.

Far from naive, Bigiyev did not see translation as a perfect form of communication and acknowledged its difficulties, demonstrating a nuanced understanding of its problematic aspects: 'Sometimes a meaning will be understood from a sentence but will be different because of the temporal context . . . In this situation, a literal translation cannot be accurate.'[101] Bigiyev understood that meanings change over time while the signs remain the same. As George Steiner suggests, linguistic change over time is perhaps the 'most salient model of Heraclitean flux'.[102] Just as you can never step in the same river twice, the meanings of particular words and expressions in language change across time and place. Bigiyev recognises this problem as well as the problem of meaning and connotation in the minds of different audiences. Because of this, he felt that translations of poems and novels often lose the beauty of the original and that in some cases translation is actually impossible.[103]

Despite the impossibility of achieving perfect translation across contexts and the impossibility of recreating the same effect on the reader when translating literature and poetry, Bigiyev defends the translation of the Qur'an. The Qur'an, he argues, is unlike other texts because the meanings of the words and the sentences are firmly established and preserved in the linguistic disciplines. Just as Bigiyev equated the fixity of the Qur'anic text with the fixity of its meaning, he also ascribed incorruptibility to Qur'anic meaning: its meaning is immune from distortion and alteration just like the consonantal text. Since the meaning is protected, he concluded that 'translating the Qur'an is definitely possible and legally obligatory' (*farz*).[104] Here, Bigiyev flips on its head the prevalent thinking among his contemporaries that Qur'anic translation is both impossible and legally impermissible: not only is it possible, but translation is also a religious obligation.

Notwithstanding his belief that translating the Qur'an was both possible and obligatory, Bigiyev did not think that just anyone could translate the text or engage in its interpretation. He spared no invective for commentators and translators whom he viewed as unqualified, and found a prime example in İsmail Ferruh whose translation of a particular Qur'anic verse he strongly disagreed with. This specific verse confronts those who, doubting

Muhammad's status as a prophet, ask why an angel has not descended to him as proof. The response found in Q. 6:9 is: *And had We made him an angel, yet assuredly We would have made him a man, and confused for them the thing which they themselves are confusing* (*wa lalabasnā 'alayhim mā yalbisūn*). However, in the *Mevakib*, Ferruh renders the last phrase, 'We would have . . . covered him with that which they wore (*onu onların giydikleriyle sitr ederdik*)'. Bigiyev fumes that this was 'written by the pen of fools' who lack the required knowledge for the task and commit 'atrocious errors'.[105] The conventional understanding of the verb *labasa* in this verse is not 'covered with clothes', the more common meaning of the verb, but rather 'confused' or 'obscured'. Bigiyev points out that the same 'mistake' appears in other printed books and, since these works passed inspection by the committee that examined Islamic works in Istanbul, Bigiyev viewed their publication as yet another indication of the lamentable state of the professional religious establishment.[106]

Though Bigiyev advocated Qur'an translation in an unprecedentedly forceful manner for the late Ottoman context, he did not support the idea of reciting translations or performing ritual prayer in any language other than Arabic.[107] Moreover, he expressed no desire to replace the Arabic Qur'an with a translation, and viewed the Qur'anic *naẓm* as the most precious asset of the Islamic tradition. He applauded the early community's zealousness in preserving it at all costs. These facts are important to keep in mind because they show that supporters of translation had diverse agendas and, in fact, that most did not embrace the vernacularisation of ritual. The majority of devout intellectuals supported translation for the purpose of learning about the Qur'an, not for transforming Muslim ritual.

For Bigiyev, translating the Qur'an formed a step in his broader mission to establish intellectual freedom, and to further the cause of rationality and education in the Muslim world. Translating the Qur'an, developing the Turkic languages and expanding the national literature were means by which Turcophone Muslims could attain modernity and become part of the civilised world while strengthening faith and improving knowledge of the sacred text.[108]

The Protestant Reformation and the Path to Modernity

For reformers like Bigiyev, the path to modernisation had a road map. He as well as other modernist observers privileged the European historical experience as the most instructive model for religious reform.[109] In particular, intellectuals referred to the Protestant Reformation as the defining moment in the development of European modernity.[110] Anti-clerical discourses from Europe, particularly from the Reformation and the French Revolution, had a pervasive influence upon late Ottoman views of institutional religion.[111] Turkish-speaking reformist ulama and devout critics adopted the view that the Ottoman ulama were responsible for the spread of atheism and the decline of Islam in Ottoman lands. In making this comparison, they drew extensively on the Protestant Reformation, constructing a narrative in which the Ottoman ulama and the Catholic priesthood were equated as self-interested priestly classes that kept the people in the dark and stunted the progress of society.[112] These priestly classes used scholarly language that the people could not understand – the priests, Latin; the ulama, Arabic – and they prevented the masses from accessing the truths of scripture on their own. On this issue, Haşim Nahid (1880–1962) writes:

> When priests [before the Reformation] magically chanted inscrutable words in an unknown language, Christians used to kneel with a feeling of subservience, kiss the aisles of the church, and prostrate themselves at the feet of these half-holy demigods who intermediated between them and Jesus. Likewise, when our turbaned *hojas* in embroidered robes and sword in hand repeat the words of God's heavenly sounds from a high, white pulpit, Turkish, Laz, Tatar, Circassian, Indian and Chinese believers listen speechless and bewitched to these heavenly tones that they do not understand. I would not compare the exalted Muslim religion with abrogated faiths. But what Christians understood then, is how much Muslims understand now.[113]

Nahid, like most reformist thinkers, reached the conclusion that Muslims lacked sufficient knowledge of their faith, and because of this ignorance remained in a state of mental and spiritual subjugation. For him, the Reformation model offered a solution to this dilemma. Nahid writes: 'A truth seeker, a "renewer" (*müceddid*) appeared among Christians. He translated the Gospel, and from the moment they understood the Gospel, the links of the heavy chains opened, the priests who had appeared as God's regents seemed smaller, and the gods of the Gospel began to ascend. Finally, they succeeded in breaking the captivity of thought and conscience.'[114] For Nahid, the German translation of the Bible by Martin Luther marked the turning point in the spiritual and intellectual liberation of Christian Europe; Christian understanding of the scripture precipitated social changes that led to the rise of European modernity. Following the Reformation model, he thought that translating the Qur'an would bring similar benefits to Muslims. With dramatic flair, Nahid proclaimed, 'The Luther of Islamdom has appeared. This renewer, this religious warrior, Musa Bigiyev, . . . is now translating the Qur'an into Turkish. This is a good tiding for the freedom of Islamic thought and conscience. A Russian Muslim has taken the first step towards the truth of religion. Let us follow him!'[115]

The idea that understanding the Qur'an via translation was essential to religious, intellectual, and ultimately political and economic revival enjoyed widespread currency in reformist circles. According to this vein of thought, the Qur'an held such inspirational power that simply communicating it would spark Muslim renewal. The writer and member of parliament Celal Nuri (1877–1938), for instance, wrote:

> Today, we are in possession of the Qur'anic texts and the Hadith of the prophet, works that are so miraculous, inimitable, blessed, sacred, and holy that communicating them in a new and useful style to the hearts of the believers is sufficient to revive our nation, to turn around our state, and to strengthen our faith. The Qur'an is tremendous. Only we are not aware of this greatness.[116]

Reconnecting with the meaning of the text would start a domino effect benefiting all aspects of society. Direct understanding of the

Qur'an and Hadith via translation, Nuri contended, would make it possible for Muslims to achieve progress and 'worldly happiness'.[117] In fact, for many, the lack of a translation answered the questions of what went wrong and what caused Muslim political and economic decline.

Writer and statesman Hüseyin Kâzım Kadri (1870–1934) remarked that whenever he saw examples of religious fanaticism among Muslims he would remind himself that 'the Qur'an has not been translated in the languages of the Muslim nations'.[118] In the effort to remedy the ills plaguing Islamicate societies, Kadri contended that Qur'anic translation was conducive to 'all the social, religious, and ethical goals of Muslim life'.[119] Likewise, the author Ubeydullah Efgani thought that individual engagement with the Qur'an through translation would increase faith, prevent the evils besetting Ottoman Muslims and inhibit the 'spread of atheism'.[120]

Despite the enthusiasm on the part of reform-minded intellectuals, the political climate remained indisposed to the publication of a freestanding translation of the Qur'an. Others doubted that a translation of the Qur'an would be the panacea that some expected. In a book criticising the reformists, Mustafa Sabri pointed out that translations of the Qur'an were not new, and that readers had disliked previous ones and found them deficient. If earlier translations had not freed Islam from its intellectual prison or sparked a revival of the Muslim world, he questioned, why then should Muslims expect a translation to have such an effect now? On the practice side of things, Sabri did not think that the reformers promoting translation had the competence to actually compose one.[121]

In 1914, prior to the beginning of World War I, editor İbrahim Hilmi published portions of a Turkish translation by an anonymous author. Hilmi was a proponent of revolutionary comprehension, the idea that understanding the Qur'an was essential for revolutionising late Ottoman society and facilitating its participation in modern civilisation. In the introduction he writes, 'As I have worked with all my ability for quite some time in order to bring about an intellectual and social revolution in our homeland, my most sincere desire was to translate, print and publish the sublime meaning of the Noble Verses.'[122] Conscious of opposition, Hilmi assured readers that a 'Turkish Qur'an' could never take the place of the original and that the Turkish version was only an explanatory translation that could not fulfil ritual purposes.[123] Despite this assurance, the very language that Hilmi used – Turkish Qur'an – offended the sensibilities of the ulama and devout Muslims.

Further complicating the matter, during the printing process Hilmi had told the public that the author was a Muslim. Later, it came to light that the unnamed author of the translation was a Catholic Christian from Syria. Devout intellectuals saw this episode as an absolute scandal. Writer Ömer Rıza Doğrul (1893–1952), who later published a Qur'an translation of his own, had the opportunity to read the text before it was printed and urged the government to halt the publication process.[124] The ulama journal *Hayrü'l-Kelam* publicly called upon the Shaykh al-Islam's office to prevent its publication, and it responded by prohibiting distribution, seizing copies from bookstores and banning the work.[125] The embattled publisher described the controversy as a conflict between the forces of progress and the reactionary ulama: 'A newspaper that was the tool of profound fanaticism spewed fire, and those who appropriate religion as a means of profit and gain did not want to digest the publication of the Turkish translation of the Holy Qur'an. Unfortunately, the government at that time had to accept their protests and wishes.'[126] The government needed the support of the ulama, and, perhaps more importantly, it did not want to exacerbate the already tense relations with the Arab provinces by allowing the publication of a self-styled 'Turkish Qur'an'. Therefore, as in the reign of Abdülhamid II, the Young Turks prevented the publication of translations. Despite this policy, when the Arab revolt occurred in 1916, the Sharif of Mecca included the translation of the Qur'an in his grievances against the Ottoman Turks.[127]

This attempt to publish a translation that was secretly composed by a Christian confirmed the suspicions of some devout critics, and added fuel to the arguments of Rashıd Rida and Mustafa Sabrı that linked translation with missionaries and attacks on Islam. Qur'an translation was already a questionable enterprise for Islamic scholars, and the deceptive nature of this first publication attempt deepened concerns that translation would lead to distortion of the text. Anti-missionary, anti-imperialist rhetoric found, in this event, another example of Christians attempting to destroy the Qur'an.[128] In addition to being Christian, the fact that the author was seen as an Arab, not a Turk, perturbed the journal *Sebilürreşad*, which felt that a native speaker of Turkish should carry out a literary enterprise of this magnitude for the Turkish language.[129] At a time of tense Turkish–Arab and Muslim–Christian relations in the Ottoman Empire, this episode exacerbated the situation and cast a shadow over the contested genre of translation.

During World War I, the Ottoman government wanted to preserve Muslim unity at all costs and prevented controversial publications. Translations of the Qur'an, with their potential to alienate the Arab provinces and their divisive effect among the ulama, again fell under this ban. In 1916, the Arab revolt led by Ḥusayn b. ʿAlī (1854–1931), the Sharif of Mecca, dealt the *coup de grâce* to Turkish–Arab unity. Though hundreds of thousands of Arabs fought on the Ottoman side in the war, the revolt shattered Turkish confidence in the Arabs and bolstered the position of Turkists who viewed the Turks as the future of the polity. Moreover, this provided fuel to the arguments for translating the Qur'an and developing a modern Islam with less dependence on the Arabic tradition.

Immediately after the war, the issue of Qur'an translation re-emerged in Turkish intellectual circles. In 1918, Ziya Gökalp penned a poem entitled 'Vatan' ('Homeland') that immortalised the concept of the Turkish Qur'an in verse.

> A country where in Turkish the call to prayer is said,
> The meaning of his prayer the villager can understand . . .
> A country in whose schools the Turkish Qur'an is read
> Everyone, young and old, understands the Guide's command . . .
> Oh Turkish son, there is your homeland![130]

Gökalp's poem endorses a radical Turkist vision of the Qur'an and its translation. Not only does it place emphasis on comprehension, it also envisions the performance of Muslim ritual in Turkish and suggests the replacement of the original text with a translation. Crucially, moving from the pragmatic to the symbolic, Gökalp casts the Turkish Qur'an not only as a useful book but as an emblem of the newly awakened Turkish nation, an emblem that plays a role in making the homeland sacred and making Islam suitably Turkish.

While Gökalp's ideas were radical, they were not necessarily anti-religious in that they did not call for the abandonment of Islam as a source of public values. He argued that there was no contradiction between Turkification, Islamisation and modernisation, and advocated the restoration of a living Islam that played an active part in the cultural life of the nation.[131] A disciple of Emile Durkheim's functionalist approach to religion – that is, that religion serves a tangible purpose in representing and uniting a community – Gökalp viewed the harmonisation of Islam with national culture as necessary if religion were to fulfil its social function. He believed it would diminish egotism and cultivate concern for the collective interests of society; and, secondly, it would reinforce the common language and cultural ties via collective rituals.[132] According to Gökalp, the inaccessible nature of Arabic-based rituals and texts defeated the purpose of religion, and made it impossible for Islam to play a vital role in national life.

Yet the texts that would make this vision possible did not yet exist. There was still no full-length translation or commentary in contemporary Turkish. During World War I, former Shaykh al-Islam Musa Kâzım (d. 1920) wrote that existing commentaries failed to convey not only the subtleties but the manifest meaning of the Qur'an. This 'great shortcoming in the national literature' deprived millions of the most basic meaning of the Qur'an.[133] To address this failing, Kâzım composed a translation and commentary of the first two Qur'anic suras titled *Safvetü'l-beyan*. Avoiding the complications of the word '*tercüme*', he called the translation sections 'the condensed meaning' (*icmalen manası*) and 'summary of explanation' (*hülasa-i tefsir*). The former was a literal translation and the latter a free translation. Additionally, the work contains longer passages of commentary in which the author explains interpretations of particular words or verses. Though evincing concern for popular comprehension, Kâzım's book remained within the parameters and format of *tafsīr*.

The perceived need to comprehend became dominant among reformists of all stripes as the ideal of Turkish–Arab political unity faded from the realm of possibility. Only a small minority of conservatives led by Sabri continued to argue that broader comprehension of the Qur'an threatened the well-being of society. However, proponents of comprehension differed over which genre, *tarjama* or *tafsīr*, was legitimate and appropriate. In an article published in 1919 and titled 'Kur'an-ı Kerim Tercüme Olunabilir mi?' ('Can the Qur'an be Translated?'), İsmail Hakkı Milaslı (1869/70–1938) describes the opposing views:

> One group of people says that there is no benefit in reading words that one does not understand, and that in order to be able to fully understand the rules and the meanings, it is necessary to translate the Holy Qur'an into Turkish. They contend that it has already been translated into a great number of foreign languages and cannot imagine any impediment to a Turkish translation.
>
> On the other hand, another group opposes translating the Qur'an into Turkish and argues that the noble meanings can only be articulated in the form of Qur'anic commentary (*tefsir*). The most fundamental reason for this opposition is their assumption that some want to use the translation in ritual prayer and beyond ritual prayer to replace the Arabic original. Actually, among those who favour translation, there are some who want translations simply for understanding just as there are others who are of the opinion that it is necessary to recite the Turkish version in place of the Arabic original in ritual prayer and supererogatory prayer (*dua*).[134]

In contrast to Gökalp, most devout intellectuals who advocated comprehension either insisted on calling the translations *tefsir* or stipulated that translations must be accompanied by commentary. Since a translation could not contain all the nuances of meaning, they viewed a parallel commentary as a necessity in order to facilitate proper understanding. They did not want to leave the interpretation of the translation to chance and felt that the masses should have access, but still required guidance. Devout intellectuals hoped to ensure continuity with the traditional understandings and prevent divergent or radical interpretations.

By the end of World War I, support for Qur'anic translation had gained substantial momentum. Nascent nationalisms and missionary activities politicised translations to an unprecedented degree, and the arguments for and against them shifted from linguistic to sociopolitical concerns. Additionally, rapidly changing political conditions capped off by World War I added a sense of urgency to the issue that was not observed prior to 1908. Yet, regardless of the heightened importance of translations in reformist and nationalist discourses, the political vicissitudes of the second constitutional period (1908–1920) did not permit them to be published. However, the wheels were in motion and a number of writers had begun composing translations even though they could not be printed.

As a result of the Allied occupation of Istanbul, which began on 13 November 1918, the British exiled many prominent figures to the island of Malta. During their imprisonment on the island, Mehmet Ubeydullah as well as the mufti and parliamentarian Hasan Fehmi (d. 1933) worked on translations of the Qur'an. Hasan Fehmi translated the entire text, which, like many others, was never published.[135] Several other writers began translations that were individual efforts, not government projects, inspired by the zeitgeist and composed with one eye on the national resistance movement that was gathering steam in Anatolia. The success of that movement and the establishment of the nation state of Turkey in 1923 created a political context that favoured nationalist ideology, and made it possible for Turkist visions of Islamic reform to be pursued and for modern translations of the Qur'an to make their debut in the public sphere.

NOTES

1 Yasir Suleiman, *The Arabic Language and National Identity* (Washington DC, Georgetown University Press, 2003), p. 125. For a variety of views on early Arab nationalism, see Rashid Khalidi *et al.*, eds., *The Origins of Arab Nationalism* (New York, Columbia University Press, 1991).

2 Dücane Cündioğlu, *Türkçe Kur'an ve Cumhuriyet İdeolojisi* (Cağaloğlu, Istanbul, Kitabevi, 1998), p. 27.
3 Midhat, *Beşair*, pp. 98–9.
4 Muḥammad Rashīd Riḍā, 'Tarjamat al-Qur'ān', in Ṣalāḥ al-Dīn Munajjid and Yūsuf Qazmā Hūrī, eds., *Fatāwā al-Imām Muḥammad Rashīd Riḍā* (Beirut, Dar al-Kitāb al-Jadīd, 1970), p. 643.
5 Riḍā, 'Tarjamat al-Qur'ān', pp. 268–74.
6 Muḥammad Rashīd Riḍā, 'Madaniyyat al-ʿarab', *al-Manār* 3 (1900), pp. 289–93, cited in Mahmoud Haddad, 'Arab Religious Nationalism in the Colonial Era: Rereading Rashīd Riḍā's Ideas on the Caliphate', *Journal of the American Oriental Society* 117, no. 2 (1997), p. 257.
7 Muḥammad Rashīd Riḍā, 'Bāb al-asʾila wa'l-ujūbat al-dīniyya', *al-Manār* 4, no. 13 (1901), p. 496.
8 Riḍā, 'Tarjamat' (1970), p. 643.
9 Ibid., p. 643.
10 Ibid., pp. 649–50.
11 Ibid.
12 Muḥammad Rashīd Riḍā, 'Fatāwā al-Manār: Wujūb taʿallum al-ʿarabiyya ʿalā kulli muslim', *al-Manār* 17, no. 8 (1914), pp. 589–92.
13 See Riḍā, 'Bāb al-asʾila', p. 497.
14 Riḍā, 'Tarjamat', in Munajjid and Hūrī, *Fatāwā*, p. 644.
15 Ibid., p. 648.
16 Ibid., p. 644.
17 Ibid.
18 Ibid.
19 Ibid.
20 Ibid., p. 647.
21 Ibid.
22 Ibid., p. 645.
23 Ibid.
24 Ibid., p. 646.
25 Ibid.
26 Ibid., p. 648.
27 Ibid.
28 Hasan Kayalı, *Arabs and Young Turks: Ottomanism, Arabism, and Islamism in the Ottoman Empire, 1908–1918* (Berkeley, University of California Press, 1997), p. 93.
29 Ahmed Naim, *İslam'da Dava-ı Kavmiyet* (Istanbul, 1913–14), pp. 51–2, cited in Berkes, *Development of Secularism in Turkey*, p. 375.
30 Mustafa Sabri, *Dini Müceddidler* (Istanbul, Evkaf Matbaası, 1338/1919–20), p. 198.
31 Ibid., p. 199.
32 Ibid., pp. 199–200.
33 Bein, *Ottoman Ulema*, p. 112.
34 Ibid., p. 197.
35 For example, Willam Goldsack, *Korān* (Calcutta, 1908–20) [Bengali]; Godfrey Dale, *Tafsiri Ya Kurani Ya Kiarabu Kwa Lugha Ya Kisawahili Pamoja Na Dibaji Na Maelezo Machache* (London, Society for Promoting Christian Knowledge, 1923) [Swahili].

36 Arthur Jeffery, 'The Presentation of Christianity to Moslems', *International Review of Missions* 13, no. 2 (1924), pp. 183–4.
37 See Chapter One in this book.
38 Samuel M. Zwemer, 'Translations of the Koran', *Moslem World* 5, no. 3 (1915), pp. 245–6.
39 Ibid., p. 246.
40 Ibid., p. 247.
41 Ibid., p. 258.
42 Ibid., p. 261.
43 Julius Richter, *A History of Protestant Missions in the Near East* (New York, Fleming H. Revell, 1910), p. 180.
44 Ibid.
45 'Büyük bir Tecavüz: Kur'an'dan Menfaat Teminine Kalkışan bir Hristiyan', *Sebilürreşad* 21, nos. 542–3 (1923), pp. 181–2.
46 *The Holy Qur'ān: With English Translation and Explanatory Notes* (Madras, Addison Press, 1915), cited in Zwemer, 'Translations of the Koran', p. 253.
47 İsmail Hakkı Bereketzade, 'Necaib-i Kur'aniye', *Sırat-ı Müstakim* 1, no. 2 (1908), p. 24.
48 Kayalı, *Arabs and Young Turks*, p. 92.
49 Ibid., pp. 94–5.
50 Eliezer Tauber, 'Rashīd Riḍā as Pan-Arabist before World War I', *Muslim World* 79, no. 2 (1989), p. 105.
51 Kayalı, *Arabs and Young Turks*, p. 181.
52 Ibid., p. 185.
53 On the post-1908 press, see Palmira Johnson Brummett, *Image and Imperialism in the Ottoman Revolutionary Press, 1908-1911* (Albany, State University of New York Press, 2000).
54 Karl Heinrich Menges, *The Turkic Languages and Peoples: An Introduction to Turkic Studies* (Wiesbaden, Harrassowitz, 1968), pp. 5–7.
55 Hanioğlu, *Brief History*, pp. 187–8.
56 This useful term, 'devout intellectual', as well as the interchangeable 'devout critic', was coined by Amit Bein, *Ottoman Ulema*, p. 27.
57 Hanioğlu, *Brief History*, pp. 140–41.
58 Bein, *Ottoman Ulema*, pp. 14–19.
59 Amit Bein, 'The Ulema, Their Institutions, and Politics in the Late Ottoman Empire (1876–1924)' (PhD Dissertation, Princeton University, 2006), p. 99. Berkes, *Development of Secularism*, p. 377.
60 Charles Kurzman, *Modernist Islam, 1840–1940: A Sourcebook* (Oxford, Oxford University Press, 2002), p. 25.
61 Ibid., p. 5.
62 Aziz al-Azmeh, *Islams and Modernities* (London, Verso, 1993), p. 79.
63 Adeeb Khalid, *The Politics of Muslim Cultural Reform: Jadidism in Central Asia* (Berkeley, University of California Press, 1998), p. 20.
64 Kurzman, *Modernist Islam*, pp. 14–15.
65 Bein, 'The Ulema', p. 102.
66 Şükrü Hanioğlu, 'Garbcılar: Their Attitudes toward Religion and Their Impact on the Official Ideology of the Turkish Republic', *Studia Islamica* 86, no. 2 (1997), pp. 133–49.

67 Hoca Şir İdris, 'Ulema-ı Kiram Hazretı'na Lozan'dan bir Hitab', *İslam Mecmuası*, 27 February 1329/12 March 1914, p. 91, cited in Bein, 'The Ulema', p. 102.
68 Hanioğlu, *Brief History*, p. 186.
69 Bein, 'The Ulema', p. 139.
70 Bein, *Ottoman Ulema*, p. 205.
71 Abdullah Cevdet, 'Son Kırk Sene Zarfında İslamiyet', cited in Dücane Cündioğlu, *Sözlü Kültür'den Yazılı Kültür'e: Anlam'ın Tarihi* (Istanbul, Tibyan, 1997), p. 219.
72 Ş. Şerif, 'Kur'an'dan Gafletimiz ve Sebepleri', *İslam Dünyası* 1, no. 14 (1913), p. 217.
73 Bereketzade, 'Necaib', pp. 23–6.
74 [Mehmet Akif], 'Mevaiz-i Diniyeden: İttihad Yaşatır, Yükseltir – Teferruk Yakar, Öldürür', *Sırat-ı Müstakim* 5, no. 116 (1326/1908), pp. 205–7.
75 Ibid., p. 206.
76 Zwemer, 'Translations of the Koran', p. 259. Ağaoğlu supported the use of translations; Ada Holly Shissler, *Between Two Empires: Ahmet Ağaoğlu and the New Turkey* (London, I.B. Tauris, 2003), p. 136.
77 Yusuf Akçura, '1329 Senesinde Türk Dünyası' (1914), in Murat Şefkatli, ed., *Türk Yurdu* (Ankara, Tutibay Yayınları, 1999), III, p. 278.
78 Kurzman, *Modernist Islam*, p. 254.
79 Ahmet Kanlıdere, *Reform within Islam: The Tajdid and Jadid Movement among the Kazan Tatars, 1809–1917: Conciliation or Conflict?* (Beyoglu, Istanbul, Eren, 1997), pp. 52–3. Though post-1908 press freedom was unprecedented in Istanbul, it had limitations.
80 Edward J. Lazzerini, 'Ğadidism at the Turn of the Twentieth Century: A View from Within', *Cahiers du Monde russe et soviétique* 16, no. 2 (1975), p. 248.
81 Ahmet Kanlıdere, *Kadimle Cedit arasında Musa Cârullah: Hayatı, Eserleri, Fikirleri* (Istanbul, Dergâh Yayınları, 2005), pp. 71–3.
82 'Petersburg'da İslam Matbaası', *İslam Dünyası* 1, no. 16 (1913), p. 256; Haşim Nahid, *Türkiye İçin Necat ve İ'tila Yolları* (Konya, Tablet Yayınları, 2006), pp. 128–9.
83 Kanlıdere, *Kadimle Cedit arasında Musa Cârullah*, p. 143.
84 Musa Carullah Bigiyev, 'Teessüf etmiştim şimdi anladım', *İslam Dünyası* 1, no. 10 (1913), p. 150.
85 'Haber: Daire-i Meşihat'te', *Tanin* 2, no. 1563 (1913), p. 6.
86 Bigiyev, 'Teessüf', p. 151.
87 Musa Carullah Bigiyev, *Halk Nazarına bir Niçe Mesele* (Kazan, Mahmud ʿAlim Efendi Maqsudov, 1912), p. 86.
88 Ibid., pp. 86–7.
89 Ibid., p. 92.
90 Ibid.
91 Ibid.
92 Ibid., p. 88.
93 Ibid., p. 90.
94 Ibid., p. 88. Q. 28:31, Q. 20:20, Q. 26:32, Q. 7:107 and Q. 27:10 also appear to deal with the staff of Moses incident.

95 The Biblical version (Exodus 7:10–12) says: 'And Moses and Aaron went in unto Pharaoh, and they did so as the Lord had commanded: and Aaron cast down his rod before Pharaoh, and before his servants, and it became a serpent. Then Pharaoh also called the wise men and the sorcerers: now the magicians of Egypt, they also did in like manner with their enchantments. For they cast down every man his rod, and they became serpents: but Aaron's rod swallowed up their rods.'
96 Bigiyev, *Halk Nazarına*, p. 91.
97 See Abū Jaʿfar Muḥammad b. Jarīr b. Yazīd al-Ṭabarī, *Tafsīr al-Ṭabarī: Al-Jāmī al-bayān ʿan taʾwīl āy al-Qurʾān*, ed. ʿAbd al-Sanad Ḥasan al-Yamāma (Cairo, Dār Hijr, n.d.), XIV, p. 527.
98 Bigiyev, *Halk Nazarına*, p. 91.
99 Ibid., pp. 91–2.
100 Ibid.
101 Ibid., p. 92.
102 Steiner, *After Babel*, p. 18. The saying by the Greek philosopher Heraclitus goes: 'No man ever steps in the same river twice, for it is not the same river and he is not the same man.'
103 Bigiyev, *Halk Nazarına*, pp. 92–3.
104 Ibid., p. 93.
105 Ibid., p. 91.
106 Ibid.
107 Ibid., p. 86.
108 Ibid., p. 37.
109 Bein, 'The Ulema', pp. 75–6.
110 Michaelle Browers and Charles Kurzman, 'Comparing Reformations', in idem, eds., *An Islamic Reformation?* (Lanham, MD, Lexington Books, 2004), pp. 1–17.
111 Bein, 'The Ulema', pp. 75–6.
112 Bigiyev, *Halk Nazarına*, p. 34.
113 Nahid, *Türkiye*, p. 128. 'Laz' refers to the populations living in the Black Sea region of Turkey, primarily those in the eastern portion thereof, and does not designate a specific ethnic group; Michael Meeker, 'The Black Sea Turks: Some Aspects of Their Ethnic and Cultural Background', *International Journal of Middle East Studies* 2, no. 4 (1971), pp. 320–21.
114 Nahid, *Türkiye*, p. 128.
115 Ibid., pp. 128–9.
116 Celal Nuri, *Hatemü'l-Enbiya* (Istanbul, Yeni Osmanlı Matbaası, 1332/1913–14), pp. 323–4.
117 Şerif, 'Kur'an'dan', p. 217.
118 Şeyh Muhsin-i Fani [Hüseyin Kâzım Kadri], *İstikbale Doğru* (Istanbul, Ahmed İhsan ve Şürekası Matbaacılık Osmanlı Şirketi, 1331/1913–14), p. 10.
119 Ibid., p. 14.
120 Ubeydullah Efgani, *Kavm-i Cedid* (Istanbul, Şems Matbaası, 1331/1912–13), p. 16.
121 Sabri, *Dini Müceddidler*, p. 196.
122 İbrahim Hilmi, 'Kur'an-ı Kerim Tercümesi', cited in Ergin, *Türkiye Maarif Tarihi*, V, p. 1610.

123 Ibid.
124 Halil Altuntaş, *Kur'an'ın Tercümesi ve Tercüme ile Namaz Meselesi* (Istanbul, Türkiye Diyanet Vakfı Yayınları, 2001), p. 88.
125 Ahmed Şirani, 'Kur'an-ı Kerim Tercümesi Hakkında', *Hayrü'l-Kelam* 1, no. 17 (1914), p. 136.
126 Altuntaş, *Kur'an'ın Tercümesi*, p. 89.
127 See Ergin, *Türkiye Maarif Tarihi*, V, p. 1927.
128 'Büyük bir Tecavüz', pp. 181–2.
129 Ibid., p. 182.
130 Gökalp, *Ziya Gökalp Külliyatı*, I, p. 113. The translation is mine.
131 Ziya Gökalp, 'Türkleşmek, İslamlaşmak, Muasırlaşmak' (1918), in Mustafa Koç, ed., *Kitaplar* (Istanbul, Yapı Kredi Yayınları, 2007), p. 49.
132 Andrew Davison, 'Secularization and Modernization in Turkey: The Ideas of Ziya Gökalp', *Economy and Society* 24, no. 2 (1995), p. 211.
133 Musa Kâzım, *Safvetü'l-beyan fi tefsiri'l-Kur'an* (Istanbul, Matbaa-i Amire, 1335/1916–17), p. 1.
134 İsmail Hakkı Milaslı, 'Kur'an-ı Kerim Tercüme Olunabilir mi?' *Sebilürreşad* 15, no. 390 (1919), p. 447.
135 Ömer Hakan Özalp, *Ulemadan bir Jöntürk: Mehmed Ubeydullah Efendi* (Istanbul, Dergâh, 2005), p. 261.

5

Translation and the Nation

A country in whose schools the Turkish Qur'an is read . . .

Ziya Gökalp (1918)

If God had intended to reveal the Qur'an in Turkish, its Gabriel would have been the author of *Safahat* (*Phases*) [Mehmet Akif].

Süleyman Nazif (1926)

NO EVENT AFFECTED THE course of Islam in modern Turkey more than the establishment of the Turkish Republic in 1923. In sharp contrast to the cosmopolitan, trans-regional character of the late Ottoman Empire, the new regime, based in Ankara, embraced nationalism and vigorously promoted the formation of Turkish identity, the use of the Turkish language and the development of national consciousness. The institutions, leadership and nationalist ideology of the new regime not only allowed for non-traditional approaches to Islam, but actively supported thoroughgoing and, at times, radical religious reform. In this context, proponents of translating the Qur'an, who were previously subject to censorship and considered dangerous intellectual mavericks, could now publish their works and win the favour of the government by doing so. In fact, the new Turkish regime made the Turkish Qur'an a cornerstone of its religious reform policy and sponsored the composition of a translation which it hoped to canonise as the official Turkish version.

Despite this favourable context, it must be stressed that the enthusiasm for a Turkish rendering of the Qur'an emerged from the late Ottoman intellectual milieu, not from the new regime. Far too often, historians, journalists and other observers have attributed the 'first' Turkish translation of the Qur'an to Mustafa Kemal Atatürk, the leader of the movement to create a Turkish nation state in the aftermath of World War I and the first president of the Turkish Republic. While Atatürk supported the Turkification of religion and created a political environment that was favourable to the emergence of the Turkish Qur'an, it was not his brainchild. After several writers and publishers sparked a public debate on translations, Atatürk became an important advocate of using translations in mosques and using Turkish as a language of Islamic ritual more broadly, but he cannot be considered responsible for the broad enthusiasm for translations that emerged from the late Ottoman period, nor for the translations which various writers composed. In fact, state involvement in Qur'an translation occurred only after private publishers printed translations of uneven quality in 1924 and ignited considerable controversy. The public outcry over these translations would lead the parliament to sponsor the composition of an officially sanctioned Turkish translation.

Islam in the New Republic

Following World War I, during which the Sharif of Mecca supported the Allies against the Ottoman state and all Arab-majority territories were lost, the policy and discourse of Islamic Unity had lost its credibility among important sectors of the Ottoman ruling class. The Ottoman Empire ended up on the losing side in World War I and, in its aftermath, British forces occupied Istanbul and arranged for the partition of the Ottoman Empire into regions ruled by different colonial regimes, as had occurred in much of the Middle East. Signed during the occupation of the Ottoman capital, the 1920 Treaty of Sevres between the Allies and the Ottomans stipulated that the Ottoman Empire would cede control of all its territories in North Africa, the Levant, the Arabian peninsula and Iraq. Additionally, it would partition Anatolia and Thrace among the Greeks, Italians, French and British, leaving only a territory in northern Anatolia bordering the Black Sea for a Turkish state. In signing this pact, the last Ottoman sultan, Mehmet Vahdettin (1861–1926), had agreed to what many considered unacceptable, humiliating terms which would reduce a major world power to a negligible colonised territory.[1]

Turkey avoided this fate due to the involvement of a group of army officers and intellectuals who rebelled against the Ottoman government and, against considerable odds, coordinated a successful resistance movement. The independence army and its leaders came to form the core of the new Turkish state, and an Ottoman military officer from Thessalonica named Mustafa Kemal emerged as the first president of the country. Inspired by the French Revolution (and perhaps also taking notes from the more recent Bolshevik Revolution in 1917), the new regime embarked on a revolutionary agenda of religious reform, the likes of which had never been seen in the Muslim world. It embraced a revolutionary approach to reforming religion and set about the task of creating a modernist, nationalist version of Islam that supported the nation-building project, and severed cultural and political ties with the broader Muslim world.

The new Turkish regime perceived the Islamic institutions present in the country – the ulama, the madrasas, the Islamic courts and the caliphate – to be inextricably linked to the Ottoman state, and to intellectual traditions and cultural orientations at odds with its vision of a progressive, European-oriented Turkish society. The ulama were the guardians of the Arabic–Islamic textual and legal traditions that formed a crucial part of the Ottoman judicial and educational systems. Despite the presence of reform-minded ulama, they embodied a conservative Islamic social order and, given their numbers and close relationship with the population, they formed a social bloc that potentially could form a strong political opposition group against the new government. For the Ankara government, the ulama represented a dangerous remnant of the old regime, whose powers needed to be curtailed drastically. Yet, the political marginalisation of the ulama did not begin during the time of the Turkish Republic. As we have seen, the Ottoman state had begun to weaken the clout of the ulama over the course of the nineteenth century; the pace had accelerated during the reign of Abdülhamid II and become even more pronounced after the revolution of 1908. However, these reforms had been incremental and never threatened the existence of Islamic institutions: intellectuals criticised the ulama, authors wrote satirical novels about the Sufi orders and the state reformed the madrasas, but their place in society never appeared to be in serious question.[2]

Under the republic, the new regime took a far more aggressive approach to the reformation of Islamic institutions. On 3 March 1924, the government demoted the governmental department of the ulama (Bab-ı Meşihat) to the Directorate of Religious Affairs (Diyanet İşleri Başkanlığı). Furthermore, it eliminated the sharia courts staffed by the ulama and abolished the office of the caliphate, the caliph being the symbolic leader of the Sunni Muslim world. Twelve days later, the doors of the madrasas – the backbone of the Islamic educational system – were closed. Since many members of the ulama worked in these schools and received their income from them, their closure created a wave of unemployment and even destitution. The pace of these reforms shocked observers around the world, generally delighting Europeans and Americans who applauded Turkey's turn towards the West, while horrifying much of the Muslim world.[3] Less than six months after the establishment of the Turkish Republic, the new regime had dismantled centuries-old educational and legal institutions which were central to Ottoman society, and had abolished an Islamic political office that dated back to the time of the Companions of the Prophet Muhammad. Within and outside of Turkey, devout Muslims feared that these reforms would permanently damage the vitality of Islam in the modern world.

Building on the late Ottoman enthusiasm for a Turkish rendering of the Qur'an, several authors published new translations in 1924, less than one month after the radical reconfiguration of Turkish Islamic institutions which occurred in March. Despite the demand for a Turkish translation, these renderings and their authors encountered an unprecedented level of criticism due to their timing, quality and claim to be 'translations' rather than mere interpretations. These Turkish translations of the Qur'an were published and received in a context of revolutionary reform and anxiety about the future of Islam.

The First Translations of the Turkish Republic

After the foundation of the republic and the dissolution of the Meşihat, the ulama establishment lost its ability to oversee and prevent the publication of translations. This political shift opened the door for the three Qur'an translations discussed here to enter the Turkish book market in 1924. These were Süleyman Tevfik's *Kur'an-ı Kerim Tercümesi*, Hüseyin Kâzım Kadri's *Nurü'l-Beyan* and Cemil Sait's translation also entitled *Kur'an-ı Kerim Tercümesi*. The translations appeared threatening to the ulama and devout intellectuals because they followed a series of rapid reforms carried out to marginalise the ulama and Islamic institutions subsequent to the Constitutional Revolution of 1908.[4] As the ulama's political power waned, it appeared possible to devout Muslims that the new regime led by Kemal might fundamentally alter or marginalise Islamic institutions, practices and texts in Turkey.[5]

The authors of these translations had similar backgrounds, all having worked the bulk of their professional lives in the service of the Ottoman state and in journalism. Not one of the three had ever worked within the religious establishment, nor did they have professional training in Qur'anic disciplines. Initially, each of them referred openly to their works as 'translations', and they all provoked a deluge of criticism. Both translators and critics claimed to champion the best interests of the people (*halk*). The translators promised to provide accessible texts in simple language to help the Turkish people understand the Qur'an. Critics, on the other hand, saw it as their duty to defend the people against poor-quality translations by unqualified authors and preserve the meaning of the Qur'an as understood by the discipline of Qur'anic commentary.[6] At the same time, each side accused the other of having malicious intentions. The devout intellectuals accused the translators and their publishers of being financially motivated, while the translators and publishers blamed devout critics for being excessively conservative and impeding the spread of Qur'anic understanding to the Turkish public.

Süleyman Tevfik (1865–1939)

The first translation to appear in print was Süleyman Tevfik's (*Translation of the Noble Qur'an*) in 1924 (See Figure 10, revised edition of Tevfik's translation). Tevfik worked for several years as a French language teacher and then in a variety of minor Ottoman bureaucratic posts until the Constitutional Revolution of 1908, after which he dedicated himself full-time to writing and journalism.[7] A prolific translator of French, Arabic and English texts, as well as the author of a number of compilations and simplified popular books on sundry topics, his translations include Arthur Conan Doyle's *Sherlock Holmes*; French novels by Victor Hugo, Alexandre Dumas and Émile Zola; and Arabic works including Ghazālī's magnum opus *Iḥyā' 'Ulūm al-Dīn* (*The Revival of Religious Scholarship*) and Fakhr al-Dīn al-Rāzī's Qur'anic commentary *al-Tafsīr al-Kabīr*. In addition to translations of European literature and Islamic works, Tevfik composed and compiled books on subjects as varied as fortune-telling, cooking, history, language, literature and how to write amulets.[8] Tevfik described himself as a 'people's writer' and a 'collector of anecdotes', and that he was.[9]

No small amount of advertising and questionable marketing surrounded the publication of his translation.[10] For each version, Tevfik used the pseudonym 'Seyyid Süleyman el-Hüseyni', a pen name that he used for many of his other works. In this case, as in previous ones, 'Seyyid' and 'el-Hüseyni' appear to have been chosen to bolster the Islamic credentials of the author, connecting him to descendants of the Prophet's family. In an advertisement for the book, the publisher Naci Kasım refers to Tevfik with even more honorifics, adding 'efendi' (sir) and 'hazretleri' (his exalted presence), the latter being a term of extreme deference, to the already inflated Seyyid Süleyman el-Hüseyni.[11] These titles seem disproportionate and ironic given that most devout intellectuals considered Tevfik to be nothing more than a popular commercial writer. Needless to say, this disingenuous presentation of the author as an Islamic authority displeased the devout critics and suggested that financial motivation was the driving force behind the selling of the book. Kasım, however, maintained that the publication was undertaken as a service for Turkish Muslims: 'It is impossible for those who do not know Arabic and Persian to understand the noble meaning of the Holy Qur'an which is the light of guidance of the civilised world.' Kasım argued that the Turkish commentaries of the nineteenth century were too archaic in style and language to be useful to Turks in the 1920s, and that these shortcomings had 'prevented the students from benefiting from them'.[12] He contrasts them with Tevfik's translation, which he describes as a 'literal translation . . . in a style that everyone can understand'.[13]

Despite these proclamations of good intentions, the book was not well-received. Most devout intellectuals criticised it vociferously and attacked Tevfik's character. His previous works on profane and esoteric subjects (including cookbooks published under female pseudonyms and works on sorcery) raised questions as to his credibility as a translator of the Qur'an. The influential Muslim-modernist journal *Sebilürreşad* denounced this translation as a 'misguided attempt' by an unqualified and morally suspect author.[14] Rather than analyse the actual translation, *Sebilürreşad* cast doubt on the reliability and moral rectitude of Tevfik by publishing passages he had previously composed on casting spells, parts of which involved the incantation of Qur'anic verses.[15] The review suggests that his work on black magic was involved in the translation, remarking, 'Sorcery is an art, but if it is mixed with Qur'anic commentary it is a great treason against religion and against the Qur'an.'[16] Though Tevfik's translation contained nothing related to sorcery, his previous works on the subject disqualified him as a reliable author on Islamic subjects in the eyes of the ulama establishment and devout critics.

Sebilürreşad's dismissal of Tevfik demonstrates that an important segment of the devout intelligentsia felt that Qur'an translators should meet the conventional requirements of moral rectitude and reliability that pertained to other Islamic scholarly disciplines; in other words, the quality of knowledge should be governed by its source and transmitter as well as by its content. It is important to note that the journal defined the translation of the Qur'an as part of the scholarly discipline of Qur'anic exegesis. This view differed from the understanding held by the translators and editors of early republican translations, who viewed translation as standing outside of the Islamic disciplines. For them, translation was a linguistic craft involving the transfer of meanings between languages, for which no special Islamic education or face-to-face transfer of knowledge was necessary. While they consulted commentaries to assist in their craft and some used the term *tefsir* in the title, they implicitly defined translation as a separate discipline informed by, but distinct from, commentary. Translators and publishers invoked the reliability and prestige of respected Qur'anic commentaries to add credibility to their works even while disavowing that they themselves qualified or even needed to qualify as commentators.

Hüseyin Kâzım Kadri (1870–1934)

Among the authors who published translations in 1924, Hüseyin Kâzım Kadri had the best chance of projecting scholarly gravitas and inspiring confidence in readers. However, the reception of his work was extremely disappointing for reasons that were largely beyond his control. His translation *Nurü'l-Beyan* (*The Light of Explication*) was released in Ramadan 1924, sparking a commercial rivalry between his publishing house and that of Süleyman Tevfik.[17] The publisher, İbrahim Hilmi, had initially intended to publish the book as a complete translation but, allegedly because of the expectations of bookstores, Hilmi decided to distribute the translation piecemeal.[18] In fact, it seems that Hilmi rushed to publish the book in order to compete on the book market with Tevfik's translation and ride the initial wave of public interest surrounding the release of the first translation of the Qur'an in the Turkish Republic. The publishers of both works placed advertisements in multiple newspapers, creating a commercial buzz that devout intellectuals and the ulama found disrespectful and scandalous for the Qur'an.[19] Like Tevfik, Kadri used a pseudonym – 'Şeyh Muhsin-i Fani' – a pen name that he had used previously with other works.

Kadri had studied at the English Commerce School in the port city of İzmir, where he learned English and French. He obtained knowledge of Arabic and Persian, as well as of Latin and Greek, through private tutors.[20] Kadri also had a keen interest in Turkic languages, studying Uygur, Chagatai and Kazan Tatar.[21] He composed a multi-volume Turkish-language dictionary that included examples of words used in 'Western Turkish' that had come from other Turkic languages as well as Arabic and Persian.[22] During the rule of Abdülhamid II, Kadri held several bureaucratic positions but left government service in 1904 and dedicated his time to agriculture and writing. He joined the CUP before its rise to power and held a seat on the central committee chosen during the first annual congress.[23] Additionally, he co-founded the newspaper *Tanin* (*Echo*), which became an organ of the CUP. After the 1908 revolution, the CUP appointed him to several governorships. However, Kadri later came into conflict with the party and was ordered to be exiled to Thessalonica; however, he and his family fled to Beirut in 1913.[24] After World War I, Kadri returned to Istanbul, where he became involved in the foundation of several political parties and served as a member of the parliament representing the province of Aydın. He held various positions in the Ottoman bureaucracy during the Allied occupation and then resigned in 1921.[25]

A bureaucrat, politician and author, Kadri harboured no illusions about his own competency in Islamic fields of knowledge. In the introduction to his translation, he acknowledges his insufficient training in Arabic, law, prophetic traditions and Qur'anic commentary, indicating that he referred to several colleagues for assistance in these matters.[26] However, Kadri explained that it was necessary to translate the Qur'an because 'the ability to compose Qur'anic commentaries' had decreased due to the difficult circumstances of recent times and the lack of security stemming from the various wars.[27] Kadri emphasises the loss of security and the difficulties of life as reasons for the emergence of simplified forms of Qur'anic commentary and translations. Kadri is referring to the Italo-Turkish War (1911–12), the Balkan Wars (1912–13), World War I (1914–18) and the Greco-Turkish War (1921–22), as well as the immense loss of life and sundry deprivations that these wars imposed upon the inhabitants of the late Ottoman Empire. For Kadri, Qur'an translation was a necessary substitute for the expansive commentary tradition; it was the genre of hard times. He writes: 'Therefore, it became necessary to obtain a large amount of information in a short amount of time and, from all quarters, people began to feel the need for a Qur'anic commentary to be written in Turkish for the Turks, which is abridged, beneficial, in line with contemporary good taste, and easy to study.'[28] Since the late nineteenth century, Ottoman citizens had turned increasingly to secular, European modes of education, leaving less time for Islamic studies. Trying to achieve a genre that provided the benefits of both commentary and translation, Kadri described *Nurü'l-Beyan* as an 'explanatory translation' (*tercüme-i tefsiri*).[29] The book's format provides the Arabic Qur'anic verse and then its translation followed by an explanatory passage.

Nurü'l-Beyan underwent a level of scrutiny and critique that few Qur'an translations in history have received. The journal *Sebilürreşad* published a series of detailed articles that enumerated the perceived errors in the translation. For instance, Eşref Edip (1882–1971), the journal's editor, acknowledged that he respected the translators as persons, but argued that they were completely unqualified to attempt a translation of the Qur'an. In several instalments, Edip identified and explained what he perceived to be errors, repeatedly asking the translators to acknowledge their mistakes and immediately 'pull their hand away from this matter without the slightest protest . . . leaving it to those who are competent'.[30] Most are instances in which Edip prefers one interpretation or word choice over another. For example, Kadri translates *ihdinā* (Q. 1:6) as 'Bize göster': '*show us* the upright path'. Edip claims that this sounds like a Muʿtazilī translation and would be better rendered as 'Bizi götür': '*take us to* the upright path'. It is difficult to agree with Edip that such an instance constitutes a 'heinous error'.[31]

Debates about fasting, and Q. 2:184

On 28 April 1924, Mehmet Rifat [Börekçi], the head of the Directorate of Religious Affairs, a newly created institution in Ankara under the direct control of the Prime Ministry, wrote an article warning Muslims that the translations of Tevfik and Kadri contained mistakes and demonstrated unawareness of the most basic elements of Arabic grammar and the discipline of Qur'anic commentary.[32] Initially, Börekçi assumed that Kadri had embarked upon the translation with good intentions but had erred due to insufficient knowledge. However, Kadri's translation of Q. 2:184 caused him to rethink this. The verse in question concerns the Ramadan fast and the provisions for those who have difficulty fulfilling the fast.

> *O believers, prescribed for you is the Fast, even as it was prescribed for those that were before you – haply you will be godfearing – for days numbered; and if any of you be sick, or if he be on a journey, then a number of other days;* ***and for those who are able to fast*** *(wa ʿalā alladhīna yutīqūnahu), a redemption by feeding a poor man. Yet better it is for him who volunteers good, and that you should fast is better for you.* (Q. 2:183–4)[33]

Commentators have debated the meaning of this passage for centuries. The crux of the matter is what the Arabic verb *yutīqūnahu* means in this context. The verb generally means 'to be able to' or 'to be able to bear', with a strong connotation of physical ability. Some commentators, and Arberry's translation above, interpret the phrase to mean that those who are physically capable of fasting but do not fast could excuse themselves by feeding a poor person. This understanding takes the text at face value, reading *those who are able* in the positive as the text has no indication of negation. According to this view, Muslims used to have the option whether to fast or provide food for the poor. In support of this view, the hadith collection, the *Saḥīḥ* of Muslim, contains a report attributed to the Companion of the Prophet, Salāma b. al-Akwaʿ (d. 74/693), in which the prophet is reported to have said 'When *and those who can shall feed one of the poor* (Q. 2:184) was revealed, those who chose to break their fast [during the month of Ramadan] fed the poor until the verse was abrogated by *Whoever is present during the month shall fast* (Q. 2:185).'[34] Most commentators who interpret Q. 2:184 as 'those who are able' argue that this verse was abrogated by Q. 2:185.[35] However, other commentators read the verse as having an implied negation, interpreting it as: *for those who are [not] able to fast*. For this reading, the Arabic negation '*lā*' is interpolated in the text.[36] This reading holds that *yuṭīqūnahu* refers to those who are *not* able to fast due to old age or chronic illness, and, therefore, there is no option for the healthy not to fast.

Following the former opinion, Kadri translates the controversial passage as follows *Takatı olduğu halde oruç tutmayanların her gün için fidye vermeleri lazımdır. Bu fidye bir miskinin itaamıdır ve tatavvu tarikiyle tezyidi hayırlıdır* (Those who are capable but do not fast need to give a redemption for each day. This redemption is feeding a poor person but the path of *tatavvu* is better).[37] Rather than recognise this as a valid interpretation supported by the commentary tradition, Börekçi described it as a mistranslation, writing that Kadri 'knowingly or unknowingly distorted the noble verse 2:184 and confused the thoughts of Muslims . . . Of course after seeing such an atrocious translation, we became suspicious of the translators.'[38] Börekçi, the highest Islamic authority in the country, questioned not only Kadri's competence and knowledge but also his integrity and good will. Börekçi insisted that reading the phrase as 'those who are not capable [of fasting]' was the only correct interpretation, and that refraining from negating the verb constituted a distortion of the text.

Having invested years of work in this project, Kadri was stunned by the accusations levelled by Börekçi. While he did not claim the translation was perfect, Kadri felt that Börekçi's critique of his translation of Q. 2:184 was both unfounded and unfair. He responded, 'Everyone knows that the text of the Qur'an is *wa ʿalā alladhīna yuṭīqūnahu* and the sublime meaning is "those who are capable but do not fast". To distort this by making it "those who do *not* have the capacity to fast" is not for me to do.'[39] Fighting fire with fire, Kadri describes Börekçi's reading of *yuṭīqūnahu* in the negative as a distortion of the text. Like Musa Bigiyev and other modernists, Kadri considered the assumption of negation to be a violation of the revealed Qur'anic *naẓm*. However, he did not base this judgement merely upon the language of the passage. Kadri cites the commentary works of Bayḍāwī, Rāzī, Ṭabarī, Ebu Suud (Abū'l-Suʿūd), Bukhārī and Suyūṭī/Maḥallī, all of which interpret the verse as 'those who are able but do not fast' and indicate that it was later abrogated. Rāzī, for instance, writes that most commentators understand *alladhīna yuṭīqūnahu* to mean 'healthy residents'.[40] He also points out that *Tafsīr al-Jalālayn* indicates that at the beginning of Islam there was a choice between fasting and providing food for the poor given that, in the second year of the Islamic calendar, Muslims were unaccustomed to the fast and this provision was offered as a means of easing their obligation.[41] Al-Bayḍāwī and Ebu Suud also submit that *yuṭīqūnahu* could refer to those who are able to fast, but break it.[42]

Given the abundant precedents for his interpretation and its linguistic plausibility, Kadri wondered how Börekçi could accuse him of distorting the Qur'an and confusing Muslims. He concluded that, for whatever reason, the head of the Directorate of Religious Affairs had malicious intentions and was set upon undermining the translation.[43] However, the writers at *Sebilürreşad* granted him no reprieve. Concurring with Börekçi that the translation had confused Muslims, Ahmet Hamdi Akseki (1887–1951), a leading figure in the Directorate of Religious Affairs, wrote that, due to Kadri's translation, some Muslims had actually broken their fasts while others had sought counsel with the ulama on the matter. Furthermore, Akseki argued that those who do not understand abrogation would think that they could 'give a few cents to a poor man and suppose that they are absolved from the fast'.[44] In addition to the alleged confusion caused by the translation of Q. 2:184, Akseki also challenged its validity, insisting that the verse commands universal fasting and never granted exemption to the healthy. Akseki contended that *yuṭīqūnahu* requires no negation because it implicitly means 'lack of capacity' or 'cessation of capacity'; he derived this interpretation from works on language, Qur'anic commentary and abrogation. In his view, the verse refers to 'those who can fast' *with great difficulty and hardship*, such as the elderly.[45]

Apart from its inaccuracy, devout intellectuals and the ulama also criticised the quality of the Turkish prose in Kadri's *Nurü'l-Beyan*, arguing that a translation of the Qur'an, if nothing else, ought to exhibit 'the full capacity of expression of the Turkish language'.[46] Leading members of the ulama felt that a Qur'an translation should be a literary masterpiece (*şaheser*) of the Turkish language. This feeling incorporated two complementary concerns, namely that the translation should convey some sense of the Qur'an's linguistic majesty and therefore not diminish the image of the Qur'an via mundane or mediocre prose, and, second, that such a translation be a landmark for the Turkish language itself, bestowing a new level of dignity and sacred legitimacy. Edip asked rhetorically where the full range of Turkish would appear if not in a translation of the Qur'an. 'In terms of language, a Qur'an translation should be a masterpiece of the Turkish language', he wrote.[47] In his view, Kadri's translation fell far short of this mark, and many passages failed to meet contemporary standards of the style of Turkish prose.

The devout intellectuals and the ulama believed the English translations of the Bible and, more recently, the translation of the Qur'an by the Ahmadi leader Muhammad Ali (1874–1951) had established precedents for literary achievement. While justified in many of their concerns, these critics had extremely high, perhaps even unrealistic, expectations for the first translations of the Qur'an. Kadri responded that the point of his composition was not to create a work of literary merit, but simply to convey the meaning to the people in a 'language that everyone [could] understand'.[48] Writing a highbrow literary translation would conflict with his primary motive of making the text accessible. For Kadri, the overly fastidious and hair-splitting critiques missed the point that the book was supposed to be comprehensible to a wide audience, and he held that it was unfair and self-defeating to interrogate every new interpreter about whether their work contained any mistakes because this would prevent anyone from attempting to write a translation or commentary on the Qur'an: erring was integral to the process and the inflated expectations, intrusive critiques and accusations served no other purpose than to stifle new efforts at understanding the text.[49] All in all, the negative reception deeply disappointed Kadri, who felt he had been personally maligned, and it prompted him to write several responses to his critics.[50]

Cemil Sait (1872–1942)

Several months after Ramadan, in September 1924, a bookish Francophile named Cemil Sait published a translation of the Qur'an. The son of a diplomat and writer, Sait grew up in a literary milieu and published his first article at age thirteen. He attended the prestigious Galatasaray Lycée in Istanbul and went on to attend the Ottoman Military Academy. Sait spent the bulk of his professional career as a military attaché at Ottoman embassies in St Petersburg and Tehran. In 1908, following the revolution, he returned to Istanbul and re-entered the literary scene. He wrote a series of articles emulating Montesquieu's *Lettres Persanes* called *İran Mektupları* (*Persian Letters*), in which he criticised current events in Istanbul. He also championed the women's movement by writing a play and a number of articles in the journal *Kadınlar Dünyası* (*Women's World*).[51]

Cemil Sait argued for the necessity of translating the Qur'an on the basis of practicality. In the introduction to his translation, he points out that Arabic speakers form a minority among the world's Muslims and that many Muslims are completely incapable of understanding the Qur'an in Arabic – a standard line of argument used in pro-translation repertoires. Given the important role of the Turkic peoples in the Muslim umma, he laments the lack of a literal (*harfi*) translation in contemporary Turkish.[52] In order to legitimise the need for translation, Sait makes a distinction between the genres of commentary and translation, and argues that traditional commentary provides the most well-known information about the Qur'an based on the Islamic sciences. However, he continues, conventional commentary does not always inform the reader about the exoteric meaning of the Arabic text so much as it provides the personal interpretation of the commentator. The reader, unaware of the exoteric or literal meaning of the original, then has no means of evaluating the interpretation in the commentary.[53]

Sait defines translation as a literal rendering of the text's exoteric meaning which complements conventional Qur'anic commentary. He disavows being an interpreter: 'My duty consists of literally translating from Arabic to Turkish. It is known that it is not good for a translator to clarify abstruse or vague points. That duty pertains to the commentators.'[54] Demarcating translation from Qur'anic commentary, Sait suggests that translation does not involve interpretation and that his task is to seamlessly transfer information from one language to another. As much as this view conflicts with the contemporary axiom that every translation is an interpretation, his non-interpretive definition legitimises the practice of Qur'an translation for writers without the conventional credentials for *tafsīr*. The notion that translation was not interpretation but a technical practice, separate and distinct from commentary, granted theoretical licence to authors of various backgrounds to engage in Qur'an translation.

Like those published during Ramadan in the same year, Sait's translation met with a brutal reception in the press. In addition to accusing him of incompetence in the task of Qur'an translation, critics argued that Sait had not actually translated directly from the Arabic.[55] It soon became almost unanimously agreed that he had composed the translation based on Albert de Biberstein-Kazimirski's French translation, which had circulated for decades in Istanbul and was the most popular translation among the Ottoman literati. In a memoir, Sait acknowledged that Kazimirski's translation had inspired him and that he had composed the work based on 'several different translations'.[56]

Akseki penned a stinging critique of Sait's translation. He excoriated Sait for translating the Beautiful Names of God, asking 'Where did you get the nerve to translate a special name of God that cannot be translated into any language? Didn't you understand anything from the commentators who wrote lengthy explanations on every word of the Qur'an but said nothing about divine names?'[57] Moreover, he accuses Sait of committing libel against God for calling the work a Qur'an translation since it is 'neither the Qur'an, nor an accurate translation of it'.[58] In terms of the actual text, he disputes Sait's claim that he translates the Qur'an literally. Akseki's critique focuses on Sait's translation of Q. 102:1–2:

> *Alhākumu'l-takāthuru ḥatta zurtum al-maqābira* (Arabic)
> *Emvalinizi tekasür etmek arzusu mezara gidinceye kadar sizi takip ediyor* (Turkish)
> 'The desire for accumulating wealth follows you to the grave.'

Akseki contends that the word '*arzu*' (desire) and the verb '*takip etmek*' (to follow) have no basis in the Arabic original. In his view, Sait had either based this on another translation or distorted the text because of his ignorance. It appears possible that Sait used Kazimirski's rendering of the verses, 'Le désir d'augmenter vos richesses vous préoccupe, jusqu'au moment où vous descendez dans la tombe.'[59] '*Le désir*' seems to be the source of '*arzu*'. However, '*takip etmek*' has no counterpart in Kazimirski's text, which uses '*préoccupe*' for the Arabic '*alhākumu*', so the translation is not completely dependent on Kazimirski. Though most critics were convinced that Sait had simply translated Kazimirski into Turkish, he appears to have used a broader array of sources and more independent initiative than previously thought.

Sait's translation of the term *takāthur* is similar to the English-language renderings of Muhammad Asad, 'You are obsessed by *greed for more and more* until you go down to your graves', and Pickthall, '*Rivalry in worldly increase* distracteth you until ye come to the graves'.[60] However, Akseki argues that this translation is incorrect because the word *takāthur* means neither accumulation of wealth nor greed, but rather 'boasting of one's own greatness' (Tr. *tefahür*). The translation of this verse hinges on the translation of the *hapax legomenon* '*takāthur*', which is also the title of this sura. For Akseki, the key to properly understanding the verses lies in the occasions of revelation (*asbāb al-nuzūl*), the narrative genre that explains the context in which particular verses of the Qur'an were revealed. Akseki points out that the occasions of revelation literature indicates that this verse was revealed when two tribes from the Medinan allies of Muhammad were arguing over which tribe was greater and had more members. In order to resolve the dispute, they went to the graveyard to count the tombs of the ancestors from their tribes, and the boasting of these two tribes occasioned the verse's revelation.[61] Based on this story, Akseki contends that the passage is not about greed or accumulating wealth, but a warning against vain boasting and pride. He goes so far as to say that Sait's translation has nothing to do with the original and is a 'fabrication' (*uydurma*).[62] Akseki recommends the translation,

> *Kesirle tefahür sizi beyhude işgal etti de kabirlere bile gittiğiniz*[63]
> 'Much boasting overcame you and you even went to the graves.'

Akseki's interpretation has a basis in the Qur'anic commentary tradition. However, Sait's translation of *takāthur* as 'desire for accumulating wealth' is also endorsed by commentaries that were respected at the time, including those of Bayḍāwī and Ṭabarī. Akseki's translation, on the other hand, appears to rely heavily on the commentary of Ebu Suud (*Irshād al-ʿaql al-salīm*), the famous Ottoman Shaykh al-Islam, which emphasises the term *tafākhur* (boasting, bragging).[64] It is difficult to go along with the outright condemnation of the translation given its linguistic plausibility as well as its support in the interpretative tradition. Akseki's fierce rejection of *takāthur* as greed is excessive, and represents another example of how Islamic leaders and devout intellectuals, in addition to reasonable critiques, sometimes went out of their way to discredit the new translations.

Moving from critiques in the press to formal announcements, Börekçi, on behalf of the Directorate of Religious Affairs, issued the following public warning to Muslims about Sait's translation:

> The work published with the signature of Cemil Sait by the name of *The Turkish Holy Qur'an* has been examined. As it is fundamentally not permissible to say 'Turkish Qur'an', it is also not permissible to rely on this work as a translation of the Holy Qur'an, [a translation] which, upon comparison with the exalted Qur'an, is clearly distorted from beginning to end. Therefore, we consider it a duty to advise Muslims not to be deceived by such works that are published with various purposes.[65]

Many others echoed Börekçi's sentiments. Given the high expectations for Turkish renderings of the Qur'an, Şeref Kâzım wrote 'these translations, despite being promoted for some time in gilded advertisements in the daily newspapers, caused a deep disenchantment in everyone'.[66] Most devout intellectuals received the Turkish translations of 1924 with a combination of disappointment and outrage. A newspaper in the city of Balıkesir reported an incident in the market in which a man saw someone holding a copy of a translation, which he seized, tore to pieces and then burned.[67] Reviews characterised these translations as 'mistake-ridden',[68] 'distorted',[69] 'atrocious'[70] and 'awful'.[71] They described the translators as 'negligent',[72] 'unqualified'[73] and 'incompetent';[74] judged their engagements with the Qur'an as 'misguided attempts' and 'deviations';[75] and branded them a 'sin'.[76]

Despite this inauspicious debut, Börekçi, like many other devout intellectuals, held on to the hope that a suitable translation and commentary would be written: 'We are of the opinion that a complete Turkish translation and commentary of the Holy Qur'an are necessary. We think that such a translation and commentary will be very auspicious and useful for our nation.'[77] Edip pointed out that if the translations had been of a higher quality he would have celebrated and commended them. Like other devout intellectuals, he supported efforts to render the text into Turkish and viewed Ali's English-language translation of the Qur'an as a model for success, admiring its format, paper quality and binding.[78] Edip wrote that the most noteworthy thing for Muslims was that the English press compared Ali's translation of the Qur'an with the English-language translations of the Torah and the Gospels, which were generally considered to be exemplars of the English language. In contrast, he viewed the Turkish translation attempts as failures in terms of both accuracy and style.[79] With these disappointments, the public looked to the state, which had long acted as the protector and guarantor of printed copies of the Qur'an, to remedy the situation.

The State-Sponsored Project

The opposition to independent translation of the Qur'an mobilised around the 1924 translations, precipitating calls for parliament to sponsor its own translation project. Producing an accurate, eloquent Qur'an translation now became a 'powerful idea among the public'.[80] On 21 February 1925, the parliament unanimously decided to fund a project to translate the Qur'an, compose a Turkish-language Qur'anic commentary and translate Bukhārī's collection of prophetic reports into Turkish.[81]

Even after the translations of 1924, which they deemed disappointing, the devout intelligentsia enthusiastically supported this project and viewed it as crucial to the spiritual life of the nation.

Edip described the translation of the Qur'an and Hadith as 'the most sacred task' and lauded the parliament's decision for being sincere and piously motivated. Additionally, he felt confident of a positive outcome because 'it was desired that the most capable and qualified writers would undertake this task'.[82] It had become clear that devout intellectuals would not accept, much less embrace, a translation composed by an author whom they viewed as unqualified, impious or motivated by commercial gain. The leaders of the Directorate of Religious Affairs, who had officially condemned the 1924 renderings, agreed wholeheartedly that the best and brightest devout intellectuals and ulama should carry out the translation. They did not disappoint the devout critics when they chose Mehmet Akif to translate the Qur'an and Elmalılı Muhammed Hamdi Yazır to compose the commentary. These authors, in sharp contrast to the three mentioned earlier, were well-respected by devout Muslims, the former as a gifted poet and Muslim-modernist journalist, the latter as a brilliant scholar from the last generation of the Ottoman ulama. It seemed that, at least in regard to the translation of the Qur'an, the fortunes of pious Muslims had taken a positive turn. Expectations were high that the collaboration of Akif and Elmalılı would produce a literary and scholarly masterpiece that would provide a textual foundation for Islamic life in the new republic.

The poet of Islam: Mehmet Akif Ersoy

Few figures loom as large on the stage of early twentieth-century Turkish Muslim literature and thought as Mehmet Akif Ersoy. A talented poet and an influential journalist, Akif was an artistic and intellectual giant of the late Ottoman Empire. He is best known for penning the lyrics of the Turkish national anthem ('İstiklal Marşı', 1921), but is also remembered for his Islamic journalism, his poignant poetry and his renderings of the Qur'an.

Akif's father was a religious scholar born in the region of today's Albania. He had emigrated to Istanbul and become a tutor there at the Fatih Madrasa, one of the premier centres of Islamic learning in the empire. Akif grew up in a devout family environment, and developed a pious outlook as well as spiritual discipline, which he maintained throughout his life. However, he did not follow the career path of the religious professional, but studied veterinary science and spent his early career working for the Ministry of Agriculture as a veterinarian investigating contagious diseases. Nevertheless, he obtained considerable knowledge of Islamic disciplines, learned Persian and Arabic as well as French, and read poetry voraciously. In particular, he developed a passion for literature, both Islamicate and European, and devoted the bulk of his artistic energies to composing Turkish-language poetry, which he published in the leading literary journals. Beginning in 1906, the ministry assigned him to teaching posts where he gave courses in literature and Turkish language.

The poems of Akif gained renown for their vivid images of late Ottoman street life and their ability to translate the contemporary pulse of life in Istanbul into verse. The poet's close friend, Midhat Cemal Kuntay, considered Akif's collection *Safahat* (*Phases*, 1911) an indispensible resource for understanding the texture of life in late Ottoman Istanbul.[83] Stylistically, Akif used all registers of Turkish, from street slang to high Ottoman, crafting verses that were lively and even carnivalesque. Additionally, Akif marshalled his poetry to comment on the state of the Muslim world. This included critiques of the ulama, scenes from mosques, images of excessive cultural Westernisation and hopes for the renewal of Islam.

In addition to his poetic life, after the 1908 revolution, Akif co-founded and edited the Muslim-modernist journal *Sırat-ı Müstakim* (*The Straight Path*), later renamed *Sebilürreşad*. He wrote original articles, including a Qur'anic commentary column, and also translated a variety of Arabic works, including those of the leading Egyptian reformist ʿAbduh, for whom he was the primary Turkish translator.[84] Like ʿAbduh, Akif hoped for a renewal of Qur'anic commentary suitable for the modern age. He supported vernacular commentary and criticised those like Sabri who felt that the classical Arabic commentaries contained all that one needed to know. Without a doubt, Akif figured among the most important exponents of moderate Muslim reformism in the late Ottoman Empire. He appreciated French poetry, championed the aims of Muslim modernism and criticised the ulama while speaking out against aggressive strains of secularism, Turkism and the abandonment of Islamic mores.

During World War I, Akif worked on several missions for the Ottoman intelligence service (Teşkilat-ı Mahsusa), travelling first to Berlin to inspect and counsel Allied Muslim prisoners who had fought against the Central Powers. In 1916, he received a counter-propaganda assignment in the Arabian peninsula, where he used his pen to combat British efforts to create an Arab uprising. While Akif and other moderates participated in the war effort, the Ottoman government seized the opportunity to carry out significant religious reforms in Istanbul. In 1917, the ulama ministry – Meşihat – was stripped of its power over courts and pious endowments (*vakıf*), both serious blows to the administrative authority of the ulama. Though Akif and other devout intellectuals had been firm critics of the ulama, even they thought that these measures excessively diminished the place of religion in the state. By 1919 Akif and his cohort abandoned their support of Islamic reform and became self-avowed conservatives.[85] In their eyes, the government had lost its credibility to carry out responsible religious reform, and appeared to be intent on marginalising Islamic leaders and institutions to the greatest possible extent.

After the war ended and British forces occupied Istanbul, Akif fled the capital and joined the independence movement led by Mustafa Kemal. He supported the Turkish War of Independence through public speeches, journalism and poetry that rallied his countrymen to the cause.[86] Yet, after the establishment of the republic in 1923, Akif made political choices that caused problems for his relationship with what would become the new regime. The Grand National Assembly was divided into two groups: the First Group headed by Kemal was secular and reform-minded while the Second Group represented a more culturally conservative faction. Akif joined the Second Group, which was quickly marginalised as Kemal's faction gained dominance and, ultimately, established a one-party regime. The Kemalist regime did not offer Akif a position in the government nor did it award him a pension for his two decades of work in the civil service. In October 1923, faced with a bleak financial situation, Akif accepted an invitation from his long-time friend and patron Abbas Halim Pasha (1866–1934), an Ottoman statesman and a son of Mehmet Ali, to spend the winter in Cairo. He repeated this sojourn in Egypt in the winter of 1924, returning to Turkey in June 1925.

It was during this period that the Directorate of Religious Affairs offered Akif a contract to translate the Qur'an into Turkish. According to many accounts, Akif did not want to take on the project because he had plans to compose a new volume of poetry and, secondly, because he did not believe that a translation was possible. He refused pleas from many of his closest friends who urged him to accept the commission. Given his talent, knowledge and standing, devout intellectuals and literary elites felt that Akif was the ideal person for the job. For the devout Turkish intellectuals, this project was the culmination of decades of discussion and growing enthusiasm for Turkish-language renderings, but the poet had mixed views on the prospect and utility of translating the Qur'an. On one hand, he clearly felt that it was important for Turkish-speaking Muslims to have access to such a text, and to become more knowledgeable of and personally engaged with the central text of Islam. On the other hand, Akif did not believe that translation of the Qur'an was technically possible and felt that the challenge of producing even an adequate rendering was daunting. Elmalılı, who was to write the accompanying commentary, persuaded Akif that the composition would not be a translation (*tercüme*) but rather a summary of the meanings (*meal*), and that such a work would be for the benefit of all.[87]

Conceding to this logic, Akif accepted the commission from the Directorate of Religious Affairs to compose a Turkish rendering. With his participation, devout proponents of Qur'an translation felt assured that the project was in the very best of hands, and, given the author, they had great expectations of a masterpiece that would be the equivalent of Martin Luther's German translation of the Bible, a rendering of a sacred text that could open the scripture to the consciousness of a nation in an entirely new way. However, Akif would not carry out this project of great national consequence in Turkey. In 1925, Akif left the country to reside in Egypt on what would become a permanent basis. For eleven years, from 1925 to

1936, Akif stayed in the suburb of Helwan outside Cairo as the guest of Egyptian royalty, and dedicated himself to the translation project and occasional teaching.[88] In fact, whether or not Akif realised it, he was moving to a Muslim-majority metropolis that would become the site of the most consequential debates on Qur'an translation of the late 1920s and 1930s. His migration to Cairo epitomised the movement of the translation conversation as well as the shift of Sunni Islamic authority from Istanbul to Egypt. With the caliphate abolished in Turkey, Egypt appeared well-positioned to claim the mantle of Sunni leadership for the twentieth century, and the question of spreading the message of the Qur'an via translation became a pressing issue for Egyptian scholars and leaders in the 1920s and 1930s. Though Akif was working on his own translation project he did not enter these Egyptian debates, as far as we know. Before examining Akif's story and the progress of the state-sponsored project (Chapter 7), it is crucial to assess the nature of Qur'anic translation debates in the broader Muslim world following the abolition of the Ottoman caliphate.

NOTES

1 Erik J. Zürcher, *Turkey: A Modern History* (London, I.B. Tauris, 2004), p. 147.
2 Yakup Kadri [Karaosmanoğlu], *Nur Baba* (Istanbul, Akşam Matbaası, 1922).
3 On Muslim responses to the abolition of the caliphate, see Mona F. Hassan, 'Loss of Caliphate: The Trauma and Aftermath of 1258 and 1924' (Unpublished PhD Thesis, Princeton University, 2009).
4 Bein, 'The Ulema', pp. 282–5.
5 Ibid., pp. 282–5.
6 [Eşref Edip], 'Kur'an-ı Kerim'in Tercümesi', *Sebilürreşad* 23, no. 597 (1924), p. 386.
7 M. Sabri Koz, 'Mehmed Tevfik ve Süleyman Tevfik', *Müteferrika* 4 (Winter 1994), p. 51.
8 For a bibliography of Tevfik's works, see Ibid., pp. 52–8.
9 Dücane Cündioğlu, 'Türkçe Kur'an Çevirilerinin Siyasî Bağlamında Bir Kur'an Mütercimi: Süleyman Tevfik', *Müteferrika* 13 (Summer 1998), p. 22.
10 Tevfik's translation *Kur'an-ı Kerim'in Tercüme ve Tefsiri* (Istanbul, Maarif Kütüphanesi, 1924) also appeared under the title *Zübdetü'l-Beyan* (Istanbul, Amidi Matbaası, 1924).
11 Naci Kasım's advertisement appeared in several newspapers including *İleri*, 7 April 1924 and 10 April 1924; *İkdam*, 7 April 1924. See Cündioğlu, 'Süleyman Tevfik', p. 33.
12 Cündioğlu, 'Türkçe Kur'an . . . Süleyman Tevfik', pp. 32–3.
13 Ibid., p. 33.

14 [Eşref Edip], 'Kur'an-ı Kerim Tercümeleri Hakkında', *Sebilürreşad* 24, no. 599 (1924), p. 11.
15 Ibid.
16 Ibid.
17 The publishing houses were Matbaa-i Amire and Maarif respectively.
18 İbrahim Hilmi, 'Nurü'l-Beyan', advertisement printed in the newspapers *İleri*, *Akşam*, *İkdam* and *Vatan* on 8, 9, 10 and 16 April 1924, cited in Cündioğlu, 'Türkçe Kur'an . . . Süleyman Tevfik', p. 33, n. 11.
19 [Eşref Edip], 'Kur'an-ı Kerim'in Tercümesi,' *Sebilürreşad* 23, no. 596 (1924), p. 377.
20 Hüseyin Kâzım Kadri, *Meşrutiyet'ten Cumhuriyet'e Hatıralarım*, ed. İsmail Kara (Istanbul, İletişim Yayınları, 1991), p. 7.
21 Ibid., p. 8.
22 Ibid., p. 24.
23 Ibid., p. 12, n. 5.
24 Ibid., p. 15.
25 Ibid., pp. 16–17.
26 Şeyh Muhsin-i Fani [Hüseyin Kâzım Kadri], *Nurü'l-Beyan: Kur'an-ı Kerim'nin Türkçe Tercümesi*, ed. İbrahim Hilmi (Istanbul, Matbaa-ı Amire, 1924), pp. i–ii.
27 Ibid.
28 Ibid.
29 Şeyh Muhsin-i Fani [Hüseyin Kâzım Kadri], 'Hazreti Şeyhin Sebil'e İlk ve Son Cevabı', reprinted in [Eşref Edip], 'Kur'an-ı Kerim Tercümeleri Hakkında', *Sebilürreşad* 24, no. 599 (1924), p. 8.
30 [Edip], 'Kur'an-ı Kerim'in Tercümesi', pp. 386–9; idem, 'Kur'an-ı Kerim Tercümeleri Hakkında', pp. 8–11; idem, 'Kur'an Tercümelerindeki Hatalar', *Sebilürreşad* 24, no. 601 (1924), pp. 35–7.
31 [Edip], 'Kur'an-ı Kerim'in Tercümesi', p. 389.
32 Mehmet Rifat [Börekçi], 'Beyan-ı Hakikat Müslümanlara', *Sebilürreşad* 24, no. 599 (1924), pp. 7–8.
33 Emphasis added in bold.
34 John Burton, 'Abrogation', *EQ*, vol. I, p. 12.
35 Jalāl al-Dīn al-Maḥallī and Jalāl al-Dīn al-Suyūṭī, *Tafsīr al-Jalālayn* (Damascus, Maṭbaʿat al-Mallāḥ, 1389/1969), Q. 2:184.
36 For example, ibid., Q. 2:184. For an overview of debates on the verse, see M. Brett Wilson, 'The Optional Ramadan Fast: Debating Q. 2.184 in the Early Turkish Republic', in Stephen Burge, ed., *The Meaning of the Word: Lexicology and Qur'anic Exegesis* (Oxford, Oxford University Press in association with The Institute of Ismaili Studies, Forthcoming).
37 Fani [Kadri], *Nurü'l-Beyan*, p. 52.
38 Mehmet Rifat, 'Beyan', p. 8.
39 Fani [Kadri], 'Diyanet İşleri Riyasetinin "Beyan-ı Hakikat" Unvanlı Makalesine Cevap', in *Nurü'l-Beyan*, Appendix, pp. 2–7.
40 Ibid., p. 5.
41 Ibid., p. 6.
42 Ibid.
43 Ibid., p. 7.

44 Ahmet Hamdi Akseki, 'Cevabı mı? İtirafı mı?' *Sebilürreşad* 24, no. 600 (1924), p. 25.
45 Ibid., pp. 24–5.
46 Mehmet Rifat, 'Beyan', p. 8.
47 [Edip], 'Kur'an-ı Kerim'in Tercümesi', p. 387.
48 Fani [Kadri], 'Diyanet', in *Nurü'l-Beyan*, p. 4.
49 Ibid.
50 Kadri sent a response letter to multiple Istanbul newspapers titled, 'Hazreti Şeyh'in Sebil'e İlk ve Son Cevabı', reprinted in [Edip], 'Kur'an-ı Kerim Tercümeleri Hakkında', p. 8; also, see his response to the Directorate of Religious Affairs: Fani, 'Diyanet', in *Nurü'l-Beyan*, pp. 2–7.
51 Dücane Cündioğlu, 'Bir Kur'an Mütercimi Cemil Said'in Kendi Kaleminden Özgeçmişi', *Dergâh* 9, no. 100 (1998), p. 46.
52 Cemil Sait [Dikel], *Kur'an-ı Kerim Tercümesi* (Istanbul, Şems Matbaası, 1924), p. 3.
53 Ibid., p. 4.
54 Ibid., p. 5.
55 Ahmet Hamdi Akseki, 'Türkçe Kur'an Namındaki Kitabın Sahibi Cemil Said'e', *Sebilürreşad* 24, no. 624 (1924), p. 404.
56 Cündioğlu, 'Bir Kur'an Mütercimi', p. 47.
57 Akseki, 'Türkçe Kur'an', p. 404.
58 Ibid., pp. 404–5.
59 M. Kazimirski, *Le Koran* (Paris, Charpentier, 1869), p. 517.
60 Muhammad Asad, *The Message of the Qur'ān* (Gibraltar, Dar al-Andalus, Brill, 1980); Marmaduke William Pickthall, *The Meaning of the Glorious Koran* (London, Knopf, 1930).
61 This story is present in al-Wāḥidī's famous work on the occasions of revelation; 'Alī b. Aḥmad al-Wāḥidī, *Asbāb al-nuzūl*, ed. Yousef Meri, tr. Mokrane Guezzou (Amman, Royal Āl al-Bayt Institute for Islamic Thought, 2008), p. 165.
62 Akseki, 'Türkçe Kur'an', p. 404.
63 Ibid.
64 Q. 102:1–2 in Ebu Suud, *Irshād al-'aql al-salīm ilā mazāyā al-Qur'ān al-Karīm* (Beirut, Dār al-Fikr, 1421/2001), V, p. 900.
65 Mehmet Rifat [Börekçi], 'İkaz', *Sebilürreşad* 24, no. 620 (1924), p. 349.
66 Şeref Kâzım, 'Yeni Neşriyat: Kur'an Tercümeleri', *Mihrab* 1, no. 11 (1924), p. 352.
67 'Yeni Tefsircilerden Müslümanların Ricası', *Sebilürreşad* 24, no. 602 (1924), p. 64.
68 Ibid.
69 Mehmet Rifat, 'İkaz', p. 349.
70 Mehmet Rifat, 'Beyan', p. 8.
71 [Edip], 'Kur'an-ı Kerim Tercümeleri Hakkında', p. 11.
72 Mehmet Rifat, 'Beyan', p. 8.
73 [Edip], 'Kur'an-ı Kerim Tercümeleri Hakkında', p. 11.
74 [Edip], 'Kur'an-ı Kerim'in Tercümesi', p. 386.
75 [Edip], 'Kur'an Tercümelerindeki Hatalar', p. 37.
76 'Yeni Tefsircilerden', p. 64.

77 Mehmet Rifat, 'Beyan', p. 7.

78 The text in question is Muhammad Ali, tr., *The Holy Qur'an: Containing Arabic Text with English Translation and Commentary* (Woking, Islamic Review Office, 1917). For more on Muhammad Ali and his translation, see Chapter Six in this book.

79 [Edip], 'Kur'an-ı Kerim'in Tercümesi', p. 387.

80 Dücane Cündioğlu, *Bir Kur'an Şairi: Mehmed Akif ve Kur'an Meali* (Istanbul, Gelenek, 2000), p. 107.

81 *Türk Büyük Millet Meclisi Zabıt Ceridesi* [*Proceedings of the Turkish Grand National Assembly*], vol. II, İntihab Devresi, İkinci İctima Celse, 21 February 1925 (Ankara, TBMM Matbaası), pp. 210–27.

82 Eşref Edip Fergan, *Mehmed Akif: Hayatı-Eserleri ve 70 Muharririn Yazıları* (Istanbul, Asari İlmiye Kütüphanesi Nesriyatı, 1938), p. 187.

83 Mehmet Akif [Ersoy], *Safahat* (Istanbul, Sırat-ı Müstakim, 1911).

84 Dücane Cündioğlu, *Mehmed Akif'in Kur'an Tercümeleri* (Istanbul, Kaknüs, 2005), p. 51.

85 Bein, *Ottoman Ulema*, pp. 45–9.

86 Ertuğrul Düzdağ and M. Orhan Okay, 'Mehmed Akif Ersoy', *TDVİA*, vol. XXVIII, pp. 432–4.

87 Fergan, *Mehmed Akif*, p. 190.

88 Ibid.

6

Caliph and Qur'an: English Translations, Egypt and the Search for a Centre

> Is not this Koran the abiding remnant of the Islamic community, after the Great War has torn asunder the countries of Islam?
>
> Muḥammad Shākir (1925)

THE ABOLITION OF THE CALIPHATE in 1924 by the Turkish government sent shock waves around the Muslim world.[1] After decades of Pan-Islamic activism by the Ottomans under Sultan Abdülhamid II and the CUP, the caliph had become a symbolic figurehead, if not the actual leader, of the global Sunni Muslim community. Though not recognised by some because the Ottomans were not of the Quraysh tribe, the Ottoman caliphate had acquired particular importance at the turn of the century as an Islamic alternative to the colonial regimes that ruled many Muslim populations after World War I. The British, French, Dutch and Italians controlled large swathes of formerly Muslim-ruled territories from Morocco to Malaysia. The end of the Ottoman caliphate opened the door to a reconfiguration of Islamic authority in the global umma. This brought about attempts to consolidate the caliphate in new locations, and caused Muslim intellectuals and leaders to place heightened attention on the role of the Qur'an as the primary guide for modern Muslim life. The loss of Muslim political power also opened the door to increased missionary activity in the Middle East – particularly in Egypt – which included polemic attacks on the Qur'an and the vigorous publication of translations of the Bible in Arabic and Turkish. With Islamic political institutions in abeyance and Christian missions on the rise, Muslim intellectuals from diverse backgrounds came to view translation as an important means of defending Islam, reinterpreting the Qur'an for modern times and spreading Islam around the globe.

In the wake of the 1924 Turkish Qur'an controversy, an international conversation sprang up among Muslims in which they wrestled with the question of what role Qur'anic translation should play in the modern Muslim world. The attempt to create a national version of the Qur'an, advocated by Gökalp and Ubeydullah, represented one end of the spectrum. According to this vision, there would be full nationalisation enabling the private practice of Islam and the distancing of the national community from the international umma. The other extreme position – championed most forcibly by Mustafa Sabri – held that the Qur'an ought not to be translated at all and maintained the hope of keeping the global community tightly bound around the axis of the Arabic Qur'an. Neither of these solutions appealed to the majority of educated Muslims. Outright nationalisation threatened to take away too much from the ritual and symbolic importance of Arabic; on the other hand, abstaining completely from translation stood at odds with the increasing literacy rates and attempts to better educate Muslims. Some intermediate position needed to be worked out, not only by individual Muslims, but also by the remaining Islamic institutions – the ulama corps, devout intellectuals and newly formed ministries of religious affairs. In the interwar period (1919–38), this intermediate position was achieved via landmark translations in the English language and by consent from the ulama in Turkey and at al-Azhar in Cairo, and by various Muslim communities in South Asia. This de facto consensus rejected the possibility that there could be a perfect translation, but accepted renderings of the Qur'an as essential for communicating its message among modern societies, for fending off Christian missionaries and for the projection of particular interpretations favoured by various individuals, movements and institutions.

In the aftermath of the Turkish Qur'an controversy, English translations and translators played an important role in shaping the translation debates of the late 1920s and 1930s, and, geographically, the Indian subcontinent and Egypt became central. In British-ruled

India, several Muslims took up their pens and set themselves to rendering the Qur'an into English, producing some of the most influential and widely read translations of modern times. No single religious agenda or political vision characterised these efforts. In fact, their purposes, commitments and backgrounds differed rather significantly. Muhammad Ali of the Lahore Ahmadiyya Movement, for example, wanted to put forth a new vision of Islam and spread this vision via translation. The novelist and English convert to Islam, Muhammad Marmaduke Pickthall, felt that no English translation befitting the Qur'an had ever been written, and he hoped to open a new window onto Islam for the Anglophone world. Abdullah Yusuf Ali (1872–1953), a Dāw'ūdī Bohra Ismaili who dedicated much of his career to the British civil service, made translation a kind of personal spiritual practice. Though they differed in their outlooks and styles, these translators were united in their cause to counter negative portrayals and to re-present the Qur'an – and by proxy, Islam as a whole – to the English-speaking world.

Courting the Caliphate

In 1914, a son of the Sharif of Mecca wrote a letter of great importance to Ronald Storrs, the oriental secretary at the British residence in Cairo. As the city was under Ottoman administration, the Meccan feared that the new Ottoman governor might attempt to depose his father, Ḥusayn b. ʿAlī, the king of the Hijaz. In the event of an anti-Ottoman uprising, he asked for British recognition of an 'Arab Khalifate of Islam' and an independent Arab state.[2] During World War I, the British supported the idea of an Arab caliphate, as they saw it as an opportunity to drive a wedge between the Arabs and the Ottoman caliphate. The idea was not new: the French had also considered it since the time of Napoleon, and by the mid-nineteenth century the Arab caliphate and specific candidates to head it were being discussed in France.[3] By dividing loyalties and aggravating existing tensions, the British used this idea during the war to carry out a divide and rule strategy to defeat the Ottoman Empire. They therefore encouraged the Sharif of Mecca in his aspirations and assisted his anti-Ottoman uprising of 1916, known as the Arab Revolt.[4] Prominent intellectuals such as Rashīd Riḍā supported the Arab caliphate scheme as well. Given Ottoman vulnerability during the war, they wagered that, with British assistance, they could wrest the caliphal title from the Ottomans and transfer it to a monarch in the Arab world. However, deciding which monarch should become caliph and how the said monarch would be recognised was a far more complicated matter.

The Egyptian jurist-scholar Muṣṭafā al-Marāghī (1881–1945), for instance, wrote a letter to the British governor general of the Sudan in 1915, arguing that the Ottoman caliphate had not improved the state of affairs in the Islamic world and suggesting that Muslims should decide whether or not the Ottomans should retain the office. The letter casts doubt upon the Ottoman caliphate and suggests that the office could, and probably should, be transferred elsewhere.[5] The great opponent of Qur'anic translation, Rashīd Riḍā, who envisioned an Arab-led revival of the Muslim world, also supported the formation of an Arab caliphate. Yet, according to these residents of Egypt, the office should not go to just any Arab territory but to the one best suited for it. Both Marāghī and Rashīd Riḍā made the case that Egypt, not the Hijaz, was the most worthy seat for the leader of Islam. Yet, despite the manoeuvring on the part of the Arabians and Egyptians, the location and status of the caliphate remained unchanged by the end of World War I.

When Turkey abolished the office in 1924, King Ḥusayn b. ʿAlī rushed to have himself proclaimed as the new caliph. This proclamation had no force and he did not gain recognition outside of the Levant, except among small groups in South East Asia and India.[6] His political position in the Arabian peninsula was tenuous due to the rising power of the Saudi state, and, additionally, other leaders sought the title. King Fuad of Egypt set plans in motion to have himself named caliph, orchestrating a caliphate conference in Cairo at which the next leader of the Muslim world would be chosen. Fuad campaigned for the support of the ulama and enlisted them to produce propaganda on his behalf. Marāghī convened the conference and Rashīd Riḍā wrote in support of the Egyptian bid. King Fuad also engaged in a public relations campaign with Muslims outside Egypt that eventually backfired. In 1924, the Egyptian king had his name embroidered on the ceremonial litter which Egypt traditionally sends to Mecca each year during the Hajj pilgrimage. The Sharif of Mecca refused to accept this brazen advertisement, and the event led to a severing of diplomatic relations.[7]

After a period of organisation and campaigning, the Cairo Caliphate Conference took place in 1926; yet, it had become clear to Marāghī that the conference attendees would not succeed in choosing a caliph. The process of inviting delegates from around the Muslim world did not go smoothly, as many Muslims believed that the exiled Ottoman caliph Abdülmecid II (1868–1944) was still the rightful holder of the office. Others, the Arabian leader Ibn Saʿūd for example, were opposed to the aspirations of Fuad and saw the conference as nothing more than a mechanism for Egypt to claim the title. Even in Egypt, many religious leaders opposed the king's aspirations. Forty members of the Egyptian ulama signed a petition stating that Egypt was not the appropriate location for the caliphate because it remained under British control and did not implement sharia.[8] Additionally, several political parties in Egypt, including the incumbent nationalist party, Wafd, opposed the idea of an Egyptian caliphate because it would elevate the monarch's power and complicate the ability of the government to rule effectively. To them, the caliphate issue threatened to reorient the Egyptian political map in favour of the king at the expense of the parliament.

When the Cairo Caliphate Conference was finally held, only forty participants from fourteen different countries attended and many important players abstained from doing so. Turkey, Iran and Afghanistan sent no delegates. Only a single representative from the Indian subcontinent attended and neither he nor the two Indonesian participants represented the most important ulama organisations from their countries. Nearly half of the forty attendees did not represent any organisation at all and participated as interested individuals. Mirroring the poor attendance, the conference proceeded disastrously due to poor organisation and the conflicting agendas brought to the table. While the Egyptians emphasised the necessity of the caliphate and claimed it was realisable, other delegates argued that it was impossible to revive the office given the political circumstances of the Muslim world and recommended that they maintain committees to work for a future realisation of the caliph.[9] Failing to achieve their desired aim, the Egyptian organisers felt that the meeting was deteriorating and decided to end the congress early. Egypt's attempt to re-establish the caliphate did not succeed, but Egyptian Muslim leaders continued to pursue ways to acquire more influence and leadership over Islamic affairs in the twentieth century.

The 1924 Cairo Edition of the Qur'an

The greatest Egyptian success in this period did not come in the form of political leadership, but rather in its efforts to amplify Egyptian religious authority. One of the crowning achievements of this era was the production of a modern edition of the Qur'an, known as the King Fuad or 'royal edition'.[10] As in the Ottoman Empire, numerous printed editions circulated in Egypt, possessing different numberings for the verses, inconsistent markings for *juz'* and also contradictions in the vowel markings. In 1924, the Egyptian Ministry of Education worked with a team of scholars to develop a standardised version that could be used in schools and replace the varying editions present in the country and beyond.[11] While the inadequacy of existing versions suggests that the project had purely practical ends, the arrangement of a new edition of the Qur'an was a project of immense importance. *Al-Manār* praised the efforts to create a revised, modernised version and argued that the new Egyptian version was superior to those printed in Istanbul (See Figure 11, page from Cairo edition).[12]

The committee based the edition not on any manuscript, but on the oral traditions that transmitted the reading of Ḥafṣ from 'Āṣim, the most widely used recitation from the eastern Mediterranean to the Indonesian archipelago. The 1924 Egyptian edition went through a revision process due to 'shortcomings', and in 1936 the Egyptian government issued the Faruq edition, named after King Faruq (r. 1936–52).[13] The Faruq edition became, and remains, the most widely used version of the Qur'an worldwide for both Sunnis and Shi'is.[14] Around the world, the vast majority of copies of the

Qur'an printed since 1924 have followed its verse numeration, diacritical markings and vocalisation. In effect, it has become the standard modern version of the text. In addition to this landmark in the history of Qur'anic recension, Egyptian scholars would also play a key role in translation debates of the early twentieth century.[15]

Muslim Missionaries: The Ahmadiyya Movement and Muhammad Ali

In 1925, roughly one year after the abolition of the caliphate, the Turkish Qur'an controversy and the Cairo edition of the Qur'an, a group of South Asian Muslims, little-known at the time, called the Ahmadiyya shipped English translations of the Qur'an to Egypt.[16] The Ahmadiyya movement had developed around Mirza Ghulam Ahmad (1835–1908), a charismatic Muslim teacher from the Punjab who made controversial claims of being the *masīḥ* (messiah), the *mahdī* (rightly guided one) and the *mujaddid* (renewer). The two main factions of Ahmadis, the Qadian group and the Lahore group, dispute whether Mirza Ghulam claimed to be a messiah/prophet (*nabī*) or rather a renewer/reformer respectively.

Mirza Ghulam and his followers often engaged in debate with Christian missionaries, and Christian proselytising strategies appear to have heavily influenced those of the Ahmadiyya movement. Ahmadis began their own missionary efforts in the West, sending teachers and books to other parts of the Muslim world, and their emissaries played pivotal roles in spreading Islam in both England and the United States. They revitalised the Woking Mosque – one of the first in the UK – outside London, making it an important centre for Muslim community building and outreach in Britain. Meanwhile, teachers from the movement who went to the United States were conduits of Islamic ideas and texts for American urban centres. The Ahmadiyya founded the first Muslim missionary centres on American soil in the early 1920s, initially working in Detroit and Chicago.[17] They won converts primarily among African Americans, and, by virtue of their presence in urban black communities, they influenced the development of American Islamic movements like the Nation of Islam.

Mirza Ghulam supported and engaged in a jihad of the pen. He and the subsequent Ahmadiyya movements wrote prolifically, and made the publication of books, journals and translations of the Qur'an a key component of their missionary efforts. In 1917, Muhammad Ali, the leader of the Lahore Ahmadiyya Movement – the branch that did not view Mirza Ghulam as a prophet – composed one of the first English-language translations by a Muslim, *The Holy Qur'an*. Vigorous efforts to promote the book abroad gave it an international renown that far outstripped other South Asian English translations. It was admired by many Turkish Muslims unfamiliar with the movement, including Mehmet Akif and Eşref Edip, who were impressed by the book's layout with side-by-side English and Arabic in parallel columns and viewed it as a model for emulation. The book, however, became infamous in Egypt where it found a hostile reception. When the Egyptian customs officials asked the professors of al-Azhar whether or not the book should be allowed to enter the country, the latter issued a fatwa banning it and ordered Muslims to burn any copies they encountered.[18] The commentary in the footnotes provides an idea of why this translation may have been offensive. It reflects some of the unconventional views of the Lahore-based Ahmadiyya group, and Rashīd Riḍā accused Ali of distorting the meaning of certain verses.[19] If in fact the Azharīs had studied the book, these words along with the footnotes would have certainly predisposed them against it. Muhammad Ali's translation also evinces a thoroughgoing modernism that would surely have irritated more conservative interpreters.

While intuitively one might surmise that the Azharī opposition arose from the fact that the work was of Ahmadi provenance, in fact, they expressed a more general rejection of translations of the Qur'an. Many of their responses condemned not the content or unconventional views, but rather the mere fact that they were translations. Most Egyptian scholars put the genre of Qur'an translation on trial and gave scant attention to the views of the Ahmadiyya. For instance, in 1925 the rector of al-Azhar, Abū'l-Faḍl al-Jizawī (d. 1927), was concerned that translations accompanied by the Arabic text would come into the possession of non-Muslims and enable them to touch the Qur'anic text, which would ritually defile it. In support of this preoccupation, he cited a prophetic tradition forbidding Muslims from carrying the Qur'an into non-Muslim territory.[20] Additionally, the importance of the Arabic Qur'an in the post-caliphate Muslim world played a leading role in these discussions. A judge and vice rector of al-Azhar, Professor Muḥammad Shākir (1866–1939), led the attack against Muhammad Ali's translation and denounced it in 1925. Shākir asked, 'Is not this Koran the abiding remnant of the Islamic community, after the Great War has torn asunder the countries of Islam? And after the Turkish republic has demolished the throne of the exalted Caliphate, and thrown aside the chief capital of Islam, just as a corpse is thrown into the grave?'[21] Without the caliphate and, in most cases, living under colonial regimes, many members of the ulama felt that the most potent symbol of Muslim unity – 'the abiding remnant' – was the Qur'an itself, the Arabic *muṣḥaf*. Turkish Muslims like Ali Suavi and Mustafa Sabri as well as Egyptians such as Rashīd Riḍā had made similar arguments prior to the elimination of the caliphate. Like these predecessors, Shākir reviled the idea of Muslim nation states using translations of the Qur'an in national and colonial languages. He accused translators of having a 'passion against the Holy Koran in the Arabic garb' and feared that the presence of a Turkish Koran in the Turkish Republic and, 'in the English colonies, an English Koran' would incite yet another battle within the Muslim world.[22] The situation would cause English Islamic populations and other colonial Muslim populations (under the Dutch, Spanish, French and Italians) to develop along different trajectories such that they would have nothing in common with the Islam of the Arabs. For Shākir, the umma – already politically dismembered and beheaded – would be further divided linguistically and religiously via translations.

In 1925 the marble courtyard of al-Azhar mosque in Cairo glowed with flames. The books that fuelled the blaze were neither Christian missionary literature nor anti-Muslim propaganda but copies of the Ahmadi translation of the Qur'an, which included the original Arabic text. Ill will towards the recent Turkish Qur'an episode of 1924, apprehensions about further divisions among Muslims and condemnation of the Ahmadiyya movement united a powerful faction of the ulama against the translation. Al-Azhar staked out a firm position against translations of the Qur'an with the result that the Egyptian state banned, confiscated and burned Muhammad Ali's book. The English Muslim translator Pickthall found this hostile reaction in Egypt to be both distasteful and misguided. Despite the fact that he had been a critic of the Ahmadi movement for some time, he was appalled that the Egyptians had burned a 'well-intentioned, reverent work' by a Muslim while openly hostile translations by Europeans continued to be sold, according to him, in Egyptian bookshops. Pickthall himself reports seeing European translations with inappropriate cover illustrations of the Prophet Muhammad and the angel Gabriel arrayed in window displays on the streets of Cairo.[23]

The displeasure with Muhammad Ali's rendering of the Qur'an spread across the Muslim world. The mufti of Beirut followed the Egyptian example and denounced the book, and in Turkey, opinions diverged as the author's association with the Ahmadiyya movement became more widely understood.[24] Though the initial reception by some important Islamic intellectuals – such as Akif and Edip, as mentioned earlier – had been warm, once they learned that Muhammad Ali was the leader of the Lahore Ahmadi community and that the translations were being used in Ahmadi missionary efforts abroad, this sentiment changed. Yet, conversely, Akif's son-in-law – Ömer Rıza Doğrul – was clearly impressed by Muhammad Ali, and he published a Turkish translation of the Qur'an titled *Tanrı Buyruğu* (1934) that included many of Muhammad Ali's views and interpretations. Just before Muhammad Ali's death, Doğrul visited Pakistan to attend the World Islamic conference in 1951. During his stay, he met with Muhammad Ali, by then an aging scholar, and described him as a superhumanly diligent author and saintly figure: 'his form had really acquired a sort of transparency and translucidity which were not of this world'.[25] Upon Muhamamd Ali's death, Doğrul penned a glowing eulogy, describing Muhammad Ali as 'certainly the greatest Muslim thinker and writer of our time'.[26]

Muhammad Ali's translation ventured to South East Asia as well, where it continued to stir up controversy. In Dutch-ruled Indonesia,

Hadji Oesman Said Tjokroaminoto (1882–1935), the leader of the nationalist Islamic party Sarekat Islam, set about translating Muhammad Ali's exegetical footnotes into Malay. Sarekat Islam was an umbrella organisation of various groups and forces working for Indonesian independence. As the president of the organisation, Tjokroaminoto was a powerful public figure and his engagement with Muhammad Ali's work was influential as well as controversial. The Egyptian-oriented reformist movement, the Muhammadiyah, in Indonesia initially approved of the Lahore-based Ahmadiyya and, therefore, endorsed Tjokroaminoto's project.[27] However, in a public debate, differences emerged between the leader of the Indonesian Ahmadiyya and a Sumatran devotee of Rashīd Riḍā. This friction caused the Muhammadiyah to oppose the translation and protest against it at the 1927 Sarekat Islam congress.[28]

Despite opposition, Tjokroaminoto persevered and completed the work, publishing the first volume in 1928. Many Indonesian reformers closely followed the writings of Rashīd Riḍā via the journal *al-Manār* and they were eager to have his opinion on Tjokroaminoto's project. A former Indonesian student of Rashīd Riḍā wrote to *al-Manār* asking whether it was permissible to use Muhammad Ali's work in the Indonesian context. Without reading the text – Rashīd Riḍā knew neither English nor Malay – Rashīd Riḍā issued a fatwa that condemned Muhammad Ali on the grounds that he was a 'Qadiani' who claimed that Ghulam was the 'awaited Messiah'.[29] This assertion was not strictly accurate, however, as Muhammad Ali had, in fact, split from the Qadian group and formed the Lahore group which considered Ghulam to be a renewer (*mujaddid*) of the Muslim community. Muhammad Ali had ceased to consider Ghulam a prophet since 1916. While he acknowledged Ghulam as a 'Muslim Messiah', he had an unconventional definition of the term 'messiah', which he defined simply as an important religious reformer.[30] From an uninformed position, Rashīd Riḍā considered Muhammad Ali's commentary to be deviant and heretical due to its Ahmadi provenance. However, the condemnation of Muhammad Ali's work in Egypt did not inhibit its popularity in Indonesia. A Dutch translation was published in 1934, just a few years after the Malay version, and subsequently

Javanese and Indonesian versions were published as well. Muhammad Ali's commentary became an important reference work for Sunni Indonesian reformers.[31] Many Indonesian reformists considered the Ahmadiyya affiliation of the work to be of little importance compared to the ideas it contained.

Through Ahmadi missionary efforts, Muhammad Ali's *The Holy Qur'an* also made its way to North America where it became a foundational text for African-American Muslim communities. For North American Muslims, the book was the only available English translation of the Qur'an written by a Muslim. It became an important reference through which black Muslims engaged with the Qur'an, and the commentary it contained shaped the way these American communities interpreted the text. The newspaper *Muhammad Speaks* printed portions of the translation frequently, though without acknowledging the author. The leader of the Nation of Islam, Elijah Muhammad (1897–1975), used the text frequently and quoted it directly in several books. He even encouraged his readers to study specific footnotes contained in Muhammad Ali's book.[32]

Muhammad Ali's translation also played an important role in England, where it was printed and distributed by the Lahore Ahmadiyya Movement. Mosque preachers used it for teaching and preaching at the Woking Muslim Mission. It was also translated into other European languages and many European converts mention *The Holy Qur'an* as part of their conversion experience. Anglophone converts like T.B. Irving and Pickthall read Muhammad Ali's translation in the early years of their Muslim lives before going on to compose their own translations. The pioneering effort of the Lahore Ahmadiyya to publish and distribute English translations on a global scale placed Muhammad Ali's rendering in the hands of Muslims from east Java, Istanbul and Cairo all the way to east London and the south side of Chicago.

As a globally distributed English translation composed by a Muslim, *The Holy Qur'an* marks an important turning point in the emergence of modern translations of the Qur'an and in the rise of English as an Islamic language. For the first time in history, a Muslim organisation disseminated printed translations of the

Qur'an on a vast scale to Western countries and across the Islamic world. The Ahmadiyya had adopted the Christian missionary strategy of producing scripture in a vernacular language and using it to spread their own message. In addition to its originality, the Qur'an distribution initiative of the Ahmadiyya surprised Muslim leaders in various countries, who had not attempted any comparable campaign. Though Muslim leaders in Egypt rejected and burned Muhammad Ali's translation, this work demonstrated that Muslims could spread their ideas and faith using modern missionary techniques, and made a lasting impression on some important figures in the Egyptian ulama. In sharp contrast to Turkey, where the translation debate had a national focus, the Ahmadiyya were globally oriented.

Novelist and Convert: Muhammad Marmaduke Pickthall

Marmaduke Pickthall, an Englishman, disembarked from a steam ship at the port of Alexandria, Egypt, in the autumn of 1929. Though he was travelling from London, he had lived for the previous four years in Muslim-ruled Hyderabad and converted to Islam a dozen years earlier, taking on the name Muhammad. He carried in his luggage the fruits of his labour of the past decade, a literary project which the Nizam of Hyderabad and many other South Asian Muslims had urged him to compose – an English translation of the Qur'an. It was by no means the first English translation. However, this rendering was to be the first composed by a Muslim whose first language was English. Pickthall's stature as a renowned writer and internationally known novelist further heightened expectations.[33] He made his visit to Egypt in order to obtain for his translation the blessing of what was arguably the most prestigious centre of Islamic learning in the world, al-Azhar. In doing so, he elevated the debate about translations of the Qur'an to a new international level and, with it, brought the English language into the spotlight. His trip to Cairo and his request for approval from al-Azhar also testified to the shifting poles of intellectual authority in modern Islam and, in the wake of the Ottoman collapse, the search for a centre of Sunni authority.

Pickthall made a name for himself, first as a novelist and later as a journalist and translator. As a young man, he spent two years in Palestine and Syria where he learned Arabic and developed what would become a lifelong love of Islamic culture. This experience provided inspiration for his most successful novel, *Saïd the Fisherman* (1903). Drawing upon stints in Turkey and Egypt, he composed several other novels with Middle Eastern settings. During the build-up to World War I, Pickthall became a supporter of the Young Turks regime in Istanbul that seized power from Abdülhamid II. He viewed the revolution as a momentous event, not just for the Ottoman Empire but for the entire Muslim world. He wrote, 'Turkey is the present head of a progressive movement extending throughout Asia and North Africa. She is also the one hope of the Islamic world.'[34] In 1912 or 1913, he travelled to Istanbul and stayed for six months. He studied the Turkish language, socialised in Ottoman high society and penned pro-Ottoman articles for publication in the British press. During the war, Pickthall became an outspoken yet isolated advocate for defending the integrity of the Ottoman Empire, which had joined the side of the Central Powers against the Allies. Despite the need during the war for British officers who knew the language and culture of the Middle East, his public support of the Ottomans prevented him from being offered an official post. He was passed over for a position at the Arab Bureau in Cairo and the job was given to none other than T.E. Lawrence (more popularly known as Lawrence of Arabia).[35]

Pickthall began to spend time with Muslim groups in Britain, primarily at the Woking Mosque, a mission centre of the Lahore Ahmadiyya Movement. In 1917, he publicly declared his conversion to Islam and, in doing so, became one of the highest-profile English converts in modern history.[36] The charismatic Khwaja Kamaluddin (1870–1932) was the leader of and vital force behind the Woking Mosque, located southeast of London. When he took leave due to illness in 1919, Pickthall took over his responsibilities for leading prayers and delivering sermons at the mosque. In this capacity, Pickthall became dissatisfied with English translations of the Qur'an which he sometimes used in sermons. The mosque used Muhammad Ali's translation, which according to Pickthall, 'seemed nonsense to the English people who came to my services'.[37] Translations by Europeans, he complained, treated the Qur'an as 'just a book not as a sacred book', turning its majestic Arabic into 'hum-drum' English,[38] and the philological focus of orientalists led them to concentrate on the meanings of individual words which resulted in inaccuracies. On the other hand, he continued, translations by Muslims often left words like *Islam* and *Muslim* untranslated, attributing to them a technical sense that they only obtained later. This tendency gave the translations a sectarian character by suggesting that the Qur'an was a book for Muslims rather than a universal message for all humankind; and so he began to compose his own renderings for use in the mosque and found that his audience received them with enthusiasm. As a professional writer, a Muslim and a native speaker of English, Pickthall saw himself as being in a unique position to compose an English translation that surpassed all previous attempts. The project of translation, however, would not be his immediate concern.

In the aftermath of World War I, the fate of the Islamic caliphate became a matter of intense meditation for Muslims across the world, particularly among South Asians, although interest in the Ottoman caliphate had begun long before World War I. While some scholars have maintained that the Ottoman rulers did not claim the caliphal title until the eighteenth century, recent research shows that Muslims in East Africa and the Indian Ocean basin had referred to the Ottoman ruler as caliph in Friday sermons (*khuṭbas*) from as early as the sixteenth century.[39] Additionally, when Muslim soldiers from British India were sent to defend the Mediterranean in the Turco-Russian war of 1877–8, the British encouraged them to revere the Ottoman caliph.[40] Moreover, the Pan-Islamic campaign of Abdülhamid II to promote loyalty to the Ottoman caliphate met with great success on the Indian subcontinent and in parts of South East Asia.

Subsequent to World War I, as part of the Treaty of Sevres (1920), the Allied Powers made plans to abolish the Ottoman Empire and deprive Turkey of all its Arab territories, including the holy cities of Mecca and Medina. The fate of the caliphate was thus uncertain, and the prospect of abolishing or disempowering the caliph profoundly disturbed Muslim communities living under British rule, so much so that it inspired the Khilafat movement in India, which attempted to convince the British not to tamper with the Ottoman Empire's territorial integrity and to preserve the Ottoman caliphate. It also became involved in the Indian nationalist movement, uniting various forces working for independence from British rule.[41] The Indian National Congress supported the Khilafatists and even Mahatma Gandhi joined the central committee. In March 1920, a delegation of the movement went to London to plead their case before the British prime minister, Lloyd George. They demanded the preservation of the temporal power of the caliph, his continued control of the holy places of Islam and the guarantee that only Muslims would govern the Arabian peninsula.[42] Though the delegation was unfavourably received by the government, they were welcomed at Woking Mosque and treated to a dinner party by none other than Pickthall.[43] The same delegation returned to the mosque in June to celebrate ʿId al-Fiṭr where Pickthall was also present.[44] Pickthall's long-standing support of the Ottoman cause thus became attached to the Khilafat movement, and his horizons began shifting towards the Indian subcontinent.

After World War I, Pickthall's steadfast Turcophilia caused him to be isolated in Britain, where many viewed him as a traitor. Though Pickthall's defence of the Ottomans had created enemies in England, it had won him friends in India, where he had become well known. In 1920, a newspaper called the *Bombay Chronicle* offered him a job as editor. Pickthall accepted and migrated to India. In addition to his editorial duties, Pickthall lectured to audiences across India on topics related to Muslim life and became actively involved in the Khilafat movement, speaking in support of the movement and even presiding over a Khilafat conference in Sind in 1921. Through these activities, he became close friends with Gandhi, and his loyalty to this friend eventually resulted in his resignation from the paper when its new owners asked him to take a hostile line towards Gandhi in 1924.[45]

Unemployment has a way of opening up time for neglected projects. For Pickthall, it meant an opportunity to return in earnest to his translation of the Qur'an. He had mentioned the project during a conversation with the manager of a media network in India and, the following day, found that many newspapers contained announcements about his 'attempt to translate the Coran into worthy English'.[46] In addition to the surprise of this unexpected publicity, Pickthall was stunned to see the enthusiasm with which the public responded, 'All Muslim India seems to be possessed with the idea that I ought to translate the [Qur'an] into real English, and that I ought to be subsidized for the purpose.'[47] Pickthall asked a friend in England to seek financial backing for the project there but also thought that wealthy Indian patrons might fund it.[48] His intuition turned out to be correct, and the richest man in India gave him not only support but also a job. The Muslim ruler of Hyderabad, Nizam Mir Osman Ali Khan (1886–1967), was reputedly not only the wealthiest individual in India but also the richest man in the world. He graced the cover of *Time* magazine and received accolades from the West for supporting the British in World War I.[49] His great wealth and famed jewellery collection made him the subject of popular fascination. He ruled the nominally independent state of Hyderabad in southern India, a domain of some twelve million subjects, the majority of whom were non-Muslim. The British resident appointed by the government in Delhi held the real political power but allowed the Nizam the autonomy to play the autocrat and to govern some aspects of local affairs.[50]

For Pickthall, Hyderabad represented an ideal Muslim polity in which a benevolent monarch ruled diverse subjects justly and an environment of interreligious tolerance prevailed.[51] The Sunni Nizam had a liberal stance towards Shi'is and non-Muslims, even helping build temples for Hindus. Pickthall's romantic imagination soared: he thought the Nizam's Hyderabad had preserved the Mughal Empire's ethos of religious plurality and harmony more than any other place on the subcontinent. Pickthall thought of the city as a 'sort of capital for all Muslims' and expected it to become the premier cultural centre of India.[52] In the post-caliphate Muslim world, Pickthall found hope in Hyderabad. In 1925, the Hyderabadi state offered Pickthall the job of headmaster at Chadarghat High School for Boys, and additionally supported his writing and scholarship.

The Nizam granted Pickthall two years of paid leave in 1928 to complete his translation of the Qur'an. Not content to rely upon his own knowledge, Pickthall consulted both European academics and traditional Islamic scholars during this period. He met with scholars in several European cities, travelling, for example, to Frankfurt to meet with the renowned scholar of Arabic Josef Horovitz (1874–1931). He also studied foundational works in European Qur'anic studies, such as Theodor Nöldeke's *Geschichte des Qorâns* (*History of the Qur'an*).[53] Additionally, Pickthall wanted to consult the ulama of Egypt and revise his manuscript under their guidance in order to avoid mistakes and 'unorthodoxy'.[54] Egypt's al-Azhar University had been an important centre of Islamic scholarship for centuries, but under British rule Cairo became the capital of Islamic modernism to which reformists from around the world flocked. The collapse of the caliphate and closure of the madrasa colleges in Istanbul further augmented Cairo's importance.[55] By going to Cairo in 1929 for guidance and approval, Pickthall was granting recognition to the enhanced authority of al-Azhar in global Islam.

The scandal surrounding Muhammad Ali's translation was known to Pickthall, but he thought that this had occurred due to the Egyptian ulama's opinion that it was a heretical Ahmadi work. Upon his arrival in Alexandria, Pickthall came to learn that the ulama were divided over the question of whether *any* translation of the Qur'an was lawful. Not only would he have to revise his translation, he would also have to make the case that translation as a genre was licit. In order to navigate the politics of the situation, Pickthall met with Shaykh Muṣṭafā al-Marāghī, a former rector of al-Azhar with a reformist outlook who supported his project. However, Marāghī had poor relations with King Fuad and had had to resign his post as rector.[56] Marāghī informed him that, in addition to the opposition of many scholars, King Fuad himself thought that translations of the Holy Book were 'sinful'.[57] Since the king was the patron of al-Azhar, no Azharī scholars were willing to assist with the revision for fear that they would lose their posts. This was confirmed by the famous Egyptian writer Taha Hussein, who suggested that Pickthall meet with the king to try to change his views on the matter. Pickthall was dismayed by the rigidity of the Egyptian ulama, their lack of cooperation as well as the condescending attitude of the Egyptian scholars towards non-Arab Muslims.[58] Ultimately, no one from al-Azhar assisted him. However, a lecturer in chemistry at the medical school – not a member of the ulama – offered to work with Pickthall on the translation, and the two revised the text for three months.[59] They worked in relative peace until the newspaper *al-Ahrām* published an article about Pickthall's project. It prompted Shākir, the leader of the attack on Muhammad Ali, to publicly condemn the translation and warn of eternal damnation for Pickthall, those who helped him, those who read the translation and those who approved of it.[60] A number of letters supporting the translation appeared in the newspaper, revealing a divide among Azharites scholars and prompting Shākir to modify his position and grudgingly admit that such a book might be beneficial. Pickthall came away from this episode thinking that public opinion in Egypt was very favourable towards Qur'anic translation.[61]

The process of seeking al-Azhar's approval appears to have been completely informal. At one point, the rector of al-Azhar, Muḥammad al-Zawāhirī (1878–1944), a Shāfiʿī scholar and opponent of translations, told Pickthall that 'there can be no objection' if the work were to be called 'the meaning of the Glorious Qur'an', not a *translation* of the Qur'an, and that if this should be the case 'we shall all be pleased with it'. In this way, the book would be presented as merely a rendering of Qur'anic meanings, not a substitute for the original. However, after Pickthall left Egypt, the very same rector declared the book unsuitable to be approved in Egypt, despite the fact that it was 'the best of all translations'.[62] The reason for this judgement was that Pickthall had allegedly translated Arabic metaphors and idioms in a literal fashion. Since the Azharites did not read English, they allegedly translated his book back into Arabic and evaluated it in that bizarre form. Though the conservative orientation of the Azharites severely disappointed the English Muslim, he found hope in the fact that they had ceased to condemn all translations of the Qur'an. 'A translation of the Qur'an by a Muslim has been examined and a literary reason has been given for its condemnation. That is a great step forward.'[63]

Ever the loyal subject, Pickthall dedicated the book to his patron, the Nizam. Through the translation, the Nizam put his imprint on a major piece of modern scholarship. With this project and his other initiatives, the Nizam appeared to be positioning himself as the most prominent Muslim ruler and patron of Islamic scholarship in the post-caliphate era. He also established *Islamic Culture*, a journal promoting modernist Islam and edited by Pickthall. In addition, the Nizam paid for the living expenses of the exiled, former Ottoman caliph, Abdülmecid II. The last caliph and his family lived in a large villa outside Nice on the French Riviera courtesy of wealthy Muslim donors like the Nizam.[64] Most striking of all, the Nizam arranged marriages between his two sons, princes of Hyderabad, and the daughter and cousin of the deposed caliph. The intermediary who organised these unions was Pickthall himself, who drew on his Ottoman connections to make these royal Muslim marriages a reality. The Nizam agreed to provide the ex-caliph with a stipend of $2,000 per month for the rest of his life and gave the daughter Dürrü Shehvar a dowry of $200,000, and the cousin a sum of $75,000.[65] Through Pickthall's mediation, the most precious brides in the Muslim world joined the house of Hyderabad.

The union of the Ottoman and Hyderabadi families was pregnant with implications, and observers speculated that the Nizam was attempting to stake a claim on the caliphate or, at the very least, obtain some of its prestige. Bringing the caliphate to Hyderabad, or anywhere, was no simple matter. Some Muslims persisted in recognising Abdülmecid II as the actual caliph and petitioned the British to have him installed in Jerusalem. Abdülmecid II didn't rule out this possibility and, even during the weddings, indicated to the press that he was in regular correspondence with the mufti of Jerusalem.[66]

Despite assisting in the marriage arrangements, it is unclear what Pickthall hoped would come of the Ottoman–Hyderabadi union. For years, Pickthall had dedicated himself to the Khilafat movement and avidly defended the Ottoman caliphate. Even after the abolition of the office, he wrote, 'I am a Khalifatist and a close personal friend, I think I may say, of the last Khalifa.'[67] The Nizam, on the other hand, had opposed the Khilafat movement and did not tolerate Khilafatists in the state of Hyderabad.[68] However, the

Nizam's financial support of the ex-caliph and his aspirations to transfer something of the caliph's prestige to Hyderabad appear to have bridged the differences between the men. Pickthall came to believe that the Nizam shared his devotion to the Ottoman caliph.[69]

If in fact the Nizam had aspirations to base a caliphate in Hyderabad, it never materialised. After Indian independence in 1948, Hyderabad was incorporated in the nation state of India and the nizamate ceased to have any political authority. With his political legacy in shambles, it now appears that the Nizam made his most lasting contribution to modern Islam through his patronage of Pickthall. The disapproval of al-Azhar did not hinder the publication and resounding success of Pickthall's translation. In fact, it became one of the most widely circulated versions in any language. *The Meaning of the Holy Qur'an* has been immensely influential upon subsequent English translations and remains widely used globally.

A Man of the Empire: Abdullah Yusuf Ali

In 1953 a south Asian man died in London. He passed away by himself, and, not knowing where he lived, his family members did not even realise that he had died. After a life of public service, the private misery of this international statesman and author came into view. He was buried in the same cemetery as Pickthall, southeast of London, their tombs nearby one another. Though both men were Muslims and had strong connections with India and Britain, their life trajectories were almost complete opposites. Nevertheless, both men became best known for writing translations of the Qur'an that gained immense popularity among Anglophone Muslims.

Whereas Pickthall was born British and converted to Islam, Yusuf Ali was born Muslim and became British. He came from a family of Dāw'udī Bohras, a South Asian Ismaili Shi'i community that traces its roots back to the Musta'lī Ismailis of medieval Islam. In many ways, Yusuf Ali's life was profoundly influenced by his career as a British civil official. Even when considering his seminal translation of the Qur'an, it becomes apparent that a sense of Britishness informed and, to some extent, inspired his engagement with the Holy Book.

For Yusuf Ali, India was a land united by empire and bound by the tie of English language. English made Pan-Indian unity possible as he believed it was 'the greatest bond which has linked together Indians of all provinces and communities. Without this bond the federation of India [would] be an ideal dream.'[70] He believed the language also gave the Indian subcontinent access to the cosmopolitan world as he considered English to be 'the medium of communication . . . with the outside world'.[71] Yusuf Ali wanted to make the Qur'an resonate within this Anglophone context and boldly stated his ambition of making 'English itself an Islamic language'.[72]

Yusuf Ali completed a BA in Classics at Bombay University in 1891 and continued his studies at St Johns College at Cambridge University in law. In 1895, he entered the Indian Civil Service, the branch of the British Empire that directly governed India.[73] In addition to his civil service career, Ali began to take on the role of international activist and statesman. M.A. Sherif's biography shows that Yusuf Ali demonstrated an unwavering loyalty to Britain, siding with the Crown against popular Muslim sentiments on many an occasion. At the Kanpur Mosque Affair of 1913, the colonial administration planned to demolish part of a mosque in order to widen a road in Kanpur. This incident sparked a united opposition from Muslims across India, but Yusuf Ali nevertheless supported the plan, aligning himself with the British. Additionally, he was an enthusiastic supporter of the British war effort against the Ottoman Empire in World War I, placing him at odds with the Indian Khilafat movement.[74]

During the late 1920s, Yusuf Ali oversaw a study group called the Progressive Islam Association, which promoted Islam as a source of ethical and spiritual inspiration in the contemporary world. It was during this period that he commenced his translation of the Qur'an. He composed the work while continuing his active public life, including sponsored lecture tours that took him throughout East and South Asia. The project was his solitary, nocturnal occupation in contrast to the public, social daily activities of meetings, conferences and lectures. He translated and composed part of the work in different climes, on various continents and between them on ocean liners, one of his favourite writing venues.[75] Involvement in various Muslim associations and educational institutions also coloured his translating period. Like Pickthall, he worked as a school headmaster (in Lahore) during the final stages of the translation, and it was his students who allegedly urged him to publish the work and also found a calligrapher and printing house for the job.[76]

The translation was first published in Lahore in 1934. Like Muhammad Ali, Yusuf Ali included a running commentary in the form of footnotes, the final tally of which exceeded 6,000. The commentary is unconventional in that it bears a heavy imprint from its author and reflects a wide array of influences. The English literary heritage makes what is perhaps an unprecedented appearance in Qur'anic commentary as the author invokes Shakespeare, Milton and Tennyson to illuminate passages.[77] Perhaps reflecting a Platonic or Ismaili sensibility, he interprets many of elements in the Qur'an metaphorically, in what Sherif calls a 'heavy handed search for symbols'.[78] While his translation has become a classic, many reprints of the work excise his highly original commentary.

The unique character of the commentary accords with the overall impression that Yusuf Ali's engagement with the Qur'an was intensely personal. He viewed Islam as an apolitical force for ethical guidance and individual inspiration, and he valued, perhaps even privileged, the Qur'an's message of comfort and inspiration for the individual. Yusuf Ali urges the reader, 'Read, study and digest the Holy Book. Read slowly, and let it sink into your heart and soul.'[79] The intimate, personal character of his magnum opus contributed greatly to its appeal. In the introduction, he mentions the devastating personal crises for which he found aid and hope in the Qur'an.[80]

A stormy personal life formed the backdrop to Yusuf Ali's successful public career. The infidelity of his first wife dealt him a crushing psychological blow, and both of his marriages failed. Due to his career in public life, he was little involved in the lives of his children and became completely estranged from them. He disinherited the two children from his first marriage, giving the majority of his estate to a fund that would provide scholarships for Indian students at the University of London.[81] Yusuf Ali thrived in his public work for institutions and political causes but struggled in relationships with those closest to him. As his health deteriorated later in life, he had neither friend nor family to care for him.[82] While virtually none of this was known to readers, his struggles influenced the translation, leading to the mystical, otherworldly sensibility that made the book special.

The chilly personal relationships of Yusuf Ali combined with his pro-British views appear to have coloured the reception of his translation. Those who knew him personally did not embrace it with the same enthusiasm as the larger English-reading Muslim public. The poet and intellectual Muhammad Iqbal knew Yusuf Ali well and had hired him as headmaster at Islamia College in Lahore. Yet the two had very different political allegiances, and Iqbal never offered a word of commendation for his translation.[83] Pickthall was acquainted with Yusuf Ali from London and had read many of his writings. Calling Yusuf Ali's translation the best English translation 'by an Indian', Pickthall penned an icy review that criticised Yusuf Ali for imposing his own literary style on the Qur'an and for his 'ecstatic comments' that resemble the style of the 'chorus in Greek tragedies'.[84] He characterised the text as 'a careless, inexact translation' and thought that its greatest merit was the unconventional, highly personal commentary.[85] Pickthall sarcastically suggested that the book would be of use to Indian Muslims who 'know English better than the teaching of their own Qur'an'.[86] With these acerbic comments, the English convert went well beyond textual criticism.

The practitioner of a decidedly non-political but devout and personal Islam, Yusuf Ali placed his political hope for the future in international institutions. He defended the League of Nations throughout the 1920s and considered it to be the best institution for promoting world peace. The League sponsored him to give a series of talks on the subject 'peace through religion', where he was called *le grand chef musulman*, and Yusuf Ali even mentions the League in his commentary on *Sūrat al-Nūr* (Q. 24) in a reference to the problem of modern slave trafficking.[87] However, the League's failure to take action against the Italian incursion on Ethiopia caused him to lose faith in the institution. He then turned to the alliance of the

United States and Britain as a hopeful candidate for ensuring peace, citing the bond of their common language.[88] The only issue on which he voiced criticism of British policy was the question of British Palestine and the creation of a Jewish state. He argued that Muslims would not accept the transfer of such an important part of Arab land to a foreign people and informed the public that this partition was a grave error.[89]

***

The three seminal English translations by Muslims in the early twentieth century aimed to help the individual to engage in personal study of the Qur'an and, additionally, to create an English-language representation of the book that gave precedence to Muslim sensibilities and countered negative portrayals created by non-Muslims. As in the Turkish case, none of the authors were traditional Islamic scholars, and each of them embraced aspects of Muslim modernism in distinct combinations. Nevertheless, the differences in background, politics and identities of the authors were vast. The leader of the Lahore Ahmadiyya Movement Muhammad Ali, the English novelist and convert Marmaduke Pickthall, and the British loyalist Abdullah Yusuf Ali were a motley crew. They composed very different kinds of translations for very different purposes. Yet, their combined efforts introduced the Qur'an to a much larger English-reading audience than ever before, and, crucially, they helped normalise the genre of Qur'an translation for Muslim authors. Despite the backlash from the Turkish Qur'an episode and the opposition of al-Azhar, the popularity of translations in a variety of languages soared.

The Debate in Egypt

After Pickthall's trip to Cairo, the translation debate escalated to new heights in Egypt. Rather than resolving the issue, the Pickthall episode resulted in Egyptian intellectuals becoming more divided than ever. Cairo became the new centre of academic debate on the subject of Qur'an translations as practical efforts to translate and disseminate the scripture gained momentum on various continents. The escalating dispute prompted many Egyptians, including some of the most important figures of the period, to write articles, treatises and books on the subject.

Why would Egyptian Muslims, who spoke Arabic and used it as their written language as well, take such an interest in translations? After all, such translations were not likely to have much, if any, effect on affairs in Egypt. The answer lies in the increasingly global orientation of the Islamic intelligentsia and al-Azhar. For Sunni Muslims around the world, Egypt became a nexus of authority after the fall of the Ottoman caliphate. The global reach of *al-Manār* and the prestige of al-Azhar made Egypt more important than ever in the post-caliphate Muslim world. In order to assert al-Azhar's influence on the development of modern Islam, some scholars, like Marāghī, held that Egyptian Islamic institutions should establish ties with non-Arab Muslim communities via translations that would counter the deleterious effects of Christian missionary activities and contribute to the spread of Islam. As with the caliphate issue, Egypt attempted to assert itself as the new leader of the Muslim world in the sphere of translations. By composing and distributing an English-language rendering, the Egyptian religious establishment hoped to project its Islamic authority both within and beyond the Muslim world.

In the 1930s, there was profound concern in Egypt over the intensification of Christian missionary activities in the country. Around the turn of the century, Christian missions began to view Egypt as a headquarters for its proselytising efforts in the Muslim world.[90] Under the protection of the British, missionary activities expanded rapidly, creating profound discomfort among Muslim leaders. In a series of articles in 1930, the newspaper *al-Fatḥ* urged Muslims to create their own methods of propaganda and evangelism.[91] In the same year, at the American mission building, a convert from Islam to Christianity named Kāmil Manṣūr gave a controversial talk in which he reportedly criticised the Qur'an and argued that Muhammad was inferior to Jesus. News of the event reached the newspapers which publicised the affair, leading to Manṣūr's arrest. Manṣūr was tried for insulting Islam, and the jury acquitted him of all charges.[92] Public disapproval of missionary activities intensified, and top ulama officials capitalised on anti-missionary sentiment. Marāghī, for instance, later established the Society for the Defence of Islam to combat evangelical activities.[93]

Missionary activities, on the part of both the Ahmadis and the Christians, contributed directly to the call for Qur'an translation in Egypt. The highly publicised conversion of a Muslim student to Christianity in January 1932 catalysed public opinion against Christian missions. In the very same month, the controversy over translations of the Qur'an flared again. A prolific reformist scholar named Farīd Wajdī (1875–1954) put forth the argument that translations of the Qur'an were essential for spreading Islam around the globe. Wajdī stressed that the Qur'an was addressed to the entire human race, not to a chosen people, and commanded Muslims to share its message in all conceivable ways.[94] He argued that modern nations prefer to obtain information directly, and that translation was indispensible for transmitting the Qur'an in the modern age.[95] Responding to the idea that Muslims worldwide could be united by teaching Arabic in schools, he wrote that linguistic unity for four hundred million Muslims was a fantasy, especially considering the fact that even in Egypt efforts to inculcate basic literacy in Arabic encountered great difficulties.[96] In Wajdī's view, Islamic missionary efforts could not be successful without translations.

The emphasis laid on propagating Islam reflected the desire to counteract the impact and methods of Christian missionaries. The Egyptian ulama felt that Christian missionaries possessed powerful techniques for communicating their message and implementing their agenda. Wajdī's call to translate the Qur'an into English fits within this context of responding to robust missionary efforts in Egypt. If Protestant missionaries could distribute Bible translations, Muslims, so the argument went, could and should disseminate translations of the Qur'an.

The rift among the Egyptian ulama deepened, pitting traditionalists who feared rapid change of the sort seen in Turkey against reformists who thought that al-Azhar remained behind the times. Marāghī joined Wajdī in championing translations. As a well-known public figure and scholar, he provided gravitas to the cause as well as political savvy. In joining the debate, Marāghī aligned himself with those who were hostile to Christian missionary activities, and wanted Muslims to respond and defend Islam. Marāghī's pro-translation campaign also contributed to his efforts to make Egypt central in the post-Ottoman Muslim world.

Marāghī contributed a scholarly argument for translation to buttress the practical, political and evangelical rhetoric of Wajdī. The shaykh drew on the work of the Andalusian scholar Abū Isḥāq al-Shāṭibī (d. 790/1388), who wrote that all Arabic words have two kinds of meaning: primary and auxiliary. The primary meaning provides the core or literal meaning of the word that is transferrable into another language. The primary meaning of the word 'bread', for instance, would indicate a food made of grain. The auxiliary meaning involves metaphorical, non-literal senses of words that are particular to the language, for example, the use of 'bread' in American English to mean money. As translators across the centuries have recognised, the auxiliary meanings cannot be easily translated into other languages. Shāṭibī concluded that translation of the Qur'an's primary meanings was possible and permissible in much the same way that commenting on the text was necessary for the sake of explanation and clarification. Building on Shāṭibī's arguments, Marāghī contended that translation was permissible, just as interpreting the Qur'an is permissible, reasoning that interpretation is not forbidden despite the fact that interpreters make errors. He reasoned that the case for translation should be no different. The risk is equal in both cases because the interpreter and translator both make discretionary choices about what meaning is appropriate and, ultimately, 'maybe the chosen meaning is what God intended and maybe it is not'.[97]

Whereas many opponents thought that the inimitable qualities (*iʿjāz*) of the Qur'an made translating it impossible, Marāghī argued that these qualities are not essential to the meaning of the text at all. Rather, he held that the inimitable aspects have to do with the unconventional literary structure of the Qur'an.[98] Therefore, these miraculous qualities pose no challenge for translating the meaning. He added the interesting opinion that neither Arabs nor non-Arabs can appreciate the inimitable qualities of the Qur'an in modern times because these elements were directed towards Arabs during the lifetime of the Prophet Muhammad.[99]

So, even if the miraculous linguistic qualities remained unique to the Arabic text, the general meaning certainly could be translated, and the successful transmission of Islam to non-Arabs had already proven the primary importance of the general meaning. He posed a well-targeted question, 'When most Muslims do not know or read Arabic and yet have clearly adopted both the foundational and auxiliary sciences of Islam, and made good of them, how can it be denied that translation effectively conveys Islam?'[100] For Marāghī, non-Arab Muslims had absorbed the essential message of the Qur'an – ethical guidance for humanity – and created vibrant Muslim communities. The scepticism over translations had, in effect, already been laid to rest by the successful embrace and practice of Islam by non-Arabs around the globe.

Marāghī acknowledged that not all verses of the Qur'an could be translated perfectly – for instance, the allegorical elements and inimitable qualities. However, most verses, particularly legal verses, could be translated effectively, and, therefore, Marāghī argued that a translation could serve as a basis for *ijtihād*. After all, legal provisions are based on the clear verses (*muḥkamāt*) not on the allegorical or symbolic verses (*mutashābihāt*), and the untranslatable verses have no importance in formulating laws, just as inimitable aspects of the language have no bearing upon it.[101]

Marāghī's support for the legal use of translations was somewhat stunning since even supporters of translation in Turkey had not suggested this. Much of the opposition in Turkey and elsewhere had argued that translations communicated none of the poetry and beauty of the Qur'an, and such a view was often taken for granted without any consideration of contrary evidence. Yet in Egypt, proponents disputed this idea and pointed out that foreign language renderings did in fact provide aesthetic, emotional and spiritual enjoyment for their readers. Wajdī reminded the public that famous foreigners had come to know and appreciate Islam through translations. He cited George Bernard Shaw, Goethe and Thomas Carlyle among those who knew no Arabic but had read translations and had come to see Islam as a positive force for humanity.[102] Despite the malicious intent of some translators, reasons Wajdī, the effect of Qur'an translations had been mixed, and, if Egypt were to publish renderings that presented a true picture of Islam, they would certainly have a positive impact on the perception of Islam in the world and assist in the conversion of non-Muslims.[103]

Fitna: Mustafa Sabri

No member of the Turkish ulama embodied opposition to the secular reforms of modern Turkey – particularly the Turkish translation of the Qur'an – to the same extent as Sabri. The former leader of the conservative Turkish ulama and a two-time Ottoman Shaykh al-Islam, he opposed religious reforms during the late Ottoman period and argued that the newly established nation state of Turkey was an atheistic, anti-Islamic state. A staunch defender of the caliphate, Sabri waged the radical argument that a colonial regime in Turkey with a caliph was preferable to an independent Turkey ruled by secular-nationalists.[104] Sabri went into exile where he continued his biting criticism of the Ankara government. After stints in Egypt, the Hijaz, Lebanon, Italy, Romania and Greece, he traversed the Mediterranean and settled in Cairo. The city on the Nile had strong ties to Istanbul, and many Turkish intellectuals and political exiles had taken refuge in its environs over the previous decades. Upon arrival, Sabri found that the Egyptian ulama and intelligentsia were engaged in a very familiar conversation: they were debating the permissibility of translating the Qur'an, and some were advocating that al-Azhar compose and distribute its own authorised English-language version. The recent arrival, a long-standing opponent of translations in Turkey, was dismayed and perplexed.

Sabri criticised the new Turkish government vociferously for its cultural reforms and dismantling of the religious establishment. Sabri went so far as to express regret that, after their entrance into the Muslim umma, the Turks had retained their language and ethnic identity unlike Egyptians and Syrians who had undergone a thorough process of Arabisation. Had the Turks been Arabised, Sabri continued, the unity of Islamic peoples could have been more easily maintained. To forcefully make his point, Sabri renounced his Turkish nationality, explaining that he preferred to retain only his Muslim identity.[105] Now in Cairo, his refuge from secular Turkish nationalism, some of the most venerable Islamic scholars in the Arab world were endorsing a piece of the Turkish reformist agenda. 'How strange it is', he remarked, 'that some Arab voices arose in support of changing the language of the Qur'an'.[106] Observing this phenomenon, in 1932 he published a book titled *Mas'alat tarjamat al-Qur'ān* (*The Issue of Translating the Qur'an*) in Arabic detailing his opposition to translation and attacking the arguments of its proponents. Sabri deems the debates about translation a *fitna*, a term that means temptation or trial but also is used to refer to the early civil wars among Muslims in the first generations of Islam.[107] Not only was Sabri surprised that some Arabs supported Qur'anic translation, he also found it troubling that members of the ulama, not secular nationalists, led the campaign. He observed that the Egyptian debates used Islamic arguments and justifications in support of translation, whereas in Turkey the issue was not seen as an Islamic legal debate.[108]

In his book, Sabri challenges the two chief Egyptian supporters of translation – Wajdī and Marāghī – and evaluates their arguments according to traditional legal thought. The difference between them, Sabri writes, is that Wajdī supports translation using a modern repertoire of social and political arguments with little knowledge of the Islamic legal tradition, while Marāghī knowingly goes against legal tradition and 'wants to clothe the naked reformism (*tajdīd*), which Farīd Wajdī wants to dress up for the people in the garb of Islamic law (*fiqh*)'.[109] Sabri argues that Ḥanafī sources strictly prohibit reciting and writing out copies of the Qur'an in Persian and, invoking a medieval scholar, consider those who rely upon these to be either heretical or insane, recommending that 'the insane receive treatment and the heretic be killed'.[110] In sum, Sabri maintained that, even within the Ḥanafī school, there was no basis for the legality of translation.

Additionally, the former Shaykh al-Islam emphasised the political agenda behind translation debates in Turkey and held out the Turkish example as a warning for Egyptian scholars. His book was published at the same time that Atatürk was experimenting with the Turkish call-to-prayer and reciting translations in mosques (see next chapter), and he argued that the goal of all this was to nationalise the book, to replace the Arabic Qur'an for ritual prayer (*ṣalāt*) and to 'sever the last bond holding together the unity of Islam'.[111] Furthermore, the replacement of the Arabic Qur'an was part of a larger transition in which, without consulting the ulama, the Turkish government replaced the sharia with the Swiss Civil Code in 1926, for example, authorising Muslim women to marry non-Muslims, and enabling men and women to receive equal inheritances. For Sabri, Marāghī's views granted licence to the translation reforms occurring in Turkey that would 'deliver a crushing blow' to the Arabic Qur'an, its meaning and its laws.[112] Additionally, Sabri criticised Wajdī's favourable views on the new Turkish regime, arguing that he was representing an atheistic government, which was hostile to Islam, as a great success and a model for the rest of the Muslim world. He writes that the project 'of translating the Qur'an is under the patronage and command of atheists'.[113]

In 1935, Marāghī again became the rector of al-Azhar. His accession injected new life into the push for Egyptian-sponsored translations. The previous writings of Wajdī and Marāghī on the topic were reprinted in book form, and Maḥmūd Shaltūt (1893–1963), another reformist Azharī, entered the fray in support of translation. They argued that al-Azhar needed to produce and publish an English translation of the Qur'an in order to reveal the true image of Islam to the Western world. Translations into other languages were discussed as well but English was a priority because it was 'the most widely used language' around the globe.[114] Even Rashīd Riḍā, the vociferous critic of Turkish translations, did an about-face and became a supporter of translations in the 1930s. He declared Egypt the most capable Muslim nation to carry out 'this duty which is considered to be the greatest service' to the non-Muslim countries, and urged the king to provide financial support.[115]

Marāghī led the effort to make these translations a reality and requested a fatwa in support of the project from the High Council of the Ulama, of which he was the chairman. He framed the question with a set of stipulations that made it hard for the committee to disagree: a translation could not be considered the Qur'an, nor replace it, nor transmit its miraculous qualities, but erroneous translations were distorting the perception of the Qur'an, and a proper rendering of the meanings could at least provide a sound explanation of its basic message. Marāghī asked whether such a translation would be permissible if it were printed in the margins of the original and indicated that it was neither the Qur'an nor a complete commentary. The council replied in the affirmative.[116]

With this licence in hand, Marāghī then obtained support from the Council of Ministers and organised a committee to develop an English-language translation for publication. However, a lack of consensus among its members and a turbulent political environment interrupted the project.[117] Though the Egyptian scholars did not produce an original English-language rendering, publishing restrictions were eased and, in 1938, an Egyptian press printed Yusuf Ali's *The Holy Qur'an*. The grand project of publishing translations in multiple languages had to be postponed, but the importance of sponsoring Qur'anic translations was established in Egyptian institutions, and presses in the country began to publish English-language translations. For an Arab-speaking country which had seized and burned translations as recently as 1925, official Egyptian support for Qur'anic translation marked a significant milestone in the spread of modern translations. The idea of publishing translations in multiple languages did not fade but gained momentum in the coming years.

The tenor of the debate on translation in Egypt differed dramatically from that in Turkey. Those Egyptians who embraced translation did so because they agreed it was a means of exporting Islam and establishing Egypt as the new centre of Islamic authority. In Turkey, proponents were not attempting to project a certain understanding of Islam to the rest of the world but rather to nationalise Islam within their own country. Turkey was pursuing reform along the lines of the Protestant reformation combined with twentieth-century linguistic nationalism, and translations were seen as relevant and useful in a Turkish Muslim sphere of Islamic practice with national boundaries, largely independent of the surrounding Muslim world.

Egyptian proponents, in contrast, championed translations as a part of the effort to spread Islam outside of traditionally Muslim regions. These translations were intended primarily for non-Muslim readers in order to foster a positive image of Islam in the West and also to win converts. Turks had debated the importance of having a sacred book in their own language while Egyptians deliberated on the merits of a translation into the language of their colonial overseer, a language that very few in Egypt could understand. In fact, the very men who debated the issue in Egypt were not conversant in the English language. Nevertheless, the efforts of the Ahmadiyya, Pickthall and Christian missionaries had convinced the reformist leadership of al-Azhar that translations were imperative to secure the future of Islam and to ensure Egypt a leading role in the Muslim world.

NOTES

1 On this, see Hassan, 'Loss of Caliphate'.
2 Elie Kedourie, *In the Anglo-Arab Labyrinth: The McMahon-Husayn Correspondence and its Interpretations, 1914–1939* (Cambridge, Cambridge University Press, 1991), pp. 4–5.
3 Aziz al-Azmeh, 'Nationalism and the Arabs', *Arab Studies Quarterly* 17, nos. 1 and 2 (Winter/Spring 1995), pp. 1–18.
4 Hassan, 'Loss of Caliphate', pp. 180–81.
5 Elie Kedourie, 'Egypt and the Caliphate', *Journal of the Royal Asiatic Society of Great Britain and Ireland* 3/4 (1963), p. 211.
6 Hassan, 'Loss of Caliphate', p. 174.
7 Kedourie, 'Egypt and the Caliphate', p. 218.
8 Israel Gershoni and James P. Jankowski, *Egypt, Islam, and the Arabs: The Search for Egyptian Nationhood, 1900–1930* (Oxford, Oxford University Press, 1986), pp. 63–4.
9 Gershoni and Jankowski, *Egypt, Islam, and the Arabs*, pp. 65–6.
10 Albin, 'Printing of the Qur'an', *EQ*, vol. IV, p. 272.
11 The committee was comprised of Shaykh Muḥammad ʿAlī al-Ḥusaynī, Ḥanafī Nāṣif, Muṣṭafā ʿAnānī and Aḥmad al-Iskandarānī; Albin, 'Printing of the Qur'an'.
12 'Taqrīẓ al-maṭbūʿāt al-ḥadītha: Al-muṣḥaf al-sharīf, ṭabaʿat al-ḥukūma al-akhīra lahu', *al-Manār* 26, no. 10 (1926), p. 796.
13 Albin, 'Printing of the Qur'an,' *EQ*, vol. IV, p. 272.
14 Gabriel Said Reynolds, *The Qur'ān in its Historical Context* (London, Routledge, 2008), pp. 2–3.
15 For a detailed account of how the 1924 Egyptian edition was produced, see Bergsträsser, 'Koranlesung in Kairo', (1932), pp. 1–42; (1933), pp. 110–34.
16 Simon Ross Valentine, *Islam and the Ahmadiyya Jamaʿat: History, Belief, Practice* (New York, Columbia University Press, 2008), p. 69. En route to perform the Hajj in 1923, the leader of the Ahmadiyya centre in Woking outside London, Khwaja Kamaluddin, and the prominent British convert to

Islam, Lord Headley, had stopped in Egypt, receiving an official welcome and speaking to several public gatherings. They may have brought copies of the translation of the Qur'an with them and then later shipped additional copies.

17 Kambiz GhaneaBassiri. *A History of Islam in America: From the New World to the New World Order* (New York, Cambridge University Press, 2010), pp. 206–10.

18 Nur Moch Ichwan, 'Differing Responses to Ahmadi Translation and Exegesis', *Archipel* 62 (2001), p. 145.

19 Ibid., p. 153.

20 Ibid., p. 145.

21 Muḥammad Shākir, 'On the Translation of the Koran into Foreign Languages', *The Moslem World* 16, no. 2 (1926), p. 164. His articles on the subject were compiled into a book; see Muḥammad Shākir, *al-Qawl al-faṣl fī tarjamat al-Qur'ān al-karīm ilā'l-lughāt al-aʿjamiyya* (Cairo, Maṭbaʿat al-Nahḍa, 1925).

22 Shākir, 'On the Translation of the Koran', p. 165.

23 Marmaduke William Pickthall, 'Arabs and Non-Arabs on the Question of Translating the Qur'an', *Islamic Culture* 5 (July 1931), p. 427.

24 Some Turkish writers appear to have confused him with the Indian activist and leader of the Khilāfat movement, Mohammad Ali Jawhar (1878–1931); Altuntaş, *Kur'an'ın Tercümesi*, p. 135.

25 Ömer Rıza Doğrul, 'A Heavy Loss for the Muslim World: Muhammad Ali and His Work', *Islamic Review* (May 1952), p. 17.

26 Ibid.

27 Ichwan, 'Differing Responses', p. 147.

28 Ibid., p. 148.

29 Ibid., pp. 150–51.

30 Ibid., pp. 153–4.

31 Ibid, p. 158.

32 Edward E. Curtis, *Black Muslim Religion in the Nation of Islam, 1960–1975* (Chapel Hill, University of North Carolina Press, 2006), pp. 46–7.

33 Marmaduke William Pickthall's works include, *Saïd the Fisherman* (London, Methuen, 1903); idem, *Enid: A Novel* (Westminster, Archibald Constable, 1904); idem, *The Children of the Nile* (London, J. Murray, 1908); idem, *Veiled Women* (London, E. Nash, 1913); idem, *Tales from Five Chimneys* (London, Mills and Boon, 1915); idem, *The House of War* (New York, Duffield, 1916); idem, *The Valley of the Kings* (New York, A.A. Knopf, 1926).

34 Peter Clark, *Marmaduke Pickthall: British Muslim* (London, Quartet Books, 1986), p. 26.

35 Ibid., p. 31.

36 Peter Clark, 'A Man of Two Cities: Pickthall, Damascus, Hyderabad', *Asian Affairs* 25, no. 3 (1994), pp. 284–5.

37 Anne Jackson Fremantle, *Loyal Enemy* (London, Hutchinson, 1938), p. 389.

38 Ibid., pp. 388–9.

39 Giancarlo Casale, *The Ottoman Age of Exploration* (Oxford, Oxford University Press, 2010), pp. 147–9.

40 Clark, *British Muslim*, p. 56

41 For more information, see Gail Minault, *The Khilafat Movement: Religious Symbolism and Political Mobilization in India* (New York, Columbia University Press, 1982).

42 'Mr. Lloyd George and the Indian Khilafat Delegation', *Islamic Review* (April 1920), p. 140.
43 'Indian Delegation at the Mosque', *Islamic Review* (April 1920), p. 139.
44 'Eid ul-Fitr', *Islamic Review* (June–July 1920), p. 225.
45 Clark, *British Muslim*, p. 57.
46 Fremantle, *Loyal Enemy*, p. 386.
47 Ibid., p. 388.
48 Ibid., p. 389.
49 *Time*, 27 February 1937.
50 Clarke, *British Muslim*, p. 59.
51 Ibid., p. 60.
52 Ibid., p. 62.
53 Fremantle, *Loyal Enemy*, pp. 404–5.
54 Pickthall, 'Arabs and Non-Arabs', p. 424.
55 Jacob Skovgaard-Petersen, 'al-Azhar, Modern Period', *EI THREE* (Brill Online).
56 Arthur Goldschmidt, *A Biographical Dictionary of Modern Egypt* (Boulder, CO, Lynne Rienner Publishers, 2000), p. 123.
57 Pickthall, 'Arabs and Non-Arabs', p. 425.
58 Ibid.
59 Muḥammad Aḥmad al-Ghamrāwī, who assisted Pickthall, also wrote a book of literary criticism on pre-Islamic poetry; Muḥammad Aḥmad al-Ghamrāwī and Amīr Shakīb Arslān, *al-Naqd al-taḥlīlī li-kitāb fī'l-adab al-jāhilī* (Cairo, al-Maṭba'a al-Salafiyya, 1929).
60 Ibid., p. 426.
61 Ibid.
62 Ibid., p. 433.
63 Ibid.
64 'Islam: Caliph's Beauteous Daughter', *Time Magazine*, 9 November 1931, http://www.time.com/time/magazine/article/0,9171,742555,00.html.
65 'India: Nizam's Azam and Moazzam', *Time Magazine*, 31 November 1931, http://www.time.com/time/magazine/article/0,9171,742647,00.html#ixzz1QhG4P5Bn.
66 Ibid.
67 Fremantle, *Loyal Enemy*, p. 436.
68 M.A. Sherif, *Searching for Solace* (Islamabad, Islamic Research Institute, 2000), p. 71.
69 Fremantle, *Loyal Enemy*, p. 393.
70 Sherif, *Searching*, p. 94.
71 Ibid.
72 Abdullah Yusuf Ali, tr., *The Holy Qur'an* (Lahore, Shaikh Muhammad Ashraf, 1934), p. iv.
73 Sherif, *Searching*, pp. 9–11.
74 Ibid., pp. 42–5.
75 Sherif, *Searching*, p. 91.
76 Yusuf Ali, *The Holy Qur'an*, p. iv.
77 Sherif, *Searching*, p. 177.
78 Ibid., pp. 175–6.
79 Yusuf Ali, *The Holy Qur'an*, p. iv.

80 Ibid.
81 Sherif, *Searching*, p. 134.
82 Ibid., pp. 139–41.
83 Ibid., pp. 102–3.
84 Marmaduke Pickthall, 'Mr. Yusuf Ali's Translation of the Qur'an', *Islamic Culture* 9 (1935), p. 519.
85 Ibid., pp. 520–21.
86 Ibid., p. 521.
87 Sherif, *Searching*, p. 121.
88 Ibid.
89 Ibid., pp. 122–3.
90 Heather J. Sharkey, *American Evangelicals in Egypt: Missionary Encounters in an Age of Empire* (Princeton, NJ, Princeton University Press, 2008), p. 49.
91 Ibid., p. 121.
92 Ibid., pp. 118–19.
93 Ibid., p. 128.
94 Muḥammad Farīd Wajdī, *al-Adilla al-ʿilmiyya ʿalā jawāz tarjamat maʿānīʾl-Qurʾān ilāʾl-lughāt al-ajnabiyya* (Cairo, Maṭbaʿat al-Raghāʾib, 1355/1936), p. 8.
95 Ibid., p. 5.
96 Ibid., pp. 17–18.
97 Muḥammad Muṣṭafā al-Marāghī, *Baḥth fī tarjamatiʾl-Qurʾān il-karīm wa aḥkāmihā* (Cairo, Maṭbaʿat al-Raghāʾib, 1355/1936), p. 5.
98 Ibid., p. 9.
99 Ibid., p. 10.
100 Ibid., p. 13.
101 Ibid.
102 Wajdī, *al-Adilla al-ʿilmiyya*, p. 11.
103 Ibid., p. 19.
104 Bein, *Ottoman Ulema*, p. 112.
105 Mustafa Sabri, *Masʾalat tarjamat al-Qurʾān* (Cairo, al-Maṭbaʿa al-Salafiyya, 1351/1932), p. 112.
106 Ibid., p. 3.
107 Ibid., p. 5.
108 Ibid.
109 Ibid., pp. 4–5.
110 Ibid., pp. 22–3. The medieval scholar that Sabri invokes is Abū Bakr Muḥammad b. al-Faḍl (d. 381/991); see Zadeh, *Vernacular Qur'an*, pp. 53–4.
111 Sabri, *Masʾalat*, p. 3.
112 Ibid., pp. 21–2.
113 Ibid., p. 72.
114 Altuntaş, *Kur'an'ın Tercümesi*, p. 145.
115 Muḥammad Rashīd Riḍā, 'Tarjamat al-Qurʾān wa kawn al-ʿarabiyya lughat al-islām', *al-Manār* 32, no. 3 (1931), pp. 184–9.
116 Altuntaş, *Kur'an'ın Tercümesi*, p. 146.
117 Ibid., p. 162.

7
The Elusive Turkish Qur'an

On the first Friday of Ramadan 1926, the imam of the Göztepe Mosque in Istanbul, Mehmet Celalettin, performed the prayer (*namaz*) and *takbīr* (*tekbir*) in Turkish of his own accord, recited Turkish translations of several chapters of the Qur'an and read out the *khuṭba* (*hutbe*) in the vernacular as well. He did the same on the following Friday.[1] This bold alteration of the ritual put the issue of the Turkish Qur'an into the public eye yet again. While the nationalist press celebrated the imam, it is clear that his use of Turkish in the mosque was neither sanctioned nor appreciated by the Directorate of Religious Affairs. To the great displeasure of many Turkist intellectuals, the Directorate of Religious Affairs quickly dismissed Celalettin from his post, arguing that there was consensus among Muslim scholars that translations of the Qur'an could not be used to perform the ritual prayer. Secondly, the decision stated that this act would 'cause division and conflict among Muslims and chaos in the country'.[2] Despite supporting the translation of the Qur'an, at this time the Turkish government did not encourage maverick activities aimed at bringing about the Turkification of Islamic ritual lest they spark social unrest and catalyse opposition to the single-party regime. The government understood the sensitivity of ritual matters and punished those who did not follow orders from the centre.

Turkists were dismayed at the decision to remove the imam from his post and wrote articles in protest. The dismissed imam defended his role in promoting vernacular worship and promised to continue leading prayers in Turkish if he could regain his position.[3] As his use of Turkish was appreciated by the new regime, he was given a teaching position, training imams.[4] The article written by the Russian-born Turkist Ahmet Ağaoğlu titled 'Is the Turkish Language Forbidden?' questioned how a government agency could punish a Turkish citizen for an act that 'served the revolution which we created and assisted in the discovery of our language and our religion'.[5] Viewing the use of the Turkish language for Islamic ritual as a natural step in the evolution of national customs and identity, Ağaoğlu and others were dismayed that the Directorate of Religious Affairs did not embrace and push forward the revolutionary agenda that had been set out by Gökalp in his nationalistic poem 'Vatan'.[6] The agenda of the Turkists met resistance in various quarters and, despite the non-democratic context, implementing religious reform proved to be a more difficult task than they had imagined.

After the parliament had commissioned the translation project in February 1925, the political fortunes in the country changed rapidly when the party led by Mustafa Kemal, Cumhuriyet Halk Partisi (CHP) (The Republican People's Party), established single-party rule, eliminated opposition parties and silenced the voices of devout intellectuals in the press. For translations of the Qur'an, this shift meant that those in good standing with the ruling party could publish translations without interference. Publishers could print new translations and even reprint the controversial renderings of 1924. Critics of unlicensed translations were undoubtedly dismayed by these developments, but, lacking any political influence, they could not prevent them. From 1926 to 1932, the abysmally received translation of journeyman writer Süleyman Tevfik was reprinted numerous times under numerous titles.[7] In these reprintings, the publishers assure readers that a committee of scholars had inspected and revised the translation; however, Tevfik admitted that it was far from perfect because the work of humans 'cannot be free of error'.[8] Despite the commissioned but unrealised state-sponsored translation project and the debacles of 1924, publishers in Istanbul were able to revise and repackage the problematic translations which had been formally denounced by the Directorate of Religious Affairs.

Not all translations of this period were so objectionable to the devout intellectuals. A well-known Islamic scholar named İzmirli

İsmail Hakkı (1868–1946) took on the task of composing a Turkish rendering called *Meani-i Kur'an (The Meanings of the Qur'an)*, which was published in 1927. An independent-minded thinker who refused to claim allegiance to any particular school of thought, İzmirli charted an original course as a scholar and practitioner of Islam. For instance, he took a deep interest in Sufism and even became a deputy (*khalīfa*) of the Shādhiliyya order, but he refused to exempt Sufi works from his critical eye and angered fellow Sufis when he argued that most hadiths quoted in Sufi literature were fabricated.[9] Among his most important works was a book called *Yeni İlm-i Kelam* (*The New Science of Theology*) (1924) in which he argued that Muslim scholars needed to engage with modern European philosophy and rediscover the Aristotelian Muslim philosophers in order to forge new theological approaches for the modern age that could refute materialist worldviews.[10] İzmirli was a close friend of Mehmet Akif and wrote for the Muslim modernist journal *Sırat-ı Müstakim*. He had the scholarly credentials and the social standing to compose a translation that could be respected in influential Muslim circles.

Critics agreed that İzmirli's *The Meanings of the Qur'an* was the most accurate translation to date, but they were disappointed that it lacked a poetic touch; as one journalist put it, 'if only the literary and linguistic level met that of the knowledge, it would be a perfect translation'.[11] A true scholar's version, the text has a cumbersome scholarly apparatus including copious footnotes, parentheses, brackets as well as underlined words and passages. For *Sūrat al-Kawthar* (Q. 108), which contains only three verses, İzmirli included a footnote for every verse, and this example is not an exception to the rule. It is clear that information and documentation, rather than aesthetic experience, were the prime objectives for the translator. İzmirli himself admitted that it might be weak in terms of literary style and made it clear that he had not attempted to replicate the stylistic beauty of the Qur'an because to do so was futile. Rather, the purpose of a translation was to make known the rulings (*aḥkām*), express the meaning of the verses and give access to the guidance contained in the Qur'an.[12] The aim of explanation, not inspiration, motivated İzmirli's project and, against the hopes of many devout intellectuals, he suggested that literary excellence was not in fact a realistic goal.

Aside from literary distaste, the critics also questioned what role İzmirli's book would play in the campaign to implement the performance of daily prayers in Turkish. His translation was published in the wake of the Turkish *namaz* event of 1926, and, in the introduction, İzmirli discusses the Ḥanafī opinion that it is permissible to translate the Qur'an and to allow those who cannot do so in Arabic to perform *namaz* in vernacular languages.[13] He does not indicate his own opinion on this matter, but the mere mention of the issue raised questions and suggested that the scholar may in fact have been sympathetic to the Turkification of ritual. Moreover, the translation contained some elements that might have given opponents of Turkification cause for concern; for instance, İzmirli did not refrain from translating the names of God and the *basmala* (the invocation *bismi'llāhi'l-raḥmāni'l-raḥīm*), though some critics opposed doing so. He rendered the *basmala* in Turkish as '*esirgeyen bağışlayan Tanrı adıyla*', translating not only the divine names Raḥmān (*esirgeyen*) and Raḥīm (*bağışlayan*), but also replacing the Arabic Allah with the Turkish word for God, Tanrı.[14] One critic suspiciously asked İzmirli to clarify, 'for the enlightenment of public opinion', whether he thought that translations could be used in prayer and if his book was such a translation that could serve as the basis for vernacular *namaz*.[15] Despite the government's reprimand of the imam who had performed prayers in Turkish, the issue clearly continued to concern devout intellectuals who sensed that the tide was turning in favour of the Turkists.

The State-Sponsored Project Continued

Neither the 1926 Turkish *namaz* event nor the newly published translations affected Akif's writing, and he continued to work intently on the state-sponsored translation project until 1931. Akif lived a scholarly life in Helwan, a suburb of Cairo, as the guest of Abbas Halim Pasha and as the neighbour of Marāghī. Though he accepted invitations from his well-heeled patrons, visited the Turkish students in the city and taught Turkish literature at the university, for the most part, Akif spent his time in his guest house with a schedule that revolved around performing the five daily prayers, translating the Qur'an and reading Rūmī's *Mathnawī*.[16] According to Akif's descriptions, translating became a ritual act which he combined with Qur'anic recitation. Akif had long been a *hāfiẓ*, someone who had memorised the entire Qur'an, but he told a close friend that this project had made him an 'iron *hāfiẓ*' (*demir hafız*).[17]

More troubling signs came in 1928 when several momentous reforms were implemented in Turkey. The legislature eliminated the stipulation in the constitution which recognised Islam as the official religion of the Turkish Republic, making Turkey officially and legally secular. Equally symbolic and having wide-ranging practical implications, the government decided to change the letters of the Turkish alphabet from the Arabic script to Latin characters in the same year. The adoption of the Latin script symbolically aligned Turkey with Europe and caused a break in the continuity of written culture, cutting off subsequent generations from Ottoman and Islamic literary traditions. The momentum to implement additional religious reforms was gathering steam and, in the same year, a controversial set of proposals appeared that envisioned the reform of Muslim ritual and mosques according to Protestant Christian models. The report recommended placing pews in mosques, playing musical instruments such as organs in services, wearing shoes inside and using the Turkish language for all ritual purposes.[18] These proposals were tantamount to a wholesale imitation of Protestant church practices and represented for Akif and like-minded intellectuals a tragic attempt to refashion Islam in the image of Euro-American Christianity. There could be no clearer example of imitating Europe than the proposals that were circulating.

For Akif, the actual and proposed reforms of 1928 appear to have raised the question of how his translation of the Qur'an would be used. The chief fear he expressed was that it would be published without a commentary, and that this would allow radical reformers and uninformed pundits to interpret it according to their whims.[19] In 1928, Akif completed a first draft of the translation, and, despite his concerns, he continued to work on the revisions. However, according to Edip, he insisted that he would only submit it when the revisions were complete. While he told his friends that this refusal was due to the quality of the work, it has been interpreted to mean that he did not trust the Turkish government with his translation and feared they would abuse it for nationalistic purposes. Eventually, Akif decided that he would never submit the work and officially annulled his contract in 1932.[20] When Akif bowed out, the Directorate of Religious Affairs gave the translation project to Elmalılı Muhammed Hamdi Yazır,[21] who was already at work on the Turkish-language commentary.

Akif's withdrawal from the translation project crushed the hopes of many devout intellectuals in Turkey that a worthy Qur'an translation by a pious, renowned poet would be produced. For seven years, the foremost Turkish poet of the era had been working in self-imposed exile on a literary-religious work of great consequence for Islam in modern Turkey. After the long wait, the ultimate outcome (though not the text itself) was extraordinarily disappointing, especially for Akif's close friends and supporters as well as for the Turkish government. Edip visited Akif in Helwan in 1932 and had the opportunity to read the entire manuscript, which he deemed a masterpiece; he wrote, 'he had polished it for years like a poem, and there were no rough edges in it whatsoever. It flowed like water. It enlivened the heart like a cascade'.[22] The poet Süleyman Nazif reported that the verses had a fluency and power which only Akif could produce in Turkish.[23]

While his friends lauded the work, they also tried to convince him to submit it, even arguing that it was not simply a personal matter for Akif but rather a work that all Turkish Muslims had a right, even a need, to read. Edip urged Akif to let him take the manuscript back to Turkey with him. The Turkish government maintained its interest in the manuscript as well and requested that those visiting Akif try to persuade him to accept payment for the manuscript, but the poet remained firm and refused to share a copy even with his closest friends.

The Ulama's Best and Brightest: Elmalılı Muhammed Hamdi Yazır (1878–1942)

Elmalılı took over the translation project in the early 1930s. Unlike Akif, Elmalılı was a distinguished member of the professional religious establishment. From the last generation of the Ottoman ulama, Elmalılı possessed a wide range of intellectual and artistic interests. He was a poet, an accomplished calligrapher, translator and author. Elmalılı had studied European philosophy and, in innovative fashion, taught in his madrasa courses the works of British philosophers John Stuart Mill and Alexander Bain as well as French philosophers Paul Janet and Gabriel Séailles. He translated these works and published his rendering of Janet and Seailles' *Histoire de la philosophie* in Turkish.[24] In addition to his intellectual and artistic pursuits, Elmalılı played an active role in politics. He joined the CUP and became a representative of Antalya in the Ottoman parliament. He held a number of bureaucratic and teaching positions within the ulama ranks and served as the minister of Pious Foundations (*evkaf*). After the closure of the madrasas in March 1924, he found himself without a job and spent the rest of his days pursuing scholarly projects largely within the confines of his home under difficult financial circumstances. Elmalılı remained highly respected as a scholar, and the Directorate of Religious Affairs chose him to compose the state-sponsored Qur'anic commentary and, later, to take over the translation project.[25]

As Elmalılı worked on his translation in the early 1930s and Egyptians debated Qur'an translation across the Mediterranean, Turkish nationalism was entering a new, far more radical, phase. The 1930s were a period of social experimentation, utopian thought and radical movements around the world. In Turkey as well, the state adopted an official policy of revolutionary reformism (*inkılapçılık*) and supported cultural projects that radically re-envisioned Turkish history, language and religion in nationalist terms. These projects were geared towards excavating the essence of the Turkish nation from the various foreign and religious influences that had usurped and obscured Turkishness over the centuries, and reconstructing a modern Turkish identity. Of course, in reality, this romantic project involved constructing a national history based upon both real and imagined elements of the distant Turkic past. Supported by the state, and at times directed by President Kemal himself, such projects flourished. Via the Turkish Language Association (*Türk Dil Kurumu*), an institution in which the president was personally invested, the new regime embarked on an initiative to 'purify' the Turkish language by purging it of Arabic and Persian vocabulary, and replacing them with neologisms built on Turkish roots.[26] On a parallel course, the Turkish History Association (*Türk Tarihi Kurumu*) developed the Turkish history thesis which posited that the Turks were the founders of world civilisation, effectively suggesting a Turkish origin for many great figures across history, including the Prophet Muhammad and Moses. For a time, the regime supported the Sun Language Theory (*Güneş Dil Teorisi*), a nationalist hypothesis that identified Turkish as the oldest language in the world and the mother of all other languages. After foreign linguists expressed doubt about this theory at a linguistics conference hosted in Turkey in 1936, support for this bizarre theory gradually diminished.[27] These were times in which a radically different past, present and future were imagined and created. As this brave new world was imagined, the status of the Qur'an as a central religio-cultural text for the nation remained uncertain.

Reforming Ritual

In tandem with other nation-building projects, efforts to recalibrate Islamic practice for the emerging nationalist worldview found their political opening in this period. The state-led initiative to use Turkish instead of Arabic in mosques moved forward in the early 1930s. Atatürk wanted to test the waters with the use of the Turkish language for the call to prayer, Qur'an recitation and daily prayer. Each of these measures, including reference to the 'Turkish Qur'an', had appeared in Gökalp's 1918 poem as characteristics of a national Islam that was intelligible, rational and accessible. However, a standard Turkish translation of the Qur'an that would form the basis of Turkish Islam and ritual life *a la Turca* did not yet exist. The first volume of Elmalılı's translation/commentary would not be published until 1935 and the complete text appeared only in 1938. This did not inhibit the enthusiasm of the president, who personally championed the recitation of Turkish translations and moved forward with a campaign to introduce them in mosque rituals.

In January 1932, during Ramadan, Mustafa Kemal summoned Qur'anic reciters from the leading mosques in Istanbul to his residence at Dolmabahçe Palace. Once assembled, he informed them that they were going to recite Turkish translations of the Qur'an in mosques. The president's point man on the project, Dr Reşit Galip (1893–1934), gave the reciters copies of Cemil Sait's 1924 translation although he added that it was less than optimal since it was based on a French work instead of the Arabic original. He assured them that a better translation was being prepared and would soon be available.[28] This introduction could hardly have inspired confidence in the reciters, yet they were in no position to refuse the president's request. Their participation was a command performance.

As Mustafa Kemal conversed with the reciters, one of the translation's deficiencies came into view when he listened to Q. 4:23, a verse which concerns the categories of women that a Muslim cannot lawfully marry. This verse states, among other things, that one cannot marry two sisters at the same time and ends with this statement: unless it be a thing of the past (*illā mā qad salafa*); God is All-Forgiving, All-Compassionate. Cemil Sait translates this phrase from the verse as,

> don't marry two sisters, but if it is a *fait accompli* God is All-Forgiving, Ever-Merciful (*İki hemşireyi nikah etmeyiniz lakin bir emr-i vaki olmuş ise Allah Gafur ve Rahimdir*).[29]

When Kemal heard this verse, he angrily replied, 'So you can go to Konya, take your wife's sister without knowing it, then later it's a *fait accompli* (*emr-i vaki*) and, *voilà*, God is All-Forgiving and Merciful! This is nonsense!'[30] The phrasing of the translation makes Kemal's interpretation plausible. The key question is how to translate the succinct phrase *illā mā qad salafa*. Sait uses the Turkish expression *emr-i vaki*, which appears to be a direct extract from Kazimirski's rendering, 'Si le fait est accompli, Dieu sera indulgent et miséricordieux.'[31]

After an uncomfortable silence, one of the reciters, a composer and *hafız* named Sadettin Kaynak (1895–1961), told Kemal that the translation was faulty and provided a traditional explanation of the verse: *illā mā qad salafa* does not mean *fait accompli*, but rather 'what had already happened' in the pre-Islamic era, *al-Jāhiliyya* (the Age of Ignorance). Only the marriages that occurred before the coming of Islam fall into this category. God was merciful and forgiving of those in this situation, Kaynak explained, because, otherwise, many women would have been left without husbands and become destitute.[32] However, there is nothing in the verse itself that demands such an interpretation, and, based purely on the wording of the text, Sait's translation remains within the bounds of plausibility. As a literal translation, Sait's *emr-i vaki* in the French sense of *fait accompli* seems accurate at first glance. However, Osman Ergin has pointed out that *emr-i vaki* bears the negative connotation of something that has happened by accident or by mistake.[33] Therefore, when Kemal heard the translation, he understood that *accidental* marriages of two sisters would be forgiven, potentially not only in the past but also in the present. Kaynak claimed the translation was incorrect, but the explanation he provided was far more of a commentary than a correction of the translation. Kemal's outrage and Kaynak's explanation bring into relief the potential conflicts between translations that state only what is in the lines and not the understanding of the interpretive tradition. The gap between the letter of the text and the understanding of the interpretive community led many to demand the joint publication of a translation and a *tefsir*, and to oppose the printing of a translation by itself. The alternative would be to produce a more *sensum per sensum* translation that incorporated contextual information and traditional commentary into the body of the text. However, this latter option conflicted with the widespread demand for a literal translation that was as close as possible to the original.

This nocturnal gathering on the Bosphorus turned into a bizarre audition. The reciters were asked to chant the Turkish text in the dramatic style prevalent in Istanbul while Kemal listened, evaluated and made suggestions. It was truly a strange moment in the history of Qur'anic recitation. Gathered in a baroque palace, religious men who had dedicated their lives to memorising and chanting the Arabic Qur'an were now reciting a French-based

Turkish translation and taking cues on their craft from a famously secular president who had eliminated the caliphate and destroyed the institutions of the ulama. The scene epitomised the dominance of secular nationalists over the ulama.

In order to implement the campaign, Turkish translations were recited in several mosques, first in Istanbul and then in other cities around the country. For the debut, a well-known musician named Hafız Yaşar Bey would recite at a small mosque in the old city. The press publicised the event with great fanfare, proclaiming that 'Hafız Yaşar will forever retain the honour of having been the first *hafız* to recite their religious books to Turks in their own tongue.'[34] The newspaper coverage of these recitations gives the impression that worshippers not only embraced the use of Turkish but also benefitted from the Qur'an as never before because they were 'listening for the first time to God's Word'.[35] The pinnacle of the campaign occurred on 3 February 1932, when reciters came to celebrate the apex of Ramadan in one of the imperial mosques of Istanbul. Every aspect of the event was pregnant with symbolism. Adjacent to Topkapı Palace in the old city, the imperial mosque par excellence, Ayasofya Cami (the former Hagia Sophia Church), was selected as the venue. The event took place on the Night of Destiny (*laylat al-qadr/Kadir Gecesi*), the high point of the Ramadan season during which it is believed that God initially revealed the Qur'an to the Prophet Muhammad.[36] Typically, worshippers perform additional prayers on this night as they are understood to be unusually efficacious during this unique time in which God had opened a channel of revelation to humankind. Yet, in terms of ritual and symbolism, it was no typical Night of Destiny. The call to prayer, the *ezan*, which was traditionally called out in Arabic beginning with *Allahu akbar* ('God is the greatest'), was performed in Turkish as *Tanrı uludur*. The reciter, Kaynak, mounted the pulpit wearing not the traditional robe and turban, but rather a two-piece suit with his head uncovered. This was the image of the new model Muslim man: dressed in European attire and practising his religion via his national language, European in form and Turkish in content.

Western observers showered the Turkish-language worship initiative with praise as it signalled alignment with Protestant notions of rational religion and modern values. Perhaps no one was as effusive as the missionary Lyman MacCallum (1893–1955), who worked for the American Bible Society in Turkey. Born in the eastern Anatolian city of Maraş to missionary parents, MacCallum also oversaw the publication of a new Turkish translation of the Bible in the newly adopted Latin script.[37] Describing the Turkish call to prayer in Ankara, he writes:

> With that cry something deep and long-pent surged from the Turkish heart . . . Islam in Turkey was still alive, solid, mighty – and national. The new and foaming wine of Mustafa Kemal was brimming the ancient bottles of Mohammed. Tonight the Turks were tearing their religious life free from the senseless clutch of the withered hand of Arabia.[38]

This ebullient description appears to reflect MacCallum's own desire to encourage the vernacularisation of religion in the Protestant spirit, activities in which he was personally involved. For American and European observers, the adoption of Turkish signified a turning point in Turkey's modernisation and alignment with Western civilisation. Their triumphalist descriptions project their own desire to promote Westernisation and nationalism against the ideal of trans-regional Muslim unity, which was maintained, in part, by the Arabic language and alphabet. For many missionaries, the transference of what they called 'Christian values', that is, Euro-American ideas and cultural practices, signalled success even when this did not involve actual religious conversion, which was extremely rare in Turkey. It should be mentioned that Protestant missionaries applied the same logic to the Armenian and Greek Christian communities in Turkey, whom they criticised for using ritual and scriptural languages that were incomprehensible to their followers. As one author put it, the Bible had become a 'closed and sealed book' in 'an unknown tongue to the masses'.[39]

Yet these descriptions fail to answer the question of how Muslim observers responded to the use of Turkish translations and all that it entailed. It is hard to measure how Turkish Muslims felt about this debut since public criticism of the single-party regime was impossible via the media, and anyone who spoke out would have faced punishment. The Kemalist press lauded the event as a great success. The reality, however, was far more complex. In fact, many Turks considered the Turkish *ezan* and use of translations to be a violation of proper Islamic practice and an unwanted imposition by the state. Opposition to the Turkish call to prayer appeared in the city of Bursa in February 1933, when a crowd of Bursans marched to the office of the minister of Pious Foundations next to the famous Uludağ Mosque and demanded that Arabic, not Turkish, be used for mosque rituals. When the director replied that the orders came from above, the group gathered an even larger crowd and moved towards the mayor's office. The police intercepted them en route and dispersed the crowd. Though unsuccessful, this protest drew the attention of President Mustafa Kemal, who immediately came to the city to assess the situation.

That the president paid personal attention to the issue indicates the importance with which he viewed what could have been dismissed as minor civil unrest. After speaking with local authorities, he issued a statement to the press in which he warned that religious politics of any kind would not be tolerated by the government and that the 'reactionaries would probably not escape the clutches of justice'.[40] Kemal told the American ambassador Charles Sherrill that the instigators of the protest were not Turkish but a trio of foreigners: an Albanian, a Bulgarian and a Russian.[41] By blaming foreigners, perhaps the president was trying to convince the ambassador that there was no domestic opposition to Turkish-language ritual. Additionally, he said that the incident primarily concerned language, not religion, and that 'the Turkish people's national language and identity' would have priority and be used in all aspects of life.[42] This forceful assertion that Turkish would reign supreme even in religious affairs seemed to suggest that the Turkification of prayer and Qur'an recitation would proceed. The reality, however, was that the Bursa incident demonstrated the unpopularity of these reforms and showed their potential to cause unrest.

Protests and armed opposition to the state were not novel. Just a few years earlier, in 1930, a group of dervishes in a small town had demanded the restoration of the sharia and attacked the local gendarmerie; also, in south-eastern Turkey, several armed uprisings occurred in the early 1930s which showed that opposition to the state was robust in certain provinces.[43] Yet, the Bursa incident revealed that religious reforms could cause unrest even in major urban centres, like Bursa, where the state thought it had control. The residents of Bursa could not get the government to rescind the Turkish call-to-prayer, which had already been implemented and publicly defended, but they were successful in swaying the state's resolve to impose Turkish for ritual prayer and Qur'an recitation in mosques, as the political risk appeared too great. While key figures in the regime favoured the Turkification of religion, the danger of the citizens' mobilisation against the reforms caused them to abandon this campaign.[44]

The protest against the imposition of Turkish language in mosque rituals, and the broader opposition to it, concerned the displacement of Arabic and government's tampering with religion. So whether or not the state had possession of an authoritative translation, even one composed by a respected figure like Mehmet Akif, it is highly unlikely that pious Muslims would have embraced Turkish-language prayer and recitation. Devout intellectuals, like Eşref Edip, who hoped for a masterpiece translation, wanted it for personal edification and study, not for ritual. In fact, they opposed the Turkification of ritual with gusto and the regime was not so naïve as to think that Akif's or Elmalılı's translation would have weakened their resolve. The threat of mobilisation against further Turkification, not the absence of a good translation, brought about the abandonment of this project, and, in terms of mosque ritual, the Turkish call to prayer was the only element of the campaign that survived the Bursa incident.

Elmalılı versus the Turkish Qur'an

Elmalılı witnessed these Turkification experiments, and the reaction against them, as he worked on his translation and commentary. The idea that his translation might be used in similar fashion disturbed him profoundly, and he did not disguise his feelings on the matter. In the introduction to his translation and commentary, the first volume of which appeared in 1935, Elmalılı unleashed these cynical verses against translations of the Qur'an:

> The one who feels not the pleasure of truth is doomed to his imagination,
> The one who cannot verify becomes a prisoner to imitation.
> The one who knows not God embraces the World,
> The one who knows not the World in a daydream is twirled,
> The one who embraces a daydream scolds this dimension.
> The one who sees not his hero swoons at her mention.
> The one who sees not the beloved faints at her reflection.
> The one who sees not ahead sobers up at the end of the game.
> The one who recognises not the law comes to in the flame.
> The one who knows not the Book awakes at the judgement in consternation.
> The one who understands not the Qur'an meanders in translations.[45]

Elmalılı deplored the phrase 'Turkish Qur'an' (*Türkçe Kur'an*), which was used by the media in their descriptions of the experimental campaign to recite Turkish translations of the Qur'an at mosques in selected cities around the country. Writing in the wake of this initiative, Elmalılı exclaimed in the initial version of his introduction, 'God forbid a Turkish Qur'an!' The editors requested that he remove this sentence and he replaced it with, 'Is there such a thing as a Turkish Qur'an, you fool?'[46]

The introduction as a whole is a scholarly, at times sarcastic, diatribe against translations of the Qur'an. As the opening words to a rendering of the Qur'an, these attacks on translation make the point that while Elmalılı was willing to write a Turkish-language commentary and rendering, he would under no circumstances consent to calling his work a translation. Drawing on an understanding which is common in ulama literature, Elmalılı defines translation as '[the expression of] the meaning of speech in another language in an equivalent expression'.[47] The concept of equivalence he invokes is not general and vague but rather specific and precise. For, in dealing with the Qur'an, he believed that every nuance of meaning and style possessed immense importance: 'It must be equivalent to the original expression in clarity and signification, in summary and in detail, in general and in particular, in liberating and in restricting, in strength and in accuracy, in beauty of style, in manner of elucidation, in the production of knowledge, and in craft.'[48] This exigent definition of translation demands no less than perfect equivalence in all registers, 'otherwise it is not a translation; it is a deficient explanation'.[49] Elmalılı employs the logic that translation means perfect replication in another language, to the extent that it can be called by the same name as the original text because it possesses all the same attributes and even produces the same effect upon the reader.[50] Given these unattainable standards, it is unsurprising that Elmalılı argues that translation of the Qur'an is impossible. Yet, he goes even further, contending that translations do more harm than good – 'The one who reads a translation', writes Elmalılı, 'is frightened at a point where they should be pleased, and pleased at a point where they should be frightened: where there should be peace, there is the proclamation of war, where there should be war, they move to make peace'.[51] He concludes by saying that his work is a summary of the meanings (*meal*) that will introduce the Qur'an, but that it can neither take the place of the original nor be used for prayer.

Given his distaste for translation and his opposition to the government's vision of Islamic reform, it is important to consider why he accepted the commission to carry out the translation project. Elmalılı, like other members of the ulama, faced a difficult situation in deciding whether or not to participate in the new religious hierarchy and reform initiatives. Some decided that any association with the Kemalist regime was completely unethical and retreated from public life. Said Nursi, for example, took this path and taught disciples illegally outside of state institutions. His covert teaching and criticism of the government's policies made him a persecuted figure who spent much of his time under house arrest. In more confrontational fashion, Sabri, the leader of the conservative ulama, fled the country and condemned those who worked with the state.

Yet, other devout Muslims feared that abstaining from the reform process would allow the state to radically alter Islam in the country and effectively cut off modern Turks from the Ottoman-Islamic heritage. They reasoned that if only the Kemalist apparatchiks participated and the ulama abstained, then the outcome would be far worse. These ulama reasoned that 'qualified cooperation' with the state would enable them to shape the reform process and ensure that religious practice remained within acceptable parameters.[52] Additionally, they also hoped to salvage the literature and traditions of the Ottoman ulama, and transmit them into the Turkish Republic. For the other side, the government needed respected Islamic scholars to carry out this work in order for the reformed Turkish Islam to retain any legitimacy. The Qur'an translation scandal of 1924 had proven that the public would not accept the work of writers lacking serious Islamic credentials. Thus, both sides had to compromise in order to pursue their aims.

Elmalılı fit within the group of ulama that made a calculated decision to work with the state, and his commentary/translation of the Qur'an is a prime example of what qualified cooperation with the government could achieve. When the book was published in 1935, there was an obvious discrepancy between the book he had produced and the book the Kemalist regime wanted. Since Gökalp, the Turkists had envisioned an everyman's Qur'an that was succinct, easy to read and accessible to all. Ideally, everyone would be able to both own it and read it. It was to be the Turkish equivalent of Martin Luther's German Bible, the translation that, in their view, made possible the Protestant Reformation. Luther's work was the most widely printed book of its time, a runaway bestseller, and the German language he used was often colloquial, folksy and eminently vernacular. In other words, the book was pitched at and accessible to a broad segment of society. Turkist intellectuals hoped that a Qur'an translation would become a classic and serve as the defining text for a new Turkish Islam. This was precisely the type of book that Elmalılı did not write.

Rather than an everyman's translation, one for the average Turkish citizen, Elmalılı produced an erudite tome that was better suited to seminary students and scholars. Despite his stated intention to write in a 'plain and terse' style, the translation uses difficult vocabulary as well as complex and inverted sentences.[53] Moreover, it contains numerous untranslated and unreferenced quotations from the Qur'an in Arabic script, which he uses to prove points throughout the piece.[54] It is evident that he wrote for an educated audience with above-average knowledge of the Qur'an and the commentary tradition. Its language resonates with the scholarly registers of late Ottoman Turkish, and employs the author's expansive vocabulary and erudition. While the text is easier to read than Elmalılı's previous writings, which were characterised by turgid prose, it was still well beyond the reach of most Turks and inaccessible to young students and the newly literate classes. A Qur'an translator in the early 1950s – Hasan Basri Çantay – wrote that Elmalılı's translation was as inaccessible as the documents of the Turkish army, and that neither general readers nor intellectuals could read it with ease.[55]

Unlike previous republican-era translations, Elmalılı's *Hak Dini Kur'an Dili* (*The Religion of God, the Language of the Qur'an*) uses the format of a traditional commentary work, whereby the Qur'an is translated and interpreted on a verse-by-verse basis. Since the text of the translation is divided into verses and small clusters of verses followed by ample sections of commentary, it is impossible for the translation to be read as a continuous text. And, in contrast to the concise, portable translations published since 1924, *Hak Dini Kur'an Dili* consists of no fewer than nine weighty volumes. The sheer physical heft of this tome rendered it inconvenient. And since the translation is subordinated to the commentary format, the result is a text that is appropriate to be studied as a reference work. It seems, though, that this is precisely what the author intended. Elmalılı did not want his synopsis and commentary to be used for religious reform projects of the radical variety and, in traditional fashion, he discouraged unguided reading of the Qur'an. Both the format and the size of his text make it unsuitable for such purposes.

Through qualified cooperation, Elmalılı managed to control the potentially revolutionary translation project and transform the product into a thoughtful but conventional piece of Islamic scholarship. While it wrestles with modern problems and voices original opinions, the work embodies traditional *tafsīr*, not modern literary translation. Populist calls for an everyman's Turkish Qur'an, a literary masterpiece that would make the spirit and word of the Qur'an current and vivid for modern Turks, were answered with a modern but scholarly commentary composed more in the spirit of the late Ottoman ulama than that of the new Turkish citizen. Elmalılı's *Hak Dini* is one of the most formidable pieces of Islamic scholarship to have been composed in the Turkish republican period. Elmalılı's translation continues to serve as a key *tefsir* text in Turkish divinity schools. The translation has been reprinted frequently, but, due to the difficult style of the original, virtually all recent versions have been simplified and reworked to make them accessible to contemporary readers. Despite the fact that most readers have never seen the original, Elmalılı's translation has achieved renown in many circles as the best Turkish translation.[56] Against the wishes of the Turkish government and those of many devout intellectuals, Elmalılı succeeded in derailing the project to create a modern literary translation of the Qur'an in the 1930s.

Though a scholarly and political success for opponents of religious reform, the publication of *Hak Dini Kur'an Dili* did not satisfy the desire of devout intellectuals for a poetic and awe-inspiring translation. They continued to hope that the 'Poet of Islam', Akif, would finish and share his translation. One year after the release of Elmalılı's translation, in 1936, Akif decided to travel to Turkey for the first time in over a decade. Before departing, he left a copy of his manuscript with his friend Yozgatlı Mehmet İhsan (1902–61) for safekeeping until his return, at which time he hoped to resume work on it. Akif had suffered from malaria over the previous years and, with his health failing, he was aware that he might never return to Egypt; in consideration of this, he left instructions with İhsan to burn the manuscript if he did not come back to Cairo. The aging poet continued to fear that he had not done justice to the translation and, additionally, that the Turkish state might obtain the translation and use it for religious reform projects. Even at the cost of losing a decade of work, he preferred its destruction to its misuse.

In Istanbul, Akif's friends inquired relentlessly about the translation, to which he responded that he had been unsuccessful, that the task had been too difficult and that the burden of responsibility too great. He spoke about the actual translational task of producing an eloquent, accurate translation and avoided talking about the potential use of the book in state religious reforms.[57] The government expressed its interest anew in the translation when Akif returned to Istanbul. Kâmil Miras (1874–1957), an Islamic scholar, a member of parliament and the author of the 1925 bill to sponsor a translation/commentary, visited Akif and inquired why he had abandoned the project. 'I'm ashamed of my translation,' replied Akif. 'The Word of God is one thing and the translation of the servant Akif is another.'[58] Atatürk sent a member of the Grand National Assembly, Hakkı Tarık Us, to inform Akif that the government was still interested in the work and to inquire as to its whereabouts. Despite these attempts, Akif successfully deflected all inquirers, telling them that he had left the manuscript with a friend in Egypt but never divulging the name.[59]

Akif passed away in Istanbul at the end of 1936 but the interest in his lost translation did not fade. In fact, his friends and family maintained their desire to obtain the elusive manuscript and crossed the Mediterranean in hopes of finding it. In 1937, Eşref Edip travelled again to Egypt and met with Mehmet İhsan, aiming to learn the fate of Akif's work. Due to the task with which he had been entrusted, İhsan had the mindset that he needed to carry out Akif's wishes and protect the book from Kemalist religious reforms, but Edip explained that not only were the revolutionary reformers interested but also the 'sincere Muslims who love the Qur'an and want to understand its meaning'.[60] Edip could not fathom the idea that İhsan had burned the only copy of the manuscript and inquired as to whether there had been another made. Edip insinuated that perhaps İhsan had made a copy and then burned the original, thereby preserving the book but technically fulfilling Akif's wishes. İhsan Bey scoffed at this idea and refused to discuss the matter. His position was clear: Akif wanted the manuscript burned and he had carried out these instructions faithfully. Yet speculation persisted as İsmail Ezherli, a Bulgarian Turk who studied at al-Azhar, claimed to have seen a copy of the work when he visited İhsan in Cairo.[61] With the same belief that the book still existed, Akif's son-in-law, Ömer Rıza Doğrul, paid İhsan a visit and pressed him for information about the manuscript, claiming that it was his rightful inheritance. Brandishing an official document that entitled him to Akif's estate, Doğrul threatened to bring a legal case against İhsan if he did not hand over the manuscript, but, again, İhsan said nothing more than that he had fulfilled the late poet's wishes.[62]

Devout intellectuals in Turkey wanted to believe that Akif's translation was still extant, perhaps stowed away in a secret place in Egypt. Against the claims of those most intimately involved, these hopes persisted into the 1990s when an eyewitness who observed the manuscript burning, İsmail Hakkı Şengüler, published an account describing the destruction of İhsan's copy.[63] According to Şengüler, when Mehmet İhsan lay on his death bed in Cairo in 1961, he instructed his son Ekmeleddin İhsanoğlu (b. 1943) to find two large notebooks in his bedroom and to burn them when he died. Several days after he passed away, a group of friends, including Turkish students and Dr İbrahim Sabri – the son of the former Ottoman Shaykh al-Islam, Mustafa Sabri – came to the house to pay their respects. As mentioned above, Mustafa Sabri had been a vocal opponent of the Turkish independence movement and the Ankara government following World War I. Additionally, he had been the most uncompromising Turkish critic of translating the Qur'an and wrote a full monograph attacking the idea. He and his son İbrahim, aged twenty-three at the time, fled Turkey in 1920 and eventually settled in Cairo. In 1924, both father and son were included on the list of 150 people who were considered *personae non-gratae* by the Turkish government and forbidden entry into the country. Marked by the experiences of his family's exile, İbrahim Sabri remained an ardent critic of the Turkish state and of those who worked with it, including Mehmet Akif. Sabri accused Akif of being a supporter of the Young Turks – tantamount to a charge of atheism – and lambasted him for supporting the 'atheistic war' for independence and for writing the national anthem of an anti-Islamic government. Essentially, İbrahim Sabri accused Akif of being a supporter of anti-religious reforms and of collaborating with what he considered the illegitimate and apostate Ankara government.[64]

İhsan's son, Ekmeleddin İhsanoğlu, still a teenager at the time, explained his father's wishes concerning the notebooks to Dr Sabri, and then took him to see them. When they opened the covers, it became clear that İhsan Bey had not burned Akif's manuscript but had preserved it and even made an additional copy with his own hand. The assembled group was stunned. Akif's outspoken critic, Dr Sabri, decided to destroy the manuscripts immediately and pushed the group into action. They took a taxi to a house with a courtyard, placed the notebooks in an aluminium bin and incinerated the iconic translation page by page.[65] This account convinced most observers that Mehmet Akif's translation had been reduced to ashes.

In September 2012, a Turkish scholar – Recep Şentürk – announced that he had in his possession a surviving portion, approximately one-third, of Mehmet Akif's translation. A student of Mehmet İhsan at al-Azhar, Mustafa Runyun (1917–1988), had preserved a copy of the manuscript, written on a typewriter in Latin characters, and it remained in the house of his son where Şentürk learned of it and obtained the text in 1988.[66] Since that time, he kept its existence a secret, calling it 'a burden that I have carried for a quarter of a century'.[67] After consulting several scholars to verify the authenticity of the text, he decided to publish the translation in a critical edition which contains the first nine suras and includes the Arabic original on the opposite page.[68]

Following the publication of *Hak Dini Kur'an Dili* and the death of Mustafa Kemal Atatürk, the Turkish Qur'an ceased to be a priority, between 1938 and 1950, for the Turkish government under President İsmet İnönü (1884–1973). The state sponsored no new translations and no other translations were published. In fact, for a time, the state appears to have suppressed all publications that promoted religion as a social force as well as those that promoted the revival of public religion via Turkification. Instead, the policy became geared towards privatising religious life and reducing its influence in public life by impeding publications and promoting secularisation.[69] In effect, the state discouraged the promotion of Islam, even nationalist approaches to Islam, as a source of public values. It made Qur'an memorisation courses illegal, made no effort to reopen the modernist School of Theological Studies in Ankara and limited religious publications. Though maintaining the Turkish call to prayer, the single-party government from 1938 to 1950 did not promote translations of the Qur'an. Instead, it encouraged the decoupling of nationalism and Islam via neglect and suppression.

Despite the Turkish state's encouragement of a thoroughly secular nationalism in this period, the broad interest in translations of the Qur'an continued unabated among Turkish intellectuals. They continued to compose translations though they could not publish them, and, when democratic elections occurred in the 1950s, a wave of new translations appeared, which were more numerous and more diverse than those of the 1920s and 1930s. It became clear that Elmalılı's scholarly magnum opus had not filled the need for an accessible, vernacular rendering of the Qur'an, and that the aspiration for such a text continued to animate the imaginations of Turkish Muslims. After 1950, under an elected government and with the support of devout intellectuals, the number of translations rose steadily. As in the 1920s, critiques were abundant but, overall, the right to compose and publish translations became enshrined in the intellectual culture and, with the exception of periods of press censorship, protected by law. After decades of debate and legal restrictions, translations of the Qur'an entered mainstream Turkish intellectual culture.

Conclusion

Despite the support of devout intellectuals, secular-nationalists and the Turkish state, a suitably modern, literary rendering of the Qur'an proved to be elusive. The politicisation of Islam and aggressive reforms in the early Turkish Republic no doubt played a formative role in making this process so difficult and so polarised. It is difficult to imagine a more politically charged context for Qur'anic translation than the first two decades of the Turkish Republic. Devout Muslims and the ulama justifiably felt that Islam itself was under attack by the state, and they adopted defensive measures and strategic compromises to protect the integrity of Islamic life in the new republic. If late Ottoman intellectuals and the state had not made the Turkification of ritual a goal, it is conceivable that the conversation about translation would have transpired much differently, and perhaps Mehmet Akif would have willingly shared his rendering with the Turcophone world. In terms of reception, the counterfactual situation is also intriguing: how would the reading public have reacted to translations in the absence of such intense politicisation of Islam? Perhaps the ulama would have welcomed and lauded some Turkish translations, as in the case of Bengali renderings.[70]

The devout intelligentsia in Turkey saw it as imperative to reject the ritual use of translations as well as the concept of translation in order to preserve the dignity and centrality of the Arabic Qur'an. A combination of qualified cooperation, non-cooperation and popular pious opposition to Turkification enabled them to succeed in this goal. With the exception of the call to prayer, the ulama and devout intellectuals derailed the vernacularisation of ritual and prevented the creation of a canonised translation.

Attempts to forge a bond between Turkish language and the Qur'an in the 1920s and 1930s possessed distinct yet related aims. Turkists sought a symbol of the nation – a Turkish Qur'an – which would form the basis for the practice and re-imagination of Islam in the vernacular. Devout intellectuals wanted an eloquent rendering that would convey the message and spirit of the Qur'an to Turcophone Muslims in order to revive Islam and counteract the deleterious forces of materialism and immorality which accompanied modernisation. Both groups supported the state-sponsored translation project, and anticipated the creation of an authorised, state-approved version which would meet their needs. Yet the politicisation of religious reform made agreement on such a version virtually impossible, and even the hired translators withdrew their support from the original aims of the project.

The attempt to canonise a modern translation of the Qur'an failed. Rather than produce an authorised version, the debate and politics concerning the Turkish Qur'an normalised a process of continual translation and public debate about what a Turkish translation could and should be. Such translations became normal and expected but, nevertheless, remained contested and contentious. As both independent authors and the Directorate of Religious Affairs published translations, they remained both decentralised and officially sanctioned. While the Directorate of Religious Affairs has published several different versions over the second half of the twentieth century, none have become authoritative, and, in fact, no one expected them to become so. In effect, Turkish Muslims ceased the search for a canonised version and adopted an understanding that translations of the Qur'an would be multiple and imperfect and, nevertheless, would play an important, ongoing role in the religious and intellectual life of the country.

NOTES

1 'Türkçe Namaz', *Milliyet*, 7 April 1926, p. 3; 'Türkçe Namaz', *Akşam*, 7 April 1926, p. 2. The first Friday in Ramadan 1926 was 19 March 1926.
2 'Diyanet İşleri Riyaseti Heyet-i Müşaveresi', *Karar Defteri* 743 (1926) in Altuntaş, *Kur'an'ın Tercümesi*, pp. 106, 191.
3 Cemaleddin Efendi, 'Münevver Hocamız', *Vakit*, 6 April 1926, p. 2.
4 Bein, *Ottoman Ulema*, p. 126.
5 Ahmet Ağaoğlu, 'Türkçe lisanı haram mıdır?' *Milliyet Gazetesi*, 11 April 1926, p. 1.
6 See Chapter Four in this book.
7 [Süleyman Tevfik], *Tercüme-i Şerife: Kur'an-ı Kerim* (Istanbul, Sühulet Kütüphanesi and Matbaa-i Ahmed Kamil, 1927); idem, *Kur'an-ı Kerim Tercümesi: Türkçe Mushaf-ı Şerif* (Istanbul, Sühulet Kütübhanesi, 1927).
8 [Süleyman Tevfik], [Introduction], *Tercüme-i Şerife*.
9 M. Sait Özervarlı, 'Alternative Approaches to Modernization in the Late Ottoman Period: İzmirli İsmail Hakkı's Religious Thought against Materialist Scientism', *International Journal of Middle East Studies* 39 (2007), p. 84.
10 Ibid., pp. 87–8.
11 Doğrul, *Kur'an Nedir*, p. 96.
12 İsmail Hakkı İzmirli, *Meani-i Kur'an – Kuran-ı Kerim'in Türkçe Tercümesi: Ayat-ı Kerimenin Mebdeleriyle, Şerh ve İzahatını Havidir* (Istanbul, Kitaphane-i Hilmi, Milli Matbaa, 1927), p. 4.
13 İzmirli, *Meani*, pp. 3–4.
14 Ibid., p. 538.
15 Yusuf Ziya, 'Meani'l-Kur'an', *Mihrab* 2, no. 28 (1341/1925), p. 163.
16 Midhat Cemal Kuntay, *Mehmet Akif: Hayatı, Sanatı, Seciyesi Seçme Şiirleri* (Istanbul, Türkiye İş Bankası Kültür Yayınları, 1986), p. 128.
17 Ibid., p. 193.
18 'İlahiyat Fakültesinde Hazırlanan Lahiye Etrafında', *Vakit*, 20 June 1928, p. 1.
19 Cündioğlu, *Bir Kur'an Şairi*, p. 136; Ruhi Naci Sağdıç, 'Kur'an Tercemeleri Münasebetiyle Mehmed Akif Merhum Hakkında Hatıralar', *Sebilürreşad* 11, no. 2 (May 1958), pp. 281–3.
20 Fergan, *Mehmed Akif*, pp. 104–5.
21 See Chapter Five of this book, and 'The Ulama's Best and Brightest' in this chapter for more on him.
22 Fergan, *Mehmed Akif*, p. 106.
23 Ibid.
24 Bein, 'The Ulema', p. 209; Paul Janet and Gabriel Séailles, *Tahlilî Tarih-i Felsefe: Metalib ve Mezahib*, tr. Elmalılı Hamdi (Istanbul, Matbaa-i Amire, 1925).

25 Yusuf Şevki Yavuz, 'Elmalılı Muhammed Hamdi', *TDVİA*, vol. XI, pp. 57–62. On Elmalılı's understanding of the concept of religion, see Ahmet Karamustafa, 'Elmalılı Muhammed Hamdi Yazır's Philosophy of Religion (1848–1946)', *Archivum Ottomanicum* 19 (2001), pp. 273–9.
26 Geoffery Lewis, *The Turkish Language Reform: A Catastrophic Success* (Oxford, Oxford University Press, 1999).
27 Lewis, *The Turkish Language*, p. 62.
28 Ergin, *Türkiye Maarif Tarihi*, V, p. 1630.
29 The verse is numbered 27 in Cemil Sait's translation as the Egyptian numeration system had not yet been applied to early republican editions of the Qur'an.
30 Ergin, *Türkiye Maarif Tarihi*, V, p. 1635. Konya, the former capital of the Anatolian Seljuk Empire, is a large city in south-central Anatolia, famous for its conservative social mores and Jalāl al-Dīn Rūmī's tomb.
31 M. Kazimirski, *Le Koran* (1869), p. 67.
32 Ergin, *Türkiye Maarif Tarihi*, V, p. 1635.
33 Ibid., n. 1.
34 *Milliyet*, 22 January 1932, cited in F. Lyman MacCallum, 'Turkey Discovers the Koran', *Muslim World* 23 (1933), p. 25. A similar article appeared in *Cumhuriyet*; 'Yerebatan camisinde Türkçe Yasin okunacak', *Cumhuriyet*, 22 January 1932, p. 1.
35 MacCallum, 'Turkey Discovers the Koran', p. 26.
36 This night is closely associated with *Sūrat al-Qadr* (Q. 97).
37 His father, a veteran missionary, Frederick W. MacCallum, composed the new translation: Frederick W. MacCallum, *İncil: Ve Diğer Kitaplar* (Istanbul, Amerikan Kitabımukaddes Şirketi ve İngiliz ve Ecnebi Kitabımukaddes Şirketi, 1933).
38 MacCallum, 'Turkey Discovers the Koran', p. 28.
39 James L. Barton, *Daybreak in Turkey* (Boston, Pilgrim Press, 1908), p. 102.
40 'Hadise Hakkında Bursa'da Gazi Hazretlerinin Tebliği', *Vakit*, 2 February 1933, p. 1.
41 Charles Sherrill, 'Ambassador Charles H. Sherrill Comments on Atatürk's Views on Religion', in Rifat N. Bali, ed., *New Documents on Atatürk: Atatürk as Viewed through the Eyes of American Diplomats* (Istanbul, Isis Press, 2007), p. 171.
42 'Hadise Hakkında', p. 1.
43 Zürcher, *Turkey*, p. 179.
44 Andrew Mango, *Atatürk* (Woodstock, NY, Overlook Press, 2002), pp. 497–8.
45 Yazır, *Hak Dini*, I, p. 9. Translation is my own. I have altered the original format in order to accentuate the rhyme pattern.
46 Yazır, *Hak Dini*, p. 15; Cündioğlu, *Türkçe Kur'an*, p. 65.
47 Cündioğlu, *Türkçe Kur'an*, p. 65.
48 Ibid., p. 9
49 Ibid.
50 Willis Barnstone, *The Poetics of Translation: History, Theory, Practice* (New Haven, CT, Yale University Press, 1993), p. 16.
51 Yazır, *Hak Dini*, p. 12.
52 Bein, *Ottoman Ulema*, p. 113.
53 Yazır, *Hak Dini*, p. 16; Cündioğlu, *Türkçe Kur'an*, p. 65.

54 Yazır, *Hak Dini*, p. 15.
55 Hasan Basri Çantay, *Kur'an-ı Hakim ve Meal-i Kerim* (Istanbul, İsmail Akgün Matbaası, 1953), I, p. 7.
56 For an example of the linguistic simplification (*sadeleştirme*) of Elmalılı's work, see the following edition: Elmalılı M. Hamdi Yazır, *Hak Dini Kur'an Dili: Meali*, ed., Sadık Kılıç and Lütfullah Cebeci (Ankara, Akçağ, 2006).
57 Cündioğlu, *Bir Kur'an Şairi*, p. 148.
58 Ibid., p. 149.
59 Ibid., pp. 149–50.
60 Eşref Edip Fergan, 'Akif'in Kur'an Meali'ne Dair', cited in Cündioğlu, *Bir Kur'an Şairi*, p. 407.
61 M. Ertuğrul Düzdağ, *Mehmed Akif: Mısır Hayatı ve Kur'an Meali* (Istanbul, Şule Yayınları, 2003), pp. 233–4.
62 Fergan, 'Akif'in Kur'an Meali'ne Dair', cited in Cündioğlu, *Bir Kur'an Şairi*, p. 407.
63 İsmail Hakkı Şengüler ed., *Mehmed Akif Külliyatı* (Istanbul, Hi. net Neşriyat, 1992), X, pp. 230–33.
64 Düzdağ, *Mehmed Akif: Mısır Hayatı*, p. 24.
65 Cündioğlu, *Bir Kur'an Şairi*, pp. 425–7; Düzdağ and Okay, 'Mehmed Akif Ersoy', p. 434.
66 Mehmed Akif Ersoy, *Kur'an Meali: Fatiha Suresi-Berae Suresi*, ed. Recep Şentürk and Asım Cüneyd Köksal (Istanbul, Mahya Yayınları, 2012), p. xv.
67 'Mehmet Akif'in Kur'an-ı Kerim Meali Yayınlandı', *Samanyolu Haber*, 5 September 2012, http://www.samanyoluhaber.com/gundem/Mehmet-Akifin-Kuran-i-Kerim-meali-yayinlandi/832511/ (accessed 10 June 2014).
68 Ersoy, *Kur'an Meali*, p. xvi.
69 Cündioğlu, *Türkçe İbadet*, p. 101.
70 Uddin, *Constructing Bangladesh*, pp. 83–9.

8

An Ubiquitous Book

It is We who have sent down the Remembrance, and We watch over it.

Q. 15:9

FOR YEARS A HEAVY leather case sat untouched in an uninhabited apartment in Istanbul. It contained a unique manuscript, the only copy of a translation of the Qur'an composed by a schoolteacher named Mithat İli. Born in the Russian Empire in Kazan, Tatarstan, İli left home as a young man to pursue an education in Damascus and later settled in Istanbul. Knowledgeable in Arabic, Russian, Uzbek and Turkish, he possessed broad learning and lived a cosmopolitan life in various parts of central and western Asia. Mithat, the son of a respected imam, cared profoundly about the Qur'an and, dissatisfied with the translations written in the 1950s, took it upon himself to produce a translation that did justice to the text in Turkish.

Many Muslims like Mithat applied their energies to translating the sacred text into Turkish in the 1950s and 1960s, and more than a few of these renderings appeared in print, but Mithat İli's remains in its case, in its handwritten manuscript form. He composed this work in the Ottoman script, the one he was most comfortable with, despite the fact that Turkey had switched to the Latin alphabet in 1928, some thirty years earlier. The manuscript remains as a family heirloom, yet it also records one instance of the impulse to translate the central text of Islam which swept over the late Ottoman Empire, the Turkish Republic and much of the Muslim world in the modern period.[1]

Translations of the Qur'an have a long history, both in the larger Muslim world and in pre-Ottoman Anatolia. Despite the fact that many Muslim scholars discouraged translations or deemed them impossible, Muslim societies have a robust history of rendering the text into Islamicate languages prior to the age of print, and, aside from occasional wars of words, these books did not receive a great deal of attention. Additionally, despite the strong opinions held by some against Qur'anic translation, there is no parallel in the history of Qur'anic translation to the persecution faced by Biblical translators. Often, as in the case of the Sāmānid dynasty and Anatolian principalities, political leaders sponsored the composition of translations, which were written by the ulama. Thus, there was no connotation of political separatism or even Islamic sectarianism in these cases, a fact that might explain why translations did not attract greater attention.

In contrast, Qur'anic printing and translation were surrounded by contention in the late nineteenth and early twentieth centuries. Changing the content and form of the Holy Book had clear political, economic and cultural ramifications that challenged the status quo of religious authority and threatened the aura of the Qur'an. In Istanbul and Cairo, the north and south poles of Sunni authority in the Mediterranean, religious authorities met printing and translation with hostility and managed to inhibit these projects until political winds and social forces turned against them. The Ottoman ulama withheld permission to print the Qur'an until foreign and illegally printed copies flooded the market. This made Istanbul, arguably the most modern Muslim metropolis of the time, trail other Muslim capitals by decades in the modernisation of Qur'anic production. In Egypt, for example, the ruler, Mehmet Ali, forced the reluctant ulama to accept Qur'anic printing and printed Turkish-language commentaries. The debates on translation were both fiercer and more public than those over printing. In both capitals, controversies raged, tempers flared and thousands of pages were written in order to introduce and either discredit or legitimise modern translations of the Qur'an.

The spread of print technology, the decline in the prestige of the ulama and the simultaneous emergence of a new class of intellectuals changed the context of the debate on Qur'anic translation and helped cultivate the conception of the Qur'an as a modern book that could be mass produced, widely owned and read in the vernacular. Print technology made *muṣḥafs* more numerous and affordable than ever before. The Ottoman sultans emphasised the need for the rich and the poor to possess a copy of the Qur'an and, what's more, they projected the printed editions as symbols of the Ottoman Empire's political and religious authority. Printed Ottoman *muṣḥafs* simultaneously became both mass produced and linked to a political entity in the Islamic Unity campaigns and to the educational initiatives of the late nineteenth century. Towards the turn of the century, owning a copy of the book became increasingly commonplace and this new economic reality fostered a different sense of access to the Holy Book.

As Arabic-language copies of the Qur'an became abundant and inexpensive, the press also reshaped traditions of Qur'anic commentary, fostering a shift towards the use of the Turkish language for interpreting and explaining the text. Printed Turkish-language works made Qur'anic commentary accessible to a broader swathe of readers, and a new group of intellectuals from outside the ulama composed many works of this type. This transitional genre, somewhere between traditional commentary and modern translation, mixed passages of translated Qur'anic verses with simplified vernacular commentary. These books became important sources for the study of the Qur'an in the nineteenth century: they were used in madrasa education and read by the non-ulama intelligentsia as well. Through these books, the practice of studying Turkish-language renderings of the Qur'an became widespread, and non-ulama authors thus carved out a niche in which they could participate in the public interpretation of the Qur'an. As the political power and intellectual prestige of the ulama declined over the course of the nineteenth and early twentieth centuries, these new intellectuals became influential commentators on the Qur'an and set a precedent for vernacular engagement with the text.

Increasing literacy rates, the rapid development of Ottoman publishing and the onset of press freedom in 1908 accelerated the vernacularisation process. A growing number of writers composed Turkish renderings and commentaries, which they published in new journals and newspapers. Due to pressure from the Shaykh al-Islam and the political need for Islamic unity, neither newspapers nor book publishers could call these works translations, so they continued to be published under the category of commentary literature. By this time, calls for the translation of the Qur'an were circulating around the Muslim world as intellectuals in Russia, Indonesia and South Asia as well as Cairo and Istanbul debated the need for and merits of Qur'anic translation. Given the spread of European colonialism across Islamicate lands, a crucial question was whether translations would aid Muslim societies by fostering close engagement with the meaning of the text or divide Muslims by encouraging nationalisation at the expense of Islamic unity. Well-meaning Muslims were found on both sides of the debate and no consensus emerged, but in general terms, the ulama leadership tended to reject the call for translation, while reform-minded intellectuals supported it. In the Ottoman case, the ulama succeeded in prohibiting the publication of such works until the fall of the empire.

The end of the Ottoman Empire transformed the political and intellectual landscape of Turkey and, in some sense, the Muslim world. The suppression of the ulama in modern Turkey opened the way for publishing translations of the Qur'an, but this florescence of publishing did not bring about the desired result. When initial renderings received widespread criticism, the parliament moved to sponsor a translation and commentary project that would meet the demands of devout intellectuals and secular-nationalists and provide a seminal translation of the Qur'an for the new nation state. The prominent scholar Elmalılı managed to create an important scholarly work in the Turkish language, but effectively undermined the state's project to provide a broadly accessible, everyman's Turkish Qur'an. However, Elmalılı won only a fleeting victory because the demand for an accessible, modern translation – independent from commentary – persisted. With the intensification of national identity in modern Turkey, this demand fuelled dozens and dozens of translation efforts in the coming decades, often by writers with far less expertise than Elmalılı.

Meanwhile, the epicentre of the translation debate shifted to the southern shore of the Mediterranean in the 1930s, engulfing

Egyptian scholars in a pitched battle. The debate there emerged from related yet distinct concerns. Whereas in Turkey, efforts were geared towards making the Qur'an accessible to the national, Turkish-speaking community, Egyptian reformists supported English-language translations in order to make the Qur'an accessible to non-Muslims and to combat the translations of Christian missionaries. Much of the conversation was bound up with anti-missionary sentiment in Egypt, and reformists like Marāghī argued that translations were an excellent means to win converts to Islam and favourably influence Western perceptions of the religion. Additionally, Egyptian scholars aimed to make Egypt a leader in the post-caliphate Islamic world and saw translations as a means to assert its influence on modern understandings of the Qur'an. Neither in Turkey nor in Egypt did the debates lead to a decisive victory for either side, but the perceived need for 'translations of the meanings' (*tarjamāt maʿānī'l-Qur'ān*) made steady progress, first among devout intellectuals and reformists and later among the ulama. Regardless of these debates, authors around the Muslim world were composing translations with increasing frequency throughout the early twentieth century.

The battles waged in the first half of the twentieth century set the stage for the widespread acceptance and expansion of printing and translation initiatives in the late twentieth and twenty-first centuries. Following the Turkish and Egyptian debates about the merits of translation, a de facto consensus developed among Muslim leaders and the ulama that translations, not scholastic commentaries, would be essential for education, private reading and Islamic missionary efforts in the modern world. Often, they would not call these works translations, but instead developed various names for translations, including the perplexing yet popular 'translation of the meanings'. Many countries liberalised rules governing the publication of translations and, in others, government agencies in charge of Islamic affairs have commissioned and published translations on a wide scale. As a result, printed copies of the Qur'an and translations, once rare commodities, have become ubiquitous in the modern Muslim world.

In Turkey, the state continued the Ottoman tradition of monitoring the publication of *muṣḥaf*s through the Muṣḥaf Examination

Committee (Mushafları İnceleme ve Kiraat Kurulu Başkanlığı) that continues to function as the state's check on copies of the Arabic Qur'an. Between 1924 and 1973, presses in Istanbul and Ankara published nearly two million copies.[2] The Directorate of Religious Affairs oversaw but did not actually publish the vast majority of these copies of the Qur'an in Arabic; in fact, for the first thirty-four years of its existence (1924–1958), it did not publish a single copy of the Qur'an and began to do so only in 1959. *Muṣḥaf* printing by the Directorate of Religious Affairs became more frequent in the 1980s following the military coup of 1980 which instigated a policy to promote a stronger sense of Islamic identity, leading to required religious education courses in all public schools, the growth of Qur'an courses and the expansion of vocational schools for imams and religious personnel.[3] Until the 1980s, the Turkish state allowed and monitored the printing (and study) of the Arabic Qur'an, but it did not go to great lengths to encourage it. In contrast, the Directorate has sponsored and published many Turkish renderings in various editions over the years (See Figure 12, translation of the Qur'an on a pulpit).[4] Despite this frequent activity, the state-sponsored translations have not been as widespread or diverse as private translation and publishing efforts.

With the democratic opening of the 1950s a wave of new translations from private publishers swept on to the book market and, ever since, new translations have been published in droves, creating an amazing variety of vernacular renderings which can be purchased in virtually every bookshop in Turkey. Sharia-minded groups, staunch nationalists, Sufi orders and Muslim minorities such as the Alevi-Bektashi have composed their own versions. One can choose from some four hundred versions, including several fully-rhyming renderings, numerous editions that reorganise the order of suras according to the chronology of the revelations, and modernised versions of the classics from the nineteenth and twentieth centuries like İsmail Ferruh Efendi's *Mevakib* and Elmalılı Hamdi Yazır's *Hak Dini Kur'an Dili*. The level of ubiquity and accessibility has reached a point at which advertisements for translations now appear on television, and newspapers often give copies of the Qur'an away to subscribers as promotions. With new versions appearing on the Turkish book market each year, some scholars and journalists have proclaimed a 'translation war' between competing versions or even a 'chaos of translation' as foretold by scholars like Mustafa Sabri in the 1930s.[5] It is estimated that publishers sell between 650,000 and 700,000 copies a year, figures that do not include the sales of *muṣḥaf*s.[6]

It is important to note that many translations include a photolithographic image of the Qur'an beside the Turkish rendering. The most commonly used version for the Arabic text is that of Hafız Osman, the calligrapher whose *muṣḥaf* was the basis for the first legally imported Qur'an in Istanbul and was reprinted many times over the course of the late nineteenth and early twentieth centuries. In versions that combine Turkish translation and Ottoman calligraphy, one can see the result of two great debates in the modern history of the Qur'an in tangible form. The coexistence of translation and the 'Arabic Qur'an' in the same book embodies a modern consensus in Turkey in which the original remains cherished alongside the vernacular renderings. Despite ominous forecasts by opponents of translation that the Arabic Qur'an would be lost or destroyed, it remains a vital part of the culture and maintains a prominent place even within translations.

Perhaps because of the ongoing debates in the country, Turkish scholars have also taken a particular interest in the history of Qur'anic translation. The Istanbul-based Research Centre for Islamic History, Art and Culture (IRCICA) undertook a large bibliography project in the 1980s to catalogue all existing printed 'translations of the meanings', that is translations, in sixty-five languages, which resulted in the most extensive reference source of its kind, the *World Bibliography of Translations of the Meanings of the Holy Qur'an*. Several subsequent efforts have produced bibliographies of manuscript translations in Persian, Turkish and Urdu.[7] The Turkish scholar Hidayet Aydar has published one of the few academic works that tracks Qur'anic translation efforts around the world in multiple languages,[8] and focused studies of particular translations and local contexts abound.

The rise of the Islamic-inspired Justice and Development Party (Adalet ve Kalkınma Partisi), which began in the 2002 election, brought about a renewed vitality of Islam as a source of public values in Turkey. In contrast to the secular thrust of previous administrations, the JDP has supported faith-based initiatives, and the consequences of this support have included expanded printing of the Qur'an as well as enhanced appreciation for Ottoman Qur'anic calligraphy and Islamic book arts. The Turkish Ministry of Tourism and Culture, as part of its strategy to build public relations with other Muslim-majority countries, has publicised Ottoman-era *muṣḥaf*s at book fairs as achievements of Ottoman-Islamic civilisation.[9] The Directorate of Religious Affairs has reinvigorated its printing of Arabic *muṣḥaf*s, and IRCICA has published a facsimile of a copy attributed to the time of the third caliph, 'Uthmān (r. 23–35/644–55), and reproduced what it considers the first edition of the Qur'an 'printed in the Muslim world', an 1803 version published in Kazan, Russia.[10]

Throughout the twentieth century, Muslim nation states competed to influence the interpretation of the Qur'an and the Islamic practice of their citizens, subjects and co-religionists around the world, and renderings of the Qur'an have played a major role in their efforts. Departments of religious affairs, missionary groups and Islamic movements of various types have embraced translations as a means of expressing and promoting their preferred understandings of the Holy Book. In the 1970s, several Arab countries picked up where the Egyptian debates of the 1930s had left off, and printed translations in various languages for use in public outreach and missionary work. After more than four decades, the ulama authorities at al-Azhar approved the translation of Marmaduke Pickthall for publication in 1973.[11] The very same year, a Libyan organisation published the rendering of Abdullah Yusuf Ali, and in 1980, that of Pickthall, followed by an English language commentary on the last *juz'* of the Qur'an by Mahmoud Ayoub.[12]

While these cases are instructive of the increasing activity in this direction, no institution exemplifies the embrace of Qur'anic printing and translation more than the King Fahd Complex for the Printing of the Holy Qur'an in Medina, Saudi Arabia. Founded by King Fahd b. 'Abd al-'Azīz in 1982, the complex prints more copies and translations of the Qur'an than any other printing house in the world.

Between 1984 and 2013, it printed over 260 million copies, including translations in more than fifty languages.[13] The complex employs over 1,700 workers and produces an average of ten million copies per year. It distributes the majority of these books to pilgrims who visit Mecca and Medina, offering a copy of the Qur'an to each and every visitor. Embassies, schools and mosques receive the remainder, which are distributed liberally and free of charge.

Saudi media frequently advertise the scope of their printing and the number of copies they distribute at the hajj and around the world. This publishing initiative forms part of the Saudi regime's strategy of building public relations with the rest of the Muslim world and serves as a way in which the monarchy projects its Islamic authority. Within the unique context of the hajj, the free copies of the Qur'an are presented as gifts from the 'Custodian of the Holy Places', King Fahd. The complex has also developed a new calligraphic rendering of the Arabic text, which it calls *The Muṣḥaf of Medina*, and publishes it according to three different styles of recitation or 'readings' (*qirā'āt*). The complex currently prints the readings of Ḥafṣ *ʿan* ʿĀṣim, Warsh *ʿan* Nāfiʿ and al-Dūrī *ʿan* Abī ʿAmr. Differences in recitation involve the length of syllables, the placement of pauses and the assimilation of certain letters, and different readings predominate in different regions of the Muslim world. In West Africa, for example, the style of Warsh is dominant, while the Ḥafṣ version is prevalent in the eastern Mediterranean and much of the Islamic east. The Egyptian editions of 1924 and 1936, which have been the most widely used recensions of modern times, exclusively use the reading of Ḥafṣ, and this has led to the de facto standardisation of this particular style. The Saudi printing of three different readings presents an interesting attempt to accommodate a broader array of Muslims, and to expand the scope of Saudi prestige and influence.

The attempt to address and influence the widest number of Muslims possible is also reflected in the King Fahd Complex's efforts to publish translations and produce new translations, often in languages that lack a complete rendering. It currently publishes translations and regularly announces the appearance of newly commissioned works. In 2009, for instance, the complex produced a translation in Tamazight, the language of the Amazigh people (commonly known as 'Berbers'), copies of which were distributed via the Saudi Embassy in Algeria.[14] It has recently released a partial translation in the Roma language as well as a newly revised Mandarin Chinese version. Upcoming publications include a Chichewa version for the country of Malawi and another in the Mandarin dialect of Sulawesi Island in Indonesia. In supporting translations into underserved languages, the King Fahd Complex has adopted the translation practice of Christian missionaries and transformed it into a tool for Islamic missionary work. Additionally, the Saudis have taken the initiative to produce new or revised translations for languages which already have translations, including Turkish, Persian, Urdu and English. Among English translations, the King Fahd Complex has published the well-known translation of Yusuf Ali in a version that cuts out his creative, unconventional footnotes.

In embarking on this venture, the Saudi complex did not evade the question of licitness. Rather than dodge the sensitive topics of the recitation and ritual use of translations, the King Fahd Complex confronted the issues head-on with a fatwa:

> Is it permissible for a Muslim to recite or memorise the Holy Qur'an in a language other than Arabic?
>
> If a Muslim cannot recite or memorise the Holy Qur'an in Arabic, it is permissible for him to do so in any other language; this is better than abandoning it altogether. Allah said, 'Allah burdens not a person beyond his scope' (Q. 2:286)[15]

Based on an opinion by Ibn Taymiyya, the fatwa not only conveys the idea that renderings of the Qur'an are permissible, it also grants licence to those unskilled in Arabic to 'recite or memorise' the Qur'an in other languages in preference to them not doing so at all. Especially for non-Ḥanafī ulama, this is a remarkably liberal opinion on the use of translations, to which neither the contemporary Egyptian nor Turkish ulama would now subscribe. In this fatwa and in the Saudi translation efforts, the ethos of access has trumped traditional reservations about composing and using translations of the Qur'an.

Reminiscent of the Pan-Islamic campaign of Abdülhamid II, the Saudi publishing efforts aim to make the Qur'an broadly accessible – economically and linguistically – meanwhile serving as a vehicle to strengthen the Islamic credentials of the sovereign. The Ottoman sultan fostered, perhaps even instigated, the age of mass Qur'anic production, but rejected the emergence of translations, which the secularist regime later encouraged in the early years of the Turkish Republic while ceasing state production of the Arabic Qur'an. The Saudi regime, and others, have combined these efforts and disseminated both *muṣḥafs* and translations as widely as possible, ushering in a new age of Qur'anic accessibility and ubiquity. This state of affairs is stunning when we consider that the Ottoman ulama rejected Qur'an printing as late as the 1870s, and that in the 1920s and 1930s many pious Muslims, including non-Arabs, felt that translations of the Qur'an were detrimental books. Just fifty years after the seminal modern debates on the translation, that is, by the last quarter of the twentieth century, efforts to make the Qur'an accessible had come full circle. Renderings of the Qur'an gained near universal usage and one of the most conservative states in the Muslim world embarked on Qur'an translation and publication projects on a large scale.

Like the Ottoman Empire, the Saudi state projects itself not only as the provider but also as the defender of the text and explains its rationale for mass producing the Qur'an as a means of protecting the Holy Book. The King Fahd Complex invokes the Qur'anic verse Q. 15:9, *It is We who have sent down the Remembrance, and We watch over it*, as scriptural support for its activities. If the verse assures divine protection of the revelation, the Saudi citation of it suggests that the King Fahd Complex acts as an agent of God in its efforts to protect, translate and disseminate the text. Whereas in many pre-print book cultures around the world, the protection of sacred texts formerly implied control of physical copies, knowledge of a sacred language and interpretation by a group of custodians – such as priests, Brahmins or the ulama – the King Fahd Complex and much of the Muslim world now embrace the idea that broad access and availability protect the text by making it ubiquitous and intelligible.

Access to the text has also amplified the role of translations for missionary use, which has increased steadily over the course of the late twentieth and twenty-first centuries. In 2012, the streets of cities across Germany bore witness to a unique Qur'an distribution effort that reveals the extent to which Muslim attitudes towards translation have changed over the past century. An organisation called the True Religion (Die Wahre Religion) set up booths across the country to give away free German-language translations to anyone who would take one, with the goal of handing out 25 million copies, enough to supply a Qur'an for every German household. Given the initiative's links to Salafī networks and publicised conversions of Germans to Islam in recent years, the land where Luther's German Bible had once spread like wild fire reacted with anxiety to this coordinated attempt to shower the country with vernacular copies of the Qur'an.[16] In 1912, the Ottoman state confiscated any translation that entered its borders and most pious Muslims considered translations haram. In 2012, proselytising Muslims took to the streets and embarked on an ambitious (and unusual) campaign to distribute millions of translations in a European language. It is no exaggeration to say that a revolution in the conception and use of Qur'anic translations has taken place in the Muslim world over the past century.

Translations, whether oral or written, have been and remain an important means by which non-Arabic speakers encounter the Qur'an. Having taken this into consideration over the past decades, Muslim intellectuals and societies have developed an approach to the genre that preserves the idea of the Qur'an as a unique book but also makes it possible to spread and project something of the meaning of the book across economic, linguistic and geographic boundaries. Neither in Istanbul nor in Cairo or Kazan is a translation equal to *the* Qur'an, but, according to the dominant approach of the late twentieth and twenty-first centuries, translations reflect something significant from the original, and publishing, studying and spreading that reflection has played a pivotal role in the elaboration of Islam in the modern world.

NOTES

1 Thanks to Erdağ Göknar for sharing this family story.

2 Nail Arslanpay, *Diyanet İşleri Başkanlığı: Kuruluşu Çalışması ve Birimlerinin Tanıtılması* (Ankara, Ayyıldız Matbaası, 1973), p. 71.

3 *Diyanet İşleri Başkanlığı Yayınları Bibliyografyası (1924–2010)*, http://www.diyanet.gov.tr/yayin/y_bibliyografya.pdf (accessed 15 March 2012); Many subsequent printings.

4 Including reprints, the Directorate published translations in the years 1935–8, 1961, 1976, 1983, 1984, 1990, 1992, 2001, 2002, 2003, 2008. Ibid.

5 Adem Demir, 'Cemaatler arası Meal Savaşı', *Newsweek Türkiye*, 5 July 2009, p. 52.

6 Ibid., p. 54.

7 Binark and Eren, *World Bibliography ... Printed Translations*; M. Nejat Sefercioğlu, *World Bibliography of Translations of the Holy Qur'an in Manuscript Form*, ed. Ekmeleddin İhsanoğlu (Istanbul, IRCICA, 2000); Ahmad Khan, *World Bibliography of Translations of the Holy Qur'an in Manuscript Form II: Translations in Urdu*, ed. Ekmeleddin İhsanoğlu (Istanbul, IRCICA, 2010).

8 Hidayet Aydar, *Kur'an-ı Kerim Tercümesi Meselesi* (Istanbul, Kur'an Okulu Yayıncılık, 1996).

9 Ailyn Algonia, 'Ottoman Era's Qur'an Copy Star Attraction at Book Fair', *Qatar Tribune*, 30 November 2010, pp. 1, 16.

10 Halit Eren, 'Editorial', *OIC Research Centre for Islamic History, Art and Culture Newsletter*, no. 80 (September–December 2009), p. 1; *Hz. Osman'a İzafe Edilen Mushaf-ı Şerif: Topkapı Sarayı Müzesi Nüshası*, ed. Tayyar Altıkulaç (Istanbul, IRCICA, 2007).

11 Marmaduke William Pickthall, *The Meaning of the Glorious Qur'ān* (Cairo, Dār al-Kitāb al-Miṣrī, 1973).

12 Abdullah Yusuf Ali, *The Glorious Kur'an* (Libyan Arab Republic, Call of Islam Society, 1973); Muhammad Marmaduke Pickthall, *The Meaning of the Glorious Koran* (Libyan Arab Republic, Islamic Call Society, 1980); Mahmoud Ayoub, *The Great Tiding: Interpretation of Juz' 'Amma, the Last Part of the Quran* (Tripoli, Libyan Arab Republic, Islamic Call Society, 1983).

13 Ali Fayyaz, '264m Copies of Qur'an Distributed', *Arab News*, 5 September 2013, http://www.arabnews.com/news/463606 (accessed 11 June 2014).

14 Dalila B., 'The Holy Qur'an in French and Amazight Distributed', *Ennahar*, http://www.ennaharonline.com/en/news/1806.html (accessed 15 August 2009).

15 King Fahd Complex for the Printing of the Holy Qur'an, 'Reciting or Memorising the Holy Qur'an in a Language Other than Arabic', *Fatwa No. 89* (1426/2005), http://www.qurancomplex.org (accessed 2 May 2012).

16 Wolfgang Dick, 'Free Koran Giveaway Sparks Debate', *Deutsche Welle*, 13 April 2012, http://www.dw.de/free-koran-giveaway-sparks-security-debate/a-15882277 (accessed 22 January 2013); Melissa Eddy and Nicholas Kulish, 'Koran Giveaway in Germany Has Some Officials Worried', *New York Times*, 16 April 2012, http://www.nytimes.com/2012/04/17/world/europe/germany-koran-giveaway-worries-officials.html (accessed 26 June 2012).

Bibliography

Primary Sources

Ahmet Cevdet Pasha. *Tarih-i Cevdet*, 12 vols. Istanbul, Matbaa-i Osmaniye, 1309/1891–2.

——. *Tezâkir*, ed. Cavid Baysun, 2nd edn, 4 vols. Ankara, Türk Tarih Kurumu Basımevi, 1986.

Ahmet Midhat. *Beşair: Sıdk-ı Muhammediye*. Istanbul, Kırk Anbar Matbaası, 1312/1894–5.

Ahmet Salih b. Abdullah. *Zübed-i asari'l-Mevahib ve'l-Envar*. Istanbul, Rıza Efendi Matbaası, 1292/1875.

Ağaoğlu, Ahmet. 'Türkçe Lisanı Haram mıdır?' *Milliyet Gazetesi*, 11 April 1926, p. 1.

Akçura, Yusuf. '1329 Senesinde Türk Dünyası' (1914), in Murat Şefkatli, ed., *Türk Yurdu*, vol. III. Ankara, Tutibay Yayınları, 1999.

Akseki, Ahmet Hamdi. 'Cevabı mı? İtirafı mı?' *Sebilürreşad* 24, no. 600 (1924), pp. 23–6.

——. 'Türkçe Kur'an Namındaki Kitabın Sahibi Cemil Said'e'. *Sebilürreşad* 24, no. 624 (1924), pp. 403–6.

Algonia, Ailyn. 'Ottoman Era's Qur'an Copy Star Attraction at Book Fair'. *Qatar Tribune*, 30 November 2010, pp. 1, 16.

Ali, Abdullah Yusuf, tr. *The Glorious Kur'an*. Libyan Arab Republic, Call of Islam Society, 1973; *The Holy Qur'an*. Lahore, Shaikh Muhammad Ashraf, 1934; *The Holy Qur'an: Text, Translation and Commentary*. Cairo, al-Manār, 1938.

Ali, Muhammad, tr. *The Holy Qur'an: Containing Arabic Text with English Translation and Commentary*. Woking, Islamic Review Office, 1917.

Ali Suavi. 'İstanbul'da Mektup'. *Ulum*, 15 Şaban 1287/9 November 1870, pp. 82–3.

Amme Cüzü [Juz' 30]. Istanbul, Matbaa-i Osmaniye, 1302/1884–5.

Ankaralı İsmail. *Fatiha Tefsiri: Fütuhat-i Ayniye*. Istanbul, Matbaa-i Ahmed Kamil, 1328/1910–11.

Ayıntâbî Mehmet. *Tercüme-i Tefsir-i Tibyan*. Cairo, Bulaq, 1257/1841–2.

Ayıntâbî Mehmet and İsmail Ferruh. *Tefsir-i Tibyan ve Tefsir-i Mevakib* [published together in one volume]. Dersaadet, Istanbul, Şirket-i Sahafiye-i Osmaniye, 1902.

Azmzâde Refik Bey. *Kıvam-ı İslam*, tr. Mehmet Ubeydullah. Cairo, 1324/1906.

Balıkesirli Devletoğlu Yusuf. *Vikaye-i Manzume*, MS İzmir 762. Süleymaniye Library, Istanbul.

Barton, James L. *Daybreak in Turkey*. Boston, Pilgrim Press, 1908.

Bereketzade, İsmail Hakkı. 'Necaib-i Kur'aniye'. *Sırat-ı Müstakim* 1, no. 2 (1908), pp. 23–6.

Biberstein-Kazimirski, Albert de, tr. *Le Koran*. Paris, Charpentier, 1841; 1869.

Bigiyev, Musa Carullah. *Halk Nazarına bir Niçe Mesele*. Kazan, Mahmud 'Alim Efendi Maqsudov, 1912.

——. 'Teesüf etmiştim şimdi anladım'. *İslam Dünyası* 1, no. 10 (1913), pp. 149–55.

Bodin, Jean. *Colloque entre sept scavans qui sont de differens sentimens: Des secrets cachez, des choses relevées*. Geneva, Droz, 1984.

[Börekçi], Mehmet Rifat. 'Beyan-ı Hakikat Müslümanlara'. *Sebilürreşad* 24, no. 599 (1924), pp. 7–8.

——. 'İkaz'. *Sebilürreşad* 24, no. 620 (1924), p. 349.

Bozkurt, Mahmut Esat. *Atatürk İhtilâli*. Istanbul, Burhaneddin Matbaası, 1940.

de Busbecq, Ogier Ghislain (Ghiselin). *The Turkish Letters of Ogier Ghiselin De Busbecq, Imperial Ambassador at Constantinople, 1554–1562*, tr. Edward Seymour Forster. Oxford, Clarendon Press, 1968.

'Büyük bir Tecavüz: Kur'an'dan Menfaat Teminine Kalkışan bir Hristiyan'. *Sebilürreşad* 21, nos. 542–3 (1923), pp. 181–2.

Çantay, Hasan Basri. *Kur'an-ı Hakim ve Meal-i Kerim*, 3 vols. Istanbul, İsmail Akgün Matbaası, 1953.

Celal Nuri. *Hatemü'l-Enbiya*. Istanbul, Yeni Osmanlı Matbaası, 1332/1913–14.

Cemaleddin Efendi. 'Münevver Hocamız'. *Vakit*, 6 April 1926, p. 2.

Cemil Sait [Dikel]. *Kur'an-ı Kerim Tercümesi*. Istanbul, Şems Matbaası, 1924.

Cevdet. *See* Ahmet Cevdet Pasha.

Dale, Godfrey. *Tafsiri Ya Kurani Ya Kiarabu Kwa Lugha Ya Kisawahili Pamoja Na Dibaji Na Maelezo Machache*. London, Society for Promoting Christian Knowledge, 1923.

Demircioğlu, Cemal. 'From Discourse to Practice: Rethinking "Translation" (*Terceme*) and Related Practices of Text Production in the Late Ottoman Literary Tradition'. PhD Thesis, Boğaziçi University, 2005.

al-Dihlawī, Muḥammad Jamāl al-Dīn. *el-Tefsirü'l-Cemali ala'l-tenzil il-Celali*, tr. Muhammad Khayr al-Dīn Hindī al-Haydarābādī. Cairo, Bulak Matbaası, 1294/1877.

Doğrul, Ömer Rıza. 'A Heavy Loss for the Muslim World: Muhammad Ali and His Work', *Islamic Review* (May 1952), pp. 17–18.

——. *Kur'an Nedir?* Istanbul, Amedi Matbaası, 1927.

——. *Tanrı Buyruğu: Kur'an-ı Kerim Tercüme ve Tefsiri*. Istanbul, Muallim Ahmet Halit Kütüphanesi, 1934.

[Ebu Suud] Abū'l-Su'ūd Muḥammad b. Muḥammad 'Imadī. *Irshād al-'aql al-salīm ilā mazāyā al-Qur'ān al-Karīm*, 5 vols. Beirut, Dar al-Fikr, 1421/2001.

Ebüzziya Tevfik. *Lûgat-i Ebüzziya*. Istanbul, Matbaa-i Ebüzziya, 1306/1888–9.

Efgani, Ubeydullah. *Kavm-i Cedid*. Istanbul, Şems Matbaası, 1331/1912–13.

'Eid ul-Fitr'. *Islamic Review* (June–July 1920), pp. 224–7.

Ersoy, Mehmet Akif. *Kur'an Meali: Fatiha Suresi-Berae Suresi*, ed. Recep Şentürk and Asım Cüneyd Köksal. Istanbul, Mahya Yayınları, 2012.

——. 'Mevaiz-i Diniyeden: İttihad Yaşatır, Yükseltir - Teferruk Yakar, Öldürür'. *Sırat-ı Müstakim* 5, no. 116 (1326/1908), pp. 205–7.

——. *Safahat: Asım*. Istanbul, Sırat-ı Müstakim, 1911; Part VI. Istanbul, İnkılap Kitabevi, 1958.

[Eşref Edip]. 'Kur'an-ı Kerim'in Tercümesi'. *See* Fergan, Eşref Edip.
——. 'Kur'an-ı Kerim Tercümeleri Hakkında'. *See* Fergan, Eşref Edip.
——. 'Kur'an Tercümelerindeki Hatalar'. *See* Fergan, Eşref Edip.
Euclid. *Euclidis elementorum geometricorum libri tredecim; Ex traditione doctissimi Nasiridini Tusini.* Rome, Typographia Medicea, 1594.
Fani, Şeyh Muhsin-i (Hüseyin Kâzım Kadri). 'Hazreti Şeyhin Sebil'e İlk ve Son Cevabı', reprinted in [Eşref Edip], 'Kur'an-ı Kerim Tercümeleri Hakkında', *Sebilürreşad* 24, no. 599 (1924), p. 8.
—— (Hüseyin Kâzım Kadri). *İstikbale Doğru.* Istanbul, Ahmed İhsan ve Şürekası Matbaacılık Osmanlı Şirketi, 1331/1913–14.
—— (Hüseyin Kâzım Kadri). *Nurü'l-Beyan: Kur'an-ı Kerim'nin Türkçe Tercümesi*, ed. İbrahim Hilmi. Istanbul, Matbaa-i Amire, 1924.
Fayyaz, Ali. '264m Copies of Qur'an Distributed'. *Arab News*, 5 September 2013. http://www.arabnews.com/news/463606 (accessed 11 June 2014).
Fergan, Eşref Edip. 'Kur'an-ı Kerim Tercümeleri Hakkında'. *Sebilürreşad* 24, no. 599 (1924), pp. 8–11.
——. 'Kur'an-ı Kerim'in Tercümesi'. *Sebilürreşad* 23, no. 596 (1924), pp. 377–8; vol. 23, no. 597 (1924), pp. 386–9.
——. 'Kur'an Tercümelerindeki Hatalar'. *Sebilürreşad* 24, no. 601 (1924), pp. 35–7.
——. *Mehmed Akif: Hayatı-Eserleri ve 70 Muharririn Yazıları.* Istanbul, Asari İlmiye Kütüphanesi Nesriyati, 1938.
Ferruh. *See* İsmail Ferruh.
al-Ghamrāwī, Muḥammad Aḥmad and Amīr Shakīb Arslān. *al-Naqd al-taḥlīlī li-kitāb fī'l-adab al-jāhilī.* Cairo, al-Maṭba'a al-Salafiyya, 1929.
al-Ghazālī, Abū Ḥāmid. *Iljām al-ʿawāmm ʿan ʿilm al-kalām.* Cairo, al-Maktaba al-Azhariyya li'l-Turāth, 1998.
Giridi Sırrı Paşa. *Ahsenü'l-kasas: Tefsir-i Sure-i Yusuf aleyhisselam.* Istanbul, Şirket-i Mürettibiyye Matbaası, 1893.
——. *Sırr-ı Furkan: Tefsir-i Sure-i Furkan.* Istanbul, Matbaa-i Osmaniye, 1312/1894–5.
——. *Sırr-ı İnsan: Tefsir-i Sure-i İnsan.* Istanbul, Eski Zabtiye Caddesinde 61 numaralı Matbaa, 1312/1894–5.
——. *Sırr-ı Meryem: Tefsir-i Sure-i Meryem.* Diyarbakır, Vilayet Matbaası, 1312/1894–5.
——. *Sırr-ı Tenzil.* Diyarbakır, Diyarbakır Matbaası, 1311/1893–4.
Gökalp, Ziya. 'Türkleşmek, İslamlaşmak, Muasırlaşmak' (1918), in Mustafa Koç, ed., *Kitaplar.* Istanbul, Yapı Kredi Yayınları, 2007, pp. 39–88.
——. *Ziya Gökalp Külliyatı*, vol. I: *Şiirler ve Halk Masalları*, ed. Fevziye Abdullah Tansel. Ankara, Türk Tarih Kurumu Basımevi, 1952.
Goldsack, Willam, tr. *Korān.* Calcutta, 1908–20.
'Haber: Daire-i Meşihat'te'. *Tanin* 2, no. 1563 (1913), p. 6.
'Hadise Hakkında Bursa'da Gazi Hazretlerinin Tebliği'. *Vakit*, 2 February 1933, p. 1.
The Holy Qur'ān, with English Translation and Explanatory Notes. Qadian, Anjuman-i-Taraqqi-i-Islam, 1915.
el-Hüseyni, Seyyid Süleyman (Süleyman Tevfik). *Kur'an-ı Kerim Tercümesi: Türkçe Mushaf-ı Şerif.* Istanbul, Sühulet Kütübhanesi, 1927.

——. (Süleyman Tevfik). *Kur'an-ı Kerim'in Tercüme ve Tefsiri*. Istanbul, Maarif Kütüphanesi, 1924.

——. (Süleyman Tevfik). *Tercüme-i Şerife: Kur'an-ı Kerim*. Istanbul, Sühulet Kütüphanesi and Matbaa-ı Ahmed Kamil, 1927.

——. (Süleyman Tevfik). *Zübdetü'l-Beyan*. Istanbul, Amidi Matbaası, 1924.

Ibn Manẓūr, Muḥammad b. Mukarram. *Lisān al-ʿarab*, 18 vols. Beirut, Dār Iḥyāʾ al-Turāth al-ʿArabī, 1997.

'İlahiyat Fakültesinde Hazırlanan Lahiye Etrafında'. *Vakit*, 20 June 1928, p. 1.

'India: Nizam's Azam and Moazzam'. *Time Magazine*, 31 November 1931. http://www.time.com/time/magazine/article/0,9171,742647,00.html#ixzz1QhG4P5Bn.

'Indian Delegation at the Mosque'. *Islamic Review* (April 1920), p. 139.

'Islam: Caliph's Beauteous Daughter'. *Time Magazine*, 9 November 1931. http://www.time.com/time/magazine/article/0,9171,742555,00.html.

İsmail Ferruh. *Tefsir-i Mevakib*. Istanbul, Matbaa-i Amire, 1281/1864.

İzmirli, İsmail Hakkı. *Meani-i Kur'an – Kuran-ı Kerim'in Türkçe Tercümesi: Ayat-ı Kerimenin Mebdeleriyle, Şerh ve İzahatını Havidir*. Istanbul, Kitaphane-i Hilmi, Milli Matbaa, 1927.

Janet, Paul and Gabriel Séailles. *Tahlilî Tarih-i Felsefe: Metalib ve Mezahib*, tr. Elmalılı Hamdi. Istanbul, Matbaa-i Amire, 1925.

Kadri, Hüseyin Kâzım (Şeyh Muhsin-i Fani, pseud.). *Meşrutiyet'ten Cumhuriyet'e Hatıralarım*, ed. İsmail Kara. Istanbul, İletişim Yayınları, 1991.

[Karaosmanoğlu], Yakup Kadri. *Nur Baba*. Istanbul, Akşam Matbaası, 1922.

Kāshifī, Ḥusayn Wāʿiẓ. *Mevakib: Terceme-i Tefsir-i Mevahib*, tr. İsmail Ferruh. Istanbul, Matbaa-i Amire, 1282/1865.

Kâtip Çelebi, Mustafa b. Abdullah. *Cihânnümâ*. Kostantiniyye, Istanbul, Darü'l-Tıbaati'l-Amire, 1144/1732.

Kayserivi, İbrahim Gözübüyükzade. *Tercüme-i Sure-i Duha*, ed. Mahmud Raci. Istanbul, Ali Şevki Efendi Matbaası, 1287/1870–71.

Kazimirski, M. *See* Biberstein-Kazimirski, Albert de.

Khan, Abu Taleb. *Travels of Mirza Abu Taleb Khan in Asia, Africa, and Europe During the Years 1799 to 1803*, tr. Charles Stewart. New Delhi, Sona Publications, 1972.

King Fahd Complex for the Printing of the Holy Qur'an. 'Reciting or Memorising the Holy Qur'an in a Language Other than Arabic'. *Fatwa No. 89* (1426/2005). http://www.qurancomplex.org (accessed 2 April 2013).

Kureyşizade Mehmet Fevzi. *El-Havasü'n-nafia fi tefsir suret el-Vakia*. Istanbul, 1313/1895–6.

MacCallum, F. Lyman. 'Turkey Discovers the Koran'. *Muslim World* 23 (1933), pp. 24–8.

MacCallum, Frederick W. *İncil: Ve Diğer Kitaplar*. Istanbul, Amerikan Kitabımukaddes Şirketi ve İngiliz ve Ecnebi Kitabımukaddes Şirketi, 1933.

al-Maḥallī, Jalāl al-Dīn and Jalāl al-Dīn al-Suyūṭī. *Tafsīr al-Jalālayn*. Damascus, Maṭbaʿat al-Mallāḥ, 1389/1969.

al-Marāghī, Muḥammad Muṣṭafā. *Baḥth fī tarjamati'l-Qur'ān il-karīm wa aḥkāmihā*. Cairo, Maṭbaʿat al-Raghāʾib, 1355/1936.

[Mehmet Akif]. 'Mevaiz-i Diniyeden'. *See* Ersoy, Mehmet Akif.
Mehmet Rifat. *See* [Börekçi], Mehmet Rifat.
Milaslı, İsmail Hakkı. 'Kur'an-ı Kerim Tercüme Olunabilir mi?' *Sebilürreşad* 15, no. 390 (1919), pp. 447–9.
'Mr. Lloyd George and the Indian Khilafat Delegation'. *Islamic Review* (April 1920), pp. 140–41.
Muallim Ömer Naci. *Hülasatü'l-İhlas*, ed. Ahmed Sabri. Istanbul, Matbaa-i Ebüzziya, 1304/1886–7.
——. *Muamma-i ilahi yahud bazı süver-i Kur'aniyenin evailindeki huruf-ı tehecci*. Istanbul, 1302/1884–5.
Musa Kâzım. *Safvetü'l-beyan fi tefsiri'l-Kur'an*. Istanbul, Matbaa-i Amire, 1335/1916–17.
Mushaf-ı Şerif. Istanbul, Matbaa-i Osmaniye, 1301/1884.
Mushaf-ı Şerif. MS Hacı Mahmud Efendi 6, Süleymaniye Library, Istanbul.
Naci. *See* Muallim Ömer Naci.
Nahid, Haşim. *Türkiye İçin: Necat ve İ'tila Yolları*. Istanbul, 1331/1912–13.
——. *Türkiye İçin Necat ve İ'tila Yolları*. Konya, Tablet Yayınları, 2006.
Namık Kemal. 'Kemal'ın Müdafaası'. *Mecmua-i Ebüzziya* 3, no. 25 (1300/1882), pp. 769–81.
'Petersburg'da İslam Matbaası'. *İslam Dünyası* 1, no. 16 (1913), p. 256.
Richter, Julius. *A History of Protestant Missions in the Near East*. New York, Fleming H. Revell, 1910.
Riḍā, Muḥammad Rashīd. 'Bāb al-as'ila wa'l-ujūbat al-dīniyya'. *al-Manār* 4, no. 13 (1901), pp. 493-500.
——. 'Fatāwā al-Manār: Wujūb ta'allum al-'arabiyya 'alā kulli muslim'. *al-Manār* 17, no. 8 (1914), pp. 589–92.
——. 'Tarjamat al-Qur'ān'. *al-Manār* 11, no. 4 (1908), pp. 268–74.
——. 'Tarjamat al-Qur'ān wa kawn al-'arabiyya lughat al-islām'. *al-Manār* 32, no. 3 (1931), pp. 184–9.
Sabri, Mustafa. *Dini Müceddidler*. Istanbul, Evkaf Matbaası, 1338/1919–20.
——. *Mas'alat tarjamat al-Qur'ān*. Cairo, al-Maṭba'a al-Salafiyya, 1351/1932.
Sağdıç, Ruhi Naci. 'Kur'an Tercemeleri Münasebetiyle Mehmed Akif Merhum Hakkında Hatıralar'. *Sebilürreşad* 11, no. 2 (1958), pp. 281–3.
Şefkatlı, Murat, ed. *Türk Yurdu*, 17 vols. Ankara, Tutibay Yayınları, 1998.
Sell, Edward. *The Faith of Islam*. London, Trübner, 1880.
Şemseddin Sami. *Kamus-i Türki*. Istanbul, İkdam Matbaası, 1317/1899; Istanbul, Çağrı Yayınları, 1987.
——. *Kamusü'l-Alam: Tarih ve Coğrafya Lûgati ve Tabir-i Esahhiyle Kâffe-i Esma-i Hassa-i Camidir*. Istanbul, Mihran Matbaası, 1306–16/1889–98.
——. *Taaşşuk-ı Tal'at ve Fıtnat*. Istanbul, Elcevaip Matbaası, 1289/1872–3.
Şeref Kâzım. 'Yeni Neşriyat: Kur'an Tercümeleri'. *Mihrab* 1, no. 11 (1924), p. 352.
Şerif, Ş. 'Kur'an'dan Gafletimiz ve Sebepleri'. *İslam Dünyası* 1, no. 14 (1913), pp. 215–17.
Shākir, Muḥammad. *al-Qawl al-faṣl fī tarjamat al-Qur'ān al-karīm ilā'l-lughāt al-a'jamiyya*. Cairo, Maṭba'at al-Nahḍa, 1925.
Sherrill, Charles H. 'Ambassador Charles H. Sherrill Comments on Atatürk's Views on Religion', in Rifat Bali, ed., *New Documents on Atatürk:*

Atatürk as Viewed through the Eyes of American Diplomats. Istanbul, Isis Press, 2007, pp. 169–72.
——. *A Year's Embassy to Mustafa Kemal*. New York, Charles Scribner's Sons, 1934.
Şirani, Ahmet. 'Kur'an-ı Kerim Tercümesi Hakkında'. *Hayrü'l-Kelam* 1, no. 17 (1914), p. 136.
Süleyman Tevfik. *See* el-Hüseyni, Seyyid Süleyman.
al-Suyūṭī, Jalāl al-Dīn. *el-Hakaik: Mimma fil-cami is-sagir vel-mesarik min hadis-i hayr il-halaik*, tr. Mehmet Zihni. Istanbul, Bab-i Ali Caddesinde 25 Numaralı Matbaa, 1310–11/1892.
al-Ṭabarī, Abū Jaʿfar Muḥammad b. Jarīr b. Yazīd. *Jāmiʿ al-bayān ʿan taʾwīl āy al-Qurʾān*, 15 vols. Beirut, Dār al-Fikr, 1984; ed. ʿAbd al-Sanad Ḥasan al-Yamāma, 26 vols. Cairo, Dār Hijr, n.d.
'Taqrīẓ al-maṭbūʿāt al-ḥadītha: Al-muṣḥaf al-sharīf, ṭabʿat al-ḥukūma al-akhīra lahu'. *al-Manār* 26, no. 10 (1926), pp. 795–6.
Tevfik, Süleyman (Seyyid Süleyman el-Hüseyni, pseud.). *Tercümeli Kur'an-ı Kerim*. Istanbul, Maarif Kütüphanesi, 1927.
Tokgöz, Ahmet İhsan. *Matbuat Hatıralarım*, ed. Alpay Kabacalı. Istanbul, İletişim Yayıncılık, 1993.
Türk Büyük Millet Meclisi Zabıt Ceridesi [*Proceedings of the Turkish Grand National Assembly*], vol. II. İntihab Devresi, İkinci İctima Celse, 21 February 1925. Ankara, TBMM Matbaası.
'Türkçe Namaz'. *Akşam*, 7 April 1926, p. 2
'Türkçe Namaz'. *Milliyet*, 7 April 1926, p. 3.
Türk-İslam Eserler Müzesi no. 40 (827/1424), Istanbul, Turkey.
al-Wāḥidī, ʿAlī b. Aḥmad. *Asbāb al-nuzūl*, ed. Yousef Meri, tr. Mokrane Guezzou. Amman, Royal Āl al-Bayt Institute for Islamic Thought, 2008.
Wajdī, Muḥammad Farīd. *al-Adilla al-ʿilmiyya ʿalā jawāz tarjamat maʿānīʾl-Qurʾān ilāʾl-lughāt al-ajnabiyya*. Cairo, Maṭbaʿat al-Raghāʾib, 1355/1936.
Yazır, Elmalılı Muhammed Hamdi. *Hak Dini Kur'an Dili: Yeni Mealli Türkçe Tefsir*, 9 vols. Istanbul, Matbaa-i Ebüzziya, 1935–9; *Hak Dini Kur'an Dili: Meali*, ed. Sadık Kılıç and Lütfullah Cebeci. Ankara, Akçağ, 2006.
'Yeni Tefsircilerden Müslümanların Ricası'. *Sebilürreşad* 24, no. 602 (1924), p. 64.
'Yerebatan camisinde Türkçe Yasin okunacak'. *Cumhuriyet*, 22 January 1932, p. 1.
Yunus Nadi. 'Türkçe Kuran, Türkçe İbadet'. *Cumhuriyet*, 25 January 1932, pp. 1, 4.
Yusuf Ali. *See* Ali, Abdullah Yusuf.
al-Zarkashī, Muḥammad b. Bahādur. *Baḥr al-muḥīṭ fī uṣūl al-fiqh*. Beirut, Dār al-Kutub al-ʿIlmiyya, 2000.
Ziya, Yusuf. 'Meani'l-Kur'an', *Mihrab* 2, no. 28 (1341/1925), pp. 162–4.

Secondary Sources

Abdul-Raof, Hussein. *Qur'an Translation: Discourse, Texture and Exegesis*. Richmond, Curzon, 2001.

——. 'The Qur'an: Limits of Translatability', in Said Faiq, ed., *Cultural Encounters in Translation from Arabic*. Clevedon, Multilingual Matters, 2004, pp. 91–106.

Altuntaş, Halil. *Kur'an'ın Tercümesi ve Tercüme ile Namaz Meselesi*. Istanbul, Türkiye Diyanet Vakfı Yayınları, 2001.

Amanat, Abbas. *Pivot of the Universe: Nasir al-Din Shah Qajar and the Iranian Monarchy, 1831–1896*. Berkeley, University of California Press, 1997.

Anderson, Benedict. *Imagined Communities: Reflections on the Origin and Spread of Nationalism*. New York, Verso, 1991.

Arberry, Arthur J., tr. *The Koran Interpreted*. London, Allen and Unwin, 1955.

al-ʿĀrif, ʿĀrif. *Tārīkh Biʾr al-Sabʿ wa qabāʾilihā*. Jerusalem, Maṭbaʿat Bayt al-Maqdis, 1934.

Arslanpay, Nail. *Diyanet İşleri Başkanlığı: Kuruluşu Çalışması ve Birimlerinin Tanıtılması*. Ankara, Ayyıldız Matbaası, 1973.

Asad, Muhammad. *The Message of the Qurʾān*. Gibraltar, Dar al-Andalus, Brill, 1980.

Atiyeh, George N., ed. *The Book in the Islamic World: The Written Word and Communication in the Middle East*. Albany, State University of New York Press, 1995.

Aydar, Hidayet. *Kur'an-ı Kerim Tercümesi Meselesi*. Istanbul, Kur'an Okulu Yayıncılık, 1996.

Ayoub, Mahmoud. *The Great Tiding: Interpretation of Juzʾ ʿAmma, the Last Part of the Quran*. Tripoli, Libyan Arab Republic, Islamic Call Society, 1983.

——. 'Translating the Meanings of the Qur'an: Traditional Opinions and Modern Debates'. *Afkar/Inquiry* 3, no. 5 (1986), pp. 34–9.

Ayvazoğlu, Beşir. *1924: Bir Fotoğrafın Uzun Hikayesi*. Istanbul, Kapı Yayınları, 2006.

al-Azmeh, Aziz. *Islams and Modernities*. London, Verso, 1993.

——. 'Nationalism and the Arabs'. *Arab Studies Quarterly* 17, nos 1 and 2 (Winter/Spring 1995), pp. 1–18.

al-Bagdadi, Nadia. 'From Heaven to Dust: Metamorphosis of the Book in Pre-Modern Arab Culture'. *Medieval History Journal* 8, no. 1 (2005), pp. 83–107.

Bali, Rifat N., ed. *New Documents on Atatürk: Atatürk as Viewed through the Eyes of American Diplomats*. Istanbul, Isis Press, 2007.

Barnstone, Willis. *The Poetics of Translation: History, Theory, Practice*. New Haven, CT, Yale University Press, 1993.

Bassnett, Susan and André Lefevere. *Translation, History, and Culture*. London, Pinter Publishers, 1990.

——. *Constructing Cultures: Essays on Literary Translation*. Clevedon, Multilingual Matters, 1998.

Bein, Amit. 'The Ulema, Their Institutions, and Politics in the Late Ottoman Empire (1876–1924)'. PhD Thesis, Princeton University, 2006.

——. *Ottoman Ulema, Turkish Republic: Agents of Change and Guardians of Tradition*. Stanford, CA, Stanford University Press, 2011.

Bergsträsser, Gotthelf. 'Koranlesung in Kairo'. *Der Islam* 20 (1932), pp. 1–42; vol. 21 (1933), pp. 110–34.

Berkes, Niyazi. *The Development of Secularism in Turkey*. New York, Routledge, 1998.
Binark, İsmet. *Eski Kitapçılık Sanatlarımız*. Ankara, Kazan Türkleri Kültür ve Yardımlaşma Derneği Yayınları, 1975.
Binark, İsmet and Halit Eren. *World Bibliography of Translations of the Meanings of the Holy Qur'an: Printed Translations, 1515–1980*, ed. Ekmeleddin İhsanoğlu. Istanbul, Research Centre for Islamic History, Art, and Culture (IRCICA), 1986.
Birge, John Kingsley. *The Bektashi Order of Dervishes*. London, Luzac, 1937.
——. 'Turkish Traslations of the Koran'. *Muslim World* 28, no. 4 (1938), pp. 394–9.
Birinci, Ali. '"Birgivi Risalesi": İlk Dinî Kitab Niçin ve Nasıl Basıldı?' *Tarih Yolunda: Yakın Mazî Sıyasî ve Fikrî Ahvâli*. Istanbul, Dergâh Yayınları, 2001, pp. 193–6.
——. 'Osman Bey ve Matbaası: Ser-Kurenâ Osman Bey'in Hikayesine ve Matbaa-i Osmaniye'nin Tarihçesine Medhal'. *Müteferrika* 39, no. 1 (Summer 2011), pp. 3–148.
Bobzin, Hartmut. '"A Treasure of Heresies": Christian Polemics against the Qur'an', in Stefan Wild, ed., *The Qur'an as Text*. Leiden, Brill, 1996, pp. 157–76.
Browers, Michaelle and Charles Kurzman. 'Comparing Reformations', in idem, eds., *An Islamic Reformation?* Lanham, MD, Lexington Books, 2004.
Brummett, Palmira Johnson. *Image and Imperialism in the Ottoman Revolutionary Press, 1908–1911*. Albany, State University of New York Press, 2000.
Burçoğlu, Nedret Kuran. 'Matbaacı Osman Bey: Saray'dan İlk Defa Kur'an-ı Kerim Basma İznini Alan Hattat'. *Tarih ve Toplum* 209 (2001), pp. 33–41.
——. 'Osman Zeki Bey and His Printing Office the Matbaa-i Osmaniye', in Philip Sadgrove and Colin Paul Mitchell, eds., *History of Printing and Publishing in the Languages and Countries of the Middle East*. New York, Middle East Studies Association of North America, 2007, pp. 35–58.
Burman, Thomas E. '*Tafsīr* and Translation: Traditional Arabic Qur'ān Exegesis and the Latin Qur'āns of Robert of Ketton and Mark of Toledo'. *Speculum* 73, no. 3 (1998), pp. 703–32.
——. *Reading the Qur'an in Latin Christendom, 1140–1560*. Philadelphia, University of Pennsylvania Press, 2007.
Casale, Giancarlo. *The Ottoman Age of Exploration*. Oxford, Oxford University Press, 2010.
Çavaş, Raşit and Fatmagül Demirel. 'Yeni Bulunan Belgelerin Işığında II. Abdülhamid'in Yaktırdığı Kitapların bir Listesi', *Müteferrika* 28, no. 2 (2005), pp. 3–24.
Chambers, Richard. 'The Education of a Nineteenth-Century Ottoman Alim, Ahmed Cevdet Paşa'. *International Journal of Middle East Studies* 4, no. 4 (1973), pp. 440–64.
Chauvin, Victor. *Bibliographie des ouvrages arabes ou relatifs aux Arabes, publiés dans l'Europe Chrétienne de 1810 à 1885*, vol. X. Liège, H. Vaillant-Carmanne, 1907.

Clark, Harry. 'The Publication of the Koran in Latin: A Reformation Dilemma'. *Sixteenth Century Journal* 15, no. 1 (1984), pp. 3–12.
Clark, Peter. *Marmaduke Pickthall: British Muslim*. London, Quartet Books, 1986.
——. 'A Man of Two Cities: Pickthall, Damascus, Hyderabad'. *Asian Affairs* 25, no. 3 (1994), pp. 270–80.
Cook, Michael. *The Koran: A Very Short Introduction*. Oxford, Oxford University Press, 2000.
Cündioğlu, Dücane. *Sözlü Kültür'den Yazılı Kültür'e: Anlam'ın Tarihi*. Istanbul, Tibyan, 1997.
——. 'Bir Kur'an Mütercimi Cemil Said'in Kendi Kaleminden Özgeçmişi'. *Dergâh* 9, no. 100 (1998), pp. 46–7.
——. 'Türkçe Kur'an Çevirilerinin Siyasî Bağlamında Bir Kur'an Mütercimi: Süleyman Tevfik'. *Müteferrika* 13 (Summer 1998), pp. 21–52.
——. *Türkçe Kur'an ve Cumhuriyet İdeolojisi*. Cağaloğlu, Istanbul, Kitabevi, 1998.
——. *Türkçe İbadet*. Istanbul, Kitabevi, 1999.
——. *Bir Kur'an Şairi: Mehmed Akif ve Kur'an Meali*. Istanbul, Gelenek, 2000.
——. '"Mason" Olduğu Söylenen Kur'an Mütercimi (1)'. *Yeni Şafak*, 3 October 2000. http://yenisafak.com.tr/arsiv/2000/ekim/03/dcundioglu.html; '"Mason" Olduğu Söylenen Kur'an Mütercimi (2)', 6 October 2000. http://yenisafak.com.tr/arsiv/2000/ekim/06/dcundioglu.html.
——. *Kur'an Çevirilerinin Dünyası*. Istanbul, Kaknüs, 2005.
——. *Mehmed Akif'in Kur'an Tercümeleri*. Istanbul, Kaknüs, 2005.
Curtis, Edward E. *Black Muslim Religion in the Nation of Islam, 1960–1975*. Chapel Hill, University of North Carolina Press, 2006.
Dalila B. 'The Holy Qur'an in French and Amazight Distributed'. *Ennahar*. http://www.ennaharonline.com/en/news/1806.html (accessed 13 March 2012).
Davison, Andrew. 'Secularization and Modernization in Turkey: The Ideas of Ziya Gökalp'. *Economy and Society* 24, no. 2 (1995), pp. 189–224.
Demir, Adem. 'Cemaatler arası Meal Savaşı'. *Newsweek Türkiye*, 5 July 2009, pp. 52–4.
Deringil, Selim. 'The Struggle against Shiism in Hamidian Iraq: A Study in Ottoman Counter-Propaganda'. *Die Welt des Islams* 30, no. 1 (1990), pp. 45–62.
——. 'Legitimacy Structures in the Ottoman State: The Reign of Abdulhamid II (1876–1909)'. *International Journal of Middle East Studies* 23, no. 3 (1991), pp. 345–59.
——. *The Well-Protected Domains: Ideology and the Legitimation of Power in the Ottoman Empire, 1876–1909*. London, I.B. Tauris, 1998.
Derman, M. Uğur. *Letters in Gold: Ottoman Calligraphy from the Sakıp Sabancı Collection, Istanbul*. New York, Metropolitan Museum of Art, 1998.
Dick, Wolfgang. 'Free Koran Giveaway Sparks Debate'. *Deutsche Welle*, 13 April 2012. http://www.dw.de/free-koran-giveaway-sparks-security-debate/a-15882277 (accessed 22 January 2013).
Diyanet İşleri Başkanlığı Yayınları Bibliyografyası (1924–2010). http://www.diyanet.gov.tr/yayin/y_bibliyografya.pdf.

Doğan, Muhammet Nur. *Fuzûli'nin Poetikası*. Cağaloğlu, Istanbul, Kitabevi, 1997.
Dressler, Markus. *Writing Religion: The Making of Turkish Alevi Islam*. Oxford, Oxford University Press, 2013.
Düzdağ, M. Ertuğrul. *Mehmed Akif: Mısır Hayatı ve Kur'an Meali*. Cağaloğlu, Istanbul, Şule Yayınları, 2003.
Eckmann, János. *Middle Turkic Glosses of the Rylands Interlinear Koran Translation*. Budapest, Akadémiai Kiadó, 1976.
Eddy, Melissa and Nicholas Kulish. 'Koran Giveaway in Germany Has Some Officials Worried'. *New York Times*, 16 April 2012. http://www.nytimes.com/2012/04/17/world/europe/germany-koran-giveaway-worries-officials.html?_r=0 (accessed 13 June 2014).
Eisenstein, Elizabeth L. *The Printing Revolution in Early Modern Europe*, 2nd edn. Cambridge, Cambridge University Press, 2005.
Eren, Halit. 'Editorial'. *OIC Research Center for Islamic History, Art and Culture Newsletter*, no. 80 (September–December 2009), p. 1.
Ergin, Osman Nuri. *Türkiye Maarif Tarihi*, vol. V. Istanbul, Osman Bey Matbaası, 1943.
Ernst, Carl. *How to Read the Qur'an*. Chapel Hill, University of North Carolina Press, 2011.
Fortna, Benjamin C. 'Islamic Morality in Late Ottoman "Secular" Schools'. *International Journal of Middle East Studies* 32, no. 3 (2001), pp. 369–93.
——. *Imperial Classroom: Islam, the State, and Education in the Late Ottoman Empire*. Oxford, Oxford University Press, 2002.
——. 'Learning to Read in the Late Ottoman Empire and Early Turkish Republic'. *Comparative Studies of South Asia, Africa and the Middle East* 21, nos 1–2 (2002), pp. 33–41.
——. *Learning to Read in the Late Ottoman Empire and the Early Turkish Republic*. New York, Palgrave-MacMillan, 2011.
Fremantle, Anne Jackson. *Loyal Enemy*. London, Hutchinson, 1938.
Gerçek, Selim Nüzhet. *Türk Matbaacılığı*, vol. I: *Müteferrika Matbaası*. Istanbul, Devlet Basımevi, 1939.
Gershoni, Israel and James P. Jankowski. *Egypt, Islam, and the Arabs: The Search for Egyptian Nationhood, 1900–1930*. Oxford, Oxford University Press, 1986.
GhaneaBassiri, Kambiz. *A History of Islam in America: From the New World to the New World Order*. New York, Cambridge University Press, 2010.
Goldschmidt, Arthur. *A Biographical Dictionary of Modern Egypt*. Boulder, CO, Lynne Rienner Publishers, 2000.
Green, Nile. 'Journeymen, Middlemen: Travel, Transculture, and Technology in the Origins of Muslim Printing'. *International Journal of Middle East Studies* 41, no. 2 (2009), pp. 203–24.
——. 'Stones from Bavaria: Iranian Lithography in Its Global Contexts'. *Iranian Studies* 43, no. 3 (2010), pp. 305–31.
——. *Bombay Islam: The Religious Economy of the West Indian Ocean, 1840–1915*. Cambridge, Cambridge University Press, 2011.

Gunasti, Susan. 'Approaches to Islam in the Thought of Elmalılı Muhammed Hamdi Yazir (1878–1942)'. Unpublished PhD Thesis, Princeton University, 2011.
——. 'Political Patronage and the Writing of Qur'an Commentaries among the Ottoman Turks'. *Journal of Islamic Studies* 24, no. 3 (2013), pp. 335–57.
Gündüz, Mahmut. 'Matbaa Tarihçesi ve İlk Kur'an-ı Kerim Basımları'. *Vakıf Dergisi* 12 (1978), pp. 335–50.
Haddad, Mahmoud. 'Arab Religious Nationalism in the Colonial Era: Rereading Rashīd Riḍā's Ideas on the Caliphate'. *Journal of the American Oriental Society* 117, no. 2 (1997), pp. 253–77.
Hagen, Gottfried. 'Translations and Translators in a Multilingual Society: A Case Study of Persian–Ottoman Translations, Late Fifteenth to Early Seventeenth Century'. *Eurasian Studies* 2, no. 1 (2003), pp. 95–134.
——. 'From Haggadic Exegesis to Myth: Popular Stories of the Prophets in Islam', in Roberta Sterman Sabbath, ed., *Sacred Tropes: Tanakh, New Testament, and Qur'an as Literature and Culture*. Leiden, Brill, 2009, pp. 301–16.
bin Hamza, Mehmet and Ahmet Topaloğlu. *XV. Yüzyıl Başlarında Yapılmış Satır-Arası Kur'an Tercümesi*. Istanbul, Devlet Kitapları, 1976.
Hanioğlu, Şükrü. 'Garbcılar: Their Attitudes toward Religion and Their Impact on the Official Ideology of the Turkish Republic'. *Studia Islamica* 86, no. 2 (1997), pp. 133–49.
——. *A Brief History of the Late Ottoman Empire*. Princeton, NJ, Princeton University Press, 2008.
Hassan, Mona F. 'Loss of Caliphate: The Trauma and Aftermath of 1258 and 1924'. Unpublished PhD Thesis, Princeton University, 2009.
Hz. Osman'a İzafe Edilen Mushaf-ı Şerif: Topkapı Sarayı Müzesi Nüshası, ed. Tayyar Altıkulaç. Istanbul, IRCICA, 2007.
Ichwan, Nur Moch. 'Differing Responses to Ahmadi Translation and Exegesis'. *Archipel* 62 (2001), pp. 143–61.
İhsanoğlu, Ekmeleddin. 'Education'. *Encyclopedia of the Ottoman Empire*, ed. Gábor Ágoston and Bruce Masters. New York, Infobase Publishing, 2001, pp. 202–3.
——. *The Turks in Egypt and Their Cultural Legacy*. Cairo, American University in Cairo Press, 2012.
Imber, Colin. *Ebu's-Su'ud: The Islamic Legal Tradition*. Stanford, CA, Stanford University Press, 1997.
Jeffery, Arthur. 'The Presentation of Christianity to Moslems'. *International Review of Missions* 13, no. 2 (1924), pp. 174–89.
Kanlıdere, Ahmet. *Reform within Islam: The Tajdid and Jadid Movement among the Kazan Tatars, 1809–1917: Conciliation or Conflict?* Beyoglu, Istanbul, Eren, 1997.
——. *Kadimle Cedit arasında Musa Cârullah: Hayatı, Eserleri, Fikirleri*. Istanbul, Dergâh Yayınları, 2005.
Kara, İsmail. 'Turban and Fez: *Ulema* as Opposition', in Elisabeth Özdalga, ed., *Late Ottoman Society: The Intellectual Legacy*. London, Routledge Curzon, 2005, pp. 162–200.

Karabacak, Esra. *An Inter-Linear Translation of the Qur'an into Old Anatolian Turkish*. Cambridge, MA, Harvard University - Department of Near Eastern Languages and Civilizations, 1994.

Karácson, Imre. 'İbrahim Müteferrika'. *Tarih-i Osmani Mecmuası* 1, no. 3 (August 1910), pp. 183–4.

Karamustafa, Ahmet. 'Elmalılı Muhammed Hamdi Yazır's Philosophy of Religion (1848–1946)'. *Archivum Ottomanicum* 19 (2001), pp. 273–9.

Karpat, Kemal. *The Politicization of Islam: Reconstructing Identity, State, Faith, and Community in the Late Ottoman State*. New York, Oxford University Press, 2001.

Kashani-Sabet, Firoozeh. *Frontier Fictions*. Princeton, NJ, Princeton University Press, 1999.

Kayalı, Hasan. *Arabs and Young Turks: Ottomanism, Arabism, and Islamism in the Ottoman Empire, 1908–1918*. Berkeley, University of California Press, 1997.

Kedourie, Elie. 'Egypt and the Caliphate'. *Journal of the Royal Asiatic Society of Great Britain and Ireland* 3/4 (1963), pp. 208–48.

——. *In the Anglo-Arab Labyrinth: The McMahon-Husayn Correspondence and its Interpretations, 1914–1939*. Cambridge, Cambridge University Press, 1991.

Khalid, Adeeb. 'Printing, Publishing, and Reform in Tsarist Central Asia'. *International Journal of Middle East Studies* 26, no. 2 (1994), pp. 187–200.

——. *The Politics of Muslim Cultural Reform: Jadidism in Central Asia*. Berkeley, University of California Press, 1998.

Khalidi, Rashid, Lisa Anderson, Muhammad Muslih and Reeva S. Simon, eds. *The Origins of Arab Nationalism*. New York, Columbia University Press, 1991.

Khan, Ahmad. *World Bibliography of Translations of the Holy Qur'an in Manuscript Form II: Translations in Urdu*, ed. Ekmeleddin İhsanoğlu. Istanbul, IRCICA, 2010.

Kidawi, A.R. 'Translating the Untranslatable: A Survey of English Translations of the Quran'. *Muslim World Book Review* 7, no. 4 (1987), pp. 66–71.

Koz, M. Sabri. 'Mehmed Tevfik ve Süleyman Tevfik'. *Müteferrika* 4 (Winter 1994), pp. 45–58.

Krstić, Tijana. *Contested Conversions to Islam: Narratives of Religious Change in the Early Modern Ottoman Empire*. Stanford, CA, Stanford University Press, 2011.

Kuntay, Midhat Cemal. *Namık Kemal: Devrinin İnsanları ve Olayları arasında*, vol. I. Istanbul, Maarif Matbaası, 1944; vol. II. Istanbul, Milli Eğitim Basımevi, 1949.

——. *Mehmet Akif: Hayatı, Sanatı, Seciyesi Seçme Şiirleri*. Istanbul, Türkiye İş Bankası Kültür Yayınları, 1986.

Kurzman, Charles. *Modernist Islam, 1840–1940: A Sourcebook*. Oxford, Oxford University Press, 2002.

Kushner, David. *To Be Governor of Jerusalem*. Istanbul, Isis, 2005.

Lawrence, Bruce B. 'Approximating Sajʿ in English Renditions of the Qur'an: A Close Reading of Sura 93 (al-Ḍuḥā) and the *basmala*'. *Journal of Qur'anic Studies* 7, no. 1 (2005), pp. 64–80.

——. *The Qur'an: A Biography*. New York, Atlantic Monthly Press, 2007.
Lazzerini, Edward J. 'Ǧadidism at the Turn of the Twentieth Century: A View from Within.' *Cahiers du Monde russe et soviétique* 16, no. 2 (1975), pp. 245–77.
Levend, Agâh Sırrı. *Şemsettin Sami*. Ankara, Üniversitesi Basımevi, 1969.
Lewis, Geoffery. *The Turkish Language Reform: A Catastrophic Success*. Oxford, Oxford University Press, 1999.
Madigan, Daniel A. *The Qur'ân's Self Image: Writing and Authority in Islam's Scripture*. Princeton, NJ, Princeton University Press, 2001.
Mango, Andrew. *Atatürk*. Woodstock, NY, Overlook Press, 2002.
Mardin, Şerif. *The Genesis of Young Ottoman Thought: A Study in the Modernization of Turkish Political Ideas*. Princeton, NJ, Princeton University Press, 1962. Reprint Syracuse, NJ, Syracuse University Press, 2000.
Meeker, Michael E. 'The Black Sea Turks: Some Aspects of Their Ethnic and Cultural Background'. *International Journal of Middle East Studies* 2, no. 4 (1971), pp. 318–45.
'Mehmet Akif'in Kur'an-ı Kerim Meali Yayınlandı'. *Samanyolu Haber*, 5 September 2012. http://www.samanyoluhaber.com/gundem/Mehmet-Akifin-Kuran-i-Kerim-meali-yayinlandi/832511/.
Menges, Karl Heinrich. *The Turkic Languages and Peoples: An Introduction to Turkic Studies*. Wiesbaden, Harrassowitz, 1968.
Messick, Brinkley. *The Calligraphic State: Textual Domination and History in a Muslim Society*. Berkeley, University of California Press, 1993.
Minault, Gail. *The Khilafat Movement: Religious Symbolism and Political Mobilization in India*. New York, Columbia University Press, 1982.
Moosa, Ebrahim. *Ghazali and the Poetics of Imagination*. Chapel Hill, NC, University of North Carolina Press, 2005.
——. 'Contrapuntal Readings in Muslim Thought: Translations and Transitions'. *Journal of the American Academy of Religion* 74, no. 1 (2006), pp. 107–18.
——. 'The Unbearable Intimacy of Language and Thought in Islam', in James Boyd, ed., *How Should We Talk About Religion? Perspectives, Contexts, Particularities*. Notre Dame, IN, University of Notre Dame Press, 2006, pp. 300–326.
Muminov, Ashirbek. 'Disputes in Bukhara on the Persian Translation of the Qur'ān'. *Mélanges de l'Université Saint-Joseph* 59 (2006), pp. 301–8.
Munajjid, Ṣalāḥ al-Dīn and Yūsuf Qazmā Hūrī, eds. *Fatāwā al-Imām Muḥammad Rashīd Riḍā*. Beirut, Dar al-Kitāb al-Jadīd, 1970.
Naff, Thomas. 'Reform and the Conduct of Ottoman Diplomacy in the Reign of Selim III, 1789–1807'. *Journal of the American Oriental Society* 83, no. 3 (1963), pp. 295–315.
Neumann, Christoph K. 'Book and Newspaper Printing in Turkish, 18th–20th Century', in Eva Hanebutt-Benz, Dagmar Glass and Geoffrey Roper, eds., *Middle Eastern Languages and the Print Revolution*. Westhofen, WVA-Verlag Skulima, 2002, pp. 227–48.
Noyan, Bedri. *Bektaşilik Alevilik Nedir?* Ankara, Doğuş Matbaacılık, 1985.

Nuovo, Angela. 'A Lost Arabic Koran Rediscovered'. *Library* 12, no. 4 (1990), pp. 273–92.
Olson, Robert. 'The Ottoman Empire in the Middle of the Eighteenth Century and the Fragmentation of Tradition: Relations of the Nationalities (Millets), Guilds (Esnaf) and the Sultan, 1740–1768'. *Die Welt des Islams* 17, no. 1/4 (1976–7), pp. 329–44.
Oxford Encyclopedia of the Reformation. Oxford, Oxford University Press, 1996.
Özalp, Ömer Hakan. *Ulemadan bir Jöntürk: Mehmed Ubeydullah Efendi*. Istanbul, Dergâh, 2005.
Özervarlı, M. Sait. 'Modification or Renewal: Elmalılı Hamdi's Alternative Modernization Project in Late Ottoman Thought', in Luca Somigli and Domenico Pietropaolo, eds., *Modernism and Modernity in the Mediterranean World*. Ottawa, Legas, 2006, pp. 43–60.
——. 'Alternative Approaches to Modernization in the Late Ottoman Period: İzmirli İsmail Hakkı's Religious Thought against Materialist Scientism'. *International Journal of Middle East Studies* 39, no. 1 (2007), pp. 77–102.
Özmucur, Süleyman and Şevket Pamuk. 'Real Wages and Standards of Living in the Ottoman Empire, 1489–1914'. *Journal of Economic History* 62, no. 2 (2002), pp. 293–321.
Paker, Saliha. 'The Age of Translation and Adaptation, 1850–1914: Turkey', in Robin Ostle, ed., *Modern Literature in the Near and Middle East, 1850–1970*. London, Routledge, 1991, pp. 17–32.
Palmer, Richard E. *Hermeneutics*. Evanston, IL, Northwestern University Press, 1969.
Peters, Rudolf. 'Religious Attitudes toward Modernization in the Ottoman Empire: A Nineteenth Century Pious Text on Steamships, Factories and the Telegraph'. *Die Welt des Islams* 26, no. 1 (1986), pp. 76–105.
Pickthall, Marmaduke William. *Saïd the Fisherman*. London, Methuen, 1903.
——. *Enid: A Novel*. Westminster, Archibald Constable, 1904.
——. *The Children of the Nile*. London, J. Murray, 1908.
——. *Veiled Women*. London, E. Nash, 1913.
——. *Tales from Five Chimneys*. London, Mills and Boon, 1915.
——. *The House of War*. New York, Duffield, 1916.
——. *The Valley of the Kings*. New York, Knopf, 1926.
——. *The Meaning of the Glorious Koran*. London, Knopf, 1930; Cairo, Dār al-Kitāb al-Miṣrī, 1973; Libyan Arab Republic, Islamic Call Society, 1980; New York, Dorset, 1985.
——. 'Arabs and Non-Arabs on the Question of Translating the Qur'an'. *Islamic Culture* 5 (July 1931), pp. 422–33.
——. 'Mr. Yusuf Ali's Translation of the Qur'an', *Islamic Culture* 9 (1935), pp. 519–21.
Pink, Johanna. 'Tradition and Ideology in Contemporary Sunnite Qur'ānic Exegesis: Qur'ānic Commentaries from the Arab World: Turkey and Indonesia and Their Interpretation of Q 5:51'. *Die Welt des Islams* 50, no. 1 (2010), pp. 3–59.

Proudfoot, Ian. 'Mass Producing Houri's Moles', in Peter G. Riddell and Tony Street, eds., *Islam: Essays on Scripture, Thought, and Society*. Leiden, Brill, 1997, pp. 161–86.

Qasim Zaman, Muhammad. 'Commentaries, Print and Patronage: "Ḥadīth" and the Madrasas in Modern South Asia'. *Bulletin of the School of Oriental and African Studies* 62, no. 1 (1999), pp. 60–81.

Reinhart, A. Kevin. 'Jurisprudence', in Andrew Rippin, ed., *The Blackwell Companion to the Qur'ān*. Malden, MA, Blackwell, 2006, pp. 434–49.

——. 'Civilization and its Discussants', in Dennis Washburn and A. Kevin Reinhart, eds., *Converting Cultures: Religion, Ideology, and Transformations of Modernity*. Leiden, Brill, 2007, pp. 267–89.

Reynolds, Gabriel Said. *The Qur'ān in its Historical Context*. London, Routledge, 2008.

Robinson, Francis. 'Islam and the Impact of Print', in idem, *Islam and Muslim History in South Asia*. Oxford, Oxford University Press, 2000, pp. 66–104.

Roxburgh, David J. *Prefacing the Image: The Writing of Art History in Sixteenth-Century Iran*. Leiden, Brill, 2001.

Sabev, Orlin. 'Private Book Collections in Ottoman Sofia, 1671–1833 (Preliminary Notes)'. *Etudes Balkaniques* 39, no. 1 (2003), pp. 34–51.

Sağol, Gülden, ed. *An Interlinear Translation of the Qur'an into Khwarzm Turkish*. Cambridge, MA, Harvard University - Department of Near Eastern Languages and Civilizations, 1993.

Sands, Kristin Zahra. 'On the Popularity of Husayn Vaʿiz-i Kashifi's *Mavāhib-i ʿaliyya*: A Persian Commentary on the Qur'an'. *Iranian Studies* 36, no. 4 (2003), pp. 469–83.

Shākir, Muḥammad. 'On the Translation of the Koran into Foreign Languages', tr. T.W. Arnold. *The Moslem World* 16, no. 2 (1926), pp. 161–5.

Schick, İrvin Cemil. 'The Iconicity of Islamic Calligraphy in Turkey'. *RES: Anthropology and Aesthetics* 53/54 (2008), pp. 211–24.

——. 'Text', in Jamal J. Elias, ed., *Key Themes for the Study of Islam*. Oxford, Oneworld, 2010, pp. 321–5.

——. 'Print Capitalism and Women's Sexual Agency in the Late Ottoman Empire'. *Comparative Studies of South Asia, Africa and the Middle East* 31, no. 1 (2011), pp. 196–216.

Schulze, Reinhart. 'The Birth of Tradition and Modernity in 18th and 19th Century Islamic Culture: The Case of Printing'. *Culture and History* 16 (1997), pp. 29–72.

Sefercioğlu, M. Nejat. *World Bibliography of Translations of the Holy Qur'an in Manuscript Form*, ed. Ekmeleddin İhsanoğlu. Istanbul, IRCICA, 2000.

Şengüler, İsmail Hakkı, ed. *Mehmed Akif Külliyatı*, 10 vols. Istanbul, Hikmet Neşriyat, 1992.

Sharkey, Heather J. *American Evangelicals in Egypt: Missionary Encounters in an Age of Empire*. Princeton, NJ, Princeton University Press, 2008.

Sherif, M.A. *Searching for Solace*. Islamabad, Islamic Research Institute, 2000.

Shissler, Ada Holly. *Between Two Empires: Ahmet Ağaoğlu and the New Turkey*. London, I.B. Tauris, 2003.

Somel, Selçuk Aksin. *The Modernization of Public Education in the Ottoman Empire, 1839–1908: Islamization, Autocracy, and Discipline*. Leiden, Brill, 2001.

Steiner, George. *After Babel: Aspects of Language and Translation*, 2nd edn. Oxford, Oxford University Press, 1992.

Stewart, Charles, tr. *Travels of Mirza Abu Taleb Khan in Asia, Africa, and Europe During the Years 1799 to 1803*. *See* Khan, Abu Taleb.

Strauss, Johann. 'Turkish Translations from Mehmed Ali's Egypt: A Pioneering Effort and Its Results', in Saliha Paker, ed., *Translations: (Re) Shaping of Literature and Culture*. Istanbul, Boğaziçi University Press, 2002, pp. 108–47.

——. 'Who Read What in the Ottoman Empire (19th–20th Centuries)?' *Middle Eastern Literatures* 6, no. 1 (2003), pp. 39–76.

Suleiman, Yasir. *The Arabic Language and National Identity*. Washington, DC, Georgetown University Press, 2003.

Tabbaa, Yasser. *The Transformation of Islamic Art during the Sunni Revival*. Seattle, University of Washington Press, 2001.

Tahir-Gürçağlar, Şehnaz. 'The Translation Bureau Revisited', in María Calzada Pérez, ed., *Apropos of Ideology: Translation Studies on Ideology - Ideologies in Translation Studies*. Manchester, St Jerome Publishing, 2003, pp. 113–29.

——. *The Politics and Poetics of Translation in Turkey, 1923–1960*. Amsterdam, Rodopi, 2008.

Tanpınar, Ahmet Hamdi. *XIX. Asır Türk Edebiyatı Tarihi*. Istanbul, Yapı Kredi Yayınları, 2006.

Tauber, Eliezer. 'Rashīd Riḍā as Pan-Arabist before World War I'. *Muslim World* 79, no. 2 (1989), pp. 102–12.

Taylor, Malissa. 'The Anxiety of Sanctity: Censorship and Sacred Texts', in Seyfi Kenan ed., *Osmanlı ve Avrupa: Seyahat, Karşılaşma ve Etkileşim (18. Yüzyıl Sonuna Kadar)/ Ottomans and Europe: Travel, Encounter and Interaction (Until the End of the 18th Century)*. Istanbul, İSAM Yayınları, 2010, pp. 513–40.

Togan, Zeki Velidi. 'The Earliest Translation of the Qur'an into Turkish'. *İslam Tetkikleri Enstitüsü Dergisi* 4 (1964), pp. 1–19.

Toledano, Ehud R. *State and Society in Mid-Nineteenth-Century Egypt*. Cambridge, Cambridge University Press, 1990.

Turkyilmaz, Zeynep. 'Anxieties of Conversion: Missionaries, State and Heterodox Communities in the Late Ottoman Empire'. Unpublished PhD Thesis, University of California, Los Angeles, 2009.

Tweed, Thomas A. *Crossing and Dwelling: A Theory of Religion*. Cambridge, MA, Harvard University Press, 2006.

Uddin, Sufia. *Constructing Bangladesh*. Chapel Hill, University of North Carolina Press, 2006.

Valentine, Simon Ross. *Islam and the Ahmadiyya Jama'at: History, Belief, Practice*. New York, Columbia University Press, 2008.

Va-Nu [Nurettin, Vala]. 'Şemseddin Sami Sinsi bir Türk Düşmanı mıydı? Haşa'. *Akşam*, 15 October 1943, p. 3.

Venuti, Lawrence. *The Scandals of Translation: Towards an Ethics of Difference*. London, Routledge, 1998.
Wild, Stefan, ed. *The Qur'an as Text*. Leiden, Brill, 1996.
——. *Self-Referentiality in the Qur'ān*. Wiesbaden, Harrassowitz, 2006.
Wilson, M. Brett. 'The First Translations of the Qur'an in Modern Turkey (1924–38)'. *International Journal of Middle East Studies* 41, no. 3 (2009), pp. 419–35.
——. 'The Optional Ramadan Fast: Debating Q. 2.184 in the Early Turkish Republic', in Stephen Burge, ed., *The Meaning of the Word: Lexicology and Qur'anic Exegesis*. Oxford, Oxford University Press in association with The Institute of Ismaili Studies, Forthcoming.
Yalçınkaya, Mehmet Alaadin. 'İsmail Ferruh Efendi'nin Londra Büyükelçiliği ve Siyasi Faaliyetleri (1797–1800)', in Kemal Çiçek, ed., *Pax Ottomana: Studies in Memoriam, Prof. Dr. Nejat Göyünç*. Ankara, Sota-Yeni Türkiye, 2001, pp. 381–407.
Zadeh, Travis. 'Translation, Geography, and the Divine Word: Mediating Frontiers in Pre-Modern Islam'. Phd Dissertation, Harvard University, 2006. Substantially amended and published as *The Vernacular Qur'an: Translation and the Rise of Persian Exegesis*. Oxford, Oxford University Press in association with The Institute of Ismaili Studies, 2012.
——. 'The Persian Fātiḥa of Salmān al-Fārisī and the Debates over Translating the Qur'an', in Stephen Burge, ed., *The Meaning of the Word: Lexicology and Tafsīr*. Oxford, Oxford University Press in association with the Institute of Ismaili Studies, Forthcoming.
Zürcher, Erik J. *Turkey: A Modern History*. London, I.B. Tauris, 2004.
Zwemer, Samuel M. 'Translations of the Koran'. *Moslem World* 5, no. 3 (1915), pp. 244–61.

Index of Qur'anic Citations

Sura	Verse	Page
1		96, 123
	6	166
2	2	94
	183–4	167
	184	166, 167, 168, 169, 181n. 35, 181n. 36
	185	167
	286	257
3	7	122
	103	116, 135
4	23	229
6	7	39
	9	143
	91	39
7	107	155n. 94
	117	140
12	2	13, 26n. 14
	108	121
14	4	1, 14, 85
15	9	248, 258
	22	122
17	16	140
	88	12
18	60	27n. 28
	109	39
20	20	155n. 94
	66	140
	113	13, 26n. 14
24		207
26	32	155n. 94
	196–7	13
27	10	155n. 94
28	31	155n. 94
31	27	39
43	3–4	1
56		100
	77–80	34
68		39
	1	39, 52n. 31
93		96
96	4	39
97		96, 246n. 36
102	1–2	172, 182n. 64
103		96
108		223
112		98, 99

Index

Note: Page references in italics indicate illustrations.
For use of square brackets in names, see author's note on p. xvii.

Abbas Halim Pasha 179
ʿAbbāsid Empire, and calligraphic Qur'an 79
ʿAbduh, Muḥammad 98, 117–18, 177
Abdülaziz, Sultan 56
Abdülhamid II, Sultan 70–2
  and censorship 79–80, 97–8, 105, 109–10, 118, 130
  and Constitutional Revolution 127, 129, 197
  Islamic Unity campaign 73, 74–80, 97–8, 105, 184, 198, 258
  and modernity 77–8, 97
  and ulama 97–8, 160
Abdullah Cevdet 133–4
Abdülmecid II, Caliph 188, 203–4
Abū'l-Faḍl al-Jizawī 191–2
Abū Ḥanīfa Nuʿmān b. Thābit 13–14, 16, 19–20, 22, 23
Abu Taleb Khan, Mirza 92
Abū Yūsuf 14
accuracy:
  and printing 66, 71
  and translation 4–5, 142, 223
Ağaoğlu, Ahmet 136, 222
Ahmad Khan, Sayyid 98
Aḥmad b. Salīm 76
Ahmadiyya movement 170, 190–6, 201, 210, 217
Ahmed Naim 124
Ahmet III, Sultan 37, 52n. 28, 67
Ahmet Cevdet Pasha:
  and Ferruh 93
  and Istanbul Qur'an 64–5, 67
  and printing 29, 63
  and Qur'an translation 107
Ahmet Midhat 105–7
Ahmet Salih b. Abdullah, *Zübed-i asari'l-Mevahib ve'l-Envar* 95
Akçura, Yusuf 109, 136
Akif, Mehmet *see* Ersoy, Mehmet Akif
el-Aksarayi, Abdurrahman 1, 84–5
Akseki, Ahmet Hamdi 169, 172–4
Alawis *see* Nusayris
Alevis:
  and Ottoman attempts to 'correct' beliefs 78
  and use of vernacular 16–17, 253
Ali, Muhammad (of Lahore) 170, 175, 186, 192–6, 197–8, 201, 205
ʿAlī b. Abī Ṭālib 39
Ali Ekrem Bey (*mutasarrif* of Jerusalem) 77, Fig. 8
Ali Jawhar, Mohammad 218n. 24
Ali Suavi 59, 60, 102–3, 192
Amanat, Abbas 46
Anatolia:
  and Qajar Empire 45–6
  and Turkish language 84–5, 249
Anderson, Benedict 15, 33
Ankarali İsmail, commentary on *Sūrat al-Fātiḥa* 96
Arab caliphate 186–9
Arab Revolt (1916) 147, 148, 178, 187
Arabic language:
  and Arab nationalism 116, 117–25
  compared with Latin 144
  compared with Turkish 84
  for daily prayer 13, 14–15, 123, 138, 143
  and divine speech 12–13, 103
  and Egyptian recension 5
  and inimitability of Qur'an 1, 5, 12, 16, 116, 122, 126
  knowledge of 19, 93–4, 102–4, 105–7, 111, 119–20, 123–4, 171, 210–11
  and Muslim unity 103, 119, 123, 124–5, 185, 192, 210, 213–15, 232
  and new Arabism 117–25
  printed books in 36–8
  and printed Qur'an 33–6, 105–6, 250, 253

for recital of Qur'an 1, 15–16, 31, 99–100, 138, 143, Fig. 1
and Revolution of 1908 129–30
Arabism 117–25
Arberry, Arthur J. 167
army, Ottoman, reforms 42–3, 86, 91
Asad, Muhammad 173
Atatürk, Mustafa Kemal:
and Qur'an in Turkish 1–2, 10, 11, 158
and religious reform 159, 161, 178, 214–15, 227–30, 233, 240
and single-party rule 222
authority:
contested 134, 249
and control of printing 70–2, 74, 75, 80, 250
and language 17–18, 21, 23–4
Aydar, Hidayet 254
Ayıntâbî Mehmet Efendi 87–90
Tefsir-i Tibyan (*The Elucidation*) 88–90, 94–5, 101, 106, 107
Ayoub, Mahmoud 255
al-Azhar University, Cairo 10
and approval of translation 213, 215, 217, 255, 285
global influence 209
and opposition to translation 208, 209–10
and Muhammad Ali 191–3, 201
and Pickthall 196, 201–2, 204, 255
see also al-Marāghī, Muḥammad

al-Bakuwī, Zayn al-ʿAbidīn Ḥājī 118
Balıkesirli Devletoğlu Yusuf, *Vikaye-i Manzume* 20
Balkans, and Turkish language 85–6
Bandini, Branton and Orazio 36
Bassnett, Susan and Lefevere, André 102
al-Bayḍāwī, ʿAbd Allāh b. ʿUmar, *Anwār al-tanzīl* 89, 95, 168–9, 174
Behçet Molla 93
Bektashi Sufi order:
persecution 92–3
and use of vernacular 16–17, 253
Benjamin, Walter 40
Bereketzade, İsmail Hakkı 128, 135, 136
Beşiktaş Scientific Society 92–3
Beşir Fuad 107
Biberstein-Kazimirski, Albert de, *Le Koran* 104, 172–3, 229
Bible:
compared with Qur'an 124–7
printed 68–9
seen as distorted 122
vernacular 3, 7, 17–19, 32–3, 68, 184, 249
Bibliander, Theodor 32, 33
Bigiyev, Musa Carullah 8, 25, 133, 136–43, 145, 168, Fig. 9
Birgivi, Mehmet 86
The Last Will and Testament (Vasiyetname) 42–3
Birinci, Ali 38
Bodin, Jean, *Colloque entre sept scavants* 35
book binding 65
book copyists 29–30, 37–42, 43, 49, 51, 59
[Börekçi], Mehmet Rifat 166–9, 174–5
Bukhara, and ritual use of translations 19
Bukhārī, Muḥammad b. Ismāʿīl 168, 175
Bulaq (Egypt), printing press 43, 88
Busbecq, Ogier Ghiselin de 36

Cairo:
and Muslim modernism 201, 214
and Qur'an edition of 1924 5, 68, 189–90, Fig. 11
and Qur'an translations 185, 208–9
and Turkish commentaries 87–8
see also al-Azhar University
Cairo Caliphate Conference (1926) 187–9
caliphate:
Arab 186–9
Ottoman
abolition 160, 180, 184, 187, 192, 198–9, 213
and Hyderabad 203–4
and sultanate 74–7, 80, 98
call to prayer, in Turkish 11, 148, 214, 227, 231–4, 242, 244

calligraphers 38–42, 47, 49, 51, 59, 71
and printed Qur'an 61, 66–8, 69–70, 254–5
see also book copyists; Hafiz Osman
Çantay, Hasan Basri 238
catechism, in Turkish 86
Celal Nuri 145–6
Cemil Sait [Dikel] 161, 170–5, 229–30
censorship:
under Abdülhamid II 79–80, 97–8, 105, 109–10, 118, 130
in Turkish Republic 243
centralisation, and Revolution of 1908 129
Cevdet Pasha *see* Ahmet Cevdet Pasha
Chauvin, Victor 81n. 37
Christianity:
and printed editions of Qur'an 33–5, 65
and translations of Qur'an 22, 32–3, 36, 125–7, 147–8
see also Bible; missionaries
colonialism 132
and Islamic unity 74–6, 116, 184
and partition of Ottoman Empire 158–9
and Qur'an translation 105, 120, 251
commentaries, Qur'an:
English 206–7
Persian 91
commentaries, Qur'an, Turkish:
by Ayıntâbî Mehmet Efendi 87–90
by Elmalılı 234–43
by İsmail Ferruh Efendi 90–5
Ottoman Empire 2, 10, 24, 25, 85–95, 98–104, 105–6, 111, 124, 149–50
popular 95–104
printed 38, 50, 65–6, 89, 249–50
Turkish Republic 165–6, 175–7
see also Qur'an translation, and commentary
Committee of Union and Progress (CUP):
and Islamic unity 184
and Kadri 165
and religious reform 134
and Turkification 129–31
cosmology, and calligraphy 40
Cumhuriyet Halk Partisi (CHP) 222

Deringil, Selim 46
dictionaries, Turkish language 84, 108, 165
al-Dihlawī, Muḥammad Jamāl al-Dīn, *el-Tefsirü'l-Cemali* 95
Directorate of Religious Affairs 160, 176, 179, 255
and Qur'an translation 9–10, 221–2, 226, 227, 244–5, 253
see also [Börekçi], Mehmet Rifat
Doğrul, Ömer Riza 147, 193, 240–1
Durkheim, Emile 149

Ebu Suud 168–9, 174
Ebüzziya Tevfik, *Lûgat-i Ebüzziya* 18
education:
and learning of Arabic 124
and learning of Turkish 129
and modernisation 73, 104, 120, 125
and print 29–30, 58, 72–3, 86, 97
and the Qur'an 31, 43–4, 48, 59, 61, 64, 72–4, 250, Fig. 5
state-controlled 73–4, 86, 90, 101, 104
Efgani, Ubeydullah 146
Egypt:
and Christian missionaries 209, 210–11
and modernisation 43–4, 97, 117–18, 214
and printed Qur'an 43, 47, 65, 68, 249
and Qur'an translation 208–13, 215–17, 252
and Sunni leadership 180, 187–9, 196, 209, 252
and Turkish commentaries 87–90
see also Cairo; Qur'an editions; ulama, Egypt
Elmalılı *see* Yazir, Elmalılı Muhammed Hamdi
English Qur'an translation 9, 25, 128, 185–6, 196–208
by Abdullah Yusuf Ali 186, 204–8
in Egypt 210–11, 215–17, 252

by Muhammad Ali 170, 175, 186, 190–2, 195–6, 197–8, 201
by Pickthall 196, 198, 199–204, 255
equivalence, and translation 12, 20–1, 235–6
Ergin, Osman Nuri 230
errors:
and calligraphy 40–1, 68
in printed Qur'an 3, 34, 48–9, 63, 66–8
in translation 166–75, 222
Ersoy, Mehmet Akif 42, 133, 223
and commentary 177
as poet 42, 176–80
and Qur'an translation 135, 136, 179–80, 191, 193, 224–6, 234, 239–42, 243–4
and *Sirat-ı Müstakim* 135, 177, 223
Esref Edip *see* Fergan, Esref Edip
Europe:
and colonialism 74–6, 105, 120, 132, 158, 184, 251
influence on Ottoman Empire 8, 21–2, 60, 86, 116
literature 24, 90, 104, 162
and Muslim modernism 132, 225–6
print culture 38, 68–9, 97
and printed Qur'an 32–6, 46, 61–4
and Reformation 7, 22, 144–5, 216, 237
Ezherli, İsmail 240

Fahd b. ʿAbd al-ʿAzīz 255–6
Fakhr al-Dīn al-Rāzī 162, 168–9
Fanton, Aristidis 57–9, 63–4
Fergan, Eşref Edip:
and Akif translation 225–6, 234, 240
and Kadri translation 166, 170
and Muhammad Ali translation 175, 191, 193
and state-sponsored translation 176
fiqh *see* law
freedom of religion 127
freedom of speech 132
Freemasonry 91–3, 130
French language:
in Ottoman Empire 104, 124, 162
Qur'an translation 104, 107, 172–3
Fuad I, king of Egypt 187–8, 189, 201–2
Fuzuli, Mehmed bin Süleyman 41

Gandhi, Mohandas Karamchand (Mahatma) 199
Gaspirali (Gasprinsky), Ismail 137
Germany, and Islam 259
al-Ghamrāwī, Muḥammad Aḥmad 202, 219n. 59
al-Ghazālī, Abū Ḥāmid 99, 122, 162
Giridi Selim Sırrı 101
God:
Beautiful Names, as untranslatable 122, 172, 224
Gökalp, Ziya 10, 131, 150, 157, 185
'Vatan' 148–9, 222, 228
Gunasti, Susan 113n. 36

Hacı Zihni Efendi (Mehmet Zihni) 107
Hadice Sultan 42–3
hadiths:
study of 134–5
Turkish translation 88, 107, 110, 175–6
Hafiz Ahmet 49–50
Hafiz Osman (calligrapher) 56–7, 61, 62, 63, 66–7, 76, 254
Hafiz Yaşar Bey 231
Haftyak (partial versions of Qur'an) 72
Hagen, Gottfried 85
Ḥanafī school 42, 78
and use of translations 14, 16, 20, 214, 224
Ḥanbalī school, and use of translations 15
Hasan Fehmi 151
Hasan Rıza (calligrapher) Fig. 6
Haşim Nahid 8, 144–5
Hayrü'l-Kelam (journal) 135–6, 147
Horovitz, Josef 201
Ḥusayn b. ʿAlī (Sharif of Mecca) 147, 148, 158, 186–8
el-Hüseyni, Seyyid Süleyman (Süleyman Tevfik) 161, 162–4, 222, Fig. 10
Hussein, Taha 201–2

Ibn al-Faḍl, Abū Bakr Muḥammad
220n. 110
Ibn Manẓūr, Muḥammad b. Mukarram,
Lisān al-ʿArab 18
Ibn Saʿūd, Abdülaziz 188
Ibn Taymiyya, Takī al-Dīn Aḥmad 257
İbrahim Gözübüyükzade Kayserivi,
Tercüme-i Süre-i Duha 96
İbrahim Hilmi 146–7, 164
İbrahim Müteferrika 37, 38, 70
İbrahim Peçevi 36
identity, national:
Arab 117, 214
in Ottoman Turkey 7–8, 80
and Revolution of 1908 11, 131
in Turkish Republic 157, 213–14,
227–8, 233, 251
İhsanoğlu, Ekmeleddin 241–2
ijtihād (independent legal reasoning)
117–18, 121, 132, 212
İli, Mithat 248
imitation (*taqlīd*) 121
India:
and Islamic unity 74, 198
and Muslim thought 98
and printed Qur'an 45, 47, 49, 79
and Qur'an translation 103–4, 128,
186
see also Khilafat movement
Indonesia:
and Islamic Unity 74–7, 79
and Qur'an translations
193–5, 251
İnönü, İsmet 242
intellectuals, Egyptian 208–9, 213
see also al-Azhar University
intellectuals, Turkish:
and censorship 79–80, 97–8,
105, 109
devout
in Ottoman Empire 24, 116, 124,
131, 136, 143, 147, 150–1
in Turkish Republic 161, 162–3,
164, 169–70, 174–5, 175–80,
222–4, 226, 234–41, 243–4
and Muslim unity 116
and print culture 23–4, 55
and Revolution of 1908 131–5
and translation of Qur'an 90–5,
99–100, 104–5, 123–4, 135–6,
221, 243
and Turkish commentaries 250
and ulama 23–4, 90–1
Young Ottomans 56, 59
interpretation:
intra-textual 140
and translation 18–19, 21, 22, 24, 101,
115n. 73, 121, 139, 166, 171–2
see also commentaries
Iqbal, Muhammad 98, 207
Iran, and printed Qur'an 45–8, 49, 50, 61,
71, 80
Iraq:
and persecution of Shiʿa 46
and printed Qur'an 49
Irving, T.B. 195
al-Isfarāʾīnī 19
İslam Mecmuası (journal) 133–4, 135
Islamic Studies:
and modern translation of Qur'an
5–6
and Ottoman-Turkish History 6
Islamic unity:
and Abdülhamid II 73, 74–80, 97–8,
105, 184, 198, 258
and Arabic language 116, 119–20,
123, 124, 185, 192, 211, 213–15,
232, 250
and nationalism 116, 192, 251
and Rashīd Riḍā 119–20, 123, 130
and Revolution of 1908 131, 135
and World War I 148, 158
İsmail Ferruh Efendi, *Mevakib* 90–5, 101,
106, 142–3, 253
Istanbul:
Allied occupation 152, 158, 178
and black-market Qur'an 49–51, 64,
71–2
copyists and bookmakers 41, 43
first Qur'an edition 64–8
illegal printed Qur'an 45–9, 61, 64,
71–2, 249
Jewish press 35
Muslim press 36–8, 42–3, 131–2
and ulama 37–8, 45–7
İzmirli İsmail Hakkı 222–4

Jāmī, Nūr al-Dīn ʿAbd al-Raḥmān 27n. 30
Jeffery, Arthur 125–6
Jews, in Ottoman Empire 35, 38
journalism, Ottoman 86, 97, 105, 250–1
Justice and Development Party 254–5

Kadırgalı (calligrapher) 68
Kadri, Hüseyin Kâzim [Şeyh Muhsin-i Fani, pseud.] 8, 146, 161, 164–70
Kamaluddin, Khwaja 197, 217n. 16
Karpat, Kemal 98
al-Kāshifī, Ḥusayn Wāʿiẓ, *Mawākib-i ʿaliyya* 91, 95
Kasım, Naci 162–3
Kâtip Çelebi, Mustafa b. Abdullah [Ḥājjī Khalīfa, pseud.] 36, 41
Kaynak, Sadettin 229–30, 231
Kazan, and Muslim publishing 72, 118, 255
Kazimirski *see* Biberstein-Kazimirski, Albert de
Kemal *see* Namik Kemal
Kethüdazade Arif Efendi 92
Khilafat movement 199, 203–4, 205
King Fahd Complex for Printing the Holy Qur'an (Medina) 3, 255–9
Krstić, Tijana 85–6
Kurdish language, use in prayers 16
Kurds:
  and Islamic Unity campaign 77
  raids on Shiʿi towns 46
Kureyşizade, Mehmet Fevzi 99–100
Kurzman, Charles 132

Lahore Ahmadiyya Movement 190, 191–6, 197, 201
language:
  and authority 17–18, 21, 23–4
  and culture 104
  and meaning 13–15, 100, 107–8, 141
  and nationalism 103, 117, 216, 227–8, 233
The Last Will and Testament (*Vasiyetname*) 42–3
Latin:
  as sacred language 17–18, 144
  translations of Qur'an 32–3, 35
law:
  Ḥanafī school 14, 16, 20, 42, 78, 214
  Ḥanbalī school 15
  Mālikī school 15
  Shāfiʿī school 16, 18–19
  unification of schools 118, 132
Lawrence, T.E. 197
Lefevere, André 89, 102
lexicon of Qur'anic vocabulary 107–8
literacy:
  in Arabic 210
  and modernisation 8–9, 30, 31, 87, 90, 101, 129, 185, 250
literalism, and translation 89, 107–8, 122, 140, 142, 163, 170, 171–3, 202, 230
literature:
  Alevi-Bektashi 16–17, 253
  European 24, 90, 104, 162
  and popular stories 85–6, 87
  and Qur'an commentaries 85–7, 88–9
  Turkish 84–7, 108, 176–80
  and Turkism 131
London edition of the Qur'an 56–64, 66, 73
Lûgat-i Ebüzziya 18
Luther, Martin 7, 23, 32–3, 126, 145, 179, 237, 259

MacCallum, Lyman 232
madrasas:
  and access to Qur'an 41, 50–1, 134
  and Ferruh's *Mevakib* 94
  and religious education 31, 79, 87
  and state-run education 2, 90, 160, 201
  and Turkish commentaries 89, 101–2, 250
Mahmud II, Sultan 92
Mālik b. Anas 15
Mālikī school 15
al-Manār 117–18, 119, 121, 132, 189, 194, 209
Manṣūr, Kāmil 209

al-Marāghī, Muḥammad Muṣṭafā 187–8, 201, 208, 210–12, 214–16, 252
Matbaa-i Amire 70, 181n. 17
Matbaa-i Osmaniye 70–2, 80
meaning:
auxiliary and primary 211–12
changes in 142
and language 13–15, 100, 107–8, 141
multiple 121
preservation 138–9
and translation 141–2, 235–6
Medina, King Fahd Complex for Printing the Holy Qur'an 3, 255–9
Mehmet Ali (governor of Egypt) 43–4, 56, 88, 179, 249
Mehmet Celalettin (imam) 221–2
Mehmet Cemaleddin Efendi (Shaykh al-Islam) 109
Mehmet Rifat *see* [Börekçi], Mehmet Rifat
Mehmet VI Vahdettin 159
Mehmet Zihni *see* Hacı Zihni Efendi
Meşihat 160, 161, 178
Messick, Brinkley 42
Midhat Cemal Kuntay 177
Milaslı, İsmail Hakkı 150
Mir Osman Ali Khan, Nizam of Hyderabad 200–1, 203–4
Miras, Kâmil 240
Mirza Ghulam Ahmad 190–1, 194
missionaries, Christian 25, 103, 105, 151, 185, 232
distribution of Bibles 53n. 56
in Egypt 184, 209, 210–11
and translation of Qur'an 22, 125–8, 147–8, 217, 252
missionaries, Muslim 190–6, 209–11, 255, 257, 259
modernisation, Turkish 5–7, 8
and army reforms 42–3, 86, 91
and education 73, 104
and Islamic printing 42–5
and literacy 7–8, 30, 31, 73, 129, 185
and national identity 131, 213–14
and printed Qur'an 60–1, 73, 77–8
and Protestant Reformation 144–5, 231–2
and Qur'an translation 21–4, 25, 80, 104–11, 120–1
see also reform, religious
modernism, Muslim 8, 101, 117, 121, 124, 130, 132–8, 144, 177–8
and Cairo 201
and English translations 208
and Lahore Ahmadiyya translation 191
and Turkish translation 135–6, 137
mosques:
and access to Qur'an 31, 64, 78, 96
state provision of Qur'an 72–3, 79
and translated Qur'an 214–15, 228–9
Muallim Ömer Naci 7, 98–9
Muhammad, Elijah 195
Muhammad Hilal Efendi 78–9
Muhammadiyah movement 194
Murat III, Sultan 36
Musa Kâzım 149–50
Muṣḥaf Examination Committee 252–3
Mustafa Fazıl Pasha 56, 58
Mustafa Kemal Atatürk *see* Atatürk, Mustafa Kemal
Mustafa Nazif (calligrapher) Fig. 7
Mustafa Sabri 14, 213–17
opposition to Qur'an translation 124, 147, 150, 185, 192, 214, 241, 253
opposition to religious reform 146, 213–14, 236
opposition to Turkish commentaries 124, 177
Muʿtazilīs 166
and Qur'an as created 16
Müteferrika *see* İbrahim Müteferrika

Naci *see* Kasım, Naci; Muallim Ömer Naci
Nadi, Yunus 109–10
Namık Kemal 56–64, 73, 77, Fig. 2
Nāṣir al-Dīn Shah 46
Nation of Islam 190, 195
nationalism:
Arab 116, 117–25
Indian 199
and language 103, 117, 216, 227–8, 233

and Muslim unity 116, 192, 251
Ottoman Turkey 6–7, 10–11, 22, 24, 25, 131
and separatism 70
Turkish Republic 151, 157, 159, 213–14, 216, 227–8, 242–3
and Turkism 131, 148–9, 151
Nazif *see* Süleyman Nazif
New Order (Nizam-ı Cedid) 42, 91
Nöldeke, Theodor 201
North America, and Qur'an translations 195
novels, Ottoman 86, 108
Nurettin, Vala [Va-Nu] 109
Nusayris 78

Oporinus, Johannes 33
Osman Zeki Bey 70–1, 72
Ottoman Empire:
and access to Qur'an 29–31, 31–2, 69–72
book ownership 8–9, 29–30, 31, 38
calligraphic tradition 39–41, 47, 51, 66–7, 71, 255
Islamic printing 42–5
and Jewish press 35, 38
and knowledge of Arabic 19, 93–4, 102–4, 105–7
and need for translations 10, 19–20, 21, 105–11
and non-Islamic printing 36–42
partition 158–9, 198–9
and print culture 7–8, 21, 23–4, 25, 34–6, 68–9, 86
and printed Qur'an 45–51, 64–8, 249, 258
Qur'an editions 55–80, 111
and Revolution of 1908 127, 129–36, 161, 197
and state control of printing 70–2, 74, 75, 80, 97–8
see also education; Europe; Islamic unity; modernisation; nationalism; Turkish Republic

Paganini, Paganino de' 33–5
Paker, Saliha 86
Pan-Islamism *see* Islamic unity
Pan-Turkism 131, 137
paraphrase, and translation 20, 88
Persian language:
commentaries 91
compared with Turkish 84
and poetry of Rūmī 17, 96
prayers in 14–15, 19
and Qur'an recitation 15
and Qur'an translation 3–4, 19–20, 93, 106, 214
photolithography 57, 63, 66–8, 76, 254
Pickthall, Muhammad Marmaduke 196–204
and caliphate 198–9, 203–4
English translation 9, 11–12, 173, 186, 196, 198, 199–204, 208, 217, 255
and Khilafat movement 199, 203–4
and Muhammad Ali's translation 193, 195, 201
and Yusuf Ali's translation 207
Poe, Edgar Allen 55
politics:
and Constitutional Revolution (1908) 127, 129–36, 161
and distribution of Qur'an 75–80
and intellectual opposition 56–7, 97, 131
and language of scripture 17–18, 22, 116
and Qur'an translation 146, 151, 214–15, 230–4
prayers, daily (*salat*) 13, 16, 104
in Arabic 13, 14–15, 123, 138, 143
in Kurdish 16
in Persian 14–15, 19
in Turkish 21, 215, 221, 224, 228, 234
see also call to prayer
press:
freedom 130–2, 133–4, 250
modernist 117–18, 124, 233
state control 70–2, 74, 75, 80, 97–8, 105
and translations 135
see also journalism; print technology
print capitalism 32, 34, 45, 59, 64, 68–9
print technology 5–6, 24–5
in Egypt 43–5
lithography 56, 59, 62, 66, 73, Figs 3, 6

metal relief printing blocks 66, Fig. 4
as mother of civilisation 29–31
in Ottoman society 36–42, 42–5, 65–6, 249
output 97
photolithography 57, 63, 66–8, 76, 254
and Qur'an 2–4, 7–8, 21–4, 30–1, 35–6, 41–2, 45–9, 61
and translations 80, 249–50
and ulama 37–8, 43, 45–6
see also press
progress, and translation 23, 25
Progressive Islam Association 205
purity, ritual:
and calligraphy 41
and location 60, 62, 192
and non-Muslim impurity 34, 60, 191–2
and printing 30, 40, 44, 49, 59–60, 62, 65

Qadian Ahmadiyya group 190, 194
Qajar Empire (Iran) 45–8, 50
Qasim Zaman, Muhammad 23
Qur'an:
abrogated verses 167, 169
access to 29–31, 31–2, 69–72, 161, 170, 237–8, 258–9
affordability 31–2, 49, 51, 55, 57, 61, 64, 69, 80
ambiguous verses 122, 140–1
and Arab identity 117
black-market copies 49–51, 64, 71–2
calligraphic 29–30, 37–42, 43, 47, 49, 51, 56–7, 60, 64, 79, 254
commodification 59
compared with Bible 125–7
as created 16
and discarded pages 50, 71
distribution in Muslim world 74–80, Fig. 8
as inimitable 1, 5, 12, 16, 33, 106–7, 116, 119, 122, 126, 145, 211–12
memorisation 7, 30, 99, 123, 138, 242, 257
monopoly of production 70–1, 80
printed 2–4, 7–8, 21–4, 30–1, 35–6, 41–2, 45–9, 61
and textual corruption 47, 48–9, 122, 142
as uncreated 15
as unique 12
untranslatable elements 122, 126, 136, 212
as veiled from the masses 7–11, 85, 99
Qur'an editions:
colophons 69, 77–8, Fig. 6
Egyptian (King Faruq) of 1936 189, 256
Egyptian (King Fuad) of 1924 5, 68, 189–90, 256, Fig. 11
first Istanbul 64–8
illegal foreign copies 45–9, 51, 64, 71–2, 79–80, 105, 249
illuminated Fig. 7
and Islamic Unity 74–5, 250
London 56–64, 66, 73
Ottoman 55–80
partial (*Haftyak*) 72
printed 2–4, 21, 32–6, 43–4, 255
standard 68
Turkish 111, 118, 147–9, 157–8, 175–80, 185, 192, 221–45
Qur'an translation 248–59
approaches to 4–7
bibliographies 254
Christian 22, 32–3, 36, 125–8, 147–8, 217
and commentary 88–9, 94–5, 106–7, 136, 171–2, 235–6, 238
as exegesis 163–4
history 9
as human speech 15–16
interlinear 20–1, 85–6, 88, 93, 106
by Kadri 161, 164–70
literal 89, 107–8, 122, 140, 142, 163, 170, 171–3, 202, 230
metaphorical 206
modern bilingual 21
in modernising Turkey 21–4, 25, 80, 104–11, 144–5, 151
and nationalism 10–11, 25, 125, 148–51, 185
as obligatory 142
possibility of 2, 3, 4–5, 11–20, 106–7, 136, 142, 179, 236

social importance 6, 7–11, 210–11
by Tevfik 161, 162–4, 222
and transparency 25–6, 134, 141–2
see also English Qur'an translation; French language, Qur'an translation; Turkish Qur'an translation

reason, and scriptures 132–3
recitation of Qur'an 53n. 44, 78, 104, 257
in Arabic 1, 15–16, 31, 99–100, 124, 138, 143, Fig. 1
in Turkish 1–2, 11, 150, 214–15, 221, 228–34, 235
reform, cultural 11, 213, 227
reform, educational 120, 125
reform, military 42–3, 86, 91
reform, religious:
and Bigiyev 136–43
in Egypt 117–19, 214, 216–17
in Ottoman Turkey 7, 8, 10–11, 22, 97–8, 116, 124, 128–9, 132–4, 148–50, 178
in Turkish Republic 157, 159–60, 161, 213–14, 216, 221–2, 225, 227–8, 228–34, 236–41, 243
Reformation, Protestant, and vernacular scriptures 7, 22, 144–5, 216, 237
Research Centre for Islamic History, Art and Culture (Istanbul; IRCICA) 254–5
Reşit Galip 229
Richter, Julius 127
Ricoldo da Monte Croce 33
Riḍā, Muḥammad Rashīd 9, 25, 98, 103, 111, 117–23, 125
and Arab caliphate 187
and Islamic unity 119–20, 123, 130, 192
and Lahore Ahmadiyya translation 191, 194
opposition to Qur'an translation 118–23, 147
support for Qur'an translation 215
ritual, and use of translations 257–8
in Bukhara 19
in Ottoman Empire 13–16, 19–20, 21, 84, 103, 119, 143, 147, 149–50
in Turkish Republic 4, 158, 215, 221, 224, 230–1
see also call to prayer; prayers; recitation of Qur'an
Robert of Ketton, *Lex Mahumet pseudoprophete* 33
Rūmī, Jalāl al-Dīn 17, 96, 225
Runyun, Mustafa 242
Russia:
and printed Qur'an 45, 47, 49, 65, 72, 79, 255
and Qur'an translation 111, 136–43, 251

Sabri, İbrahim 241–2
Sabri, Mustafa *see* Mustafa Sabri
Said Nursi (Bediüzzaman) 236
Sait, Cemil *see* Cemil Sait
Salāma b. al-Akwa 167
al-Samarī, Aḥsan Shāh Aḥmad 118
Sami, Şemseddin *see* Şemseddin Sami
Samih Rifat 109
Şanizade Ataullah Efendi 92–3
Sarekat Islam (Indonesia) 194
Saudi Arabia, and translation of Qur'an 255–8
schools *see* education
scribes *see* book copyists; calligraphers
script 248, 255
cursive 79
Latin 225, 232
naskh (*nesih*) 67
Sebilürreşad (journal) 124, 132, 148, 163–4, 166, 169, 177
secularism, in Turkey 6, 11, 117, 178, 213, 225, 231, 242–3, 255
Şekerzade Mehmed Efendi (calligrapher) 67–8, 69, 76
Selim III 42, 91
Şemseddin Sami 108–10
Sengüler, İsmail Hakkı 241
Şentürk, Recep 242
Şeref Kâzım 174
Sevres Treaty (1920) 158–9, 198
Şeyh Hamdullah (calligrapher) 67

Şeyh Muhsin-i Fani [pseud.] *see* Kadri, Hüseyin Kâzım
Seyyid Abdullah Efendi 67
al-Shāfiʿī, Abū Abdullah Muḥammad 13, 15–16
Shāfiʿī school 16, 18–19
Shāh Walī Allāh, *Fatḥ al-Raḥmān* 95
Shākir, Muḥammad 184, 192, 202
Shaltūt, Maḥmūd 215
Shams al-Dīn Muḥammad b. Qudāma al-Maqdisī 15
sharia courts:
  in late Ottoman Empire 134
  in Turkish Republic 160, 215, 233–4
Sharif of Mecca *see* Ḥusayn b. ʿAlī
al-Shāṭibī, Abū Isḥāq 211
al-Shaybānī, Muḥammad 14
Shaykh al-Islam 124, 134, 213
  ban on translations 105, 109–10, 147, 251
  and Bigiyev 137, 138
  and legal disputes 49
  and printed Qur'an 50, 63, 71, 74
  and Revolution of 1908 130
  see also Mustafa Sabri
Sherif, M.A. 205–6
Sherrill, Charles 233
Shiʿism:
  and Qajar Empire 46
  see also Twelver Shiʿism; Zaydī Shiʿism
Sırat-ı Müstakim (journal) 135, 177, 223
Society for the Defence of Islam 210
South Asia, and Qur'an translation 190–1, 251
South East Asia:
  and Ahmadiyya translation 193–4
  and Ottoman distribution of Qur'an 73–4, 76–7
Steiner, George 142
Storrs, Ronald 186
Strauss, Johann 95–6
Suavi, Ali *see* Ali Suavi
Sufi orders 160, 223
  and Turkish commentaries 96
Süleyman Nazif 157, 226
Süleyman Tevfik [Seyyid Süleyman el-Hüseyni, pseud.] 161, 162–4, 166, 222, Fig. 10
sultanate, and caliphate 74–7, 80, 98
Sunni Islam:
  and caliphate 184
  in Egypt 180, 187–9, 196, 209
  in India 200
  and printed Qur'an 78–9
  and use of translations 16

al-Ṭabarī, Abū Jaʿfar Muḥammad b. Jarīr b. Yazīd 52n. 31, 141, 168, 174
Tabbaa, Yasser 79
tafsīr (interpretation):
  in Ottoman Empire 18–19, 22, 24, 101, 115n. 73, 121, 139–41, 149
  in Turkish Republic 164, 172, 230, 238–9
Tahir-Gürçağlar, Şehnaz 23
al-Tamīmī, Shaykh 44
Tanzimat reforms 29–30, 98
taqlīd (imitation) 121
tarjama (translation) 12, 18–19, 22–4, 150
ta'wīl (esoteric interpretation) 141
Taylor, Malissa 68
Tevfik, Süleyman *see* Süleyman Tevfik
Tjokroaminoto, Hadji Oesman Said 194
translation:
  and accuracy 4–5, 142
  and equivalence 12, 20–1, 235–6
  of European works 86–7, 97, 104
  free 149
  and interpretation 18–19, 22, 24, 101, 115n. 73, 121, 139, 166, 171–2
  and modernisation 23
  and paraphrase 20, 88
  of Qur'an *see* Qur'an translation
  as tool of progress 23, 25, 86
  word-for-word 20, 93, 149
Turkey *see* Ottoman Empire; Turkish Republic
Turkish language:
  compared with Arabic 84
  dictionaries 84, 108, 165

and European biographies 86
and Islamic works 87, 97
lexicon of Qur'anic vocabulary 107–8
Old Anatolian 20
and poetry 177
and Revolution of 1908 129–30
ritual use 4, 16, 20, 25, 84, 103, 119, 143, 147, 149–50, 158, 222, 243–4
call to prayer 11, 148, 214, 227, 231–4
prayer 21, 215, 221, 224, 228, 234
recitation of Qur'an 1–2, 11, 150, 214–15, 221, 228–34, 235
and script 225, 248
status in Ottoman state 20, 116–17
status in Turkish Republic 157–80, 213, 227–8
Turkish Qur'an translation 248–59, Fig. 12
and Akif 179–80, 224–6, 234, 239–42, 243–4
and catechisms 86
early translations 20–1
in Egypt 87–8
and Elmalılı 234–9, 243, 251, 253
and İli 248
and missionaries 125–9, 147–8, 151, 232
and modernisation 6–7, 21–4, 25, 80, 104–11, 120–1
and modernism 135–6, 137
and nationalism 10–11, 25, 125, 148–51, 185, 242–3
opposition to 127, 130, 133, 136, 161, 243, 249
by Elmalılı 235–6
by Rashīd Riḍā 118–23, 147
by Sabri 124, 147, 150, 185, 192, 214, 241, 253
state-sponsored 25, 175–80, 222, 224–6, 227–8, 244, 251, 253
in Turkish Republic 157–80, 192, 193, 214–15, 222–3, 230–3, 234–43
and ulama 9–10, 14, 21, 30, 105, 111, 213
see also commentaries
Turkish Republic:
and nationalism 151, 157, 159, 213–14
opposition to religious reforms 213–17, 221–2, 233–4, 236, 238–40
and Qur'an translation 157–80, 192, 193, 214–15
as secular state 225, 231, 242–3
see also Directorate of Religious Affairs
Turkism 131, 148–9, 161, 178
al-Ṭūsī, Nāṣir al-Dīn 36
Twelver Shiʿism, and use of translations 16
Tyndale, William 18

Ubeydullah Efendi, Mehmet 110–11, 118, 151, 185
ulama, Egypt:
and Arab caliphate 187–8
and Christian missionaries 209–10
and Mustafa Sabri 213–14
and printed Qur'an 44–5
and Qur'an translation 192–3, 196, 201–2, 213–16, 257
ulama, India 103–4
ulama, Turkey:
and Abdülhamid II 97–8, 160
and black-market printed copies 50–1
and copyists and bookmakers 41–2, 43, 51
decline in influence 23–4, 60, 104, 134, 159–60, 178, 251
and education 90
and illegal printed Qur'an 45–7
and intellectuals 23–4, 90–1, 116, 133–4, 243
and the masses 99, 101, 123, 124, 133, 144, 151
and Muslim press 37–8, 45
and printed Ottoman editions 55–6, 63, 65, 67–8, 70, 80, 249
and Qur'an translation
Ottoman Empire 9–10, 14, 21, 30, 105, 111, 133, 136, 147, 237, 249, 251
Turkish Republic 161, 163, 169–70, 185, 237, 243–4, 257

reformist 144, 159
and Turkish language 84–5
Us, Hakkı Tarık 240

Vikaye-i Manzume 20

Wajdī, Farīd 210–13, 214, 215
Walī Allāh, Shāh 3–4
Woking Mosque 195, 197, 199, 217n. 16
World War I 165, 178, 197, 205
and Islamic unity 148, 158, 184

Yazidis 78
Yazır, Elmalılı Muhammed Hamdi 2, 10, 176–7, 179, 226–8, 234–9, 243, 251, 253
Yemen:
ban on printed books 42
and Ottoman distribution of Qur'an 78–9
Young Ottomans 56, 59
Young Turks 110, 127, 129–31, 147, 197, 241
Yozgatlı Mehmet İhsan 239–42
Yusuf Ali, Abdullah 186, 204–8, 216, 255, 257

Zadeh, Travis 16, 19
al-Zarkashī, Muḥammad b. Bahādur 18–19
al-Zawāhirī, Muḥammad 202
Zaydī Shiʿism 78
Zwemer, Samuel M. 126–7